Sunday Missal

✝

for 1994-1995
with Prayers and Hymns

Approved for use in Canada

NOVALIS

Acknowledgements: The *Living with Christ Sunday Missal for 1994-1995* is approved for use in Canada by the National Liturgy Office, Canadian Conference of Catholic Bishops.

Liturgical texts: Excerpts from the *Lectionary for Mass* © 1969, 1980, 1981, 1992, International Committee on English in the Liturgy, Inc. (ICEL); excerpts from *The Roman Missal* © 1973, ICEL; *Eucharistic Prayers for Masses with Children* and *Eucharistic Prayers for Masses of Reconciliation* © 1975, 1980, ICEL; *Eucharistic Prayers* © 1980, ICEL; excerpts from the *Rite of Penance* © 1974, ICEL. All rights reserved. English translation of Glory to God, Creeds, and Holy, Holy by the International Consultation on English Texts. Scripture quotations are adapted from the New Revised Standard Version of the Bible © 1989, Division of Christian Education of the National Council of the Churches of Christ in the United States of America, and are used by permission. All rights reserved. Lectionary texts are from the *Lectionary, Sundays and Solemnities* © 1992, Concanan, Inc. Used by permission. All rights reserved.

Editorial texts: The Sunday introductions, special prayer intentions and all other editorial texts are non-official material provided by the publisher. With the illustrations and format, they are © 1994, Novalis, Saint Paul University, 223 Main St., Ottawa, Canada K1S 1C4. All rights reserved.

Editor: Louise Pambrun

Editor-in-Chief: Michael O'Hearn

Music editor: Bernadette Gasslein

Psalm settings: © 1994 Gordon Johnston/Novalis (GJ)

Music: All credits accompany the music texts.

Cover design: Christiane Lemire

Illustrations: Malgosia Chelkowska

Layout: Francine Petitclerc

ISBN: 2-89088-705-7

ISSN: 0832-5324

Printed in Canada

Contents

*The Church, therefore,
earnestly desires
that Christ's faithful,
when present
at this mystery of faith,
should not be there
as strangers
or silent spectators.
On the contrary, through
a proper appreciation
of the rites and prayers
they should participate
knowingly, devoutly
and actively.*

(Constitution on the Sacred Liturgy, §48)

Introductory Rites

GATHERING SONG *(Turn to the appropriate day)*

GREETING

In the name of the Father, and of the Son, and of the Holy Spirit. **Amen**.

The grace of our Lord Jesus Christ and the love of God and the fellowship of the Holy Spirit be with you all. **And also with you.**

or: The grace and peace of God our Father and the Lord Jesus Christ be with you. **And also with you.**

or: The Lord be with you. **And also with you.**

RITE OF BLESSING AND SPRINKLING HOLY WATER *(or PENITENTIAL RITE, p. 7)*

Dear friends, this water will be used to remind us of our baptism. Ask God to bless it, and to keep us faithful to the Spirit he has given us.

1 God our Father, your gift of water brings life and freshness to the earth; it washes away our sins and bring us eternal life.

We ask you now to bless this water, and to give us your protection on this day which you have made your own. Renew the living spring of your life within us and protect us in spirit and body, that we may be free from sin and come into your presence to receive your gift of salvation. We ask this through Christ our Lord.

2 Lord God almighty, creator of all life, of body and soul, we ask you to bless this water: as we us it in faith, forgive our sins and save us from all illness and the power of evil.

Lord, in your mercy give us living water, always springing up as a fountain of salvation: free us, body and soul, from every danger, and admit us to your presence in purity of heart. Grant this through Christ our Lord.

3 *During the Easter season:*
Lord God almighty, hear the prayers of your people: we celebrate our creation and redemption. Hear our prayers and bless this water which gives fruitfulness to the fields, and refreshment and cleansing to us. You chose water to show your goodness when you led your people to freedom through the Red Sea and satisfied their thirst in the desert with water from the rock. Water was the symbol used by the prophets to foretell your new covenant with us. You made the water of baptism holy by Christ's baptism in the Jordan: by it you give us a new birth and renew us in holiness. May this water remind us of our baptism and let us share the joy of all who have been baptized at Easter. We ask this through Christ our Lord.

Where it is customary to bless salt also, add:

Almighty God, we ask you to bless this salt as once you blessed the salt scattered over the water by the prophet Elisha. Wherever this salt and water are sprinkled, drive away the power of evil, and protect us always by the presence of your Holy Spirit. Grant this through Christ our Lord.

While the celebrant sprinkles all present, an appropriate song may be sung. Afterwards, he continues:

May almighty God cleanse us of our sins, and through the eucharist we celebrate make us worthy to sit at his table in his heavenly kingdom. **Amen.**

(Turn to the GLORY TO GOD, *p. 10)*

PENITENTIAL RITE

My brothers and sisters, to prepare ourselves to celebrate the sacred mysteries, let us call to mind our sins.

1 **I confess to almighty God, and to you, my brothers and sisters, that I have sinned through my own fault, in my thoughts and in my words, in what I have done, and in what I have failed to do; and I ask blessed Mary, ever virgin, all the angels and saints, and you, my brothers and sisters, to pray for me to the Lord our God.**

   May almighty God have mercy on us, forgive us our sins, and bring us to everlasting life. **Amen.**

Lord, have mercy. **Lord, have mercy.**

Christ, have mercy. **Christ, have mercy.**

Lord, have mercy. **Lord, have mercy.**

2 Lord, we have sinned against you: Lord, have mercy. **Lord, have mercy.**

Lord, show us your mercy and love. **And grant us your salvation.**

May almighty God have mercy on us, forgive us our sins, and bring us to everlasting life. **Amen.**

3a You were sent to heal the contrite: Lord, have mercy. **Lord, have mercy.**

You came to call sinners: Christ, have mercy. **Christ, have mercy.**

You plead for us at the right hand of the Father: Lord, have mercy. **Lord, have mercy.**

May almighty God have mercy on us, forgive us our sins, and bring us to everlasting life. **Amen.**

3b Lord Jesus, you came to reconcile us to one another and to the Father: Lord, have mercy. **Lord, have mercy.**

Lord Jesus, you heal the wounds of sin and division: Christ, have mercy. **Christ, have mercy.**

Lord Jesus, you intercede for us with your Father: Lord, have mercy. **Lord, have mercy.**

May almighty God have mercy on us, forgive us our sins, and bring us to everlasting life. **Amen.**

3c You raise the dead to life in the Spirit: Lord, have mercy. **Lord, have mercy.**

You bring pardon and peace to the sinner: Christ, have mercy. **Christ, have mercy.**

You bring light to those in darkness: Lord, have mercy. **Lord, have mercy.**

May almighty God have mercy on us, forgive us our sins, and bring us to everlasting life. **Amen.**

3d Lord Jesus, you raise us to new life: Lord, have mercy. **Lord, have mercy.**

Lord Jesus, you forgive us our sins: Christ, have mercy. **Christ, have mercy.**

Lord Jesus, you feed us with your body and blood: Lord, have mercy. **Lord, have mercy.**

May almighty God have mercy on us, forgive us our sins, and bring us to everlasting life. **Amen.**

3e Lord Jesus, you healed the sick: Lord, have mercy. **Lord, have mercy.**

Lord Jesus, you forgave sinners: Christ, have mercy. **Christ, have mercy.**

Lord Jesus, you give us yourself to heal us and bring us strength: Lord, have mercy. **Lord, have mercy.**

May almighty God have mercy on us, forgive us our sins, and bring us to everlasting life. **Amen.**

GLORY TO GOD

Glory to God in the highest, and peace to his people on earth.

Lord God, heavenly King, almighty God and Father, we worship you, we give you thanks, we praise you for your glory.

Lord Jesus Christ, only Son of the Father, Lord God, Lamb of God, you take away the sin of the world: have mercy on us; you are seated at the right hand of the Father: receive our prayer.

For you alone are the Holy One, you alone are the Lord, you alone are the Most High, Jesus Christ, with the Holy Spirit, in the glory of God the Father. Amen.

OPENING PRAYER   *(Turn to the appropriate day)*

Liturgy of
the Word

**READINGS — PSALM — ACCLAMATION —
GOSPEL** *(Turn to the appropriate day)*

HOMILY

PROFESSION OF FAITH: APOSTLES' CREED

I believe in God, the Father almighty, creator of
heaven and earth.

I believe in Jesus Christ, his only Son, our Lord.
He was conceived by the power of the Holy Spirit
and born of the Virgin Mary.

He suffered under Pontius Pilate, was crucified,
died, and was buried. He descended to the dead.
On the third day he rose again. He ascended into
heaven, and is seated at the right hand of the
Father. He will come again to judge the living
and the dead.

I believe in the Holy Spirit, the holy catholic
Church, the communion of saints, the forgiveness of sins, the resurrection of the body, and the
life everlasting.

PROFESSION OF FAITH: NICENE CREED

We believe in one God, the Father, the almighty, maker of heaven and earth, of all that is seen and unseen.

We believe in one Lord, Jesus Christ, the only Son of God, eternally begotten of the Father, God from God, Light from Light, true God from true God, begotten, not made, one in Being with the Father. Through him all things were made. For us men and for our salvation he came down from heaven: by the power of the Holy Spirit he was born of the Virgin Mary, and became man. For our sake he was crucified under Pontius Pilate; he suffered, died, and was buried. On the third day he rose again in fulfilment of the Scriptures; he ascended into heaven and is seated at the right hand of the Father. He will come again in glory to judge the living and the dead, and his kingdom will have no end.

We believe in the Holy Spirit, the Lord, the giver of life, who proceeds from the Father and the Son. With the Father and the Son he is worshipped and glorified.

He has spoken through the Prophets. We believe in one holy catholic and apostolic Church. We acknowledge one baptism for the forgiveness of sins. We look for the resurrection of the dead, and the life of the world to come. Amen.

PRAYER OF THE FAITHFUL

(Turn to the appropriate day)

PREPARATION OF THE GIFTS

Blessed are you, Lord, God of all creation. Through your goodness we have this bread to offer, which earth has given and human hands have made. It will become for us the bread of life.

Blessed be God for ever.

By the mystery of this water and wine may we come to share in the divinity of Christ, who humbled himself to share in our humanity.

Blessed are you, Lord, God of all creation. Through your goodness we have this wine to offer, fruit of the vine and work of human hands. It will become our spiritual drink.

Blessed be God for ever.

Lord God, we ask you to receive us and be pleased with the sacrifice we offer you with humble and contrite hearts.

Lord, wash away my iniquity; cleanse me from my sin.

Pray, friends, that our sacrifice may be acceptable to God, the almighty Father.

May the Lord accept the sacrifice at your hands
for the praise and glory of his name,
for our good, and the good of all his Church.

PRAYER OVER THE GIFTS

(Turn to the appropriate day)

EUCHARISTIC PRAYER

The Lord be with you. **And also with you.**

Lift up your hearts. **We lift them up to the Lord.**

Let us give thanks to the Lord our God. **It is right to give him thanks and praise.**

PREFACES

Eucharistic Prayers for Masses of Reconciliation and Children's Masses incorporate specific prefaces.

Reconciliation I *(with preface)*   p. 47
Reconciliation II *(with preface)*   p. 50
Children I *(with preface)*   p. 54
Children II *(with preface)*   p. 57
Children III *(with preface)*   p. 60

These prefaces are for use with Eucharistic Prayers I-IV:

EUCHARISTIC PRAYER II

Father, it is our duty and our salvation, always and everywhere to give you thanks through your beloved Son, Jesus Christ.

He is the Word through whom you made the universe, the Saviour you sent to redeem us. By

14

the power of the Holy Spirit he took flesh and was born of the Virgin Mary.

For our sake he opened his arms on the cross; he put an end to death and revealed the resurrection. In this he fulfilled your will and won for you a holy people.

And so we join the angels and the saints in proclaiming your glory as we say: **Holy, Holy** *(p. 32)*

EUCHARISTIC PRAYER IV

Father in heaven, it is right that we should give you thanks and glory: you alone are God, living and true.

Through all eternity you live in unapproachable light. Source of life and goodness, you have created all things, to fill your creatures with every blessing and lead all men to the joyful vision of your light.

Countless hosts of angels stand before you to do your will; they look upon your splendour and praise you, night and day.

United with them, and in the name of every creature under heaven, we too praise your glory as we say: **Holy, Holy** *(p. 32)*

ADVENT I

Father, all-powerful and ever-living God, we do well always and everywhere to give you thanks through Jesus Christ our Lord.

When he humbled himself to come among us as a human being, he fulfilled the plan you formed long ago and opened for us the way to salvation. Now we watch for the day, hoping that the salvation promised us will be ours when Christ our Lord will come again in his glory.

And so, with all the choirs of angels in heaven we proclaim your glory and join in their unending hymn of praise: **Holy, Holy** *(p. 32)*

ADVENT II

Father, all-powerful and ever-living God, we do well always and everywhere to give you thanks through Jesus Christ our Lord.

His future coming was proclaimed by all the prophets. The virgin mother bore him in her womb with love beyond all telling. John the Baptist was his herald and made him known when at last he came. In his love Christ has filled us with joy as we prepare to celebrate his birth, so that when he comes he may find us watching in prayer, our hearts filled with wonder and praise.

And so, with all the choirs of angels in heaven, we proclaim your glory and join in their unending hymn of praise: **Holy, Holy** *(p. 32)*

CHRISTMAS I

Father, all-powerful and ever-living God, we do well always and everywhere to give you thanks through Jesus Christ our Lord.

In the wonder of the incarnation your eternal Word has brought to the eyes of faith a new and radiant vision of your glory. In him we see our God made visible and so are caught up in love of the God we cannot see.

And so, with all the choirs of angels in heaven, we proclaim your glory and join in their unending hymn of praise: **Holy, Holy** *(p. 32)*

16

CHRISTMAS II

Father, all-powerful and ever-living God, we do well always and everywhere to give you thanks through Jesus Christ our Lord.

Today you fill our hearts with joy as we recognize in Christ the revelation of your love. No eye can see his glory as our God, yet now he is seen as one like us.

Christ is your Son before all ages, yet now he is born in time. He has come to lift up all things to himself, to restore unity to creation, and to lead us from exile into your heavenly kingdom.

With all the angels of heaven we sing our joyful hymn of praise: **Holy, Holy** *(p. 32)*

CHRISTMAS III

Father, all-powerful and ever-living God, we do well always and everywhere to give you thanks through Jesus Christ our Lord.

Today in him a new light has dawned upon the world: God has become one with humanity, and we have become one again with God.

Your Eternal Word has taken upon himself our human weakness, giving our mortal nature immortal value. So marvellous is this oneness between God and humanity that Christ our brother restores the gift of everlasting life to his brothers and sisters.

In our joy we sing to your glory with all the choirs of angels: **Holy, Holy** *(p. 32)*

EPIPHANY

Father, all-powerful and ever-living God, we do well always and everywhere to give you thanks.

Today you revealed in Christ your eternal plan of salvation and showed him as the light of all peoples. Now that his glory has shone among us you have renewed humanity in his immortal image.

Now, with angels and archangels, and the whole company of heaven, we sing the unending hymn of your praise: **Holy, Holy** *(p. 32)*

TRANSFIGURATION OF THE LORD

Father, all-powerful and ever-living God, we do well always and everywhere to give you thanks through Jesus Christ our Lord.

He revealed his glory to the disciples to strengthen them for the scandal of the cross. His glory shone from a body like our own, to show that the Church, which is the body of Christ, would one day share his glory.

In our unending joy we echo on earth the song of the angels in heaven as they praise your glory for ever: **Holy, holy** *(p. 32)*

SUNDAYS IN ORDINARY TIME I

Father, all-powerful and ever-living God, we do well always and everywhere to give you thanks through Jesus Christ our Lord.

Through his cross and resurrection he freed us from sin and death and called us to the glory that has made us a chosen race, a royal priesthood, a holy nation, a people set apart.

Everywhere we proclaim your mighty works, for you have called us out of darkness into your own wonderful light.

And so, with all the choirs of angels in heaven, we proclaim your glory and join in their unending hymn of praise: **Holy, Holy** *(p. 32)*

SUNDAYS IN ORDINARY TIME II

Father, all-powerful and ever-living God, we do well always and everywhere to give you thanks through Jesus Christ our Lord.

Out of love for sinners, he humbled himself to be born of the Virgin. By suffering on the cross he freed us from unending death, and by rising from the dead he gave us eternal life.

And so, with all the choirs of angels in heaven we proclaim your glory and join in their unending hymn of praise: **Holy, Holy** *(p. 32)*

SUNDAYS IN ORDINARY TIME III

Father, all-powerful and ever-living God, we do well always and everywhere to give you thanks.

We see your infinite power in your loving plan of salvation. You came to our rescue by your power as God, but you wanted us to be saved by one like us. The human family refused your friendship, but it was restored by our Lord and brother Jesus Christ.

Through him the angels of heaven offer their prayer of adoration as they rejoice in your presence for ever. May our voices be one with theirs in their triumphant hymn of praise: **Holy, Holy** *(p. 32)*

SUNDAYS IN ORDINARY TIME IV

Father, all-powerful and ever-living God, we do well always and everywhere to give you thanks through Jesus Christ our Lord.

By his birth we are reborn. In his suffering we are freed from sin. By his rising from the dead we rise to everlasting life. In his return to you in glory we enter into your heavenly kingdom.

And so, we join the angels and the saints as they sing their unending hymn of praise: **Holy, Holy** *(p. 32)*

SUNDAYS IN ORDINARY TIME V

Father, all-powerful and ever-living God, we do well always and everywhere to give you thanks.

All things are of your making, all times and seasons obey your laws, but you chose to create us in your own image, setting us over the whole world in all its wonder. You made us the stewards of creation, to praise you day by day for the marvels of your wisdom and power, through Jesus Christ our Lord.

We praise you, Lord, with all the angels in their song of joy: **Holy, Holy** *(p. 32)*

SUNDAYS IN ORDINARY TIME VI

Father, all-powerful and ever-living God, we do well always and everywhere to give you thanks.

In you we live and move and have our being. Each day you show us a Father's love; your Holy Spirit, dwelling within us, gives us on earth the hope of unending joy. Your gift of the Spirit, who raised

Jesus from the dead, is the foretaste and promise of the paschal feast of heaven.

With thankful praise, in company with the angels, we glorify the wonders of your power: **Holy, Holy** *(p. 32)*

SUNDAYS IN ORDINARY TIME VII

Father, all-powerful and ever-living God, we do well always and everywhere to give you thanks.

So great was your love that you gave us your Son as our redeemer. You sent him as one like ourselves, though free from sin, that you might see and love in us what you see and love in Christ. Your gifts of grace, lost by disobedience, are now restored by the obedience of your Son.

We praise you, Lord, with all the angels and saints in their song of joy: **Holy, Holy** *(p. 32)*

SUNDAYS IN ORDINARY TIME VIII

Father, all-powerful and ever-living God, we do well always and everywhere to give you thanks.

When your children sinned and wandered far from your friendship, you reunited them with yourself through the blood of your Son and the power of the Holy Spirit. You gather them into your Church, to be one as you, Father, are one with your Son and the Holy Spirit. You call them to be your people, to praise your wisdom in all your works. You make them the body of Christ and the dwelling-place of the Holy Spirit.

In our joy we sing to your glory with all the choirs of angels: **Holy, Holy** *(p. 32)*

LENT I

Father, all-powerful and ever-living God, we do well always and everywhere to give you thanks through Jesus Christ our Lord.

Each year you give us this joyful season when we prepare to celebrate the paschal mystery with mind and heart renewed. You give us a spirit of loving reverence for you, our Father, and of willing service to our neighbour.

As we recall the great events that gave us new life in Christ, you bring the image of your Son to perfection within us.

Now, with angels and archangels, and the whole company of heaven, we sing the unending hymn of your praise: **Holy, Holy** *(p. 32)*

LENT II

Father, all-powerful and ever-living God, we do well always and everywhere to give you thanks.

This great season of grace is your gift to your family to renew us in spirit. You give us strength to purify our hearts, to control our desires, and so to serve you in freedom. You teach us how to live in this passing world, with our heart set on the world that will never end.

Now, with all the saints and angels, we praise you for ever: **Holy, Holy** *(p. 32)*

LENT IV

Father, all-powerful and ever-living God, we do well always and everywhere to give you thanks.

Through our observance of Lent you correct our faults and raise our minds to you, you help us grow in holiness and offer us the reward of everlasting life through Jesus Christ our Lord.

Through him the angels and all the choirs of heaven worship in awe before your presence. May our voices be one with theirs as they sing with joy the hymn of your glory: **Holy, Holy** *(p. 32)*

FIRST SUNDAY OF LENT

Father, all-powerful and ever-living God, we do well always and everywhere to give you thanks through Jesus Christ our Lord.

His fast of forty days makes this a holy season of self-denial. By rejecting the devil's temptations he has taught us to rid ourselves of the hidden corruption of evil, and so to share his paschal meal in purity of heart, until we come to its fulfilment in the promised land of heaven.

Now we join the angels and the saints as they sing their unending hymn of praise: **Holy, Holy** *(p. 32)*

SECOND SUNDAY OF LENT

Father, all-powerful and ever-living God, we do well always and everywhere to give you thanks through Jesus Christ our Lord.

On your holy mountain he revealed himself in glory in the presence of his disciples. He had already prepared them for his approaching death. He wanted to teach them through the Law and the Prophets that the promised Christ had first to suffer and so come to the glory of his resurrection.

In our unending joy we echo on earth the song of the angels in heaven as they praise your glory for ever: **Holy, Holy** *(p. 32)*

THIRD SUNDAY OF LENT

This preface is said with the Year A gospel about the Samaritan woman; otherwise, one of the prefaces of Lent is said.

Father, all-powerful and ever-living God, we do well always and everywhere to give you thanks, through Jesus Christ our Lord.

When he asked the woman of Samaria for water to drink, Christ had already prepared for her the gift of faith. In his thirst to receive her faith he awakened in her heart the fire of your love.

With thankful praise, in company with the angels, we glorify the wonders of your power: **Holy, Holy** *(p. 32)*

FOURTH SUNDAY OF LENT

This preface is said with the Year A gospel about the man born blind; otherwise, one of the prefaces of Lent is said.

Father, all-powerful and ever-living God, we do well always and everywhere to give you thanks, through Jesus Christ our Lord.

He came among us as a man, to lead us from darkness into the light of faith.

Through Adam's fall we were born as slaves of sin, but now through baptism in Christ we are reborn as your adopted children.

Earth unites with heaven to sing the new song of creation, as we adore and praise you for ever: **Holy, Holy** *(p. 32)*

FIFTH SUNDAY OF LENT

This preface is said with the Year A gospel about Lazarus; otherwise, one of the prefaces of Lent is said.

Father, all-powerful and ever-living God, we do well always and everywhere to give you thanks, through Jesus Christ our Lord.

As a man like us, Jesus wept for Lazarus his friend. As the eternal God, he raised Lazarus from the dead. In his love for us all, Christ gives us the sacraments to lift us up to everlasting life.

Through him the angels of heaven offer their prayer of adoration as they rejoice in your presence for ever. May our voices be one with theirs in their triumphant hymn of praise: **Holy, Holy** *(p. 32)*

PASSION SUNDAY

Father, all-powerful and ever-living God, we do well always and everywhere to give you thanks through Jesus Christ our Lord.

Though he was sinless, he suffered willingly for sinners. Though innocent, he accepted death to save the guilty. By his dying he has destroyed our sins. By his rising he has raised us up to holiness of life. We praise you, Lord, with all the angels in their song of joy: **Holy, Holy** *(p. 32)*

EASTER I

Father, all-powerful and ever-living God, we do well always and everywhere to give you thanks through Jesus Christ our Lord.

We praise you with greater joy than ever on this Easter night (day), when Christ became our paschal sacrifice.

He is the true Lamb who took away the sins of the world. By dying he destroyed our death; by rising he restored our life.

And so, with all the choirs of angels in heaven we proclaim your glory and join in their unending hymn of praise: **Holy, Holy** *(p. 32)*

EASTER II

Father, all-powerful and ever-living God, we do well always and everywhere to give you thanks through Jesus Christ our Lord.

We praise you with greater joy than ever in this Easter season, when Christ became our paschal sacrifice.

He has made us children of the light, rising to new and everlasting life. He has opened the gates of heaven to receive his faithful people. His death is our ransom from death; his resurrection is our rising to life.

The joy of the resurrection renews the whole world, while the choirs of heaven sing for ever to your glory: **Holy, Holy** *(p. 32)*

EASTER III

Father, all-powerful and ever-living God, we do well always and everywhere to give you thanks through Jesus Christ our Lord.

We praise you with greater joy than ever in this Easter season, when Christ became our paschal sacrifice.

He is still our priest, our advocate who always pleads our cause. Christ is the victim who dies no more, the Lamb, once slain, who lives for ever.

The joy of the resurrection renews the whole world, while the choirs of heaven sing for ever to your glory: **Holy, Holy** *(p. 32)*

EASTER IV

Father, all-powerful and ever-living God, we do well always and everywhere to give you thanks through Jesus Christ our Lord.

We praise you with greater joy than ever in this Easter season, when Christ became our paschal sacrifice.

In him a new age has dawned, the long reign of sin is ended, a broken world has been renewed, and we are once again made whole.

The joy of the resurrection renews the whole world, while the choirs of heaven sing for ever to your glory: **Holy, Holy** *(p. 32)*

EASTER V

Father, all-powerful and ever-living God, we do well always and everywhere to give you thanks through Jesus Christ our Lord.

We praise you with greater joy than ever in this Easter season, when Christ became our paschal sacrifice.

As he offered his body on the cross, his perfect sacrifice fulfilled all others. As he gave himself into your hands for our salvation, he showed himself to be the priest, the altar, and the lamb of sacrifice.

The joy of the resurrection renews the whole world, while the choirs of heaven sing for ever to your glory: **Holy, Holy** *(p. 32)*

ASCENSION I

Father, all-powerful and ever-living God, we do well always and everywhere to give you thanks.

(Today) the Lord Jesus, the king of glory, the conqueror of sin and death, ascended to heaven while the angels sang his praises.

Christ, the mediator between God and man, judge of the world and Lord of all, has passed beyond our sight, not to abandon us but to be our hope. Christ is the beginning, the head of the Church; where he has gone, we hope to follow.

The joy of the resurrection and ascension renews the whole world, while the choirs of heaven sing for ever to your glory: **Holy, Holy** *(p. 32)*

ASCENSION II

Father, all-powerful and ever-living God, we do well always and everywhere to give you thanks through Jesus Christ our Lord.

In his risen body he plainly showed himself to his disciples and was taken up to heaven in their sight to claim for us a share in his divine life.

And so, with all the choirs of angels in heaven, we proclaim your glory and join in their unending hymn of praise: **Holy, Holy** *(p. 32)*

PENTECOST

Father, all-powerful and ever-living God, we do well always and everywhere to give you thanks.

Today you sent the Holy Spirit on those marked out to be your children by sharing the life of your only Son, and so you brought the paschal mystery to its completion.

Today we celebrate the great beginnings of your Church when the Holy Spirit made known to all peoples the one true God, and created from the many languages of earth one voice to profess one faith.

The joy of the resurrection renews the whole world, while the choirs of heaven sing for ever to your glory: **Holy, Holy** *(p. 32)*

TRINITY

Father, all-powerful and ever-living God, we do well always and everywhere to give you thanks.

We joyfully proclaim our faith in the mystery of your Godhead. You have revealed your glory as the glory also of your Son and of the Holy Spirit: three Persons equal in majesty, undivided in splendour, yet one Lord, one God, ever to be adored in your everlasting glory.

And so, with all the choirs of angels in heaven, we proclaim your glory and join in their unending hymn of praise: **Holy, Holy** *(p. 32)*

HOLY EUCHARIST I

Father, all-powerful and ever-living God, we do well always and everywhere to give you thanks through Jesus Christ our Lord.

He is the true and eternal priest who established this unending sacrifice. He offered himself as a victim for our deliverance and taught us to make this offering in his memory. As we eat his body which he gave for us, we grow in strength. As we

29

drink his blood which he poured out for us, we are washed clean.

Now, with angels and archangels, and the whole company of heaven, we sing the unending hymn of your praise: **Holy, Holy** *(p. 32)*

HOLY EUCHARIST II

Father, all-powerful and ever-living God, we do well always and everywhere to give you thanks through Jesus Christ our Lord.

At the last supper, as he sat at table with his apostles, he offered himself to you as the spotless lamb, the acceptable gift that gives you perfect praise. Christ has given us this memorial of his passion to bring us its saving power until the end of time. In this great sacrament you feed your people and strengthen them in holiness, so that the family of mankind may come to walk in the light of one faith, in one communion of love. We come then to this wonderful sacrament to be fed at your table and grow into the likeness of the risen Christ.

Earth unites with heaven to sing the new song of creation as we adore and praise you for ever: **Holy, Holy** *(p. 32)*

CHRIST THE KING

Father, all-powerful and ever-living God, we do well always and everywhere to give you thanks.

You anointed Jesus Christ, your only Son, with the oil of gladness, as the eternal priest and universal king. As priest he offered his life on the altar of the cross and redeemed the human race by this one perfect sacrifice of peace.

As king he claims dominion over all creation, that he may present to you, his almighty Father, an eternal and universal kingdom: a kingdom of truth and life, a kingdom of holiness and grace, a kingdom of justice, love, and peace.

And so, with all the choirs of angels in heaven we proclaim your glory and join in their unending hymn of praise: **Holy, Holy** *(p. 32)*

BLESSED VIRGIN MARY I

Father, all-powerful and ever-living God, we do well always and everywhere to give you thanks as we honour the Blessed Virgin Mary.

Through the power of the Holy Spirit, she became the virgin mother of your only Son, our Lord Jesus Christ, who is for ever the light of the world.

Through him the choirs of angels and all the powers of heaven, praise and worship your glory. May our voices blend with theirs as we join in their unending hymn: **Holy, Holy** *(p. 32)*

CHRISTIAN UNITY

Father, all-powerful and ever-living God, we do well always and everywhere to give you thanks through Jesus Christ our Lord.

Through Christ you bring us to the knowledge of your truth, that we may be united by one faith and one baptism to become his body. Through Christ you have given the Holy Spirit to all peoples.

How wonderful are the works of the Spirit, revealed in so many gifts! Yet how marvellous is the unity the Spirit creates from their diversity, as he dwells in the hearts of your children, filling the whole Church with his presence and guiding it with his wisdom!

In our joy we sing to your glory with all the choirs of angels:

HOLY, HOLY

Holy, holy, holy Lord, God of power and might, heaven and earth are full of your glory. Hosanna in the highest. Blessed is he who comes in the name of the Lord. Hosanna in the highest.

Praise to the Father

We come to you, Father, with praise and thanksgiving, through Jesus Christ your Son. Through him we ask you to accept and bless these gifts we offer you in sacrifice.

For the Church

We offer them for your holy catholic Church. Watch over it, Lord, and guide it; grant it peace and unity throughout the world. We offer them for N., our pope, for N., our bishop, and for all who hold and teach the catholic faith that comes to us from the apostles.

For the living

Remember, Lord, your people, especially those for whom we now pray, N. and N.

> *Christian Initiation (Scrutinies and Baptism):*
> Remember, Lord, these godparents who (will) present your chosen men and women for baptism, N. and N.

Remember all of us gathered here before you. You know how firmly we believe in you and dedicate ourselves to you. We offer you this sacrifice of praise for ourselves and those who are dear to us. We pray to you, our living and true God, for our well-being and redemption.

To honour the saints

In union with the whole Church,

Christmas and Octave of Christmas:
we celebrate that day (night) when Mary without loss of her virginity gave the world its Saviour.

Epiphany:
we celebrate that day when your only Son, sharing your eternal glory, showed himself in a human body.

Holy Thursday:
we celebrate that day when Jesus Christ, our Lord, was betrayed for us.

Easter Vigil to Second Sunday of Easter:
we celebrate that day (night) when Jesus Christ, our Lord, rose from the dead in his human body.

Ascension:
we celebrate that day when your only Son, our Lord, took his place with you and raised our frail human nature to glory.

Pentecost:
we celebrate the day of Pentecost when the Holy Spirit appeared to the apostles in the form of countless tongues.

we honour Mary, the ever-virgin mother of Jesus Christ our Lord and God. We honour Joseph, her husband, the apostles and martyrs Peter and Paul, Andrew,

James, John, Thomas, James, Philip, Bartholomew, Matthew, Simon and Jude; we honour Linus, Cletus, Clement, Sixtus, Cornelius, Cyprian, Lawrence, Chrysogonus, John and Paul, Cosmas and Damian

and all the saints. May their merits and prayers gain us your constant help and protection.

Invocation of the Holy Spirit

Father, accept this offering from your whole family.

Christian Initiation (Scrutinies):
We offer it especially for the men and women you call to share your life through the living waters of baptism.

Christian Initiation (Baptism):
and from those born into new life by water and the Holy Spirit with all their sins forgiven. Keep them one in Christ Jesus the Lord, and may their names be written in the book of life.

Holy Thursday:
in memory of the day when Jesus Christ, our Lord, gave the mysteries of his body and blood for his disciples to celebrate.

Easter Vigil to Second Sunday of Easter:
and from those born into the new life of water and the Holy Spirit, with all their sins forgiven.

Grant us your peace in this life, save us from final damnation, and count us among those you have chosen.

Bless and approve our offering; make it acceptable to you, an offering in spirit and in truth. Let it become for us the body and blood of Jesus Christ, your only Son, our Lord.

The Lord's Supper

The day before he suffered

Holy Thursday:
to save us and all people, that is today,

he took bread in his sacred hands and looking up to heaven, to you, his almighty Father, he gave you thanks and praise. He broke the bread, gave it to his disciples, and said:

Take this, all of you, and eat it:
this is my body which will be given up for you.

When supper was ended, he took the cup. Again he gave you thanks and praise, gave the cup to his disciples, and said:

Take this, all of you, and drink from it:
this is the cup of my blood,
the blood of the new and everlasting covenant.
It will be shed for you and for all
so that sins may be forgiven.
Do this in memory of me.

Memorial Acclamation

1 Let us proclaim the mystery of faith: **Christ has died, Christ is risen, Christ will come again.**

2 Praise to you, Lord Jesus, firstborn from the dead! **Dying you destroyed our death, rising you restored our life. Lord Jesus, come in glory.**

3 We are faithful, Lord, to your command: **When we eat this bread and drink this cup, we proclaim your death, Lord Jesus, until you come in glory.**

4 Christ is Lord of all ages! **Lord, by your cross and resurrection, you have set us free. You are the Saviour of the world.**

Memorial Prayer

Father, we celebrate the memory of Christ, your Son. We, your people and your ministers, recall his passion, his resurrection from the dead, and his ascension into glory; and from the many gifts you have given us we offer to you, God of glory and majesty, this holy and perfect sacrifice: the bread of life and the cup of eternal salvation.

Look with favour on these offerings and accept them as once you accepted the gifts of your servant Abel, the sacrifice of Abraham, our father in faith, and the bread and wine offered by your priest Melchisedech.

Almighty God, we pray that your angel may take this sacrifice to your altar in heaven. Then, as we receive from this altar the sacred body and blood of your Son, let us be filled with every grace and blessing.

For the dead

Remember, Lord, those who have died and have gone before us marked with the sign of faith, especially those for whom we now pray, N. and N.

May these, and all who sleep in Christ, find in your presence light, happiness, and peace.

In communion with the saints

For ourselves, too, we ask some share in the fellowship of your apostles and martyrs, with John the Baptist, Stephen, Matthias, Barnabas,

Ignatius, Alexander, Marcellinus, Peter, Felicity, Perpetua, Agatha, Lucy, Agnes, Cecilia, Anastasia

and all the saints.

Though we are sinners, we trust in your mercy and love. Do not consider what we truly deserve, but grant us your forgiveness.

Through Christ our Lord you give us all these gifts, you fill them with life and goodness, you bless them and make them holy.

In praise of God

Through him, with him, in him, in the unity of the Holy Spirit, all glory and honour is yours, almighty Father, for ever and ever. **Amen.**

(Turn to the LORD'S PRAYER, p. 63)

EUCHARISTIC PRAYER II

Invocation of the Holy Spirit

Lord, you are holy indeed, the fountain of all holiness. Let your Spirit come upon these gifts to make them holy, so that they may become for us the body and blood of our Lord, Jesus Christ.

The Lord's Supper

Before he was given up to death, a death he freely accepted, he took bread and gave you thanks. He broke the bread, gave it to his disciples, and said:

Take this, all of you, and eat it:
this is my body which will be given up for you.

When supper was ended, he took the cup. Again he gave you thanks and praise, gave the cup to his disciples, and said:

Take this, all of you, and drink from it:
this is the cup of my blood,
the blood of the new and everlasting covenant.

It will be shed for you and for all
so that sins may be forgiven.
Do this in memory of me.

Memorial Acclamation

1 Let us proclaim the mystery of faith: **Christ has died, Christ is risen, Christ will come again.**

2 Praise to you, Lord Jesus, firstborn from the dead! **Dying you destroyed our death, rising you restored our life. Lord Jesus, come in glory.**

3 We are faithful, Lord, to your command: **When we eat this bread and drink this cup, we proclaim your death, Lord Jesus, until you come in glory.**

4 Christ is Lord of all ages! **Lord, by your cross and resurrection, you have set us free. You are the Saviour of the world.**

Memorial Prayer

In memory of his death and resurrection, we offer you, Father, this life-giving bread, this saving cup. We thank you for counting us worthy to stand in your presence and serve you. May all of us who share in the body and blood of Christ be brought together in unity by the Holy Spirit.

For the Church

Lord, remember your Church throughout the world; make us grow in love, together with N., our pope, N. our bishop, and all the clergy.

Christian Initiation (Baptism):
Remember all those who have been baptized (and confirmed) today as members of your family. Help them to follow Christ your Son with loving hearts.

For the dead

Remember our brothers and sisters who have gone to their rest in the hope of rising again; bring them and all the departed into the light of your presence.

In communion with the saints

Have mercy on us all; make us worthy to share eternal life with Mary, the virgin Mother of God, with the apostles, and with all the saints who have done your will throughout the ages. May we praise you in union with them, and give you glory through your Son, Jesus Christ.

In praise of God

Through him, with him, in him, in the unity of the Holy Spirit, all glory and honour is yours, almighty Father, for ever and ever. **Amen.**

(Turn to the LORD'S PRAYER, *p. 63)*

EUCHARISTIC PRAYER III

Praise to the Father

Father, you are holy indeed, and all creation rightly gives you praise. All life, all holiness comes from you through your Son, Jesus Christ our Lord, by the working of the Holy Spirit. From age to age you gather a people to yourself, so that from east to west a perfect offering may be made to the glory of your name.

Invocation of the Holy Spirit

And so, Father, we bring you these gifts. We ask you to make them holy by the power of your Spirit, that they may become the body and blood of your Son, our Lord Jesus Christ, at whose command we celebrate this eucharist.

The Lord's Supper

On the night he was betrayed, he took bread and gave you thanks and praise. He broke the bread, gave it to his disciples, and said:

> Take this, all of you, and eat it:
> this is my body which will be given up for you.

When supper was ended, he took the cup. Again he gave you thanks and praise, gave the cup to his disciples, and said:

> Take this, all of you, and drink from it:
> this is the cup of my blood,
> the blood of the new and everlasting covenant.
> It will be shed for you and for all
> so that sins may be forgiven.
> Do this in memory of me.

Memorial Acclamation

1 Let us proclaim the mystery of faith: **Christ has died, Christ is risen, Christ will come again.**

2 Praise to you, Lord Jesus, firstborn from the dead! **Dying you destroyed our death, rising you restored our life. Lord Jesus, come in glory.**

41

3 We are faithful, Lord, to your command: **When we eat this bread and drink this cup, we proclaim your death, Lord Jesus, until you come in glory.**

4 Christ is Lord of all ages! **Lord, by your cross and resurrection, you have set us free. You are the Saviour of the world.**

Memorial Prayer

Father, calling to mind the death your Son endured for our salvation, his glorious resurrection and ascension into heaven, and ready to greet him when he comes again, we offer you in thanksgiving this holy and living sacrifice.

Look with favour on your Church's offering, and see the Victim whose death has reconciled us to yourself. Grant that we, who are nourished by his body and blood, may be filled with his Holy Spirit, and become one body, one spirit in Christ.

May he make us an everlasting gift to you and enable us to share in the inheritance of your saints, with Mary, the virgin Mother of God; with the apostles, the martyrs, (Saint N.) and all your saints, on whose constant intercession we rely for help.

For the Church

Lord, may this sacrifice, which has made our peace with you, advance the peace and salvation of all the world. Strengthen in faith and love your pilgrim Church on earth; your servant, Pope N., our bishop N., and all the bishops, with the clergy and the entire people your Son has gained for you. Father, hear the prayers of the family you have gathered here before you.

Christian Initiation (Baptism):
Strengthen those who have now become your people by the waters of rebirth (and the gift of the Holy Spirit). Help them to walk in newness of life.

In mercy and love unite all your children wherever they may be.

For the dead

Welcome into your kingdom our departed brothers and sisters, and all who have left this world in your friendship. We hope to enjoy for ever the vision of your glory, through Christ our Lord, from whom all good things come.

In praise of God

Through him, with him, in him, in the unity of the Holy Spirit, all glory and honour is yours, almighty Father, for ever and ever. **Amen**.

(Turn to the LORD'S PRAYER, *p. 63)*

EUCHARISTIC PRAYER IV

Praise to the Father

Father, we acknowledge your greatness: all your actions show your wisdom and love. You formed man in your own likeness and set him over the whole world to serve you, his creator, and to rule over all creatures.

Even when he disobeyed you and lost your friendship you did not abandon him to the power of death, but helped all men to seek and find you.

Again and again you offered a covenant to man, and through the prophets taught him to hope for salvation.

Father, you so loved the world that in the fullness of time you sent your only Son to be our Saviour. He was conceived through the power of the Holy Spirit and born of the Virgin Mary, a man like us in all things but sin.

To the poor he proclaimed the good news of salvation, to prisoners, freedom, and to those in sorrow, joy. In fulfilment of your will he gave himself up to death; but by rising from the dead, he destroyed death and restored life.

And that we might live no longer for ourselves but for him, he sent the Holy Spirit from you, Father, as his first gift to those who believe, to complete his work on earth and bring us the fullness of grace.

Invocation of the Holy Spirit

Father, may this Holy Spirit sanctify these offerings. Let them become the body and blood of Jesus Christ our Lord as we celebrate the great mystery which he left us as an everlasting covenant.

The Lord's Supper

He always loved those who were his own in the world. When the time came for him to be glorified by you, his heavenly Father, he showed the depth of his love.

While they were at supper, he took bread, said the blessing, broke the bread, and gave it to his disciples, saying:

44

Take this, all of you, and eat it:
this is my body which will be given up for you.

In the same way, he took the cup, filled with wine. He gave you thanks, and giving the cup to his disciples, said:

Take this, all of you, and drink from it:
this is the cup of my blood,
the blood of the new and everlasting covenant.
It will be shed for you and for all
so that sins may be forgiven.
Do this in memory of me.

Memorial Acclamation

1 Let us proclaim the mystery of faith: **Christ has died, Christ is risen, Christ will come again.**

2 Praise to you, Lord Jesus, firstborn from the dead! **Dying you destroyed our death, rising you restored our life. Lord Jesus, come in glory.**

3 We are faithful, Lord, to your command: **When we eat this bread and drink this cup, we proclaim your death, Lord Jesus, until you come in glory.**

4 Christ is Lord of all ages! **Lord, by your cross and resurrection, you have set us free. You are the Saviour of the world.**

Memorial Prayer

Father, we now celebrate this memorial of our redemption. We recall Christ's death, his descent among the dead, his resurrection, and his ascension to your right hand; and, looking forward to his coming in glory, we offer you his body and blood, the acceptable sacrifice which brings salvation to the whole world.

For the Church

Lord, look upon this sacrifice which you have given to your Church; and by your Holy Spirit, gather all who share this one bread and one cup into the one body of Christ, a living sacrifice of praise.

Lord, remember those for whom we offer this sacrifice, especially N. our pope, N. our bishop, and bishops and clergy everywhere. Remember those who take part in this offering, those here present,

> *Christian Initiation (Baptism):*
> those born again today by water and the Holy Spirit,

and all your people, and all who seek you with a sincere heart.

For the dead

Remember those who have died in the peace of Christ and all the dead whose faith is known to you alone.

In communion with the saints

Father, in your mercy grant also to us, your children, to enter into our heavenly inheritance in the company of the Virgin Mary, the Mother of God, and your apostles and saints. Then, in your kingdom, freed from the corruption of sin and death, we shall sing your glory with every creature through Christ our Lord, through whom you give us everything that is good.

In praise of God

Through him, with him, in him, in the unity of the Holy Spirit, all glory and honour is yours, almighty Father, for ever and ever. **Amen.**

(Turn to the LORD'S PRAYER, *p. 63)*

EUCHARISTIC PRAYER FOR MASS OF RECONCILIATION I

Preface

Father, all-powerful and ever-living God, we do well always and everywhere to give you thanks and praise. You never cease to call us to a new and more abundant life.

God of love and mercy, you are always ready to forgive; we are sinners, and you invite us to trust in your mercy.

Time and time again we broke your covenant, but you did not abandon us. Instead, through your Son, Jesus our Lord, you bound yourself even more closely to the human family by a bond that can never be broken.

Now is the time for your people to turn back to you and be renewed in Christ your Son, a time of grace and reconciliation.

You invite us to serve the family of mankind by opening our hearts to the fullness of your Holy Spirit.

In wonder and gratitude, we join our voices with the choirs of heaven to proclaim the power of your love and to sing of our salvation in Christ:

Holy, holy, holy Lord, God of power and might, heaven and earth are full of your glory. Hosanna in the highest. Blessed is he who comes in the name of the Lord. Hosanna in the highest.

Praise to the Father

Father, from the beginning of time you have always done what is good for man so that we may be holy as you are holy.

Look with kindness on your people gathered here before you: send forth the power of your Spirit so that these gifts may become for us the body and blood of your beloved Son, Jesus the Christ, in whom we have become your sons and daughters.

When we were lost and could not find the way to you, you loved us more than ever: Jesus, your Son, innocent and without sin, gave himself into our hands and was nailed to a cross. Yet before he stretched out his arms between heaven and earth in the everlasting sign of your covenant, he desired to celebrate the Paschal feast in the company of his disciples.

While they were at supper, he took bread and gave you thanks and praise. He broke the bread, gave it to his disciples, and said:

Take this, all of you, and eat it:
this is my body which will be given up for you.

At the end of the meal, knowing that he was to reconcile all things in himself by the blood of his

48

cross, he took the cup, filled with wine. Again he gave you thanks, handed the cup to his friends, and said:

> Take this, all of you, and drink from it:
> this is the cup of my blood,
> the blood of the new and everlasting covenant.
> It will be shed for you and for all
> so that sins may be forgiven.
> Do this in memory of me.

Memorial Acclamation

1 Let us proclaim the mystery of faith: **Christ has died, Christ is risen, Christ will come again.**

2 Praise to you, Lord Jesus, firstborn from the dead! **Dying you destroyed our death, rising you restored our life. Lord Jesus, come in glory.**

3 We are faithful, Lord, to your command: **When we eat this bread and drink this cup, we proclaim your death, Lord Jesus, until you come in glory.**

4 Christ is Lord of all ages! **Lord, by your cross and resurrection, you have set us free. You are the Saviour of the world.**

Memorial Prayer

We do this in memory of Jesus Christ, our Passover and our lasting peace. We celebrate his death and resurrection and look for the coming of that day when he will return to give us the fulness of joy. Therefore we offer you, God ever faithful and true, the sacrifice which restores man to your friendship.

For the Church

Father, look with love on those you have called to share in the one sacrifice of Christ. By the power of your Holy Spirit make them one body, healed of all division.

Keep us all in communion of mind and heart with N., our pope, and N., our bishop. Help us to work together for the coming of your kingdom, until at last we stand in your presence to share the life of the saints, in the company of the Virgin Mary and the apostles, and of our departed brothers and sisters whom we commend to your mercy.

Then, freed from every shadow of death, we shall take our place in the new creation and give you thanks with Christ, our risen Lord.

In praise of God

Through him, with him, in him, in the unity of the Holy Spirit, all glory and honour is yours, almighty Father, for ever and ever. **Amen.**

(Turn to the LORD'S PRAYER, *p. 63)*

EUCHARISTIC PRAYER FOR MASS OF RECONCILIATION II

Preface

Father, all-powerful and ever-living God, we praise and thank you through Jesus Christ our Lord for your presence and action in the world. In the midst of conflict and division, we know it is you who turn our minds to thoughts of peace.

Your Spirit changes our hearts: enemies begin to speak to one another, those who were estranged join hands in friendship, and nations seek the way of peace together.

Your Spirit is at work when understanding puts an end to strife, when hatred is quenched by mercy, and vengeance gives way to forgiveness.

For this we should never cease to thank and praise you. We join with all the choirs of heaven as they sing for ever to your glory!

Holy, holy, holy Lord, God of power and might, heaven and earth are full of your glory. Hosanna in the highest. Blessed is he who comes in the name of the Lord. Hosanna in the highest.

God of power and might, we praise you through your Son, Jesus Christ, who comes in your name. He is the Word that brings salvation. He is the hand you stretch out to sinners. He is the way that leads to your peace.

God our Father, we had wandered far from you, but through your Son you have brought us back. You gave him up to death so that we might turn again to you and find our way to one another.

Therefore we celebrate the reconciliation Christ has gained for us.

We ask you to sanctify these gifts by the power of your Spirit, as we now fulfil your Son's command.

While he was at supper on the night before he died for us, he took bread in his hands, and gave you thanks and praise. He broke the bread, gave it to his disciples, and said:

Take this, all of you, and eat it:
this is my body which will be given up for you.

At the end of the meal he took the cup. Again he praised you for your goodness, gave the cup to his disciples, and said:

Take this, all of you, and drink from it:
this is the cup of my blood,
the blood of the new and everlasting covenant.
It will be shed for you and for all
so that sins may be forgiven.
Do this in memory of me.

Memorial Acclamation

1 Let us proclaim the mystery of faith: **Christ has died, Christ is risen, Christ will come again.**

2 Praise to you, Lord Jesus, firstborn from the dead! **Dying you destroyed our death, rising you restored our life. Lord Jesus, come in glory.**

3 We are faithful, Lord, to your command: **When we eat this bread and drink this cup, we proclaim your death, Lord Jesus, until you come in glory.**

4 Christ is Lord of all ages! **Lord, by your cross and resurrection, you have set us free. You are the Saviour of the world.**

Memorial Prayer

Lord our God, your Son has entrusted to us this pledge of his love. We celebrate the memory of his death and resurrection and bring you the gift you have given us, the sacrifice of reconciliation. Therefore, we ask you, Father, to accept us, together with your Son.

Fill us with his Spirit through our sharing in this meal. May he take away all that divides us.

For the Church

May this Spirit keep us always in communion with N., our pope, N., our bishop, with all the bishops and all your people. Father, make your Church throughout the world a sign of unity and an instrument of your peace.

In communion with the saints

You have gathered us here around the table of your Son, in fellowship with the Virgin Mary, Mother of God, and all the saints. In that new world where the fullness of your peace will be revealed, gather people of every race, language, and way of life to share in the one eternal banquet with Jesus Christ the Lord.

In praise of God

Through him, with him, in him, in the unity of the Holy Spirit, all glory and honour is yours, almighty Father, for ever and ever. **Amen.**

(Turn to the LORD'S PRAYER, *p. 63)*

EUCHARISTIC PRAYER FOR MASS WITH CHILDREN I

Preface

God our Father, you have brought us here together so that we can give you thanks and praise for all the wonderful things you have done.

We thank you for all that is beautiful in the world and for the happiness you have given us. We praise you for daylight and for your word which lights up our minds. We praise you for the earth, and all the people who live on it, and for our life which comes from you.

We know that you are good. You love us and do great things for us. So we all sing together:

Holy, holy, holy Lord, God of power and might, heaven and earth are full of your glory. Hosanna in the highest.

Father, you are always thinking about your people; you never forget us. You sent us your Son Jesus, who gave his life for us and who came to save us. He cured sick people; he cared for those who were poor and wept with those who were sad. He forgave sinners and taught us to forgive each other. He loved everyone and showed us how to be kind. He took children in his arms and blessed them. So we all sing together:

Blessed is he who comes in the name of the Lord. Hosanna in the highest.

God our Father, all over the world your people praise you. So now we pray with the whole Church: with N., our pope, and N., our bishop. In heaven the blessed Virgin Mary, the apostles and all the saints always sing your praise. Now we join with them and with the angels to adore you as we sing:

Holy, holy, holy Lord, God of power and might, heaven and earth are full of your glory. Hosanna in the highest. Blessed is he who comes in the name of the Lord. Hosanna in the highest.

God our Father, you are most holy and we want to show you that we are grateful.

We bring you bread and wine and ask you to send your Holy Spirit to make these gifts the body and blood of Jesus your Son. Then we can offer to you what you have given to us.

On the night before he died, Jesus was having supper with his apostles. He took bread from the table. He gave you thanks and praise. Then he broke the bread, gave it to his friends, and said:

Take this, all of you, and eat it:
this is my body which will be given up for you.

When supper was ended, Jesus took the cup that was filled with wine. He thanked you, gave it to his friends, and said:

Take this, all of you, and drink from it:
this is the cup of my blood,
the blood of the new and everlasting covenant.
It will be shed for you and for all
so that sins may be forgiven.

Then he said to them:

Do this in memory of me.

We do now what Jesus told us to do. We remember his death and his resurrection and we offer you, Father, the bread that gives us life, and the cup that saves us. Jesus brings us to you; welcome us as you welcome him.

1 Let us proclaim the mystery of faith: **Christ has died, Christ is risen, Christ will come again.**

2 Praise to you, Lord Jesus, firstborn from the dead! **Dying you destroyed our death, rising you restored our life. Lord Jesus, come in glory.**

3 We are faithful, Lord, to your command: **When we eat this bread and drink this cup, we proclaim your death, Lord Jesus, until you come in glory.**

4 Christ is Lord of all ages! **Lord, by your cross and resurrection, you have set us free. You are the Saviour of the world.**

Father, because you love us, you invite us to come to your table. Fill us with the joy of the Holy Spirit as we receive the body and blood of your Son.

Lord, you never forget any of your children. We ask you to take care of those we love, especially of N. and N.; and we pray for those who have died.

Remember everyone who is suffering from pain or sorrow. Remember Christians everywhere and all other people in the world.

We are filled with wonder and praise when we see what you do for us through Jesus your Son, and so we sing:

Through him, with him, in him, in the unity of the Holy Spirit, all glory and honour is yours, almighty Father, for ever and ever. **Amen.**

(Turn to the LORD'S PRAYER, *p. 63)*

EUCHARISTIC PRAYER FOR MASS WITH CHILDREN II

Preface

God, our loving Father, we are glad to give you thanks and praise because you love us. With Jesus we sing your praise:

Glory to God in the highest.
or: **Hosanna in the highest.**

Because you love us, you gave us this great and beautiful world. With Jesus we sing your praise:

Glory to God in the highest.
or: **Hosanna in the highest.**

Because you love us, you sent Jesus your Son to bring us to you and to gather us around him as the children of one family. With Jesus we sing your praise:

Glory to God in the highest.
or: **Hosanna in the highest.**

For such great love we thank you with the angels and saints as they praise you and sing:

Holy, holy, holy Lord, God of power and might, heaven and earth are full of your glory. Hosanna in the highest. Blessed is he who comes in the name of the Lord. Hosanna in the highest.

Blessed be Jesus, whom you sent to be the friend of children and of the poor.

He came to show us how we can love you, Father, by loving one another. He came to take away sin, which keeps us from being friends, and hate, which makes us all unhappy.

He promised to send the Holy Spirit, to be with us always so that we can live as your children.

Blessed is he who comes in the name of the Lord. Hosanna in the highest.

God our Father, we now ask you to send your Holy Spirit to change these gifts of bread and wine into the body and blood of Jesus Christ, our Lord.

The night before he died, Jesus your Son showed us how much you love us. When he was at supper with his disciples, he took bread, and gave you thanks and praise. Then he broke the bread, gave it to his friends, and said:

Take this, all of you, and eat it:
this is my body which will be given up for you.

Jesus has given his life for us.

When supper was ended, Jesus took the cup that was filled with wine. He thanked you, gave it to his friends, and said:

Take this, all of you, and drink from it:
this is the cup of my blood,
the blood of the new and everlasting covenant.

It will be shed for you and for all
so that sins may be forgiven.

Jesus has given his life for us.

Then he said to them:

Do this in memory of me.

And so, loving Father, we remember that Jesus died and rose again to save the world. He put himself into our hands to be the sacrifice we offer you.

We praise you. We bless you. We thank you.

Lord our God, listen to our prayer. Send the Holy Spirit to all of us who share in this meal. May this Spirit bring us closer together in the family of the Church, with N., our pope, N., our bishop, all other bishops, and all who serve your people.

We praise you. We bless you. We thank you.

Remember, Father, our families and friends and all those we do not love as we should. Remember those who have died. Bring them home to you, to be with you for ever.

We praise you. We bless you. We thank you.

Gather us all together into your kingdom. There we shall be happy for ever with the Virgin Mary, Mother of God and our mother. There all the friends of Jesus the Lord will sing a song of joy.

We praise you. We bless you. We thank you.

Through him, with him, in him, in the unity of the Holy Spirit, all glory and honour is yours, almighty Father, for ever and ever. **Amen.**

(Turn to the LORD'S PRAYER, *p. 63)*

59

Preface

Outside the Easter Season:

We thank you, God our Father. You made us to live for you and for each other. We can see and speak to one another, and become friends, and share our joys and sorrows.

During the Easter Season:

We thank you, God our Father. You are the living God; you have called us to share in your life, and to be happy with you for ever. You raised up Jesus, your Son, the first among us to rise from the dead, and gave him new life. You have promised to give us new life also, a life that will never end, a life with no more anxiety and suffering.

And so, Father, we gladly thank you with everyone who believes in you; with the saints and angels, we rejoice and praise you, singing:

Holy, holy, holy Lord, God of power and might, heaven and earth are full of your glory. Hosanna in the highest. Blessed is he who comes in the name of the Lord. Hosanna in the highest.

Yes, Lord, you are holy; you are kind to us and to all. For this we thank you. We thank you above all for your Son, Jesus Christ.

Outside the Easter season:
You sent him into this world because people had turned away from you and no longer loved each other. He opened our eyes and our hearts to understand that we are brothers and sisters, and that you are Father of us all.

During the Easter season:
He brought us the Good News of life to be lived with you for ever in heaven. He showed us the way to that life, the way of love. He himself has gone that way before us.

He now brings us together to one table and asks us to do what he did.

Father, we ask you to bless these gifts of bread and wine and make them holy. Change them for us into the body and blood of Jesus Christ, your Son.

On the night before he died for us he had supper for the last time with his disciples. He took bread and gave you thanks. He broke the bread and gave it to his friends, saying:

Take this, all of you, and eat it:
this is my body which will be given up for you.

In the same way he took a cup of wine. He gave you thanks and handed the cup to his disciples, saying:

Take this, all of you, and drink from it:
this is the cup of my blood,
the blood of the new and everlasting covenant.
It will be shed for you and for all men
so that sins may be forgiven.

Then he said to them:

Do this in memory of me.

God our Father, we remember with joy all that Jesus did to save us. In this holy sacrifice, which he gave as a gift to his Church, we remember his death and resurrection.

Father in heaven, accept us together with your beloved Son. He willingly died for us, but you raised him to life again. We thank you and say:

Glory to God in the highest.

Jesus now lives with you in glory, but he is also here on earth, among us. We thank you and say:

Glory to God in the highest.

One day he will come in glory and in his kingdom there will be no more suffering, no more tears, no more sadness. We thank you and say:

Glory to God in the highest.

Father in heaven, you have called us to receive the body and blood of Christ at this table and to be filled with the joy of the Holy Spirit. Through this sacred meal give us strength to please you more and more.

Lord, our God, remember N., our pope, N., our bishop, and all other bishops.

Outside the Easter season:
Help all who follow Jesus to work for peace and to bring happiness to others.

> *During the Easter season:*
> Fill all Christians with the gladness of Easter. Help us to bring this joy to all who are sorrowful.

Bring us all at last, together with Mary, the Mother of God, and all the saints, to live with you and to be one with Christ in heaven.

Through him, with him, in him, in the unity of the Holy Spirit, all glory and honour is yours, almighty Father, forever and ever. **Amen.**

COMMUNION RITE

LORD'S PRAYER

Let us pray with confidence to the Father in the words our Saviour gave us:

Our Father, who art in heaven, hallowed be thy name; thy kingdom come; thy will be done on earth as it is in heaven. Give us this day our daily bread; and forgive us our trespasses as we forgive those who trespass against us; and lead us not into temptation, but deliver us from evil.

Deliver us, Lord, from every evil, and grant us peace in our day. In your mercy keep us free from sin and protect us from all anxiety as we wait in joyful hope for the coming of our Saviour, Jesus Christ.

For the kingdom, the power and the glory are yours, now and forever.

SIGN OF PEACE

Lord Jesus Christ, you said to your apostles: I leave you peace, my peace I give you. Look not on our sins, but on the faith of your Church, and grant us the peace and unity of your kingdom where you live for ever and ever. **Amen.**

The peace of the Lord be with you always. **And also with you.**

Let us offer each other a sign of peace.

BREAKING OF THE BREAD

Lamb of God, you take away the sins of the world: have mercy on us.

Lamb of God, you take away the sins of the world: have mercy on us.

Lamb of God, you take away the sins of the world: grant us peace.

May this mingling of the body and blood of our Lord Jesus Christ bring eternal life to us who receive it.

COMMUNION

1 Lord Jesus Christ, Son of the living God, by the will of the Father and the work of the Holy Spirit your death brought life to the world. By your holy body and blood free me from all my sins and from every evil. Keep me faithful to your teaching and never let me be parted from you.

2 Lord Jesus Christ, with faith in your love and mercy, I eat your body and drink your blood. Let it not bring me condemnation, but health in mind and body.

This is the Lamb of God who takes away the sins of the world. Happy are those who are called to his supper.

Lord, I am not worthy to receive you, but only say the word and I shall be healed.

May the body (blood) of Christ bring me to ever-lasting life.

The body of Christ. **Amen.**

The blood of Christ. **Amen.**

COMMUNION ANTIPHON

(Turn to the appropriate day)

PRAYER AFTER COMMUNION

(Turn to the appropriate day)

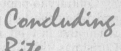

Concluding Rite

BLESSING

The Lord be with you. **And also with you.**

May almighty God bless you, the Father, and the Son, and the Holy Spirit. **Amen.**

DISMISSAL

Go in the peace of Christ.

or: The Mass is ended, go in peace.

or: Go in peace to love and serve the Lord.

Thanks be to God.

Amid the flurry of preparing for Christmas, today's gospel reminds us to remain "alert" and to not let our hearts be "weighed down with the worries of this life." For many, these 'worries' may involve the hectic juggling of Christmas shopping, parties, card-writing and baking. For others, they may be the worries of providing for their loved ones—will there be a warm place to gather, a Christmas meal and presents for the children?

Contrary to popular belief, Christmas doesn't end when the last present has been opened or when the last bit of baking has disappeared. Christmas, the arrival of Jesus in our world, is only just the beginning. The new life that we receive in Jesus continues each and every day as we await, with watchful anticipation, the second coming of Jesus, in power and glory.

And while we await that second coming, we live as a people of hope. Advent offers us an opportunity to pause in our busy-ness, to recognize our longing for Jesus' message of love and new beginnings. We pray that our lives may be transformed anew this season and that we may find ways to bring hope to those who live in loneliness or despair.

Caryl Green, Chelsea, QC

ENTRANCE ANTIPHON *(Psalm 25:1-3)*

To you, my God, I lift my soul, I trust in you; let me never come to shame. Do not let my enemies laugh at me. No one who waits for you is ever put to shame.

INTRODUCTORY RITES *(p. 5)*
The Glory to God *is not said during Advent.*

OPENING PRAYER

All-powerful God, increase our strength of will for doing good that Christ may find an eager welcome at his coming and call us to his side in the kingdom of heaven.

FIRST READING *(Jeremiah 33:14-16)*

The days are surely coming, says the Lord, when I will fulfil the promise I made to the house of Israel and the house of Judah.

In those days and at that time I will cause a righteous Branch to spring up for David; and he shall execute justice and righteousness in the land.

In those days Judah will be saved and Jerusalem will live in safety. And this is the name by which it will be called: "The Lord is our righteousness."

The word of the Lord. **Thanks be to God.**

RESPONSORIAL PSALM *(Psalm 25)*

To you, O Lord, I lift my— soul.

GJ

℟. **To you, O Lord, I lift my soul.**

Make me to know your ways, O • **Lord,**
teach me your • **paths.**
Lead me in your truth and • **teach_me,**
for you are the God of my • **sal**-vation. ℟.

Good and upright is the • **Lord,**
therefore he instructs sinners in the • **way.**
He leads the humble in what is • **right,**
and teaches the humble • **his** way. ℟.

All the paths of the Lord are steadfast love
    and • **faithfulness,**
for those who keep his covenant
    and his • **decrees.**
The friendship of the Lord is for those
    who • **fear_him,**
and he makes his covenant known • **to** them. ℟.

SECOND READING *(1 Thessalonians 3:12–4:2)*

Beloved: May the Lord make you increase and
abound in love for one another and for all, just as
we abound in love for you. And may he so
strengthen your hearts in holiness that you may
be blameless before our God and Father at the
coming of our Lord Jesus with all his saints.

Finally, brothers and sisters, we ask and urge you in the Lord Jesus that, as you learned from us how you ought to live and to please God, as, in fact, you are doing, you should do so more and more. For you know what instructions we gave you through the Lord Jesus.

The word of the Lord. **Thanks be to God.**

GOSPEL ACCLAMATION *(Psalm 85)*

If not sung, this acclamation is omitted.

Lord, show us your mercy and love, and grant us your salvation.

GOSPEL *(Luke 21:25-28, 34-36)*

A reading from the holy gospel according to Luke. **Glory to you, Lord.**

Jesus spoke to his disciples about his return in glory. "There will be signs in the sun, the moon, and the stars and on the earth distress among nations confused by the roaring of the sea and the waves. People will faint from fear and foreboding of what is coming upon the world, for the powers of the heavens will be shaken.

"Then they will see 'the Son of Man coming in a cloud' with power and great glory. Now when these things begin to take place, stand up and raise your heads, because your redemption is drawing near.

"Be on guard so that your hearts are not weighed down with dissipation and drunkenness and the worries of this life, and that day catch you unexpectedly, like a trap. For it will come upon all who live on the face of the whole earth. Be alert at all times, praying that you may have the strength to escape all these things that will take place, and to stand before the Son of Man."

The gospel of the Lord. **Praise to you, Lord Jesus Christ.**

PROFESSION OF FAITH *(Creed, pp. 11-12)*

PRAYER OF THE FAITHFUL

The following intentions are suggestions only.

℞: **Lord, hear our prayer.**

For the Church, witness to God's word in our world, we pray to the Lord: ℞.

For government leaders guided by principles of justice and mercy, we pray to the Lord: ℞.

For those who search for hope amidst despair, we pray to the Lord: ℞.

For ourselves, God's people, called to welcome those who have lost hope, we pray to the Lord: ℞.

PREPARATION OF THE GIFTS *(p. 13)*

PRAYER OVER THE GIFTS

Father, from all you give us we present this bread and wine. As we serve you now, accept our offering and sustain us with your promise of eternal life.

PREFACE *(Advent I, p. 15)*

COMMUNION ANTIPHON *(Psalm 85:12)*

The Lord will shower his gifts, and our land will yield its fruit.

PRAYER AFTER COMMUNION

Father, may our communion teach us to love heaven. May its promise and hope guide our way on earth.

SOLEMN BLESSING FOR ADVENT *(Optional)*

Bow your heads and pray for God's blessing.

You believe that the Son of God once came to us; you look for him to come again. May his coming bring you the light of his holiness and free you with his blessing. **Amen.**

May God make you steadfast in faith, joyful in hope, and untiring in love all the days of your life. **Amen.**

You rejoice that our Redeemer came in the flesh. When he comes again in glory, may he reward you with endless life. **Amen.**

May almighty God bless you, the Father, and the Son, and the Holy Spirit. **Amen.**

DISMISSAL *(p. 65)*

December 4 Second Sunday of Advent

Today we continue the theme of preparation. We are called to readiness, invited to journey to conversion as we prepare for the coming of the Lord.

Advent is a time to prepare ourselves not only for this year's Christmas season, but also for the day we will meet Jesus face to face. Often we become so wrapped up with our worldly cares and goods that we fail to hear the call of prophets like John. We become blinded to the truth and to the God who sustains and encompasses all.

As we prepare for the Nativity, Jesus gives each of us a personal invitation to follow him more closely, to be like John, setting an example by word and action, calling others to a life in Christ. We are reminded to base our life on Christ.

The valleys and mountains of life at times may almost overpower us, but Jesus gives meaning and hope to life as he, like John, calls us to repentance and promises us salvation. Our love of God overflows to others to help them through the valleys of life, the ups and downs, and to restore faith and hope to a sometimes discouraged world.

Murray J. Hanowski, Neudorf, SK

ENTRANCE ANTIPHON *(See Isaiah 30:19, 30)*

People of Zion, the Lord will come to save all nations, and your hearts will exult to hear his majestic voice.

INTRODUCTORY RITES *(p. 5)*
The Glory to God *is not said during Advent.*

OPENING PRAYER

God of power and mercy, open our hearts in welcome. Remove the things that hinder us from receiving Christ with joy, so that we may share his wisdom and become one with him when he comes in glory.

FIRST READING *(Baruch 5:1-9)*

Take off the garment of your sorrow
 and affliction, O Jerusalem,
and put on forever the beauty
 of the glory from God.
Put on the robe of the righteousness
 that comes from God;
put on your head the diadem of the glory
 of the Everlasting;
for God will show your splendour
 everywhere under heaven.
For God will give you evermore the name,
"Righteous Peace, Godly Glory."

Arise, O Jerusalem, stand upon the height;
look toward the east,
and see your children
 gathered from west and east
at the word of the Holy One,
rejoicing that God has remembered them.

For they went out from you on foot,
led away by their enemies;
but God will bring them back to you,
carried in glory, as on a royal throne.

For God has ordered that every high mountain
and the everlasting hills be made low
and the valleys filled up, to make level ground,
so that Israel may walk safely in the glory of God.
The woods and every fragrant tree
have shaded Israel at God's command.
For God will lead Israel with joy,
in the light of his glory,
with the mercy and righteousness
    that come from him.

The word of the Lord. **Thanks be to God.**

RESPONSORIAL PSALM (*Psalm 126*)

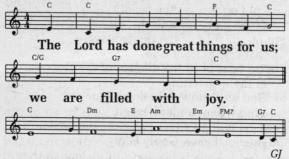

GJ

℟. **The Lord has done great things for us;**
we are filled with joy.

When the Lord restored the fortunes of • **Zion,**
we were like those who • **dream.**
Then our mouth was filled with • **laughter,**
and our tongue with shouts • **of** joy. ℟.

74

Then it was said among the • **nations,**
The Lord has done great things for • **them.**
The Lord has done great things for • **us,**
and we • **re**-joiced. ℟.

Restore our fortunes, O • **Lord,**
like the watercourses in the desert
    of the • **Negev.**
May those who sow in • **tears**
reap with shouts • **of** joy. ℟.

Those who go out • **weeping,**
bearing the seed for • **sowing,**
shall come home with shouts of • **joy,**
carrying • **their** sheaves. ℟.

SECOND READING *(Philippians 1:3-6, 8-11)*

My brothers and sisters, I thank my God every
time I remember you, constantly praying with joy
in every one of my prayers for all of you, because
of your sharing in the gospel from the first day
until now.

I am confident of this, that the one who began a
good work among you will bring it to completion
by the day of Jesus Christ.

For God is my witness, how I long for all of you
with the compassion of Christ Jesus. And this is
my prayer, that your love may overflow more and
more with knowledge and full insight so that in
the day of Christ you may be pure and blameless,
having produced the harvest of righteousness
that comes through Jesus Christ for the glory and
praise of God.

The word of the Lord. **Thanks be to God.**

GOSPEL ACCLAMATION *(Luke 3:4, 6)*

If not sung, this acclamation is omitted.

Prepare the way of the Lord, make straight his paths: all people shall see the salvation of God.

GOSPEL *(Luke 3:1-6)*

A reading from the holy gospel according to Luke. **Glory to you, Lord.**

In the fifteenth year of the reign of Emperor Tiberius, when Pontius Pilate was governor of Judea, and Herod was ruler of Galilee, and his brother Philip ruler of the region of Ituraea and Trachonitis, and Lysanias ruler of Abilene, during the high priesthood of Annas and Caiaphas, the word of God came to John son of Zechariah in the wilderness.

He went into all the region around the Jordan, proclaiming a baptism of repentance for the forgiveness of sins, as it is written in the book of the words of the prophet Isaiah, "The voice of one crying out in the wilderness: 'Prepare the way of the Lord, make his paths straight. Every valley shall be filled, and every mountain and hill shall be made low, and the crooked shall be made straight, and the rough ways made smooth; and all flesh shall see the salvation of God.' "

The gospel of the Lord. **Praise to you, Lord Jesus Christ.**

PROFESSION OF FAITH *(Creed, pp. 11-12)*

PRAYER OF THE FAITHFUL

The following intentions are suggestions only.

℟: **Lord, hear our prayer.**

For all Christians, called to work together to prepare the Lord's way, we pray to the Lord: ℟.

For an end to persecution and wars, we pray to the Lord: ℟.

For those caught up in turmoil and uncertainty, and for all who assist them, we pray to the Lord: ℟.

For us, God's people gathered here, called to walk the path of new life, we pray to the Lord: ℟.

PREPARATION OF THE GIFTS *(p. 13)*

PRAYER OVER THE GIFTS

Lord, we are nothing without you. As you sustain us with your mercy, receive our prayers and offerings.

PREFACE *(Advent I, p. 15)*

COMMUNION ANTIPHON *(Baruch 5:5; 4:36)*

Rise up, Jerusalem, stand on the heights, and see the joy that is coming to you from God.

PRAYER AFTER COMMUNION

Father, you give us food from heaven. By our sharing in this mystery, teach us to judge wisely the things of earth and to love the things of heaven.

SOLEMN BLESSING AND DISMISSAL *(p. 71)*

December 11 Third Sunday of Advent

It is difficult to *talk* about joy; we have to *show* it. Israel had no shortage of images to show why they rejoiced in God: God was a merciful judge, a defender of Israel, a great ruler in their midst, a force against evil, a victor in war, a joyous and loving dancer who rejoiced in them. Israel simply overflowed with joy for God.

Paul sums up the Christian life with this simple exhortation: "Rejoice in the Lord always. The Lord is near." From joy come prayer, gratitude, gentleness and peace of mind. From joy also come the will and the power to keep worries about material goods in perspective.

On this Third Sunday of Advent, the Church waits in joyful expectation for its Saviour. John the Baptist calls us to show the depth of our joy by sharing our goods with the less fortunate, abandoning greed, and exercising fairness in all our dealings with others. Because we have received the baptism of Jesus Christ, in the fire of the Holy Spirit, we do our best to live in joyful witness. With all we have been given, may our joy express itself in the justness and fruitfulness of our lives.

Christine Mader, Toronto, ON

ENTRANCE ANTIPHON *(Philippians 4:4, 5)*

Rejoice in the Lord always; again I say, rejoice! The Lord is near.

INTRODUCTORY RITES *(p. 5)*
The Glory to God *is not said during Advent.*

OPENING PRAYER

Lord God, may we, your people, who look forward to the birthday of Christ, experience the joy of salvation and celebrate that feast with love and thanksgiving.

FIRST READING *(Zephaniah 3:14-18)*

Sing aloud, O daughter Zion; shout, O Israel!
Rejoice and exult with all your heart,
O daughter of Jerusalem!
The Lord has taken away
    the judgments against you,
he has turned away your enemies.
The king of Israel, the Lord, is in your midst;
you shall fear disaster no more.

On that day it shall be said to Jerusalem:
Do not fear, O Zion;
do not let your hands grow weak.
The Lord, your God, is in your midst,
a warrior who gives victory;
he will rejoice over you with gladness,
he will renew you in his love.
The Lord, your God, will exult over you
    with loud singing
as on a day of festival.

The word of the Lord. **Thanks be to God.**

79

RESPONSORIAL CANTICLE *(Isaiah 12)*

Cry out for joy,_____

for God is a-mong you.

GJ

℟. **Cry out for joy and gladness: for among you is the great and Holy One of Israel.**

Surely God is my salvation;
   I will trust, and will not • **be** a-fraid,
for the Lord God is my strength
    • **and** my might;
he has become • **my** sal-vation.
With joy you will draw water
    from the • **wells_of** sal-vation. ℟.

Give thanks • **to** the Lord,
call • **on** his name;
make known his deeds a•-**mong** the nations;
proclaim that his name • **is** ex-alted. ℟.

Sing praises to the Lord,
    for he • **has** done gloriously;
let this be known in • **all** the earth.
Shout aloud and sing for joy, O • **roy**-al Zion,
for great in your midst
    is the • **Holy_One** of Israel. ℟.

SECOND READING *(Philippians 4:4-7)*

Rejoice in the Lord always; again I will say, Rejoice.

Let your gentleness be known to everyone. The Lord is near. Do not worry about anything, but in everything let your requests be made known to God by prayer and supplication with thanksgiving.

And the peace of God, which surpasses all understanding, will guard your hearts and your minds in Christ Jesus.

The word of the Lord. **Thanks be to God.**

GOSPEL ACCLAMATION *(Isaiah 61:1; Luke 4:18)*

If not sung, this acclamation is omitted.

The Spirit of the Lord now upon me has sent me to bring good news to the poor.

GOSPEL *(Luke 3:10-18)*

A reading from the holy gospel according to Luke. **Glory to you, Lord.**

The crowds, who were gathering to be baptized by John, asked him, "What should we do?" In reply John said to them, "Whoever has two coats must share with anyone who has none; and whoever has food must do likewise."

Even tax collectors came to be baptized, and they asked him, "Teacher, what should we do?" He said to them, "Collect no more than the amount prescribed for you." Soldiers also asked him, "And we, what should we do?" He said to them, "Do not extort money from anyone by threats or false accusation, and be satisfied with your wages."

As the people were filled with expectation, and all were questioning in their hearts concerning John, whether he might be the Messiah, John answered all of them by saying, "I baptize you with water; but one who is more powerful than I is coming; I am not worthy to untie the thong of his sandals. He will baptize you with the Holy Spirit and fire. His winnowing fork is in his hand, to clear his threshing floor and to gather the wheat into his granary; but the chaff he will burn with unquenchable fire."

So, with many other exhortations, John proclaimed the good news to the people.

The gospel of the Lord. **Praise to you, Lord Jesus Christ.**

PROFESSION OF FAITH *(Creed, pp. 11-12)*

PRAYER OF THE FAITHFUL

The following intentions are suggestions only.

℟: **Lord, hear our prayer.**

For Christians everywhere, called to witness to God's love by joyful and practical service in the world, we pray to the Lord: ℟.

For the swift coming of God's rule of peace and justice among all nations, we pray to the Lord: ℟.

For people among us who are lonely or separated from family and friends, we pray to the Lord: ℟.

For all who work to help families experience true peace and joy, we pray to the Lord: ℟.

PREPARATION OF THE GIFTS *(p. 13)*

PRAYER OVER THE GIFTS

Lord, may the gift we offer in faith and love be a continual sacrifice in your honour and truly become our eucharist and our salvation.

PREFACE *(Advent I-II, p. 15)*

COMMUNION ANTIPHON *(See Isaiah 35:4)*

Say to the anxious: be strong and fear not, our God will come to save us.

PRAYER AFTER COMMUNION

God of mercy, may this eucharist bring us your divine help, free us from our sins, and prepare us for the birthday of our Saviour, who is Lord for ever and ever.

SOLEMN BLESSING AND DISMISSAL *(p. 71)*

Life was such a simple affair on the family farm that I could easily focus on a few special traditional experiences. These generally stood out for me, head and shoulders above the rest. The 'visit' was one of these.

I *loved* visiting and, even more, being visited! I enjoyed aunts and uncles and especially young cousins—even neighbours—dropping by. My heart always 'leaped within me!' What great times we had sharing family stories, spending endless hours playing cards, checkers, crokinole and other games.

Such was the simple entertainment of prairie farm life—so long ago! Of course, during the Christmas season we pulled out all the stops! Seasonal baking, special cooking, home-made drinks appeared daily on our family table, as 'company' dropped by to wish us season's greetings.

So I am naturally struck by Mary's visit to her cousin Elizabeth in today's gospel. I imagine, in the midst of that 'rural' culture and given Mary's pregnant circumstances, Elizabeth's feelings as she greeted her cousin at the door.

In fact, Luke recalls Elizabeth being so taken up by this event that something extraordinary happens. United with the child within her, who also "leaped for joy," Elizabeth utters prophecies that are filled with blessings.

And so we see here the ultimate experience in visiting—with the Spirit released to delight and affirm all of them that day "in the hill country."

Christmas will be a time of visiting. Let us release the Spirit of God among us as we bear Jesus to one another!

Jerome Herauf, Halifax, NS

ENTRANCE ANTIPHON *(Isaiah 45:8)*

Let the clouds rain down the Just One, and the earth bring forth a Saviour.

INTRODUCTORY RITES *(p. 5)*
The Glory to God *is not said during Advent.*

OPENING PRAYER

Lord, fill our hearts with your love, and as you revealed to us by an angel the coming of your Son as man, so lead us through his suffering and death to the glory of his resurrection.

FIRST READING *(Micah 5:2-5)*

The Lord says to his people:
"You, O Bethlehem of Ephrathah,
who are one of the little clans of Judea,
from you shall come forth for me
one who is to rule in Israel,
whose origin is from of old, from ancient days."

Therefore he shall give them up until the time
when she who is in labour has brought forth;
then the rest of his kindred
shall return to the people of Israel.
And he shall stand and feed his flock

in the strength of the Lord,
in the majesty of the name of the Lord his God.

And they shall live secure,
for now he shall be great to the ends of the earth;
and he shall be the one of peace.

The word of the Lord. **Thanks be to God.**

RESPONSORIAL PSALM *(Psalm 80)*

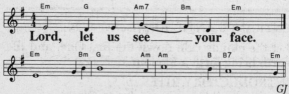

Lord, let us see_____your face.

GJ

℟. **Lord, make us turn to you;**
   let us see your face and we shall be saved.

Give ear, O Shepherd • **of** Israel,
you who are enthroned upon the cherubim,
   shine • **forth.**
Stir up your • **might,**
and come to • **save_us.** ℟.

Turn again, O God • **of** hosts,
look down from heaven and • **see;**
have regard for this • **vine,**
the stock that your right hand has • **planted.** ℟.

Let your hand be upon the one at • **your** right,
the one whom you have made strong
   for your• -**self.**
Then we will never turn back from • **you;**
give us life, and we will call on your • **name.** ℟.

SECOND READING *(Hebrews 10:5-10)*

When Christ came into the world, he said, "Sacrifices and offerings you have not desired, but a body you have prepared for me; in burnt offerings and sin offerings you have taken no pleasure. Then I said, as it is written of me in the scroll of the book, 'See, God, I have come to do your will, O God.' "

When Christ said, "You have neither desired nor taken pleasure in sacrifices and offerings and burnt offerings and sin offerings" (these are offered according to the law), then he added, "See, I have come to do your will." He abolishes the first in order to establish the second.

And it is by God's will that we have been sanctified through the offering of the body of Jesus Christ once for all.

The word of the Lord. **Thanks be to God.**

GOSPEL ACCLAMATION *(Luke 1:38)*

If not sung, this acclamation is omitted.

I am the servant of the Lord: let it be done to me according to your word.

GOSPEL *(Luke 1:39-45)*

A reading from the holy gospel according to Luke. **Glory to you, Lord.**

Mary set out and went with haste to a Judean town in the hill country, where she entered the house of Zechariah and greeted Elizabeth.

When Elizabeth heard Mary's greeting, the child leaped in her womb. And Elizabeth was filled with the Holy Spirit and exclaimed with a loud cry, "Blessed are you among women, and blessed is the fruit of your womb. And why has this happened to me, that the mother of my Lord comes to me? For as soon as I heard the sound of your greeting, the child in my womb leaped for joy. And blessed is she who believed that there would be a fulfilment of what was spoken to her by the Lord."

The gospel of the Lord. **Praise to you, Lord Jesus Christ.**

PROFESSION OF FAITH *(Creed, pp. 11-12)*

PRAYER OF THE FAITHFUL

The following intentions are suggestions only.

℞: **Lord, hear our prayer.**

For the Church, called as Mary was, to give Christ to our world, we pray to the Lord: ℞.

For the swift coming of God's rule of peace and justice among all nations, we pray to the Lord: ℞.

For people in our midst who reach out for our love and our hope, we pray to the Lord: ℞.

For us, God's people gathered here, called to bring the presence of Christ to each other, we pray to the Lord: ℞.

PREPARATION OF THE GIFTS *(p. 13)*

PRAYER OVER THE GIFTS

Lord, may the power of the Spirit, which sanctified Mary the mother of your Son, make holy the gifts we place upon this altar.

PREFACE *(Advent II, p. 16)*

COMMUNION ANTIPHON *(Isaiah 7:14)*

The Virgin is with child and shall bear a son, and she will call him Emmanuel.

PRAYER AFTER COMMUNION

Lord, in this sacrament we receive the promise of salvation; as Christmas draws near make us grow in faith and love to celebrate the coming of Christ our Saviour, who is Lord for ever and ever.

SOLEMN BLESSING AND DISMISSAL *(p. 71)*

"And the Word became flesh and lived among us..." Has the phrase become so familiar that we no longer recognize its profound implications?

Notice the kinds of images which pervade the Christmas readings. Light banishes the darkness; voices resound with songs of praise; the seas, the mountains, the trees proclaim their joy. This is not the discourse of theoretical abstraction but the language of the senses, of nature, language which resonates with our human experience.

And at the centre of all this is that perfectly human event, the birth of a baby—a baby, however, who is the Mighty God, the Prince of Peace, the "imprint of God's very being."

We need to remind ourselves that "Incarnation" refers not just to one event but to the ongoing reality of God's presence in our midst. The life of this God, who is at once cosmic and personal, infuses and transforms every dimension of our existence.

May we, like Mary, treasure and ponder the true meaning of this festival time. Let us pray for a re-awakened awareness of the Word-made-flesh living among us, not just 2,000 years ago, but here and now and always.

Krystyna Higgins, Kitchener, ON

MASS DURING THE NIGHT

ENTRANCE ANTIPHON

Let us all rejoice in the Lord, for our Saviour is born to the world. True peace has descended from heaven.

INTRODUCTORY RITES *(p. 5)*

OPENING PRAYER

Father, you make this holy night radiant with the splendour of Jesus Christ our light. We welcome him as Lord, the true light of the world. Bring us to eternal joy in the kingdom of heaven.

FIRST READING *(Isaiah 9:2-4, 6-7)*

The people who walked in darkness
have seen a great light;
those who lived in a land of deep darkness —
on them light has shone.
You have multiplied the nation,
you have increased its joy;
they rejoice before you
as with joy at the harvest,
as people exult when dividing plunder.

For the yoke of their burden,
and the bar across their shoulders,
the rod of their oppressor,
you have broken as on the day of Midian.

For a child has been born for us,
a son given to us;
authority rests upon his shoulders;
and he is named
Wonderful Counsellor, Mighty God,
Everlasting Father, Prince of Peace.
His authority shall grow continually,
and there shall be endless peace
for the throne of David and his kingdom.
He will establish and uphold it
with justice and with righteousness
from this time onward and forevermore.
The zeal of the Lord of hosts will do this.

The word of the Lord. **Thanks be to God.**

RESPONSORIAL PSALM *(Psalm 96)*

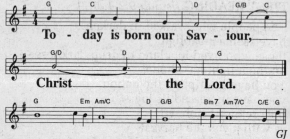

GJ

℟. **Today is born our Saviour, Christ the Lord.**

O sing to the Lord a • **new** song;
sing to the Lord, all • **the** earth.
Sing to the Lord, bless • **his** name;
tell of his salvation from day • **to** day. ℟.

Declare his glory among • **the** nations,
his marvellous works among all • **the** peoples.
For great is the Lord,
    and greatly to • **be** praised;
he is to be revered above • **all** gods. ℟.

Let the heavens be glad, and
    let the earth • **re-**joice;
let the sea roar, and all • **that** fills_it;
let the field exult, and every•**-thing** in_it.
Then shall all the trees of the forest
    sing • **for** joy. ℟.

Rejoice before the Lord; for he • **is** coming,
for he is coming to judge • **the** earth.
He will judge the world • **with** righteousness,
and the peoples with • **his** truth. ℟.

SECOND READING *(Titus 2:11-14)*

The grace of God has appeared, bringing salvation to all, training us to renounce impiety and worldly passions, and in the present age to live lives that are self-controlled, upright, and godly, while we wait for the blessed hope and the manifestation of the glory of our great God and Saviour, Jesus Christ.

He it is who gave himself for us that he might redeem us from all iniquity and purify for himself a people of his own who are zealous for good deeds.

The word of the Lord. **Thanks be to God.**

GOSPEL ACCLAMATION *(Luke 2:10-11)*

If not sung, this acclamation is omitted.

Good news and great joy to all the world: today is born our Saviour, Christ the Lord.

GOSPEL *(Luke 2:1-16)*

A reading from the holy gospel according to Luke.
Glory to you, Lord.

In those days a decree went out from Emperor Augustus that all the world should be registered. This was the first registration and was taken while Quirinius was governor of Syria. All went to their own towns to be registered. Joseph also went from the town of Nazareth in Galilee to Judea, to the city of David called Bethlehem, because he was descended from the house and family of David. He went to be registered with Mary, to whom he was engaged and who was expecting a child.

While they were there, the time came for her to deliver her child. And she gave birth to her firstborn son and wrapped him in bands of cloth, and laid him in a manger, because there was no place for them in the inn.

In that region there were shepherds living in the fields, keeping watch over their flock by night. Then an angel of the Lord stood before them, and the glory of the Lord shone around them, and they were terrified. But the angel said to them, "Do not be afraid; for see—I am bringing you good news of great joy for all the people: to you is born this day in the city of David a Saviour, who is the Messiah, the Lord. This will be a sign for you: you will find a child wrapped in bands of cloth and lying in a manger."

And suddenly there was with the angel a multitude of the heavenly host, praising God and saying, "Glory to God in the highest heaven, and on earth peace among those whom he favours!"

When the angels had left them and gone into heaven, the shepherds said to one another, "Let us go now to Bethlehem and see this thing that has taken place, which the Lord has made known to us." So they went with haste and found Mary and Joseph, and the child lying in the manger.

The gospel of the Lord. **Praise to you, Lord Jesus Christ.**

PROFESSION OF FAITH *(Nicene Creed, p. 12)*

PRAYER OF THE FAITHFUL

The following intentions are suggestions only.

℞: **Lord, hear our prayer.**

For the Church, called to see with the eyes of faith God's living presence in our midst, we pray to the Lord: ℞.

For all the world's children, gracious sacraments of God's gift of life, we pray to the Lord: ℞.

For people in our midst who, in this season of joyful light, walk in darkness, loneliness and despair, we pray to the Lord: ℞.

For us, God's people gathered here, called to recognize God's presence in all things, we pray to the Lord: ℞.

PREPARATION OF THE GIFTS *(p. 13)*

PRAYER OVER THE GIFTS

Lord, accept our gifts on this joyful feast of our salvation. By our communion with God made man, may we become more like him who joins our lives to yours.

PREFACE *(Christmas I-III, p. 16)*

COMMUNION ANTIPHON *(John 1:14)*

The Word of God became man; we have seen his glory.

PRAYER AFTER COMMUNION

God our Father, we rejoice in the birth of our Saviour. May we share his life completely by living as he has taught.

SOLEMN BLESSING FOR CHRISTMAS *(Optional)*

Bow your heads and pray for God's blessing.

When he came to us as our brother, the Son of God scattered the darkness of this world, and filled this holy night (day) with his glory. May the God of infinite goodness scatter the darkness of sin and brighten your hearts with holiness. **Amen.**

God sent his angels to shepherds to herald the great joy of our Saviour's birth. May he fill you with joy and make you heralds of his gospel. **Amen.**

When the Word became flesh, earth was joined to heaven. May he give you his peace and good will, and fellowship with all the heavenly host. **Amen.**

May almighty God bless you, the Father, and the Son, and the Holy Spirit. **Amen.**

DISMISSAL *(p. 65)*

MASS AT DAWN

ENTRANCE ANTIPHON *(See Isaiah 9; Luke 1)*

A light will shine on us this day, the Lord is born for us: he shall be called Wonderful God, Prince of peace, Father of the world to come; and his kingship will never end.

INTRODUCTORY RITES *(p. 5)*

OPENING PRAYER

Father, we are filled with the new light by the coming of your Word among us. May the light of faith shine in our words and actions.

FIRST READING *(Isaiah 62:11-12)*

The Lord has proclaimed to the end of the earth:
"Say to daughter Zion,
See, your salvation comes;
his reward is with him,
and his recompense before him.

"They shall be called 'The Holy People,'
'The Redeemed of the Lord';
and you shall be called 'Sought Out,'
'A City Not Forsaken.' "

The word of the Lord. **Thanks be to God.**

RESPONSORIAL PSALM *(Psalm 97)*

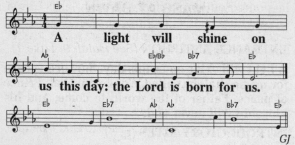

R̘. **A light will shine on us this day:**
The Lord is born for us.

The Lord is king! Let the earth re•-joice;
let the many coastlands be • glad!
Clouds and thick darkness
    are all a•-round_him;
righteousness and justice
    are the foundation of his • throne. R̘.

The mountains melt like wax before the • Lord,
before the Lord of all the • earth.
The heavens proclaim his • righteousness;
and all the peoples behold his • glory. R̘.

Light dawns for the • righteous,
and joy for the upright in • heart.
Rejoice in the Lord, O you • righteous,
and give thanks to his holy • name! R̘.

SECOND READING *(Titus 3:4-7)*

When the goodness and loving kindness of God
our Saviour appeared, he saved us, not because of
any works of righteousness that we had done, but
according to his mercy, through the water of

98

rebirth and renewal by the Holy Spirit. This Spirit he poured out on us richly through Jesus Christ our Saviour, so that, having been justified by his grace, we might become heirs according to the hope of eternal life.

The word of the Lord. **Thanks be to God.**

GOSPEL ACCLAMATION *(Luke 2:14)*

If not sung, this acclamation is omitted.

Glory to God in the highest, peace to God's people on earth.

GOSPEL *(Luke 2:15-20)*

A reading from the holy gospel according to Luke. **Glory to you, Lord.**

When the angels had left them and gone into heaven, the shepherds said to one another, "Let us go now to Bethlehem and see this thing that has taken place, which the Lord has made known to us."

So they went with haste and found Mary and Joseph, and the child lying in the manger. When they saw this, they made known what had been told them about this child; and all who heard it were amazed at what the shepherds told them.

But Mary treasured all these words and pondered them in her heart. The shepherds returned, glorifying and praising God for all they had heard and seen, as it had been told them.

The gospel of the Lord. **Praise to you, Lord Jesus Christ.**

PROFESSION OF FAITH *(Nicene Creed, p. 12)*

PRAYER OF THE FAITHFUL *(p. 95)*

PREPARATION OF THE GIFTS *(p. 13)*

PRAYER OVER THE GIFTS

Father, may we follow the example of your Son who became man and lived among us. May we receive the gift of divine life through these offerings here on earth.

PREFACE *(Christmas I-III, p. 16)*

COMMUNION ANTIPHON *(See Zechariah 9:9)*

Daughter of Zion, exult; shout aloud, daughter of Jerusalem! Our King is coming, the Holy One, the Saviour of the world.

PRAYER AFTER COMMUNION

Lord, with faith and joy we celebrate the birthday of your Son. Increase our understanding and our love of the riches you have revealed in him.

SOLEMN BLESSING AND DISMISSAL *(p. 96)*

MASS DURING THE DAY

ENTRANCE ANTIPHON *(Isaiah 9:6)*

A child is born for us, a son given to us; dominion is laid on his shoulder, and he shall be called Wonderful Counsellor.

INTRODUCTORY RITES *(p. 5)*

OPENING PRAYER

Lord God, we praise you for creating us, and still more for restoring us in Christ. Your Son shared our weakness: may we share his glory.

FIRST READING *(Isaiah 52:7-10)*

How beautiful upon the mountains are the feet of the messenger who announces peace, who brings good news, who announces salvation, who says to Zion, "Your God reigns."

Listen! Your sentinels lift up their voices, together they sing for joy; for in plain sight they see the return of the Lord to Zion.

Break forth together into singing, you ruins of Jerusalem; for the Lord has comforted his people, he has redeemed Jerusalem. The Lord has bared his holy arm before the eyes of all the nations; and all the ends of the earth shall see the salvation of our God.

The word of the Lord. **Thanks be to God.**

RESPONSORIAL PSALM *(Psalm 98)*

All the ends of the earth have seen the
sav - ing pow-er of God.

GJ

℟. **All the ends of the earth have seen
the saving power of God.**

O sing to the Lord a • **new** song,
for he has done marvel•**-lous** things.
His right hand and his holy • **arm**
have brought • **him** victory. ℟.

The Lord has made known • **his** victory;
he has revealed his vindication
    in the sight of • **the** nations.
He has remembered his steadfast • **love**
and faithfulness to the house • **of** Israel. ℟.

All the ends of the earth • **have** seen
the victory of • **our** God.
Make a joyful noise to the Lord, all the • **earth;**
break forth into joyous song
    and • **sing** praises. ℟.

Sing praises to the Lord with • **the** lyre,
with the lyre and the sound • **of** melody.
With trumpets and the sound of the • **horn**
make a joyful noise before the King,
    • **the** Lord. ℟.

SECOND READING *(Hebrews 1:1-6)*

Long ago God spoke to our ancestors in many and various ways by the prophets, but in these last days he has spoken to us by a Son, whom he appointed heir of all things, through whom he also created the worlds.

He is the reflection of God's glory and the exact imprint of God's very being, and he sustains all things by his powerful word. When he had made purification for sins, he sat down at the right hand of the Majesty on high, having become as much superior to angels as the name he has inherited is more excellent than theirs.

For to which of the angels did God ever say, "You are my Son; today I have begotten you"? Or again, "I will be his Father, and he will be my Son"? And again, when he brings the firstborn into the world, he says, "Let all God's angels worship him."

The word of the Lord. **Thanks be to God.**

GOSPEL ACCLAMATION

If not sung, this acclamation is omitted.

A holy day has dawned upon us. Come you nations and adore the Lord. Today a great light has come upon the earth.

GOSPEL *(John 1:1-18)*

A reading from the holy gospel according to John. **Glory to you, Lord.**

In the beginning was the Word, and the Word was with God, and the Word was God. He was in the beginning with God. All things came into being through him, and without him not one thing came into being. What has come into being in him was life, and the life was the light of all people.

The light shines in the darkness, and the darkness did not overcome it. There was a man sent from God, whose name was John. He came as a witness to testify to the light, so that all might believe through him. He himself was not the light, but he came to testify to the light.

The true light, which enlightens everyone, was coming into the world. He was in the world, and the world came into being through him; yet the world did not know him. He came to what was his own, and his own people did not accept him. But to all who received him, who believed in his name, he gave power to become children of God, who were born, not of blood or of the will of the flesh or of the will of man, but of God.

And the Word became flesh and lived among us, and we have seen his glory, the glory as of a father's only son, full of grace and truth.

John testified to him and cried out, "This was he of whom I said, 'He who comes after me ranks ahead of me because he was before me.' "

From his fullness we have all received, grace upon grace. The law indeed was given through Moses; grace and truth came through Jesus Christ. No one has ever seen God. It is God the only Son, who is close to the Father's heart, who has made him known.

The gospel of the Lord. **Praise to you, Lord Jesus Christ.**

PROFESSION OF FAITH *(Nicene Creed, p. 12)*

PRAYER OF THE FAITHFUL *(p. 95)*

PREPARATION OF THE GIFTS *(p. 13)*

PRAYER OVER THE GIFTS

Almighty God, the saving work of Christ made our peace with you. May our offering today renew that peace within us and give you perfect praise.

PREFACE *(Christmas I-III, p. 16)*

COMMUNION ANTIPHON *(Psalm 98:3)*

All the ends of the earth have seen the saving power of God.

PRAYER AFTER COMMUNION

Father, the child born today is the Saviour of the world. He made us your children. May he welcome us into your kingdom.

SOLEMN BLESSING AND DISMISSAL *(p. 96)*

The shepherds in today's gospel are the first to proclaim the Good News: "all who heard it were amazed at what the shepherds told them." What is even more astonishing is the fact that it is shepherds who are doing this. In those days, shepherds were generally viewed as dirty and smelly, best banned from polite company. Nonetheless, they bravely ventured beyond their usual role in order to share what the angels had told them. They took a great risk—of being shunned, rejected and turned away. And yet, they stepped forward in faith and became the first evangelists.

Mary, too, gives us a splendid example of what it means to step out in faith. Think of the nine months before Jesus' birth: the suspicious circumstances surrounding her pregnancy, the journey to Bethlehem, the lack of shelter, the distance from family and home. And then, the awesome responsibility of giving birth to God. How difficult it must have been for her to remain faithful to God during those months!

It is precisely because of her faithfulness that Mary is presented to us as a model to be followed. Mary was not all that different from us. She too was simply a human being, struggling to be faithful to God. She too must have had misgivings and doubts. And yet, she continued to trust, to step out in faith and to be open to God. When we honour Mary, then, we emphasize the full potential of human beings to give themselves to God.

And so, today, on the first day of the new year, a challenge is set before us. Can we, like the shepherds, courageously move beyond our accustomed roles in order to share the Good News with others? Like Mary, can we open ourselves to God to such an extent that we too bring forth new life to others? By our own words and actions, can we make the love of God incarnate in our world?

Teresa Whalen, Regina, SK

ENTRANCE ANTIPHON *(See Isaiah 9:2, 6)*

A light will shine on us this day, the Lord is born for us: he shall be called Wonderful God, Prince of peace, Father of the world to come; and his kingship will never end.

INTRODUCTORY RITES *(p. 5)*

OPENING PRAYER

God our Father, may we always profit by the prayers of the Virgin Mother Mary, for you bring us life and salvation through Jesus Christ her Son.

FIRST READING *(Numbers 6:22-27)*

The Lord spoke to Moses: "Speak to Aaron and his sons, saying, 'Thus you shall bless the Israelites: You shall say to them,

'The Lord bless you and keep you;
the Lord make his face to shine upon you,
and be gracious to you;

the Lord lift up his countenance upon you,
and give you peace.'

"So they shall put my name on the Israelites, and
I will bless them."

The word of the Lord. **Thanks be to God.**

RESPONSORIAL PSALM *(Psalm 67)*

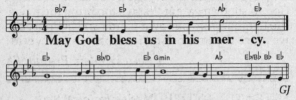

GJ

℟. **May God bless us in his mercy.**

May God be gracious to us • **and** bless_us
and make his face to shine • **up**-on_us,
that your way may be known up•-on earth,
your saving power a•-mong all nations. ℟.

Let the nations be glad and sing • **for** joy,
for you judge the peoples with equity
   and guide the nations up•-on earth.
Let the peoples praise you, • **O** God;
let all the • **peo**-ples praise_you. ℟.

The earth has yielded • **its** increase;
God, our God, • **has** blessed_us.
May God continue • **to** bless_us;
let all the ends of the • **earth** re-vere_him. ℟.

SECOND READING *(Galatians 4:4-7)*

When the fullness of time had come, God sent his Son, born of a woman, born under the law, in order to redeem those who were under the law, so that we might receive adoption as children.

And because you are children, God has sent the Spirit of his Son into our hearts, crying, "Abba! Father!" So you are no longer a slave but a child, and if a child then also an heir, through God.

The word of the Lord. **Thanks be to God.**

GOSPEL ACCLAMATION *(Hebrew 1:1-2)*

If not sung, this acclamation is omitted.

In the past God spoke to our ancestors through the prophets; now God speaks to us through the Son.

GOSPEL *(Luke 2:16-21)*

A reading from the holy gospel according to Luke. **Glory to you, Lord.**

When the angels had left them the shepherds said to one another, "Let us go now to Bethlehem and see this thing that has taken place, which the Lord has made known to us."

So they went with haste and found Mary and Joseph, and the child lying in the manger. When they saw this, they made known what had been told them about this child; and all who heard it were amazed at what the shepherds told them.

But Mary treasured all these words and pondered them in her heart.

The shepherds returned, glorifying and praising God for all they had heard and seen, as it had been told them.

After eight days had passed, it was time to circumcise the child; and he was called Jesus, the name given by the angel before he was conceived in the womb.

The gospel of the Lord. **Praise to you, Lord Jesus Christ.**

PROFESSION OF FAITH *(Creed, pp. 11-12)*

PRAYER OF THE FAITHFUL

The following intentions are suggestions only.

℟: **Lord, hear our prayer.**

For all Christians, called to be a sign of unity as we work together for justice, we pray to the Lord: ℟.

For peace in our world broken by violence, abuse, hatred and the misuse of the world's resources, we pray to the Lord: ℟.

For all who hunger and thirst for freedom from the shackles of poverty, unemployment and prejudice, we pray to the Lord: ℟.

For those who, like Mary, display strength, courage and perseverance, we pray to the Lord: ℟.

PREPARATION OF THE GIFTS *(p. 13)*

PRAYER OVER THE GIFTS

God our Father, we celebrate at this season the beginning of our salvation. On this feast of Mary, the Mother of God, we ask that our salvation will be brought to its fulfilment.

PREFACE *(Blessed Virgin Mary I, p. 31)*

COMMUNION ANTIPHON *(Hebrews 13:8)*

Jesus Christ is the same yesterday, today, and for ever.

PRAYER AFTER COMMUNION

Father, as we proclaim the Virgin Mary to be the mother of Christ and the mother of the Church, may our communion with her Son bring us to salvation.

SOLEMN BLESSING—NEW YEAR *(Optional)*

Bow your heads and pray for God's blessing.

Every good gift comes from the Father of light. May he grant you his grace and every blessing, and keep you safe throughout the coming year. **Amen.**

May he grant you unwavering faith, constant hope, and love that endures to the end. **Amen.**

May he order your days and work in his peace, hear your every prayer, and lead you to everlasting life and joy. **Amen.**

May almighty God bless you, the Father, and the Son, and the Holy Spirit. **Amen.**

DISMISSAL *(p. 65)*

As we pass by store windows and homes this week, we probably won't see many coloured lights. Christmas trees lie toppled over next to garbage cans. Carols are silenced. Exchanges on gifts have been made and the baking and visitors are gone. The snow (at least on the Prairies) is here to stay and the doldrums threaten to set in as we face a long winter and the inevitable return to everyday routine. In the face of these realities, what does this Feast of Epiphany offer us?

The familiar story of the wise ones from the East reminds us that Jesus is the epiphany, the manifestation of the all-embracing, all-inclusive God. From beginning to end, Jesus manifested a special and unceasing care for *all*. Jesus is Saviour of the *whole* world. The seekers from afar were not only expert in astrology but also wise spiritually, open to and discerning signs of God everywhere. No difference in race or religion, no scheming despot, no tribulation of the journey daunted them in their search for a light in the darkness.

As we return to ordinariness, we are assured that God is shown to all who seek. Perhaps the long journey has dulled our senses and we fail to see the signs that enlighten our way to Christ. Seekers, draw fresh hope: God lives among us. Are you looking? Are you asking? Can you imagine the possibility that seekers from unfamiliar places may help lead you to the Truth? This is a wake-up call! Stay on the journey. Stay in the company of other seekers journeying toward a God who is always eager to be found, a God who is full and rich and great enough to be Saviour of *all*.

Mary Coswin, Winnipeg, MB

ENTRANCE ANTIPHON *(See Malachi 3:1)*

The Lord and ruler is coming; kingship is his, and government and power.

INTRODUCTORY RITES *(p. 5)*

OPENING PRAYER

Father, you revealed your Son to the nations by the guidance of a star. Lead us to your glory in heaven by the light of faith.

FIRST READING *(Isaiah 60:1-6)*

Arise, shine, for your light has come,
and the glory of the Lord has risen upon you!
For darkness shall cover the earth,
and thick darkness the peoples;
but the Lord will arise upon you,
and his glory will appear over you.

Nations shall come to your light,
and kings to the brightness of your dawn.
Lift up your eyes and look around;
they all gather together, they come to you;
your sons shall come from far away,
and your daughters shall be carried
on their nurses' arms.

113

Then you shall see and be radiant;
your heart shall thrill and rejoice,
because the abundance of the sea
shall be brought to you,
the wealth of the nations shall come to you.
A multitude of camels shall cover you,
the young camels of Midian and Ephah;
all those from Sheba shall come.
They shall bring gold and frankincense,
and shall proclaim the praise of the Lord.

The word of the Lord. **Thanks be to God.**

RESPONSORIAL PSALM *(Psalm 72)*

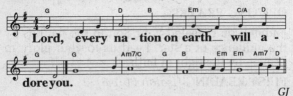

GJ

℟. **Lord, every nation on earth will adore you.**

Give the king your justice, O • **God,**
and your righteousness to a king's • **son.**
May he judge your • **people** with righteousness,
and your • **poor** with justice. ℟.

In his days may righteousness • **flourish**
and peace abound, until the moon is no • **more.**
May he have dominion from • **sea** to sea,
and from the River to the • **ends_of** the earth. ℟.

May the kings of Tarshish and of the isles
render him • **tribute,**
may the kings of Sheba and Seba brings • **gifts.**
May all kings fall • **down** before him,
all nations • **give** him service. ℟.

114

For he delivers the needy when they • **call,**
the poor and those who have no • **helper.**
He has pity on the • **weak_and** the needy,
and saves the • **lives_of** the needy. ℞.

SECOND READING *(Ephesians 3:2-3, 5-6)*

Surely you have already heard of the commission
of God's grace that was given me for you, and how
the mystery was made known to me by revelation.

In former generations this mystery was not made
known to humanity as it has now been revealed to
his holy apostles and prophets by the Spirit: that
is, the Gentiles have become fellow heirs, members of the same body, and sharers in the promise
in Christ Jesus through the gospel.

The word of the Lord. **Thanks be to God.**

GOSPEL ACCLAMATION *(See Matthew 2:2)*

If not sung, this acclamation is omitted.

We have seen his star in the east and have come to
adore the Lord.

GOSPEL *(Matthew 2:1-12)*

A reading from the holy gospel according to Matthew. **Glory to you, Lord.**

In the time of King Herod, after Jesus was born in
Bethlehem of Judea, wise men from the East came
to Jerusalem, asking, "Where is the child who has
been born king of the Jews? For we observed his
star at its rising, and have come to pay him
homage."

When King Herod heard this, he was frightened,
and all Jerusalem with him; and calling together

115

all the chief priests and scribes of the people, he inquired of them where the Messiah was to be born. They told him, "In Bethlehem of Judea; for so it has been written by the prophet: 'And you, Bethlehem, in the land of Judah, are by no means least among the rulers of Judah; for from you shall come a ruler who is to shepherd my people Israel'."

Then Herod secretly called for the wise men and learned from them the exact time when the star had appeared. Then he sent them to Bethlehem, saying, "Go and search diligently for the child; and when you have found him, bring me word so that I may also go and pay him homage."

When they had heard the king, they set out; and there, ahead of them, went the star that they had seen at its rising, until it stopped over the place where the child was. When they saw that the star had stopped, they were overwhelmed with joy.

On entering the house, they saw the child with Mary his mother; and they knelt down and paid him homage. Then, opening their treasure chests, they offered him gifts of gold, frankincense, and myrrh.

And having been warned in a dream not to return to Herod, they left for their own country by another road.

The gospel of the Lord. **Praise to you, Lord Jesus Christ.**

PROFESSION OF FAITH *(Nicene Creed, p. 12)*

PRAYER OF THE FAITHFUL

The following intentions are suggestions only.

℟: Lord, hear our prayer.

For the Church, light of the nations, witness to the message of Jesus, we pray to the Lord: ℟.

For a deep and mutual respect among the members of all faith traditions, we pray to the Lord: ℟.

For those who seek a welcome at our table and a place in our communities, we pray to the Lord: ℟.

For us, God's people, yearning for fresh hope as we seek the Light, we pray to the Lord: ℟.

PREPARATION OF THE GIFTS *(p. 13)*

PRAYER OVER THE GIFTS

Lord, accept the offerings of your Church, not gold, frankincense and myrrh, but the sacrifice and food they symbolize: Jesus Christ.

PREFACE *(Epiphany, p. 18)*

COMMUNION ANTIPHON *(See Matthew 2:2)*

We have seen his star in the east, and have come with gifts to adore the Lord.

PRAYER AFTER COMMUNION

Father, guide us with your light. Help us to recognize Christ in this eucharist and welcome him with love.

SOLEMN BLESSING FOR EPIPHANY *(Optional)*

Bow your heads and pray for God's blessing.

God has called you out of darkness, into his wonderful light. May you experience his kindness and blessings, and be strong in faith, in hope, and in love. **Amen.**

Because you are followers of Christ, who appeared on this day as a light shining in darkness, may he make you a light to all your sisters and brothers. **Amen.**

The wise men followed the star, and found Christ, who is light from light. May you too find the Lord when your pilgrimage is ended. **Amen.**

May almighty God bless you, the Father, and the Son, and the Holy Spirit. **Amen.**

DISMISSAL *(p. 65)*

January 15   Second Sunday in Ordinary Time

Today's gospel demonstrates Mary's implicit trust in her son. Her statement invites Jesus to do something and he performs his first miracle at that wedding, surrounded by family and friends.

One thing this account says is that our prayers, like Mary's request, are most likely to be answered in everyday situations, in familiar places, and among those who are an integral part of our lives.

Attentive to signs of Jesus' presence, we become increasingly aware of little miracles which occur unexpectedly. As others share their life experience with us, we find answers to our own questions. God puts us in touch with special people who make a powerful impact on our lives. This does not mean that major problems and concerns will disappear in an instant. Rather, our pain is eased and we cope more easily when we are surrounded by loving, caring members of our home, work and church communities.

As we listen to his word and 'do whatever he tells us,' Jesus performs miracles in our hearts. Just as he transformed water into an abundance of the finest wine, so will he transform us, with all our faults and weaknesses, into the grace-filled, loving people that he means us to be.

It's all a matter of asking, of listening, and of trusting!

Barbara K. d'Artois, Pierrefonds, QC

ENTRANCE ANTIPHON *(Psalm 66:4)*

May all the earth give you worship and praise, and break into song to your name, O God, Most High.

INTRODUCTORY RITES *(p. 5)*

OPENING PRAYER

Father of heaven and earth, hear our prayers, and show us the way to peace in the world.

FIRST READING *(Isaiah 62:1-5)*

The Lord says this:
"For Zion's sake I will not keep silent,
and for Jerusalem's sake I will not rest,
until her vindication shines out like the dawn,
and her salvation like a burning torch.

"The nations shall see your vindication,
and all the kings your glory;
and you shall be called by a new name
that the mouth of the Lord will give.
You shall be a crown of beauty
    in the hand of the Lord,
and a royal diadem in the hand of your God.

"You shall no more be termed 'Forsaken,'
and your land shall no more be termed 'Desolate';
but you shall be called 'My Delight Is in Her,'
and your land 'Married';
for the Lord delights in you,
and your land shall be married.

"For as a young man marries a young woman,
so shall your builder marry you,

and as the bridegroom rejoices over the bride,
so shall your God rejoice over you."

The word of the Lord. **Thanks be to God.**

RESPONSORIAL PSALM *(Psalm 96)*

GJ

℟. **Proclaim God's marvellous deeds
to all the nations.**

O sing to the Lord • a new song;
sing to the Lord, • all the earth.
Sing to the Lord, • bless his name;
tell of his salvation from • day to day. ℟.

Declare his glory a•-mong the nations,
his marvellous works among • all the peoples.
For great is the Lord, and greatly • to be praised;
he is to be revered a•-bove all gods. ℟.

Ascribe to the Lord, O families • of the peoples,
ascribe to the Lord • glory and strength.
Ascribe to the Lord the glory • due his name;
bring an offering, and come • into his courts. ℟.

Worship the Lord in • ho-ly splendour;
tremble before him, • all the earth.
Say among the nations, "The • Lord is king!
He will judge the • peoples with equity." ℟.

121

SECOND READING *(1 Corinthians 12:4-11)*

There are varieties of gifts, but the same Spirit; and there are varieties of services, but the same Lord; and there are varieties of activities, but it is the same God who activates all of them in everyone.

To each is given the manifestation of the Spirit for the common good. To one is given through the Spirit the utterance of wisdom, and to another the utterance of knowledge according to the same Spirit, to another faith by the same Spirit, to another gifts of healing by the one Spirit, to another the working of miracles, to another prophecy, to another the discernment of spirits, to another various kinds of tongues, to another the interpretation of tongues.

All these are activated by one and the same Spirit, who allots to each one individually just as the Spirit chooses.

The word of the Lord. **Thanks be to God.**

GOSPEL ACCLAMATION *(2 Thessalonians 2:14)*

If not sung, this acclamation is omitted.

God has called us with the gospel, to share in the glory of our Lord Jesus Christ.

GOSPEL *(John 2:1-12)*

A reading from the holy gospel according to John. **Glory to you, Lord.**

There was a wedding in Cana of Galilee, and the mother of Jesus was there. Jesus and his disciples had also been invited to the wedding.

When the wine gave out, the mother of Jesus said to him, "They have no wine." And Jesus said to her, "Woman, what concern is that to you and to me? My hour has not yet come." His mother said to the servants, "Do whatever he tells you."

Now standing there were six stone water jars for the Jewish rites of purification, each holding about a hundred litres. Jesus said to the servants, "Fill the jars with water." And they filled them up to the brim. He said to them, "Now draw some out, and take it to the chief steward." So they took it.

When the steward tasted the water that had become wine, and did not know where it came from (though the servants who had drawn the water knew), the steward called the bridegroom and said to him, "Everyone serves the good wine first, and then the inferior wine after the guests have become drunk. But you have kept the good wine until now."

Jesus did this, the first of his signs, in Cana of Galilee, and revealed his glory; and his disciples believed in him. After this he went down to Capernaum with his mother, his brothers, and his disciples; and they remained there a few days.

The gospel of the Lord. **Praise to you, Lord Jesus Christ.**

PROFESSION OF FAITH *(Creed, pp. 11-12)*

PRAYER OF THE FAITHFUL

The following intentions are suggestions only.

℞: **Lord, hear our prayer.**

For the Church, called to share the gifts of the Spirit for the good of all, we pray to the Lord: ℞.

For leaders of nations and peoples, called to govern with prudence, justice and wisdom, we pray to the Lord: ℞.

For the elderly among us who are lonely, shut-in or ignored, we pray to the Lord: ℞.

For us, your people gathered here, seeking healing and renewal in this celebration of the Lord's death and resurrection, we pray to the Lord: ℞.

PREPARATION OF THE GIFTS *(p. 13)*

PRAYER OVER THE GIFTS

Father, may we celebrate the eucharist with reverence and love, for when we proclaim the death of the Lord you continue the work of his redemption.

PREFACE *(Sundays in Ordinary Time, p. 18)*

COMMUNION ANTIPHON *(Psalm 23:5)*

The Lord has prepared a feast for me; given wine in plenty for me to drink.

PRAYER AFTER COMMUNION

Lord, you have nourished us with bread from heaven. Fill us with your spirit, and make us one in peace and love.

BLESSING AND DISMISSAL *(p. 65)*

Mohandas Gandhi had a mission in life: to set India free. To accomplish this mission he sacrificed wealth and personal success. His only 'weapon' was nonviolence. In spite of years of tireless labour and many obstacles, Gandhi never lost hope. At the time of his death, Gandhi's only possessions were a rice bowl, a pair of glasses and a pair of sandals... but Gandhi did leave India free.

In today's gospel, Jesus responds to questions about his mission in life. He reads from the book of the prophet Isaiah, "The Spirit of the Lord is upon me, because he has anointed me to bring good news to the poor. He has sent me to proclaim release to the captives and recovery of sight to the blind, to let the oppressed go free, to proclaim the year of the Lord's favour."

To accomplish his mission in life Jesus had to be rejected, tortured and crucified. At the time of his death, Jesus' only possessions were a few items of clothing... but he did leave the world free.

As followers of Jesus, each of us has a mission: to imitate him... to bring good news to the poor... to work for justice and peace. This is indeed a major task. It requires sacrifice and tireless labour. It may even cost us our wealth and personal success... but it will set us free. Can we call ourselves Christians if we ignore this challenge?

━━━━━━ *Jim McSheffrey, St. John's, NF*

125

ENTRANCE ANTIPHON *(Psalm 96:1, 6)*

Sing a new song to the Lord! Sing to the Lord, all the earth. Truth and beauty surround him, he lives in holiness and glory.

INTRODUCTORY RITES *(p. 5)*

OPENING PRAYER

All-powerful and ever-living God, direct your love that is within us, that our efforts in the name of your Son may bring the human family to unity and peace.

FIRST READING *(Nehemiah 8:1-4, 5-6, 8-10)*

All the people gathered together into the square before the Water Gate. They told the scribe Ezra to bring the book of the law of Moses, which the Lord had given to Israel. Accordingly, the priest Ezra brought the law before the assembly, both men and women and all who could hear with understanding. This was on the first day of the seventh month. He read from it facing the square before the Water Gate from early morning until midday, in the presence of the men and the women and those who could understand; and the ears of all the people were attentive to the book of the law. The scribe Ezra stood on a wooden platform that had been made for the purpose.

And Ezra opened the book in the sight of all the people, for he was standing above all the people; and when he opened it, all the people stood up. Then Ezra blessed the Lord, the great God, and all the people answered, "Amen, Amen," lifting up their hands. Then they bowed their heads and worshipped the Lord with their faces to the ground.

So the Levites read from the book, from the law of God, with interpretation. They gave the sense, so that the people understood the reading. And Nehemiah, who was the governor, and Ezra the priest and scribe, and the Levites who taught the people said to all the people, "This day is holy to the Lord your God; do not mourn or weep." For all the people wept when they heard the words of the law.

Then Ezra said to them, "Go your way, eat the fat and drink sweet wine and send portions of them to those for whom nothing is prepared, for this day is holy to our Lord; and do not be grieved, for the joy of the Lord is your strength."

The word of the Lord. **Thanks be to God.**

RESPONSORIAL PSALM *(Psalm 19)*

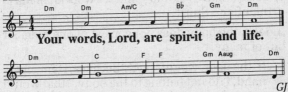

GJ

℟. **Your words, Lord, are spirit and life.**

The law of the Lord is • **perfect,**
reviving the • **soul;**
the decrees of the Lord are • **sure,**
making wise the • **simple.** ℟.

The precepts of the Lord are • **right,**
rejoicing the • **heart;**
the commandment of the Lord is • **clear,**
enlightening the • **eyes.** ℟.

127

The fear of the Lord is • **pure,**
enduring for•-**ever;**
the ordinances of the Lord are • **true**
and righteous alto•-**gether.** ℟.

Let the words of my • **mouth**
and the meditation of my • **heart**
be acceptable to • **you,**
O Lord, my rock and my re•-**deemer.** ℟.

SECOND READING *(1 Corinthians 12:12-30)*

For the shorter version, omit the indented parts.

Just as the body is one and has many members,
and all the members of the body, though many,
are one body, so it is with Christ. For in the one
Spirit we were all baptized into one body—Jews
or Greeks, slaves or free—and we were all made to
drink of one Spirit.

Indeed, the body does not consist of one member
but of many.

If the foot would say, "Because I am not a
hand, I do not belong to the body," that would
not make it any less a part of the body. And if
the ear would say, "Because I am not an eye, I
do not belong to the body," that would not
make it any less a part of the body. If the whole
body were an eye, where would the hearing
be? If the whole body were hearing, where
would the sense of smell be?

But as it is, God arranged the members in the
body, each one of them, as he chose. If all were
a single member, where would the body be?

As it is, there are many members, yet one body. The eye cannot say to the hand, "I have no need of you," nor again the head to the feet, "I have no need of you." On the contrary, the members of the body that seem to be weaker are indispensable, and those members of the body that we think less honourable we clothe with greater honour, and our less respectable members are treated with greater respect; whereas our more respectable members do not need this.

But God has so arranged the body, giving the greater honour to the inferior member, that there may be no dissension within the body, but the members may have the same care for one another. If one member suffers, all suffer together with it; if one member is honoured, all rejoice together with it.

Now you are the body of Christ and individually members of it.

And God has appointed in the church first apostles, second prophets, third teachers; then deeds of power, then gifts of healing, forms of assistance, forms of leadership, various kinds of tongues.

Are all apostles? Are all prophets? Are all teachers? Do all work miracles? Do all possess gifts of healing? Do all speak in tongues? Do all interpret?

The word of the Lord. **Thanks be to God.**

GOSPEL ACCLAMATION *(Luke 4:18-19)*

If not sung, this acclamation is omitted.

The Lord sent me to bring good news to the poor
and freedom to prisoners.

GOSPEL *(Luke 1:1-4; 4:14-21)*

A reading from the holy gospel according to Luke.
Glory to you, Lord.

Since many have undertaken to set down an
orderly account of the events that have been
fulfilled among us, just as they were handed on to
us by those who from the beginning were eyewitnesses and servants of the word, I too decided,
after investigating everything carefully from the
very first, to write an orderly account for you,
most excellent Theophilus, so that you may know
the truth concerning the things about which you
have been instructed.

Jesus, filled with the power of the Spirit, returned
to Galilee, and a report about him spread through
all the surrounding country. He began to teach in
their synagogues and was praised by everyone.
When he came to Nazareth, where he had been
brought up, Jesus went to the synagogue on the
sabbath day, as was his custom.

He stood up to read, and the scroll of the prophet
Isaiah was given to him. He unrolled the scroll
and found the place where it was written: "The
Spirit of the Lord is upon me, because he has
anointed me to bring good news to the poor. He
has sent me to proclaim release to the captives
and recovery of sight to the blind, to let the

oppressed go free, to proclaim the year of the Lord's favour."

And Jesus rolled up the scroll, gave it back to the attendant, and sat down. The eyes of all in the synagogue were fixed on him.

Then Jesus began to say to them, "Today this scripture has been fulfilled in your hearing."

The gospel of the Lord. **Praise to you, Lord Jesus Christ.**

PROFESSION OF FAITH *(Creed, pp. 11-12)*

PRAYER OF THE FAITHFUL

The following intentions are suggestions only.

℞: **Lord, hear our prayer.**

For the Church, called to faithfully proclaim the mission of Jesus, we pray to the Lord: ℞.

For leaders of nations, entrusted with the political and economic futures of their peoples, we pray to the Lord: ℞.

For those who seek justice and freedom from poverty, unemployment and oppression, we pray to the Lord: ℞.

For our parish community, called in baptism to be responsible for one another, we pray to the Lord: ℞.

PREPARATION OF THE GIFTS *(p. 13)*

PRAYER OVER THE GIFTS

Lord, receive our gifts. Let our offerings make us holy and bring us salvation.

PREFACE *(Sundays in Ordinary Time, p. 18)*

COMMUNION ANTIPHON *(Psalm 34:5)*

Look up at the Lord with gladness and smile; your face will never be ashamed.

PRAYER AFTER COMMUNION

God, all-powerful Father, may the new life you give us increase our love and keep us in the joy of your kingdom.

BLESSING AND DISMISSAL *(p. 65)*

Mass for the Unity of Christians

This Mass (517) may be celebrated during the week. However, for pastoral reasons, it may be celebrated on Sunday. Readings are from the Lectionary, Sundays and Solemnities, *#41, 2, 53.*

ENTRANCE ANTIPHON *(Psalm 106:47)*

Save us, Lord our God, and gather us together from the nations, that we may proclaim your holy name, and glory in your praise.

INTRODUCTORY RITES *(p. 5)*

OPENING PRAYER

Lord, hear the prayers of your people and bring the hearts of believers together in your praise and in common sorrow for their sins. Heal all divisions among Christians that we may rejoice in the perfect unity of your Church and move together as one to eternal life in your kingdom.

FIRST READING *(Ezekiel 36:24-28)*

I will take you from the nations, and gather you from all the countries, and bring you into your own land. I will sprinkle clean water upon you, and you shall be clean from all your uncleanness, and from all your idols I will cleanse you. A new heart I will give you, and a new spirit I will put within you; and I will remove from your body the heart of stone and give you a heart of flesh. I will put my spirit within you, and make you follow my statutes and be careful to observe my ordinances. Then you shall live in the land that I gave to your ancestors; and you shall be my people, and I will be your God.

The word of the Lord. **Thanks be to God.**

RESPONSORIAL PSALM *(Psalm 80)*

Lord, let us see your face.

GJ

℞. **Lord, make us turn to you;**
    let us see your face and we shall be saved.

Give ear, O Shepherd • of Israel,
you who are enthroned upon the cherubim,
    shine • **forth.**
Stir up your • **might,**
and come to • **save_us.** ℞.

Turn again, O God • **of** hosts,
look down from heaven and • **see;**
have regard for this • **vine,**
the stock that your right hand has • **planted.** ℞.

Let your hand be upon the one at • **your** right,
the one whom you have made strong
   for your•-**self.**
Then we will never turn back from • **you;**
give us life, and we will call on your • **name.** ℞.

SECOND READING *(1 Corinthians 1:3-9)*

My brothers and sisters: Grace to you and peace from God our Father and the Lord Jesus Christ.

I give thanks to my God always for you because of the grace of God that has been given you in Christ Jesus, for in every way you have been enriched in him, in speech and knowledge of every kind— just as the testimony of Christ has been strengthened among you—so that you are not lacking in any spiritual gift as you wait for the revealing of our Lord Jesus Christ.

He will also strengthen you to the end, so that you may be blameless on the day of our Lord Jesus Christ. God is faithful; by him you were called into fellowship with his Son, Jesus Christ our Lord.

The word of the Lord. **Thanks be to God.**

GOSPEL ACCLAMATION *(John 15:4-5)*

If not sung, this acclamation is omitted.

Live in me and let me live in you, says the Lord; my branches bear much fruit.

134

GOSPEL *(John 15:1-8)*

Jesus said to his disciples: "I am the true vine, and my Father is the vinegrower. He removes every branch in me that bears no fruit. Every branch that bears fruit he prunes to make it bear more fruit. You have already been cleansed by the word that I have spoken to you.

"Abide in me as I abide in you. Just as the branch cannot bear fruit by itself unless it abides in the vine, neither can you unless you abide in me. I am the vine, you are the branches. Those who abide in me and I in them bear much fruit, because apart from me you can do nothing.

"Whoever does not abide in me is thrown away like a branch and withers; such branches are gathered, thrown into the fire, and burned.

"If you abide in me, and my words abide in you, ask for whatever you wish, and it will be done for you. My Father is glorified by this, that you bear much fruit and become my disciples."

The gospel of the Lord. **Praise to you, Lord Jesus Christ.**

PROFESSION OF FAITH *(Creed, pp. 11-12)*

PRAYER OF THE FAITHFUL *(p. 131)*

PREPARATION OF THE GIFTS *(p. 13)*

PRAYER OVER THE GIFTS

Lord, hear our prayer for your mercy as we celebrate this memorial of our salvation. May this sacrament of your love be our sign of unity and our bond of charity.

PREFACE *(Christian Unity, p. 31)*

COMMUNION ANTIPHON *(Colossians 3:14-15)*

To crown all things there must be love, to bind them together and bring them to completion; and may the peace of Christ rule in your hearts, that peace to which all of you are called as one body.

PRAYER AFTER COMMUNION

Lord, fill us with the Spirit of love; by the power of this sacrifice bring together in love and peace all who believe in you.

BLESSING AND DISMISSAL *(p. 65)*

The hometown reaction to Jesus is striking: the people of Nazareth are "amazed" at his words. They "spoke well of him" but could not quite grasp the idea that this Jesus, whom they have known for years, could utter such "gracious words." After all, this is only "Joseph's son."

Jeremiah's dialogue with God offers another perspective. Jeremiah is commissioned to speak the words that God commands him to speak. He is God's mouthpiece, destined for this: before he was formed, before he was born, God knew him, God appointed him a prophet to the nations. The depth and breadth of God's knowledge and call exceed all we know of ourselves and of each other.

How tragic it is when we refuse to see and hear one another because we think we know everything there is to know about the other, because we think we have understood all there is to understand. Jeremiah's call and his commission exceeded his own sense of himself, just as Jesus' fulfilment of the scriptures far exceeded the limits that the people of Nazareth allowed him.

Both Jeremiah and Jesus remain true to God's commission. It is a hard and terrible call, the call to grow and to live in truth. Paul exhorts the Corinthians to love since love is, ultimately, encounter with God.

It is fitting to listen to our own call to grow in deep relationship with God and with each other. We are called to grow in a manner that is at once expansive, inclusive and utterly amazing when we realize that we are only 'Joseph's son.'

Christine Jamieson, Ottawa, ON

ENTRANCE ANTIPHON *(Psalm 106:47)*

Save us, Lord our God, and gather us together from the nations, that we may proclaim your holy name and glory in your praise.

INTRODUCTORY RITES *(p. 5)*

OPENING PRAYER

Lord our God, help us to love you with all our hearts and to love all people as you love them.

FIRST READING *(Jeremiah 1:4-5, 17-19)*

Now the word of the Lord came to me saying, "Before I formed you in the womb, I knew you, and before you were born, I consecrated you; I appointed you a prophet to the nations.

"Therefore, gird up your loins; stand up and tell the people everything that I command you. Do not break down before them, or I will break you before them. And I for my part have made you today a fortified city, an iron pillar, and a bronze wall, against the whole land—against the kings of Judah, its princes, its priests, and the people of the land.

"They will fight against you; but they shall not prevail against you, for I am with you, says the Lord, to deliver you.

The word of the Lord. **Thanks be to God.**

RESPONSORIAL PSALM *(Psalm 71)*

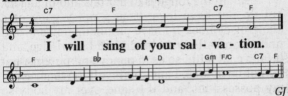

GJ

℟. **I will sing of your salvation.**

In you, O Lord, I • **take** refuge;
let me never be • **put** to shame.
In your righteousness,
   de•-**liver_me** and rescue_me;
incline your ear to • **me** and save_me. ℟.

Be to me a rock • **of** refuge,
a strong • **fortress,** to save_me,
for you are my rock • **and** my fortress.
Rescue me, O my God,
   from the hand • **of** the wicked. ℟.

For you, O Lord, are • **my** hope,
my trust, O Lord, • **from** my youth.
Upon you I have leaned • **from** my birth;
it was you who took me
   from my • **mo**-ther's womb. ℟.

My mouth will tell of your right•-**eous** acts,
of your deeds of salvation • **all** day long.
O God, from my youth • **you** have taught_me,
and I still proclaim your • **wond**-rous deeds. ℟.

139

SECOND READING *(1 Corinthians 12:31–13:13)*

The shorter version begins at the asterisks.

Brothers and sisters, strive for the greater gifts. And I will show you a still more excellent way.

If I speak in the tongues of mortals and of angels, but do not have love, I am a noisy gong or a clanging cymbal. If I have prophetic powers, and understand all mysteries and all knowledge, and if I have all faith, so as to remove mountains, but do not have love, I am nothing. If I give away all my possessions, and if I hand over my body so that I may boast, but do not have love, I gain nothing.

***

Love is patient; love is kind; love is not envious or boastful or arrogant or rude. It does not insist on its own way; it is not irritable or resentful; it does not rejoice in wrongdoing, but rejoices in the truth. It bears all things, believes all things, hopes all things, endures all things. Love never ends.

But as for prophecies, they will come to an end; as for tongues, they will cease; as for knowledge, it will come to an end.

For we know only in part, and we prophesy only in part; but when the complete comes, the partial will come to an end.

When I was a child, I spoke like a child, I thought like a child, I reasoned like a child; when I became an adult, I put an end to childish ways.

For now we see in a mirror, dimly, but then we will see face to face. Now I know only in part; then I will know fully, even as I have been fully known.

Now faith, hope, and love abide, these three; and the greatest of these is love.

The word of the Lord. **Thanks be to God.**

GOSPEL ACCLAMATION *(Luke 4:18-19)*

If not sung, this acclamation is omitted.

The Lord sent me to bring good news to the poor and freedom to prisoners.

GOSPEL *(Luke 4:21-30)*

A reading from the holy gospel according to Luke. **Glory to you, Lord.**

Jesus, filled with the power of the Spirit, came to Nazareth, where he had been brought up. He went to the synagogue on the sabbath day, as was his custom, and read from the prophet Isaiah. The eyes of all were fixed on him. Then he began to say to them, "Today this scripture has been fulfilled in your hearing." All spoke well of him and were amazed at the gracious words that came from his mouth. They said, "Is not this Joseph's son?"

Jesus said to them, "Doubtless you will quote to me this proverb, 'Doctor, cure yourself!' And you will say, 'Do here also in your hometown the things that we have heard you did at Capernaum.'"

And he said, "Truly I tell you, no prophet is accepted in the prophet's hometown. But the truth is, there were many widows in Israel in the time of Elijah, when the heaven was shut up three years and six months, and there was a severe famine over all the land; yet Elijah was sent to none of them except to a widow at Zarephath in Sidon. There were also many lepers in Israel in the time of the prophet Elisha, and none of them was cleansed except Naaman the Syrian."

When they heard this, all in the synagogue were filled with rage. They got up, drove Jesus out of the town, and led him to the brow of the hill on which their town was built, so that they might hurl him off the cliff. But Jesus passed through the midst of them and went on his way.

The gospel of the Lord. **Praise to you, Lord Jesus Christ.**

PROFESSION OF FAITH *(Creed, pp. 11-12)*

PRAYER OF THE FAITHFUL

The following intentions are suggestions only.

℟: **Lord, hear our prayer.**

For the Church, called to serve all nations, we pray to the Lord: ℟.

For open and ongoing dialogue among nations, we pray to the Lord: ℟.

For those who suffer persecution and loneliness, we pray to the Lord: ℟.

For us, called in baptism to be prophets of God's word, we pray to the Lord: ℟.

PREPARATION OF THE GIFTS *(p. 13)*

PRAYER OVER THE GIFTS

Lord, be pleased with the gifts we bring to your altar, and make them the sacrament of our salvation.

PREFACE *(Sundays in Ord. Time, p. 18)*

COMMUNION ANTIPHON *(Psalm 31:16-17)*

Let your face shine on your servant, and save me by your love. Lord, keep me from shame, for I have called to you.

PRAYER AFTER COMMUNION

Lord, you invigorate us with this help to our salvation. By this eucharist give the true faith continued growth throughout the world.

BLESSING AND DISMISSAL *(p. 65)*

The people Jesus called as his disciples had been working all night with very little to show for their effort. They were cleaning up, ready to call it a day. How like us in so many ways, busy with the routine tasks of our living.

It has become a habit to observe that Jesus called his first disciples in the midst of their busy lives. It has become a cliché to say he calls us in the same way. But did you notice in the gospel reading that Jesus also called the disciples *into* their busy lives? He told them to take the tools of their trade—their skills, their knowledge and their understanding—and use them to discover the authenticity of his call. "Let down your nets for a catch," he said. Dip your nets again where you have dipped before.

Do we expect Jesus to use the ordinary things in our lives to show us the authenticity of his call? If we are expecting much of God at all, we may be hoping for a saint's mystic calling or at least for a little mystery. But Jesus most often finds us in our ordinary daily duties and transforms them into the very work of his kingdom. Perhaps this transformation of the ordinary is one of the meanings of faith: where Jesus is present even the routine of labour and work, our successes and our frustrations, the ordinary stuff of living, become intimations of God's presence and avenues to the kingdom.

How often do we need to dip our nets again to grasp the presence of Christ in even the ordinary rounds of our living? Allowing Christ to fill the ordinary and the everyday is what real discipleship is about. Allowing Christ to transform the ordinary is really what is extraordinary about the Good News.

James B. Sauer, San Antonio, TX

ENTRANCE ANTIPHON *(Psalm 95:6-7)*

Come, let us worship the Lord. Let us bow down in the presence of our maker, for he is the Lord our God.

INTRODUCTORY RITES *(p. 5)*

OPENING PRAYER

Father, watch over your family and keep us safe in your care, for all our hope is in you.

FIRST READING *(Isaiah 6:1-2, 3-8)*

In the year that King Uzziah died, I saw the Lord sitting on a throne, high and lofty; and the hem of his robe filled the temple. Seraphs were in attendance above him; each had six wings. And one called to another and said: "Holy, holy, holy is the Lord of hosts; the whole earth is full of his glory." The pivots on the thresholds shook at the voices of those who called, and the house filled with smoke.

And I said: "Woe is me! I am lost, for I am a man of unclean lips, and I live among a people of unclean lips; yet my eyes have seen the King, the Lord of hosts!"

Then one of the seraphs flew to me, holding a live coal that had been taken from the altar with a pair of tongs. The seraph touched my mouth with it and said: "Now that this has touched your lips, your guilt has departed and your sin is blotted out."

Then I heard the voice of the Lord saying, "Whom shall I send, and who will go for us?" And I said, "Here am I; send me!"

The word of the Lord. **Thanks be to God**.

RESPONSORIAL PSALM *(Psalm 138)*

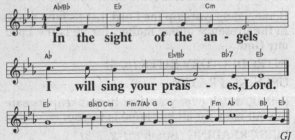

GJ

℟. **In the sight of the angels**
   I will sing your praises, Lord.

I give you thanks, O Lord,
    with my • **whole** heart;
before the gods I sing • **your** praise;
I bow down toward your ho•-**ly** temple.
I give thanks to your name for your
    steadfast love • **and** your faithfulness. ℟.

For you have exalted • **your** name
and your word a•-**bove** everything.
On the day I called, • **you** answered_me,
you increased my • **strength** of soul. ℞.

All the kings of the earth
    shall praise you, • O Lord,
for they have heard the words of • **your** mouth.
They shall sing of the ways of • **the** Lord,
for great is the • **glory_of** the Lord. ℞.

You stretch out your hand,
    and your right hand • **de**-livers_me.
The Lord will fulfil his purpose • **for** me;
your steadfast love, O Lord, endures • **for**-ever.
Do not forsake the • **work_of** your hands. ℞.

SECOND READING *(1 Corinthians 15:1-11)*

For the shorter version, omit the idented parts.

My brothers and sisters,

I would remind you of the good news that I proclaimed to you, which you in turn received, in which also you stand. This is the good news through which also you are being saved, if you hold firmly to the message that I proclaimed to you—unless you have come to believe in vain. For

I handed on to you as of first importance what I in turn had received: that Christ died for our sins in accordance with the scriptures, and that he was buried, and that he was raised on the third day in accordance with the scriptures, and that he appeared to Cephas, then to the twelve.

147

Then Christ appeared to more than five hundred brothers and sisters at one time, most of whom are still alive, though some have died. Then he appeared to James, then to all the apostles. Last of all, as to one untimely born, Christ appeared also to me.

> For I am the least of the apostles, unfit to be called an apostle, because I persecuted the church of God. But by the grace of God I am what I am, and his grace toward me has not been in vain. On the contrary, I worked harder than any of the apostles—though it was not I, but the grace of God that is with me.

Whether then it was I or they, so we proclaim and so you have come to believe.

The word of the Lord. **Thanks be to God.**

GOSPEL ACCLAMATION *(Matthew 4:19)*

If not sung, this acclamation is omitted.

Come follow me, says the Lord, and I will make you fishers of my people.

GOSPEL *(Luke 5:1-11)*

A reading from the holy gospel according to Luke. **Glory to you, Lord.**

While Jesus was standing beside the lake of Gennesaret, and the crowd was pressing in on him to hear the word of God, he saw two boats there at the shore of the lake; the fishermen had gone out of them and were washing their nets.

Jesus got into one of the boats, the one belonging to Simon, and asked him to put out a little way from the shore. Then he sat down and taught the crowds from the boat. When he had finished speaking, he said to Simon, "Put out into the deep water and let down your nets for a catch." Simon answered, "Master, we have worked all night long but have caught nothing. Yet if you say so, I will let down the nets." When they had done this, they caught so many fish that their nets were beginning to break. So they signalled their partners in the other boat to come and help them. And they came and filled both boats, so that they began to sink.

But when Simon Peter saw it, he fell down at Jesus' knees, saying, "Go away from me, Lord, for I am a sinful man!"

For Simon Peter and all who were with him were amazed at the catch of fish that they had taken; and so also were James and John, sons of Zebedee, who were partners with Simon. Then Jesus said to Simon, "Do not be afraid; from now on you will be catching people."

When they had brought their boats to shore, they left everything and followed Jesus.

The gospel of the Lord. **Praise to you, Lord Jesus Christ.**

PROFESSION OF FAITH *(Creed, pp. 11-12)*

PRAYER OF THE FAITHFUL

The following intentions are suggestions only.

℟: **Lord, hear our prayer.**

For the Church, community of disciples, called to follow Jesus in all things, we pray to the Lord: ℟.

For nations and peoples as they struggle to build a world of peace and justice, we pray to the Lord: ℟.

For those among us who seek healing, support and peace, we pray to the Lord: ℟.

For us, God's people, invited to discover God in the routine of our lives, we pray to the Lord: ℟.

PREPARATION OF THE GIFTS *(p. 13)*

PRAYER OVER THE GIFTS

Lord our God, may the bread and wine you give us for our nourishment on earth become the sacrament of our eternal life.

PREFACE *(Sundays in Ord. Time, p. 18)*

COMMUNION ANTIPHON *(Matthew 5:5-6)*

Blessed are the sorrowing; they shall be consoled. Blessed those who hunger and thirst for what is right; they shall be satisfied.

PRAYER AFTER COMMUNION

God our Father, you give us a share in the one bread and the one cup and make us one in Christ. Help us to bring your salvation and joy to all the world.

BLESSING AND DISMISSAL *(p. 65)*

Can you recall an experience where you really had to stretch yourself, maybe at work or in a relationship? You may have thought you had given all you could, but more was asked, more was expected.

Probably the uncompromising and definitive words of Jesus in today's gospel were that type of experience for the disciples. They had placed their trust in him and now Jesus was challenging them to face ridicule, hatred or suffering if need be, for his sake and for the sake of his message, in the hope of some remote promises to come.

These same words are directed to us today as disciples. We are being asked to step out of our comfortable world into the realm of 'risk,' to put ourselves on the line for the sake of the kingdom. This involves difficult choices and is certainly different from what our culture offers. But, after all, this is what the life of a Christian is all about: to choose a different way than the one most travelled, a way that puts us in touch with the larger context, the complete picture, a way that prepares us to die well in Christ and to rise to new life with him. We are being asked to stretch ourselves. Are we up to the challenge?

Connie Paré, Chatham, ON

ENTRANCE ANTIPHON *(Psalm 31:3)*

Lord, be my rock of safety, the stronghold that saves me. For the honour of your name, lead me and guide me.

INTRODUCTORY RITES *(p. 5)*

OPENING PRAYER

God our Father, you have promised to remain for ever with those who do what is just and right. Help us to live in your presence.

FIRST READING *(Jeremiah 17:5-8)*

Thus says the Lord:
"Cursed are those who trust in mere mortals
and make mere flesh their strength,
whose hearts turn away from the Lord.
They shall be like a shrub in the desert,
and shall not see when relief comes.
They shall live in the parched places
    of the wilderness,
in an uninhabited salt land.

"Blessed are those who trust in the Lord,
whose trust is the Lord.
They shall be like a tree planted by water,
sending out its roots by the stream.
This tree shall not fear when heat comes,
and its leaves shall stay green;
in the year of drought it is not anxious,
and it does not cease to bear fruit."

The word of the Lord. **Thanks be to God.**

RESPONSORIAL PSALM *(Psalm 1)*

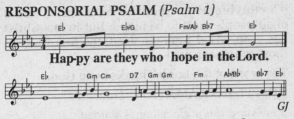

GJ

℟. **Happy are they who hope in the Lord.**

Happy are those who do not follow
    the advice • **of** the wicked,
or take the path that sinners tread,
    or sit in the • **seat** of scoffers;
but their delight is in the • **law_of** the Lord,
and on his law they meditate • **day** and night. ℟.

They are like trees planted by • **streams** of water,
which yield their fruit • **in** its season,
and their leaves • **do** not wither.
In all that they • **do,** they prosper. ℟.

The wicked • **are** not so,
but are like chaff that the wind • **drives** a-way.
For the Lord watches over
    the • **way_of** the righteous,
but the way of the • **wicked** will perish. ℟.

SECOND READING *(1 Corinthians 15:12, 16-20)*

If Christ is proclaimed as raised from the dead,
how can some of you say there is no resurrection
of the dead?

For if the dead are not raised, then Christ has not
been raised. If Christ has not been raised, your
faith is futile and you are still in your sins. Then
those also who have died in Christ have perished.

153

If for this life only we have hoped in Christ, we are of all people most to be pitied. But in fact Christ has been raised from the dead, the first fruits of those who have died.

The word of the Lord. **Thanks be to God.**

GOSPEL ACCLAMATION *(Luke 6:23)*

If not sung, this acclamation is omitted.

Rejoice and be glad; your reward will be great in heaven.

GOSPEL *(Luke 6:17, 20-26)*

A reading from the holy gospel according to Luke. **Glory to you, Lord.**

Jesus came down with the twelve and stood on a level place, with a great crowd of his disciples and a great multitude of people from all Judea, Jerusalem, and the coast of Tyre and Sidon. Then Jesus looked up at his disciples and said:

"Blessed are you who are poor,
for yours is the kingdom of God.
Blessed are you who are hungry now,
for you will be filled.
Blessed are you who weep now,
for you will laugh.
Blessed are you when people hate you,
and when they exclude you, revile you,
    and defame you
on account of the Son of Man.

"Rejoice in that day and leap for joy,
for surely your reward is great in heaven;
for that is what their ancestors did to the prophets.

"But woe to you who are rich,
for you have received your consolation.
Woe to you who are full now,
for you will be hungry.
Woe to you who are laughing now,
for you will mourn and weep.
Woe to you when all speak well of you,
for that is what their ancestors did
   to the false prophets."

The gospel of the Lord. **Praise to you, Lord Jesus Christ.**

PROFESSION OF FAITH *(Creed, pp. 11-12)*

PRAYER OF THE FAITHFUL

The following intentions are suggestions only.

℞: **Lord, hear our prayer.**

For the Church, called to trust in its Lord who alone brings salvation, we pray to the Lord: ℞.

For those who shoulder the burden of public service and the challenge of promoting the good of all, we pray to the Lord: ℞.

For those men and women whose riches, power and success have left them unsatisfied, we pray to the Lord: ℞.

For us, baptized into discipleship, called to stand with the poor, the hungry and the unemployed in their search for justice, we pray to the Lord: ℞.

PREPARATION OF THE GIFTS *(p. 13)*

155

PRAYER OVER THE GIFTS

Lord, we make this offering in obedience to your word. May it cleanse and renew us, and lead us to our eternal reward.

PREFACE *(Sundays in Ord. Time, p. 18)*

COMMUNION ANTIPHON *(Psalm 78:29-30)*

They ate and were filled; the Lord gave them what they wanted: they were not deprived of their desire.

PRAYER AFTER COMMUNION

Lord, you give us food from heaven. May we always hunger for the bread of life.

BLESSING AND DISMISSAL *(p. 65)*

At first glance, today's gospel may seem too radical to be taken seriously. Having stunned the crowds already with his Beatitudes, Jesus continues by challenging people to, of all things, love their enemies! "Bless those who curse you," he says. "Pray for those who abuse you... Do good, and lend, expecting nothing in return."

How are we to understand these challenging words? Is Jesus advocating that those who are oppressed accept their oppression? Is he suggesting that those who are being abused not seek justice? Unfortunately, people have often misinterpreted Jesus' words as condoning submission to oppression, abuse and injustices of all kinds. However, this interpretation conveniently ignores the fact that Jesus' whole life was dedicated to liberating the victims of such things.

Far from being a call to be submissive in the face of oppression, Jesus' challenge to "love your enemies" is a call to empowerment. Jesus knew that those who are oppressed or abused would gain nothing by simply 'buying into' the cycle of reaction which the world expects of them. Such a cycle promotes victimization, turning victim into victimizer. Such a cycle feeds on hatred, not love. And hatred, whether fostered by victim or victimizer, is what kills the soul. Jesus knew that real empowerment—real liberation—comes not from cultivating more and more hatred for one's enemies, but from cutting off this cycle of reaction with a loving response.

To respond with love is to condemn the sin instead of the sinner. It is to be merciful and forgiving, just as God is merciful and forgiving. Admittedly, those of us who have suffered oppression or abuse may not be able to offer full mercy and forgiveness for some time. However, as long as we are striving to free ourselves from any hatred that may bind us, as long as we remain open to the possibility of loving our enemies, then we are on the road to real liberation.

John O'Donnell, Halifax, NS

ENTRANCE ANTIPHON *(Psalm 13:5-6)*

Lord, your mercy is my hope, my heart rejoices in your saving power. I will sing to the Lord for his goodness to me.

INTRODUCTORY RITES *(p. 5)*

OPENING PRAYER

Father, keep before us the wisdom and love you have revealed in your Son. Help us to be like him in word and deed.

FIRST READING *(1 Samuel 26:2, 7-9, 12-13, 22-25)*

Having heard that David was hiding out in the desert, Saul rose and went down to the Wilderness of Ziph, with three thousand chosen men of Israel, to seek David in the Wilderness of Ziph.

David and Abishai went into Saul's army by night; there Saul lay sleeping within the encampment, with his spear stuck in the ground at his head; and Abner and the army lay around him. Abishai said to David, "God has given your enemy into your hand today; now therefore let me pin him to the ground with one stroke of the spear; I will not strike him twice." But David said to Abishai, "Do not destroy him; for who can raise his hand against the Lord's anointed, and be guiltless?"

So David took the spear that was at Saul's head and the water jar, and they went away. No one saw it, or knew it, nor did anyone awake; for they were all asleep, because a deep sleep from the Lord had fallen upon them.

Then David went over to the other side, and stood on top of a hill far away, with a great distance between them. David called aloud to Saul, "Here is the spear, O king! Let one of the young men come over and get it. The Lord rewards everyone for his righteousness and his faithfulness; for the Lord gave you into my hand today, but I would not raise my hand against the Lord's anointed. As your life was precious today in my sight, so may my life be precious in the sight of the Lord, and may he rescue me from all tribulation."

Then Saul said to David, "Blessed be you, my son David! You will do many things and will succeed in them."

So David went his way, and Saul returned to his place.

The word of the Lord. **Thanks be to God.**

RESPONSORIAL PSALM *(Psalm 103)*

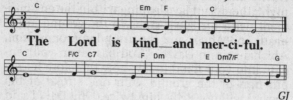

GJ

℟. **The Lord is kind and merciful.**

Bless the Lord, O my • **soul,**
and all that is within me, bless his ho•**-ly** name.
Bless the Lord, O my • **soul,**
and do not forget all • **his** benefits. ℟.

It is the Lord who forgives all your in•**-iquity,**
who heals all your • **dis-**eases,
who redeems your life from the • **Pit,**
who crowns you
 with steadfast love • **and** mercy. ℟.

The Lord is merciful and • **gracious,**
slow to anger and abounding
 in stead•**-fast** love.
He does not deal with us according to our • **sins,**
nor repay us according to our • **in-**iquities. ℟.

As far as the east is from the • **west,**
so far he removes our transgressions • **from** us.
As a father has compassion for his • **children,**
so the Lord has compassion
 for those • **who** fear_him. ℟.

SECOND READING *(1 Corinthians 15:45-50)*

It is written: "The first Adam, became a living being"; the last Adam became a life-giving spirit. But it is not the spiritual that is first, but the physical, and then the spiritual.

The first was from the earth, made of dust; the second is from heaven. As was the one of dust, so are those who are of the dust; and as is the one of heaven, so are those who are of heaven.

Just as we have borne the image of the one of dust, we will also bear the image of the one of heaven.

What I am saying, brothers and sisters, is this: flesh and blood cannot inherit the kingdom of God, nor does the perishable inherit the imperishable.

The word of the Lord. **Thanks be to God.**

GOSPEL ACCLAMATION *(John 13:34)*

If not sung, this acclamation is omitted.

I give you a new commandment: love one another as I have loved you.

GOSPEL *(Luke 6:27-38)*

A reading from the holy gospel according to Luke. **Glory to you, Lord.**

Jesus addressed a great crowd of his disciples, together with the multitude from Judea, Jerusalem, Tyre and Sidon. "I say to you who listen: Love your enemies, do good to those who hate you, bless those who curse you, pray for those who abuse you. If anyone strikes you on the cheek, offer the other also; and from anyone who takes away your coat do not withhold even your shirt. Give to everyone who begs from you; and if anyone takes away your goods, do not ask for them again. Do to others as you would have them do to you.

"If you love those who love you, what credit is that to you? For even sinners love those who love them. If you do good to those who do good to you, what credit is that to you? For even sinners do the same. If you lend to those from whom you hope to receive, what credit is that to you? Even sinners lend to sinners, to receive as much again. But love your enemies, do good, and lend, expecting nothing in return. Your reward will be great, and you will be children of the Most High; for he is kind to the ungrateful and the wicked. Be merciful, just as your Father is merciful.

"Do not judge, and you will not be judged; do not condemn, and you will not be condemned. Forgive, and you will be forgiven; give, and it will be given to you. A good measure, pressed down, shaken together, running over, will be put into your lap; for the measure you give will be the measure you get back."

The gospel of the Lord. **Praise to you, Lord Jesus Christ.**

PROFESSION OF FAITH *(Creed, pp. 11-12)*

PRAYER OF THE FAITHFUL

The following intentions are suggestions only.

℟: **Lord, hear our prayer.**

For the Church and its leaders, called to stand in solidarity with victims of oppression and abuse, we pray to the Lord: ℟.

For world peace built on non-violence, we pray to the Lord: ℟.

For the healing and empowerment of the victims of violence and oppression, we pray to the Lord: ℟.

For us, God's holy people, challenged to love our enemies, we pray to the Lord: ℟.

PREPARATION OF THE GIFTS *(p. 13)*

PRAYER OVER THE GIFTS

Lord, as we make this offering, may our worship in Spirit and truth bring us salvation.

PREFACE *(Sundays in Ord. Time, p. 18)*

COMMUNION ANTIPHON *(Psalm 9:1-2)*

I will tell all your marvellous works. I will rejoice and be glad in you, and sing to your name, Most High.

PRAYER AFTER COMMUNION

Almighty God, help us to live the example of love we celebrate in this eucharist, that we may come to its fulfilment in your presence.

BLESSING AND DISMISSAL *(p. 65)*

In the late 1800's, a boy was working 14 hours a day in a store in London, England. After two years of this, he told his mother one day that he would kill himself if he had to go on any longer.

After his talk with his mother, the boy wrote to a former teacher, explaining how miserable he felt. The teacher wrote back, praising him as a person and assuring him that he was very gifted.

This encouragement changed the boy's life, and he went on to become one of England's most gifted authors. His name was H.G. Wells.

Today's gospel is an occasion for us to reflect on how we approach others. Do we rescue them from their misery by affirming and encouraging them? or do we drive them into a deeper despair by nagging and criticizing? It is a question of how much, after all, we care for *them*.

But this gospel probes even deeper—into what is really in our hearts. For that is what comes most easily to our lips. Whether we affirm or criticize ultimately depends upon how we perceive ourselves. It is a question then of how much, after all, we care about *ourselves*.

The gospel, then, encourages all of us, assuring us of our giftedness, stating, in no uncertain terms, that we must *love ourselves*   as much as we *love others*.

Jerome Herauf, Halifax, NS

ENTRANCE ANTIPHON *(Psalm 18:18-19)*

The Lord has been my strength; he has led me into freedom. He saved me because he loves me.

INTRODUCTORY RITES *(p. 5)*

OPENING PRAYER

Lord, guide the course of world events and give your Church the joy and peace of serving you in freedom.

FIRST READING *(Sirach 27:4-7)*

When a sieve is shaken, the rubbish appears; so do a person's faults when one speaks. The kiln tests the potter's vessels; so the test of a person is in conversation.

Its fruit discloses the cultivation of a tree; so a person's speech discloses the cultivation of the mind. Do not praise people before they speak, for this is the way people are tested.

The word of the Lord. **Thanks be to God.**

RESPONSORIAL PSALM *(Psalm 92)*

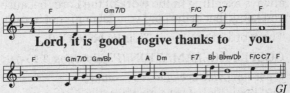

GJ

℟. **Lord, it is good to give thanks to you.**

It is good to give thanks • **to** the Lord,
to sing praises to your name, • **O** Most High;
to declare your steadfast love • **in** the morning,
and your • **faithfulness** by night. ℟.

165

The righteous flourish • **like** the palm_tree,
and grow like a • **cedar** in Lebanon.
They are planted in the house • **of** the Lord;
they flourish in the • **courts_of** our God. ℞.

In old age they still • **pro**-duce fruit;
they are always green and • **full** of sap,
showing that the • **Lord** is upright;
he is my rock, and there is
   no un•-**righteousness** in him. ℞.

SECOND READING *(1 Corinthians 15:54-58)*

When this perishable body puts on imperishability, and this mortal body puts on immortality, then the saying that is written will be fulfilled: "Death has been swallowed up in victory." "Where, O death, is your victory? Where, O death, is your sting?"

The sting of death is sin, and the power of sin is the law. But thanks be to God, who gives us the victory through our Lord Jesus Christ.

Therefore, my beloved, be steadfast, immovable, always excelling in the work of the Lord, because you know that in the Lord your labour is not in vain.

The word of the Lord. **Thanks be to God.**

GOSPEL ACCLAMATION *(Philippians 2:15-16)*

If not sung, this acclamation is omitted.

Shine on the world like bright stars; you are offering it the word of life.

GOSPEL *(Luke 6:39-45)*

A reading from the holy gospel according to Luke.
Glory to you, Lord.

Jesus told his disciples a parable: "Can a blind person guide a blind person? Will not both fall into a pit? A disciple is not above the teacher, but everyone who is fully qualified will be like the teacher.

"Why do you see the speck in your neighbour's eye, but do not notice the log in your own eye? Or how can you say to your neighbour, 'Friend, let me take out the speck in your eye,' when you yourself do not see the log in your own eye? You hypocrite, first take the log out of your own eye, and then you will see clearly to take the speck out of your neighbour's eye.

"No good tree bears bad fruit, nor again does a bad tree bear good fruit; for each tree is known by its own fruit. Figs are not gathered from thorns, nor are grapes picked from a bramble bush.

"Out of the good treasure of the heart, the good person produces good, and out of evil treasure, the evil person produces evil; for it is out of the abundance of the heart that the mouth speaks."

The gospel of the Lord. **Praise to you, Lord Jesus Christ.**

PROFESSION OF FAITH *(Creed, pp. 11-12)*

PRAYER OF THE FAITHFUL

The following intentions are suggestions only.

℟: **Lord, hear our prayer.**

For the Church, called to integrity of speech and action, we pray to the Lord: ℟.

For peace and justice among nations, built on mutual assistance, we pray to the Lord: ℟.

For the healing of those who suffer harsh and unfair criticism, we pray to the Lord: ℟.

For us, God's people gathered here, called to speak words of goodness and love, we pray to the Lord: ℟.

PREPARATION OF THE GIFTS *(p. 13)*

PRAYER OVER THE GIFTS

God our creator, may this bread and wine we offer as a sign of our love and worship lead us to salvation.

PREFACE *(Sundays in Ord. Time, p. 18)*

COMMUNION ANTIPHON *(Psalm 13:6)*

I will sing to the Lord for his goodness to me, I will sing the name of the Lord, Most High.

PRAYER AFTER COMMUNION

God of salvation, may this sacrament which strengthens us here on earth bring us to eternal life.

BLESSING AND DISMISSAL *(p. 65)*

This gospel is chosen for a day on which we publicly receive ashes on our foreheads as a sign of sinfulness and repentance. Yet Matthew lets us know that Jesus objects to making a public show of good works. Jesus' objection reminds me of the words T. S. Eliott gives Thomas Becket in *Murder in the Cathedral:* "To do the right deed for the wrong reason." Jesus condemns the public display of almsgiving, prayer and fasting, because it involves the wrong reason for doing the right thing—good works.

What is the right reason, then, for doing good works? Why should they be done "in secret"? Jesus is telling us something about his Father, "who sees in secret." Giving alms, praying and fasting are responses of intimacy—special actions and sacred moments between a loving Father and ourselves as beloved. Nothing must be allowed to interfere with this privileged relationship. Giving alms, praying and fasting are ways of acknowledging, nourishing and protecting our relationship to the Father who loves us first and unconditionally. Such good works are about intimacy, not public display; about care, not publicity; about the gift of self, not self-glorification. Being one with our Father "who sees in secret" is itself the reward.

John Thompson, Saskatoon, SK

NOTE: During Lent, the Glory to God *and* Alleluia *are not said. Seasonal gospel acclamations may be found on p. 632.*

ENTRANCE ANTIPHON *(Wisdom 11:24-25, 27)*

Lord, you are merciful to all, and hate nothing you have created. You overlook the sins of men to bring them to repentance. You are the Lord our God.

GREETING *(p. 5)*

OPENING PRAYER

Lord, protect us in our struggle against evil. As we begin the discipline of Lent, make this day holy by our self-denial.

FIRST READING *(Joel 2:12-18)*

"Even now," says the Lord, "return to me with all your heart, with fasting, with weeping, and with mourning; rend your hearts and not your clothing.

"Return to the Lord, your God, for he is gracious and merciful, slow to anger, and abounding in steadfast love, and relents from punishing."

Who knows whether the Lord will not turn and relent, and leave a blessing behind him: a grain offering and a drink offering to be presented to the Lord, your God?

Blow the trumpet in Zion; sanctify a fast; call a solemn assembly; gather the people. Sanctify the congregation; assemble the aged; gather the children, even infants at the breast. Let the bridegroom leave his room, and the bride her canopy.

Between the vestibule and the altar let the priests, the ministers of the Lord, weep. Let them say, "Spare your people, O Lord, and do not make your heritage a mockery, a byword among the nations. Why should it be said among the peoples, 'Where is their God?' "

Then the Lord became jealous for his land, and had pity on his people.

The word of the Lord. **Thanks be to God.**

RESPONSORIAL PSALM *(Psalm 51)*

GJ

℟. **Be merciful, O Lord, for we have sinned.**

Have mercy on me, O God,
  according to your steadfast • **love;**
according to your abundant mercy
  blot out my trans•-**gressions.**
Wash me thoroughly from my in•-**iquity,**
and cleanse me from my • **sin.** ℟.

For I know my trans•-**gressions,**
and my sin is ever be•-**fore_me.**
Against you, you alone, have I • **sinned,**
and done what is evil in your • **sight.** ℟.

Create in me a clean heart, O • **God,**
and put a new and right spirit with•-**in_me.**
Do not cast me away from your • **presence,**
and do not take your holy spirit • **from_me.** ℟.

171

Restore to me the joy of your sal•-**vation,**
and sustain in me a willing • **spirit.**
O Lord, open my • **lips,**
and my mouth will declare your • **praise.** ℞.

SECOND READING *(2 Corinthians 5:20–6:2)*

We are ambassadors for Christ, since God is making his appeal through us; we entreat you on behalf of Christ, be reconciled to God. For our sake God made Christ to be sin who knew no sin, so that in Christ we might become the righteousness of God. As we work together with him, we urge you also not to accept the grace of God in vain. For the Lord says, "At an acceptable time I have listened to you, and on a day of salvation I have helped you." See, now is the acceptable time; see, now is the day of salvation!

The word of the Lord. **Thanks be to God.**

GOSPEL ACCLAMATION *(Psalm 95:7-8)*

If not sung, this acclamation is omitted.

If today you hear God's voice, harden not your hearts.

GOSPEL *(Matthew 6:1-6, 16-18)*

A reading from the holy gospel according to Matthew. **Glory to you, Lord.**

Jesus said to the disciples, "Beware of practising your piety before others in order to be seen by them; for then you have no reward from your Father in heaven.

"So whenever you give alms, do not sound a trumpet before you, as the hypocrites do in the synagogues and in the streets, so that they may be praised by others. Truly I tell you, they have received their reward. But when you give alms, do not let your left hand know what your right hand is doing, so that your alms may be done in secret; and your Father who sees in secret will reward you.

"And whenever you pray, do not be like the hypocrites; for they love to stand and pray in the synagogues and at the street corners, so that they may be seen by others. Truly I tell you, they have received their reward. But whenever you pray, go into your room and shut the door and pray to your Father who is in secret; and your Father who sees in secret will reward you.

"And whenever you fast, do not look dismal, like the hypocrites, for they disfigure their faces so as to show others that they are fasting. Truly I tell you, they have received their reward. But when you fast, put oil on your head and wash your face, so that your fasting may be seen not by others but by your Father who is in secret; and your Father who sees in secret will reward you."

The gospel of the Lord. **Praise to you, Lord Jesus Christ.**

The Profession of Faith *is omitted today.*

BLESSING AND DISTRIBUTION OF ASHES

Lord, bless the sinner who asks for your forgiveness and bless all those who receive these ashes. May they keep this Lenten season in preparation for the joy of Easter.

PRAYER OF THE FAITHFUL

The following intentions are suggestions only.

℞: **Lord, hear our prayer.**

For the Church, called in this season of Lent to open our hearts to God's kingdom among us, we pray to the Lord: ℞.

For renewed generosity among nations for the sake of our brothers and sisters who are poor and dispossessed, we pray to the Lord: ℞.

For all who suffer loneliness and loss, we pray to the Lord: ℞.

For us, God's people gathered here, called to care for each other as God cares for us, we pray to the Lord: ℞.

PREPARATION OF THE GIFTS *(p. 13)*

PRAYER OVER THE GIFTS

Lord, help us to resist temptation by our Lenten works of charity and penance. By this sacrifice may we be prepared to celebrate the death and resurrection of Christ our Saviour and be cleansed from sin and renewed in spirit.

PREFACE *(Lent IV, p. 22)*

COMMUNION ANTIPHON *(Psalm 1:2-3)*

The one who meditates day and night on the law of the Lord will yield fruit in due season.

PRAYER AFTER COMMUNION

Lord, through this communion may our lenten penance give you glory and bring us your protection.

BLESSING AND DISMISSAL *(p. 65)*

Isn't it interesting that we need both structure and variety in our lives? How boring life would be if each day were a repetition of the last and there were no change in our patterns. On the other hand, how chaotic it would be if every day were different from the last and there were no sense of order or planning. We need both structure and variety in order to have balance, peace and joy in our lives.

Today we are within familiar structures. We listen to readings we have heard many times before and we repeat familiar rituals. There is a comfort in this repetition... and a danger that the familiarity may impede our hearing the readings— we hear the first line and go off on a mental 'trip'!

How do we bring newness to this oft-repeated listening? There is a clue in the second reading: "the word is near you..." Let us enter into the wilderness with Jesus and allow the word that is near us to touch us. To what wilderness is the Spirit leading us at this time? Is the wilderness a place of blessing for us? What are we learning about ourselves there?

Jesus responded to temptation by returning to scripture passages that strengthened him. Is there a word near us, that strengthens us at this time? Within the familiar structure of Lent, let us seek to respond to God in new ways.

— *Sandra Barrett, Saint John, NB*

Parishes engaged in the Rite of Christian Initiation of Adults celebrate the Rite of Election today.

175

ENTRANCE ANTIPHON *(Psalm 91:15-16)*

When he calls to me, I will answer; I will rescue him and give him honour. Long life and contentment will be his.

INTRODUCTORY RITES *(p. 5)*

The Glory to God *and* Alleluia *are not said during Lent.*

OPENING PRAYER

Father, through our observance of Lent, help us to understand the meaning of your Son's death and resurrection, and teach us to reflect it in our lives.

FIRST READING *(Deuteronomy 26:4-10)*

Moses spoke to the people, saying: "When the priest takes the basket from your hand and sets it down before the altar of the Lord your God, you shall make this response before the Lord your God:

" 'A wandering Aramean was my ancestor; he went down into Egypt and lived there as an alien, few in number, and there he became a great nation, mighty and populous. When the Egyptians treated us harshly and afflicted us, by imposing hard labour on us, we cried to the Lord, the God of our ancestors; the Lord heard our voice and saw our affliction, our toil, and our oppression.

" 'The Lord brought us out of Egypt with a mighty hand and an outstretched arm, with a terrifying display of power, and with signs and wonders; and he brought us into this place and gave us this land, a land flowing with milk and honey. So now I bring the first of the fruit of the ground that you, O Lord, have given me.' "

And Moses continued, "You shall set it down before the Lord your God and bow down before the Lord your God."

The word of the Lord. **Thanks be to God.**

RESPONSORIAL PSALM *(Psalm 91)*

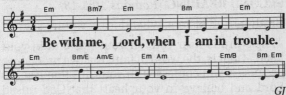

Be with me, Lord, when I am in trouble.

GJ

℟. **Be with me, Lord, when I am in trouble.**

You who live in the shelter of the Most • **High,**
who abide in the shadow of the • **Al**-mighty,
will say to the Lord,
    "My refuge and my • **fortress;**
my God, in whom • **I** trust." ℟.

No evil shall be•**-fall_you,**
no scourge come near • **your** tent.
For he will command his angels
    con•**-cerning_you**
to guard you in all • **your** ways. ℟.

On their hands they will bear you • **up,**
so that you will not dash your foot
    against • **a** stone.
You will tread on the lion and the • **adder,**
the young lion and the serpent
    you will trample un•**-der** foot. ℟.

Those who love me, I will de•-liver;
I will protect those who know • **my** name.
When they call to me, I will • **answer_them;**
I will be with them in trouble,
I will rescue them • **and** honour_them. ℞.

SECOND READING *(Romans 10:8-13)*

Brothers and sisters, what does scripture say?

"The word is near you, on your lips and in your heart" (that is, the word of faith that we proclaim); because if you confess with your lips that Jesus is Lord and believe in your heart that God raised him from the dead, you will be saved.

For one believes with the heart and so is justified, and one confesses with the mouth and so is saved.

The scripture says, "No one who believes in him will be put to shame." For there is no distinction between Jew and Greek; the same Lord is Lord of all and is generous to all who call on him. For, "Everyone who calls on the name of the Lord shall be saved."

The word of the Lord. **Thanks be to God.**

GOSPEL ACCLAMATION *(Matthew 4:4)*

If not sung, this acclamation is omitted.

No one lives on bread alone, but on every word that comes from the mouth of God.

GOSPEL *(Luke 4:1-13)*

A reading from the holy gospel according to Luke. **Glory to you, Lord.**

Jesus, full of the Holy Spirit, returned from the Jordan and was led by the Spirit in the wilderness, where for forty days he was tempted by the devil. He ate nothing at all during those days, and when they were over, he was famished.

The devil said to him, "If you are the Son of God, command this stone to become a loaf of bread." Jesus answered him, "It is written, 'One does not live by bread alone.' "

Then the devil led him up and showed him in an instant all the kingdoms of the world. And the devil said to him, "To you I will give their glory and all this authority; for it has been given over to me, and I give it to anyone I please. If you, then, will worship me, it will all be yours." Jesus answered him, "It is written, 'Worship the Lord your God, and serve only him.' "

Then the devil took him to Jerusalem, and placed him on the pinnacle of the temple, saying to him, "If you are the Son of God, throw yourself down from here, for it is written, 'He will command his angels concerning you, to protect you,' and 'On their hands they will bear you up, so that you will not dash your foot against a stone.' " Jesus answered him, "It is said, 'Do not put the Lord your God to the test.' "

When the devil had finished every test, he departed from him until an opportune time.

The gospel of the Lord. **Praise to you, Lord Jesus Christ.**

RITE OF ELECTION

PROFESSION OF FAITH (*Nicene Creed, p. 12*)

PRAYER OF THE FAITHFUL

The following intentions are suggestions only.

℟: **Lord, hear our prayer.**

For the Church, cherished community to whom the Lord speaks, we pray to the Lord: ℟.

For leaders of nations, entrusted with the political and economic futures of their peoples, we pray to the Lord: ℟.

For those who are discouraged by temptation, we pray to the Lord: ℟.

For us, God's people gathered here, called to renew our baptismal promises at the end of our Lenten journey, we pray to the Lord: ℟.

PREPARATION OF THE GIFTS *(p. 13)*

PRAYER OVER THE GIFTS

Lord, make us worthy to bring you these gifts. May this sacrifice help to change our lives.

PREFACE *(Lent I-II or First Sunday of Lent, p. 22)*

COMMUNION ANTIPHON *(Psalm 91:4)*

The Lord will overshadow you, and you will find refuge under his wings.

PRAYER AFTER COMMUNION

Father, you increase our faith and hope, you deepen our love in this communion. Help us to live by your words and to seek Christ, our bread of life.

BLESSING AND DISMISSAL *(p. 65)*

Peter, didn't get it—despite the powerful signs! His sleepiness was no excuse. The gospel criticism is sharp, "he did not know what he was saying," chattering on about raising tents, perhaps lost in daydreams of the good times of the harvest festival.

Jesus is greater than Moses the Lawgiver, greater than Elijah the Prophet! Jesus is the Messiah, come to fulfill the hopes and expectations of the Hebrew people. Do *we* get it? Son of Man, Son of God!

The mountain-top experiences of both Moses and Jesus are described in today's readings in cosmic and mystical language. We can almost feel the breath of an all-powerful God. But the experiences have their dark, shadow side.

Caught up in the desire for total happiness, looking for an unclouded religious experience of pure joy, demanding extraordinary enthusiasm from faith, we sometimes attempt to sidestep or, like Peter, to trivialize the shadow side of religious experience. We too, like Moses, fear the terrifying darkness.

We need Jesus transfigured, greater than Moses! The Exodus, led by Moses, is outdone by the great liberation by Jesus, for us.

John Walsh, Scarborough, ON

ENTRANCE ANTIPHON *(Psalm 27:8-9)*

My heart has prompted me to seek your face; I seek it, Lord; do not hide from me.

INTRODUCTORY RITES *(p. 5)*
The Glory to God *and* Alleluia *are not said during Lent.*

OPENING PRAYER

God our Father, help us to hear your Son. Enlighten us with your word, that we may find the way to your glory.

FIRST READING *(Genesis 15:5-12, 17-18)*

The Lord brought Abram outside and said, "Look toward heaven and count the stars, if you are able to count them." Then the Lord said to him, "So shall your descendants be." And Abram believed the Lord; and the Lord reckoned it to him as righteousness.

Then the Lord said to Abram, "I am the Lord who brought you from Ur of the Chaldeans, to give you this land to possess."

But Abram said, "O Lord God, how am I to know that I shall possess it?"

The Lord said to him, "Bring me a heifer three years old, a female goat three years old, a ram three years old, a turtledove, and a young pigeon." Abram brought the Lord all these and cut them in two, laying each half over against the other; but he did not cut the birds in two. And when birds of prey came down on the carcasses, Abram drove them away.

As the sun was going down, a deep sleep fell upon Abram, and a deep and terrifying darkness descended upon him. When the sun had gone down and it was dark, a smoking fire pot and a flaming torch passed between these pieces.

On that day the Lord made a covenant with Abram, saying, "To your descendants I give this land, from the river of Egypt to the great river, the river Euphrates."

The word of the Lord. **Thanks be to God.**

RESPONSORIAL PSALM *(Psalm 27)*

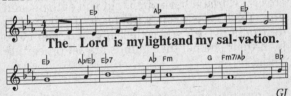

GJ

℞. **The Lord is my light and my salvation.**

The Lord is my light and my sal•-vation;
whom shall • I fear?
The Lord is the stronghold of my • **life**;
of whom shall I be • **a-fraid?** ℞.

Hear, O Lord, when I cry a•-**loud**,
be gracious to me • **and** answer_me!
"Come," my heart says, "seek his • **face!**"
Your face, Lord, do • **I** seek. ℞.

Do not hide your face from • **me**.
Do not turn your servant away • **in** anger,
you who have been my • **help**.
Do not cast me off, do not forsake me,
   O God of my • **sal**-vation! ℞.

183

I believe that I shall see the goodness
    of the • **Lord**
in the land of • **the** living.
Wait for the Lord; be • **strong,**
and let your heart take courage;
    wait for • **the** Lord! ℞.

SECOND READING *(Philippians 3:17–4:1)*

The shorter version begins at the asterisks.

Brothers and sisters, join in imitating me, and observe those who live according to the example you have in us. For many live as enemies of the cross of Christ; I have often told you of them, and now I tell you even with tears. Their end is destruction; their god is the belly; and their glory is in their shame; their minds are set on earthly things.

* * *

But our citizenship is in heaven, and it is from there that we are expecting a Saviour, the Lord Jesus Christ. He will transform the body of our humiliation that it may be conformed to the body of his glory, by the power that also enables him to make all things subject to himself.

Therefore, my brothers and sisters, whom I love and long for, my joy and crown, stand firm, my beloved, in the Lord in this way.

The word of the Lord. **Thanks be to God.**

GOSPEL ACCLAMATION *(Luke 9:35)*

If not sung, this acclamation is omitted.

From the shining cloud the Father's voice is heard: This is my beloved Son, hear him.

GOSPEL *(Luke 9:28-36)*

A reading from the holy gospel according to Luke.
Glory to you, Lord.

Jesus took with him Peter and John and James, and went up on the mountain to pray. And while he was praying, the appearance of his face changed, and his clothes became dazzling white.

Suddenly they saw two men, Moses and Elijah, talking to Jesus. They appeared in glory and were speaking of his departure, which he was about to accomplish at Jerusalem.

Now Peter and his companions were weighed down with sleep; but since they had stayed awake, they saw his glory and the two men who stood with him.

Just as Moses and Elijah were leaving Jesus, Peter said to him, "Master, it is good for us to be here; let us make three tents, one for you, one for Moses, and one for Elijah." Peter did not know what he was saying.

While Peter was saying this, a cloud came and overshadowed them; and they were terrified as they entered the cloud. Then from the cloud came a voice that said, "This is my Son, my Chosen; listen to him!" When the voice had spoken, Jesus was found alone.

And the disciples kept silent and in those days told no one any of the things they had seen.

The gospel of the Lord. **Praise to you, Lord Jesus Christ.**

PROFESSION OF FAITH *(Creed, pp. 11-12)*

PRAYER OF THE FAITHFUL

The following intentions are suggestions only.

℞: **Lord, hear our prayer.**

For the Church, journeying toward Easter rebirth in fasting and prayer, we pray to the Lord: ℞.

For the liberation of those who suffer political and economic depression, we pray to the Lord: ℞.

For those among us who are sick, lonely, or unemployed, we pray to the Lord: ℞.

For us, God's people gathered here, called to be a sign of liberation to our neighbours, we pray to the Lord: ℞.

PREPARATION OF THE GIFTS *(p. 13)*

PRAYER OVER THE GIFTS

Lord, make us holy. May this eucharist take away our sins that we may be prepared to celebrate the resurrection.

PREFACE *(Lent I-II or Second Sunday of Lent, p. 22)*

COMMUNION ANTIPHON *(Matthew 17:5)*

This is my Son, my beloved, in whom is all my delight: listen to him.

PRAYER AFTER COMMUNION

Lord, we give thanks for these holy mysteries which bring to us here on earth a share in the life to come, through Christ our Lord.

BLESSING AND DISMISSAL *(p. 65)*

The words of God to Moses are the words of God today to all those enslaved in pain and misery. Jesus hears the cry of the poor and the lonely in institutions, in psychiatric hospitals, men and women with AIDS, out of work or depressed, and many others. Jesus calls us and sends us, just as he sent Moses, to visit the weak and the poor, to announce to them the good news of love.

So often we are afraid to give them a hand of love and of compassion, to look them in the eye, to see in them a brother, a sister in humanity. We wonder 'What will happen to me if I enter into relationship with a person in need or in misery? Where might it lead me? Wouldn't it be dangerous? And anyway, what can I do for him or her?'

Jesus tells us, "Do not be afraid; I will be with you." We cannot do it alone. We need the power of God, the Holy Spirit of love and compassion. The commandment of Jesus is simple, "As the Father loves me, I love you... and my commandment is that you love one another as I have loved you."

Let us ask Jesus to give us the gift of trust in his love and in his words, that we may have the strength to risk loving.

Jean Vanier, Trosly-Breuil, France

Parishes engaged in the Rite of Christian Initiation of Adults celebrate the First Scrutiny today (p. 193).

ENTRANCE ANTIPHON *(Psalm 25:15-16)*

My eyes are ever fixed on the Lord, for he re
leases my feet from the snare. O look at me and b
merciful, for I am wretched and alone.

INTRODUCTORY RITES *(p. 5)*
The Glory to God *and* Alleluia *are not said during Len*

OPENING PRAYER

Father, you have taught us to overcome our sin
by prayer, fasting and works of mercy. When w
are discouraged by our weakness, give us confi
dence in your love.

FIRST READING *(Exodus 3:1-8, 13-15)*

Moses was keeping the flock of his father-in-law
Jethro, the priest of Midian; he led his floc
beyond the wilderness, and came to Horeb, th
mountain of God. There the angel of the Lor
appeared to him in a flame of fire out of a bush
Moses looked, and the bush was blazing, yet i
was not consumed.

Then Moses said, "I must turn aside and look at thi
great sight, and see why the bush is not burned up.

When the Lord saw that Moses had turned aside
to see, God called to him out of the bush, "Moses
Moses!" And Moses said, "Here I am." Then God
said, "Come no closer! Remove the sandals from
your feet, for the place on which you are standing
is holy ground."

God said further, "I am the God of your father, the
God of Abraham, the God of Isaac, and the God o
Jacob." And Moses hid his face, for he was afraid
to look at God.

'hen the Lord said, "I have observed the misery
f my people who are in Egypt; I have heard their
ry on account of their taskmasters. Indeed, I
now their sufferings, and I have come down to
leliver them from the Egyptians, and to bring
hem up out of that land to a good and broad land,
, land flowing with milk and honey."

But Moses said to God, "If I come to the Israelites
nd say to them, 'The God of your ancestors has
ent me to you,' and they ask me, 'What is his
ame?' what shall I say to them?"

God said to Moses, "I AM WHO I AM." He said fur-
her, "Thus you shall say to the Israelites, 'I AM has
ent me to you.'"

God also said to Moses, "Thus you shall say to the
sraelites, 'The Lord, the God of your ancestors,
he God of Abraham, the God of Isaac, and the
God of Jacob, has sent me to you.' This is my name
orever, and this my title for all generations."

The word of the Lord. **Thanks be to God.**

RESPONSORIAL PSALM *(Psalm 103)*

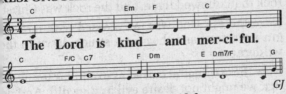

The Lord is kind and merciful.

GJ

℟. **The Lord is kind and merciful.**

Bless the Lord, O my • **soul,**
and all that is within me, bless his ho•-ly name.
Bless the Lord, O my • **soul,**
and do not forget all • **his** benefits. ℟.

189

It is the Lord who forgives all your in•-iquit
heals all your • dis-eases,
who redeems your life from • **the** Pit,
and crowns you
   with steadfast love • **and** mercy. ℞.

The Lord works vindi•-**cation**
and justice for all who are • **op**-pressed.
He made known his ways to • **Moses**,
his acts to the people • **of** Israel. ℞.

The Lord is merciful and • **gracious**,
slow to anger and abounding in stead•-**fast** lov
For as the heavens are high above the • **earth**
so great is his steadfast love
   toward those • **who** fear_him. ℞.

SECOND READING *(1 Corinthians 10:1-6, 10-12*

I do not want you to be unaware, brothers an
sisters, that our ancestors were all under th
cloud; all passed through the sea; all were bap
tized into Moses in the cloud and in the sea; all at
the same spiritual food, and all drank the sam
spiritual drink. For they drank from the spiritua
rock that followed them, and the rock was Christ

Nevertheless, God was not pleased with most o
our ancestors, and they were struck down in th
wilderness.

Now these things occurred as examples for us, sc
that we might not desire evil as they did. And d
not complain as some of them did, and wer
destroyed by the destroyer.

These things happened to our ancestors to serv
as an example, and they were written down tc

nstruct us, on whom the ends of the ages have
ome. So if you think you are standing, watch out
hat you do not fall.

he word of the Lord. **Thanks be to God.**

GOSPEL ACCLAMATION *(Matthew 4:17)*

f not sung, this acclamation is omitted.

Repent, says the Lord; the kingdom of heaven is at
hand.

GOSPEL *(Luke 13:1-9)*

A reading from the holy gospel according to Luke.
Glory to you, Lord.

esus was teaching the crowds; some of those
present told Jesus about the Galileans whose
blood Pilate had mingled with their sacrifices.

esus asked them, "Do you think that because
hese Galileans suffered in this way they were
worse sinners than all other Galileans? No, I tell
you; but unless you repent, you will all perish as
hey did. Or those eighteen who were killed when
he tower of Siloam fell on them—do you think
hat they were worse offenders than all the others
iving in Jerusalem? No, I tell you; but unless you
repent, you will all perish just as they did."

Then Jesus told this parable: "A man had a fig tree
planted in his vineyard; and he came looking for
ruit on it and found none. So he said to the gardener, 'See here! For three years I have come look-
ng for fruit on this fig tree, and still I find none. Cut
t down! Why should it be wasting the soil?'

191

The gardener replied, 'Sir, let it alone for or more year, until I dig around it and put manure o it. If it bears fruit next year, well and good; but not, you can cut it down.' "

The gospel of the Lord. **Praise to you, Lord Jesu Christ.**

PROFESSION OF FAITH *(Creed, pp. 11-12)*

PRAYER OF THE FAITHFUL

The following intentions are suggestions only.

℞: **Lord, hear our prayer.**

For the Church, herald of the good news to thos who are oppressed and poor, we pray to the Lord: ℞

For leaders of nations, struggling to witness t love and compassion in a world of suffering an loneliness, we pray to the Lord: ℞.

For God's beloved sons and daughters who are i pain and distress, or enslaved by fear or depres sion, we pray to the Lord: ℞.

For us, God's people gathered here, invited t grow in caring and fidelity to our families and ou Christian communities, we pray to the Lord: ℞

PREPARATION OF THE GIFTS *(p. 13)*

PRAYER OVER THE GIFTS

Lord, by the grace of this sacrifice may we wh(ask forgiveness be ready to forgive one another.

PREFACE *(Lent I-II, p. 22)*

COMMUNION ANTIPHON *(Psalm 84:3-4)*

The sparrow even finds a home, the swallow finds a nest wherein to place her young, near to your altars, Lord of hosts, my King, my God! How happy they who dwell in your house! For ever they are praising you.

PRAYER AFTER COMMUNION

Lord, in sharing this sacrament may we receive your forgiveness and be brought together in unity and peace.

BLESSING AND DISMISSAL *(p. 65)*

Christian Initiation: First Scrutiny

ENTRANCE ANTIPHON *(Ezekiel 36:23-26)*

I will prove my holiness through you. I will gather you from the ends of the earth; I will pour clean water on you and wash away all your sins. I will give you a new spirit within you, says the Lord.

INTRODUCTORY RITES *(p. 5)*

OPENING PRAYER

Lord, you call these chosen ones to the glory of a new birth in Christ, the second Adam. Help them grow in wisdom and love as they prepare to profess their faith in you.

FIRST READING *(Exodus 17:3-7)*

In the wilderness the people thirsted for water; and the people complained against Moses and said, "Why did you bring us out of Egypt, to kill us and our children and livestock with thirst?" So Moses cried out to the Lord, "What shall I do with this people? They are almost ready to stone me."

The Lord said to Moses, "Go on ahead of the people, and take some of the elders of Israel with you; take in your hand the staff with which you struck the Nile, and go. I will be standing there in front of you on the rock at Horeb. Strike the rock, and water will come out of it, so that the people may drink." Moses did so, in the sight of the elders of Israel.

He called the place Massah and Meribah, because the Israelites quarrelled and tested the Lord, saying, "Is the Lord among us or not?"

The word of the Lord. **Thanks be to God.**

RESPONSORIAL PSALM *(Psalm 95)*

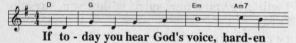

If to - day you hear God's voice, hard-en

not your hearts.

GJ

℟. **If today you hear God's voice,
harden not your hearts.**

O come, let us sing to • **the** Lord;
let us make a joyful noise
    to the rock of our • **sal**-vation!
Let us come into his presence
    • **with** thanksgiving;
let us make a joyful noise to him
    with songs • **of** praise! ℞.

O come, let us worship and • **bow** down,
let us kneel before the Lord, • **our** Maker!
For he is our God, and we are the people
    of • **his** pasture,
and the sheep of • **his** hand. ℞.

O that today you would listen to • **his** voice!
Do not harden your hearts, as at Meribah, as
    on the day at Massah in • **the** wilderness,
when your ancestors tested me,
    and put me to • **the** proof,
though they had seen • **my** work. ℞.

SECOND READING *(Romans 5:1-2, 5-8)*

Since we are justified by faith, we have peace
with God through our Lord Jesus Christ, through
whom we have obtained access to this grace in
which we stand; and we boast in our hope of
sharing the glory of God.

And hope does not disappoint us, because God's
love has been poured into our hearts through the
Holy Spirit that has been given to us. For while
we were still weak, at the right time Christ died
for the ungodly. Indeed, rarely will anyone die for
a righteous person, though perhaps for a good
person someone might actually dare to die. But

God proves his love for us in that while we still were sinners Christ died for us.

The word of the Lord. **Thanks be to God.**

GOSPEL ACCLAMATION *(John 4:42, 15)*

If not sung, this acclamation is omitted.

Lord, you are truly the Saviour of the world; give me living water, that I may never thirst again.

GOSPEL *(John 4:5-42)*

For the shorter version, omit the indented parts.

A reading from the holy gospel according to John. **Glory to you, Lord.**

Jesus came to a Samaritan city called Sychar, near the plot of ground that Jacob had given to his son Joseph. Jacob's well was there, and Jesus, tired out by his journey, was sitting by the well. It was about noon.

A Samaritan woman came to draw water, and Jesus said to her, "Give me a drink." (His disciples had gone to the city to buy food.)

The Samaritan woman said to him, "How is it that you, a Jew, ask a drink of me, a woman of Samaria?" (Jews do not share things in common with Samaritans.) Jesus answered her, "If you knew the gift of God, and who it is that is saying to you, 'Give me a drink,' you would have asked him, and he would have given you living water."

The woman said to him, "Sir, you have no bucket, and the well is deep. Where do you get that living water? Are you greater than our ancestor Jacob, who gave us the well, and with his children and his flocks drank from it?" Jesus said to her, "Everyone who drinks of this water will be thirsty again, but those who drink of the water that I will give them will never be thirsty. The water that I will give will become in them a spring of water gushing up to eternal life." The woman said to him, "Sir, give me this water, so that I may never be thirsty or have to keep coming here to draw water."

Jesus said to her, "Go, call your husband, and come back." The woman answered him, "I have no husband." Jesus said to her, "You are right in saying, 'I have no husband'; for you have had five husbands, and the one you have now is not your husband. What you have said is true!"

The woman said to him, "Sir, I see that you are a prophet. Our ancestors worshipped on this mountain, but you say that the place where people must worship is in Jerusalem."

Jesus said to her, "Woman, believe me, the hour is coming when you will worship the Father neither on this mountain nor in Jerusalem. You worship what you do not know; we worship what we know, for salvation is from the Jews. But the hour is coming, and is now here, when the true worshippers will worship the Father in spirit and truth, for the Father seeks such as these to worship him. God is spirit, and those who worship him must worship in spirit and truth."

The woman said to him, "I know that the Messiah is coming" (who is called the Christ). "When he comes, he will proclaim all things to us." Jesus said to her, "I am he, the one who is speaking to you."

Just then his disciples came. They were astonished that he was speaking with a woman, but no one said, "What do you want?" or, "Why are you speaking with her?" Then the woman left her water jar and went back to the city. She said to the people, "Come and see a man who told me everything I have ever done! He cannot be the Messiah, can he?" They left the city and were on their way to him. Meanwhile the disciples were urging him, "Rabbi, eat something." But he said to them, "I have food to eat that you do not know about." So the disciples said to one another, "Surely no one has brought him something to eat?"

Jesus said to them, "My food is to do the will of him who sent me and to complete his work. Do you not say, 'Four months more, then comes the harvest'? But I tell you, look around you, and see how the fields are ripe for harvesting. The reaper is already receiving wages and is gathering fruit for eternal life, so that sower and reaper may rejoice together. For here the saying holds true, 'One sows and another reaps.' I sent you to reap that for which you did not labour. Others have laboured, and you have entered into their labour."

Many Samaritans from that city believed in Jesus because of the woman's testimony, "He told me everything I have ever done." So when the Samaritans came to him, they asked him to stay with them; and he stayed there two days. And many more believed because of his word. They said to the woman, "It is no longer because of what you said that we believe, for we have heard for ourselves, and we know that this is truly the Saviour of the world."

The gospel of the Lord. **Praise to you, Lord Jesus Christ.**

PROFESSION OF FAITH *(Creed, pp. 11-12)*

PRAYER OF THE FAITHFUL *(p. 192)*

PREPARATION OF THE GIFTS *(p. 13)*

PRAYER OVER THE GIFTS

Lord God, give faith and love to your children and lead them safely to the banquet you have prepared for them. We ask this in the name of Jesus the Lord.

PREFACE *(Third Sunday of Lent, p. 24)*

COMMUNION ANTIPHON *(John 4:13-14)*

Whoever drinks the water that I shall give him, says the Lord, will have a spring inside him, welling up for eternal life.

PRAYER AFTER COMMUNION

Lord, be present in our lives with your gifts of salvation. Prepare these men and women for your sacraments and protect them in your love. We ask this through Christ our Lord.

BLESSING AND DISMISSAL *(p. 65)*

This very familiar story of the prodigal son can be heard from such different points of view: from that of the younger son, the older brother, the forgiving father...

In my twenties, I went off travelling to 'distant lands'... searching. Some might say I lived 'irresponsibly.' I travelled far from family and friends, from God and from myself.

As time passed, an event in my life caused me to stop running. I realized that I had nowhere else to go. I had to face myself, my family, my God. I'd reached the end of my running. Where to turn? Where was God? Where was love?

In experiencing God's love at perhaps the darkest hour ever of my life, I was able to take that important first step back—to myself and to my family. I returned home to reconcile with my mother. Amid tears and with tentative sharing, we reached across a gulf of hurt that had existed for many years.

In the deep healing of my mother's love, I can but glimpse God's infinite love and acceptance. I know that I am loved. I can love more fully. The God of Love makes this possible.

Caryl Green, Chelsea, QC

Parishes engaged in the Rite of Christian Initiation of Adults celebrate the Second Scrutiny today (p. 206).

ENTRANCE ANTIPHON *(See Isaiah 66:10-11)*

Rejoice, Jerusalem! Be glad for her, you who love her; rejoice with her, you who mourned for her, and you will find contentment at her consoling breasts.

INTRODUCTORY RITES *(p. 5)*
The Glory to God *and* Alleluia *are not said during Lent.*

OPENING PRAYER

Father of peace, we are joyful in your Word, your Son Jesus Christ, who reconciles us to you. Let us hasten toward Easter with the eagerness of faith and love.

FIRST READING *(Joshua 5:9, 10-12)*

After the Israelites had crossed over the Jordan river, and entered the promised land, the Lord said to Joshua, "Today I have rolled away from you the disgrace of Egypt."

While the Israelites were camped in Gilgal they kept the Passover in the evening on the fourteenth day of the month in the plains of Jericho.

On the day after the Passover, on that very day, they ate the produce of the land, unleavened cakes and parched grain. The manna ceased on the day they ate the produce of the land, and the Israelites no longer had manna; they ate the crops of the land of Canaan that year.

The word of the Lord. **Thanks be to God.**

RESPONSORIAL PSALM *(Psalm 34)*

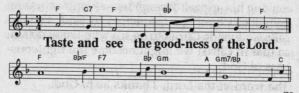

Taste and see the good-ness of the Lord.

GJ

℞. **Taste and see the goodness of the Lord.**

I will bless the Lord at all • **times;**
his praise continually shall be in • **my** mouth.
My soul makes its boast in the • **Lord;**
let the humble hear and • **be** glad. ℞.

O magnify the Lord with • **me,**
and let us exalt his name • **to**-gether.
I sought the Lord, and he • **answered_me,**
and delivered me from all • **my** fears. ℞.

Look to him, and be • **radiant;**
so your faces shall never be • **a**-shamed.
This poor soul cried, and was heard
   by the • **Lord,**
and was saved from ev•-**ery** trouble. ℞.

SECOND READING *(2 Corinthians 5:17-21)*

If anyone is in Christ, there is a new creation:
everything old has passed away; see, everything
has become new! All this is from God, who reconciled us to himself through Christ, and has given
us the ministry of reconciliation; that is, in Christ,
God was reconciling the world to himself, not
counting their trespasses against them, and en-
trusting the message of reconciliation to us.

So we are ambassadors for Christ, since God is making his appeal through us; we entreat you on behalf of Christ, be reconciled to God. For our sake God made Christ to be sin who knew no sin, so that in Christ we might become the righteousness of God.

The word of the Lord. **Thanks be to God.**

GOSPEL ACCLAMATION *(Luke 15:18)*

If not sung, this acclamation is omitted.

I will rise and go to my father and tell him: Father, I have sinned against heaven and against you.

GOSPEL *(Luke 15:1-3, 11-32)*

A reading from the holy gospel according to Luke. **Glory to you, Lord.**

All the tax collectors and sinners were coming near to listen to Jesus. And the Pharisees and the scribes were grumbling and saying, "This fellow welcomes sinners and eats with them."

So he told them a parable: "There was a man who had two sons. The younger of them said to his father, 'Father, give me the share of the property that will belong to me.' So the father divided his property between them. A few days later the younger son gathered all he had and travelled to a distant country, and there he squandered his property in dissolute living.

"When he had spent everything, a severe famine took place throughout that country, and he began to be in need. So he went and hired himself out to one of the citizens of that country, who sent him to his fields to feed the pigs. The young man

203

would gladly have filled himself with the pods that the pigs were eating; and no one gave him anything.

"But when he came to himself he said, 'How many of my father's hired hands have bread enough and to spare, but here I am dying of hunger! I will get up and go to my father, and I will say to him, "Father, I have sinned against heaven and before you; I am no longer worthy to be called your son; treat me like one of your hired hands." '

"So he set off and went to his father. But while he was still far off, his father saw him and was filled with compassion; he ran and put his arms around him and kissed him.

"Then the son said to him, 'Father, I have sinned against heaven and before you; I am no longer worthy to be called your son.' But the father said to his slaves, 'Quickly, bring out a robe—the best one—and put it on him; put a ring on his finger and sandals on his feet. And get the fatted calf and kill it, and let us eat and celebrate; for this son of mine was dead and is alive again; he was lost and is found!' And they began to celebrate.

"Now his elder son was in the field; and when he came and approached the house, he heard music and dancing. He called one of the slaves and asked what was going on. The slave replied, 'Your brother has come, and your father has killed the fatted calf, because he has got him back safe and sound.'

"Then the elder son became angry and refused to go in. His father came out and began to plead with him. But he answered his father, 'Listen! For all these years I have been working like a slave for you, and I have never disobeyed your command; yet you have never given me even a young goat so that I might celebrate with my friends. But when this son of yours came back, who has devoured your property with prostitutes, you killed the fatted calf for him!'

"Then the father said to him, 'Son, you are always with me, and all that is mine is yours. But we had to celebrate and rejoice, because this brother of yours was dead and has come to life; he was lost and has been found.' "

The gospel of the Lord. **Praise to you, Lord Jesus Christ.**

PROFESSION OF FAITH *(Creed, pp. 11-12)*

PRAYER OF THE FAITHFUL

The following intentions are suggestions only.

℞: **Lord, hear our prayer.**

For the Church, weak yet strong, healing yet seeking wholeness, we pray to the Lord: ℞.

For the world's peoples who seek safe haven, and for our own country, strong in its tradition of welcoming strangers, we pray to the Lord: ℞.

For those searching for a word of hope, we pray to the Lord: ℞.

For those seeking initiation into the Christian community, we pray to the Lord: ℞.

PREPARATION OF THE GIFTS *(p. 13)*

PRAYER OVER THE GIFTS

Lord, we offer you these gifts which bring us peace and joy. Increase our reverence by this eucharist, and bring salvation to the world.

PREFACE *(Lent I-II, p. 22)*

COMMUNION ANTIPHON *(Luke 15:32)*

My son, you should rejoice, because your brother was dead and has come back to life; he was lost and is found.

PRAYER AFTER COMMUNION

Father, you enlighten all who come into the world. Fill our hearts with the light of your gospel, that our thoughts may please you, and our love be sincere.

BLESSING AND DISMISSAL *(p. 65)*

Christian Initiation: Second Scrutiny

ENTRANCE ANTIPHON *(Ezekiel 36:23-26)*

I will prove my holiness through you. I will gather you from the ends of the earth; I will pour clean water on you and wash away all your sins. I will give you a new spirit within you, says the Lord.

INTRODUCTORY RITES *(p. 5)*

OPENING PRAYER

Almighty and eternal God, may your Church increase in true joy. May these candidates for baptism, and all the family of man, be reborn into the life of your kingdom.

FIRST READING *(1 Samuel 16:1, 6-7, 10-13)*

The Lord said to Samuel, "Fill your horn with oil and set out; I will send you to Jesse of Bethlehem, for I have provided for myself a king among his sons."

When the sons of Jesse came, Samuel looked on Eliab and thought, "Surely the Lord's anointed is now before the Lord." But the Lord said to Samuel, "Do not look on his appearance or on the height of his stature, because I have rejected him; for the Lord does not see as mortals see; they look on the outward appearance, but the Lord looks on the heart."

Jesse made seven of his sons pass before Samuel, and Samuel said to Jesse, "The Lord has not chosen any of these." Samuel said to Jesse, "Are all your sons here?" And he said, "There remains yet the youngest, but he is keeping the sheep." And Samuel said to Jesse, "Send and bring him; for we will not sit down until he comes here." Jesse sent and brought David in. Now he was ruddy, and had beautiful eyes, and was handsome. The Lord said, "Rise and anoint him; for this is the one."

Then Samuel took the horn of oil, and anointed him in the presence of his brothers; and the spirit of the Lord came mightily upon David from that day forward.

The word of the Lord. **Thanks be to God.**

RESPONSORIAL PSALM *(Psalm 23)*

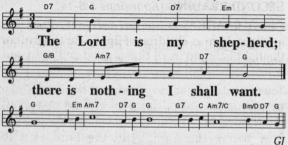

GJ

℟. **The Lord is my shepherd;**
there is nothing I shall want.

The Lord is my shepherd, I shall • **not** want.
He makes me lie down in • **green** pastures;
he leads me be•-**side** still waters;
he re•-**stores** my soul. ℟.

He leads me in right paths
    for his • **name's** sake.
Even though I walk through
    the dark•-**est** valley,
I fear no evil, for • **you** are with_me;
your rod and your • **staff**—they comfort_me. ℟.

You prepare a table • **be**-fore_me
in the presence of • **my** enemies;
you anoint my • **head** with oil;
my cup • **o**-ver-flows. ℟.

208

Surely goodness and mercy • **shall** follow_me
all the days of • **my** life,
and I shall dwell in the • **house_of** the Lord
my • **whole** life long. ℟.

SECOND READING *(Ephesians 5:8-14)*

Once you were darkness, but now in the Lord you
are light. Live as children of light—for the fruit of
the light is found in all that is good and right and
true.

Try to find out what is pleasing to the Lord. Take
no part in the unfruitful works of darkness, but
instead expose them. For it is shameful even to
mention what such people do secretly; but everything exposed by the light becomes visible, for
everything that becomes visible is light. Therefore it is said, "Sleeper, awake! Rise from the
dead, and Christ will shine on you."

The word of the Lord. **Thanks be to God.**

GOSPEL ACCLAMATION *(John 8:12)*

If not sung, this acclamation is omitted.

I am the light of the world, says the Lord; whoever
follows me will have the light of life.

GOSPEL *(John 9:1-41)*

For the shorter version, omit the indented parts.

A reading from the holy gospel according to John.
Glory to you, Lord.

As Jesus walked along, he saw a man blind from
birth.

His disciples asked him, "Rabbi, who sinned, this man or his parents, that he was born blind?"

Jesus answered, "Neither this man nor his parents sinned; he was born blind so that God's works might be revealed in him. We must work the works of him who sent me while it is day; night is coming when no one can work. As long as I am in the world, I am the light of the world." When he had said this,

He spat on the ground and made mud with the saliva and spread the mud on the man's eyes, saying to him, "Go, wash in the pool of Siloam" (which means Sent).

Then the man who was blind went and washed, and came back able to see. The neighbours and those who had seen him before as a beggar began to ask, "Is this not the man who used to sit and beg?" Some were saying, "It is he." Others were saying, "No, but it is someone like him." He kept saying, "I am the man."

But they kept asking him, "Then how were your eyes opened?" He answered, "The man called Jesus made mud, spread it on my eyes, and said to me, 'Go to Siloam and wash.' Then I went and washed and received my sight." They said to him, "Where is he?" He said, "I do not know."

They brought to the Pharisees the man who had formerly been blind. Now it was a sabbath day when Jesus made the mud and opened his eyes. Then the Pharisees also began to ask him how he had received his sight. He said to them, "He put mud on my eyes. Then I washed, and now I see." Some of the Pharisees said, "This man is not from God, for he does not observe the sabbath." But others said, "How can a man who is a sinner perform such signs?" And they were divided. So they said again to the blind man, "What do you say about him? It was your eyes he opened." He said, "He is a prophet."

They did not believe that he had been blind and had received his sight until they called the parents of the man who had received his sight and asked them, "Is this your son, who you say was born blind? How then does he now see?" His parents answered, "We know that this is our son, and that he was born blind; but we do not know how it is that now he sees, nor do we know who opened his eyes. Ask him; he is of age. He will speak for himself." His parents said this because they were afraid of the Jewish authorities, who had already agreed that anyone who confessed Jesus to be the Messiah would be put out of the synagogue. Therefore his parents said, "He is of age; ask him."

So for the second time they called the man who had been blind, and they said to him, "Give glory to God! We know that this man is a sinner." He answered, "I do not know whether he is a sinner. One thing I do know, that though I was blind, now I see." They said to him, "What did he do to you? How did he open your eyes?" He answered them, "I have

211

told you already, and you would not listen. Why do you want to hear it again? Do you also want to become his disciples?" Then they reviled him, saying, "You are his disciple, but we are disciples of Moses. We know that God has spoken to Moses, but as for this man, we do not know where he comes from."

The man answered, "Here is an astonishing thing! You do not know where he comes from, and yet he opened my eyes. We know that God does not listen to sinners, but he does listen to one who worships him and obeys his will. Never since the world began has it been heard that anyone opened the eyes of a person born blind. If this man were not from God, he could do nothing."

They answered him, "You were born entirely in sins, and are you trying to teach us?" And they drove him out.

Jesus heard that they had driven him out, and when he found him, he said, "Do you believe in the Son of Man?" He answered, "And who is he, sir? Tell me, so that I may believe in him." Jesus said to him, "You have seen him, and the one speaking with you is he." He said, "Lord, I believe." And he worshipped him.

Jesus said, "I came into this world for judgment so that those who do not see may see, and those who do see may become blind." Some of the Pharisees near him heard this and said to him, "Surely we are not blind, are we?" Jesus said to them, "If you were blind, you would have no sin. But now that you say, 'We see,' your sin remains."

The gospel of the Lord. **Praise to you, Lord Jesus Christ.**

PROFESSION OF FAITH *(Creed, pp. 11-12)*

PRAYER OF THE FAITHFUL *(p. 205)*

PREPARATION OF THE GIFTS *(p. 13)*

PRAYER OVER THE GIFTS

Lord, we offer these gifts in joy and thanksgiving for our salvation. May the example of our faith and love help your chosen ones on their way to salvation. Grant this through Christ our Lord.

PREFACE *(Fourth Sunday of Lent, p. 24)*

COMMUNION ANTIPHON *(See John 9:11)*

The Lord rubbed my eyes: I went away and washed, then I could see, and I believed in God.

PRAYER AFTER COMMUNION

Lord, be close to your family. Rule and guide us on our way to your kingdom and bring us to the joy of salvation. Grant this in the name of Jesus the Lord.

BLESSING AND DISMISSAL *(p. 65)*

Solidarity Day

Some uses for stones (besides throwing them at others): kicking one down the street on a leisurely morning walk; making a border around a flower garden; skipping a perfect one across the nearest body of water; paving a walkway; constructing a fireplace; building a house; erecting a memorial... I am making this list because if we take today's gospel seriously there will be a lot of extra stones around and we will have to find constructive ways to use them!

This gospel is about sin (the fact that none of us is without it) and what we shouldn't do because we are sinful people (judge others). It is also about what we *should do* (hence the new uses for stones). Jesus says that he will not condemn the woman brought before him—but he also stands *with* her, taking her side against unjust aggression and sending her away with a feeling of hope and dignity. Jesus' actions provide a simple example of what is often called 'solidarity.'

Today is *Solidarity Day,* a time when Catholics across Canada join in support of—in *solidarity* with—our sisters and brothers in Asia, Africa, South America and the Caribbean. It is a time to acknowledge our sinfulness and our support of sinful structures and practices. It is a time to *stand with* and *take the side of* people who are oppressed, people who are victims of injustice, people who, through no fault of their own, face often insurmountable obstacles just to live one more day. It is a time to think about how we can use all those extra stones to build a better world.

Susan Eaton, Toronto, ON

Parishes engaged in the Rite of Christian Initiation of Adults celebrate the Third Scrutiny today (p. 220)

ENTRANCE ANTIPHON *(Psalm 43:1-2)*

Give me justice, O God, and defend my cause against the wicked; rescue me from unjust and deceitful men. You, O God, are my refuge.

INTRODUCTORY RITES *(p. 5)*

The Glory to God *and* Alleluia *are not said during Lent.*

OPENING PRAYER

Father, help us to be like Christ your Son, who loved the world and died for our salvation. Inspire us by his love, guide us by his example.

FIRST READING *(Isaiah 43:16-21)*

Thus says the Lord,
who makes a way in the sea,
a path in the mighty waters,
who brings out chariot and horse,
 army and warrior;
they lie down, they cannot rise,
they are extinguished, quenched like a wick:
Do not remember the former things,
or consider the things of old.

I am about to do a new thing;
now it springs forth, do you not perceive it?

I will make a way in the wilderness
and rivers in the desert.

The wild animals will honour me,
the jackals and the ostriches;
for I give water in the wilderness,
    rivers in the desert,
to give drink to my chosen people,
the people whom I formed for myself
so that they might declare my praise.

The word of the Lord. **Thanks be to God.**

RESPONSORIAL PSALM *(Psalm 126)*

℞. **The Lord has done great things for us;**
  we are filled with joy.

When the Lord restored the fortunes of • **Zion,**
we were like those who • **dream.**
Then our mouth was filled with • **laughter,**
and our tongue with shouts • **of** joy. ℞.

Then it was said among the • **nations,**
The Lord has done great things for • **them.**
The Lord has done great things for • **us,**
and we • **re**-joiced. ℞.

Restore our fortunes, O • **Lord,**
like the watercourses in the desert
   of the • **Negev.**
May those who sow in • **tears**
reap with shouts • **of** joy. ℟.

Those who go out • **weeping,**
bearing the seed for • **sowing,**
shall come home with shouts of • **joy,**
carrying • **their** sheaves. ℟.

SECOND READING *(Philippians 3:8-14)*

I regard everything as loss because of the surpassing value of knowing Christ Jesus my Lord. For his sake I have suffered the loss of all things, and I regard them as rubbish, in order that I may gain Christ and be found in him, not having a righteousness of my own that comes from the law, but one that comes through faith in Christ, the righteousness from God based on faith.

I want to know Christ and the power of his resurrection and the sharing of his sufferings by becoming like him in his death, if somehow I may attain the resurrection from the dead.

Not that I have already obtained this or have already reached the goal; but I press on to make it my own, because Christ Jesus has made me his own.

Beloved, I do not consider that I have made it my own; but this one thing I do: forgetting what lies behind and straining forward to what lies ahead, I press on toward the goal for the prize of the heavenly call of God in Christ Jesus.

The word of the Lord. **Thanks be to God.**

GOSPEL ACCLAMATION *(Joel 2:12-13)*

If not sung, this acclamation is omitted.

With all your heart turn to me, says the Lord, for I am tender and compassionate.

GOSPEL *(John 8:1-11)*

A reading from the holy gospel according to John.
Glory to you, Lord.

Jesus went to the Mount of Olives. Early in the morning he came again to the temple. All the people came to him and he sat down and began to teach them.

The scribes and the Pharisees brought a woman who had been caught in adultery; and making her stand before the people, they said to Jesus, "Teacher, this woman was caught in the very act of committing adultery. In the law, Moses commanded us to stone such women. Now what do you say?" They said this to test Jesus, so that they might have some charge to bring against him.

Jesus bent down and wrote with his finger on the ground. When the scribes and Pharisees kept on questioning him, Jesus straightened up and said to them, "Let anyone among you who is without sin be the first to throw a stone at her." And once again Jesus bent down and wrote on the ground.

When the scribes and Pharisees heard what Jesus had said, they went away, one by one, beginning with the elders; and Jesus was left alone with the woman standing before him.

218

Jesus straightened up and said to her, "Woman, where are they? Has no one condemned you?" She said, "No one, sir." And Jesus said, "Neither do I condemn you. Go your way, and from now on do not sin again."

The gospel of the Lord. **Praise to you, Lord Jesus Christ.**

PROFESSION OF FAITH *(Creed, pp. 11-12)*

PRAYER OF THE FAITHFUL

The following intentions are suggestions only.

℞: **Lord, hear our prayer.**

For the Church, called to be a community of solidarity with those who are oppressed, we pray to the Lord: ℞.

For leaders of nations, entrusted with the task of building a just world, we pray to the Lord: ℞.

For our brothers and sisters in Asia, Africa and the Americas, who call on us to support their efforts to improve their lives, we pray to the Lord: ℞.

For us, God's holy people, witnesses to the dignity and respect owed each human person, we pray to the Lord: ℞.

PREPARATION OF THE GIFTS *(p. 13)*

PRAYER OVER THE GIFTS

Almighty God, may the sacrifice we offer take away the sins of those whom you enlighten with the Christian faith.

PREFACE *(Lent I-II, p. 22)*

COMMUNION ANTIPHON *(John 8:10-11)*

Has no one condemned you? The woman answered: No one, Lord. Neither do I condemn you: go and do not sin again.

PRAYER AFTER COMMUNION

Almighty Father, by this sacrifice may we always remain one with your Son, Jesus Christ, whose body and blood we share.

BLESSING AND DISMISSAL *(p. 65)*

Christian Initiation: Third Scrutiny

ENTRANCE ANTIPHON *(Ezekiel 36:23-26)*

I will prove my holiness through you. I will gather you from the ends of the earth; I will pour clean water on you and wash away all your sins. I will give you a new spirit within you, says the Lord.

INTRODUCTORY RITES *(p. 5)*

OPENING PRAYER

Lord, enlighten your chosen ones with the word of life. Give them a new birth in the waters of baptism and make them living members of the Church.

FIRST READING *(Ezekiel 37:12-14)*

Thus says the Lord God: "I am going to open your graves, and bring you up from your graves, O my people; and I will bring you back to the land of Israel. And you shall know that I am the Lord, when I open your graves, and bring you up from your graves, O my people.

"I will put my spirit within you, and you shall live, and I will place you on your own soil; then you shall know that I, the Lord, have spoken and will act," says the Lord.

The word of the Lord. **Thanks be to God.**

RESPONSORIAL PSALM *(Psalm 130)*

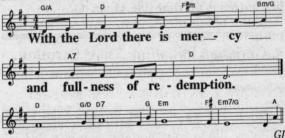

℟. **With the Lord there is mercy and fullness of redemption.**

Out of the depths I cry to you, O • **Lord.**
Lord, hear • **my** voice!
Let your ears be at•-**tentive**
to the voice of my sup•-**pli**-cations! ℟.

If you, O Lord, should mark in•-**iquities,**
Lord, who • **could** stand?
But there is forgiveness with • **you,**
so that you may be • **re**-vered. ℟.

221

I wait for the • **Lord,**
my soul waits, and in his word • **I** hope;
my soul waits for the • **Lord**
more than those who watch for • **the** morning. ℟.

For with the Lord there is steadfast • **love,**
and with him is great power to • **re-**deem.
It is he who will redeem • **Israel**
from all its • **in-**iquities. ℟.

SECOND READING *(Romans 8:8-11)*

Those who are in the flesh cannot please God. But you are not in the flesh; you are in the Spirit, since the Spirit of God dwells in you. Anyone who does not have the Spirit of Christ does not belong to him.

But if Christ is in you, though the body is dead because of sin, the Spirit is life because of righteousness.

If the Spirit of God who raised Jesus from the dead dwells in you, he who raised Christ from the dead will give life to your mortal bodies also through his Spirit that dwells in you.

The word of the Lord. **Thanks be to God.**

GOSPEL ACCLAMATION *(John 11:25, 26)*

If not sung, this acclamation is omitted.

I am the resurrection and the life, says the Lord; whoever believes in me will not die for ever.

GOSPEL *(John 11:1-45)*

For the shorter version, omit the indented parts.

A reading from the holy gospel according to John.
Glory to you, Lord.

> Now a certain man, Lazarus, was ill. He was
> from Bethany, the village of Mary and her
> sister Martha. Mary was the one who anointed
> the Lord with perfume and wiped his feet with
> her hair; her brother Lazarus was ill. So

The sisters of Lazarus sent a message to Jesus,
"Lord, he whom you love is ill." But when Jesus
heard this, he said, "This illness does not lead to
death; rather it is for God's glory, so that the Son
of God may be glorified through it." Accordingly,
though Jesus loved Martha and her sister and
Lazarus, after having heard that Lazarus was ill,
he stayed two days longer in the place where he
was. Then after this Jesus said to the disciples,
"Let us go to Judea again."

> The disciples said to him, "Rabbi, the people
> there were just now trying to stone you, and
> are you going there again?" Jesus answered,
> "Are there not twelve hours of daylight?
> Those who walk during the day do not stum-
> ble, because they see the light of this world.
> But those who walk at night stumble, because
> the light is not in them."

After saying this, he told them, "Our friend
Lazarus has fallen asleep, but I am going there
to awaken him." The disciples said to him,
"Lord, if he has fallen asleep, he will be all

right." Jesus, however, had been speaking about his death, but they thought that he was referring merely to sleep. Then Jesus told them plainly, "Lazarus is dead. For your sake I am glad I was not there, so that you may believe. But let us go to him." Thomas, who was called the Twin, said to his fellow disciples, "Let us also go, that we may die with him."

When Jesus arrived, he found that Lazarus had already been in the tomb four days.

Now Bethany was near Jerusalem, some two miles away, and many Jews had come to Martha and Mary to console them about their brother.

When Martha heard that Jesus was coming, she went and met him, while Mary stayed at home. Martha said to Jesus, "Lord, if you had been here, my brother would not have died. But even now I know that God will give you whatever you ask of him." Jesus said to her, "Your brother will rise again." Martha said to him, "I know that he will rise again in the resurrection on the last day." Jesus said to her, "I am the resurrection and the life. Those who believe in me, even though they die, will live, and everyone who lives and believes in me will never die. Do you believe this?" She said to him, "Yes, Lord, I believe that you are the Messiah, the Son of God, the one coming into the world."

When she had said this, she went back and called her sister Mary, and told her privately,

"The Teacher is here and is calling for you." And when Mary heard it, she got up quickly and went to him. Now Jesus had not yet come to the village, but was still at the place where Martha had met him. The Jews who were with her in the house, consoling her, saw Mary get up quickly and go out. They followed her because they thought that she was going to the tomb to weep there.

When Mary came where Jesus was and saw him, she knelt at his feet and said to him, "Lord, if you had been here, my brother would not have died." When Jesus saw her weeping, and the Jews who came with her also weeping,

He was greatly disturbed in spirit and deeply moved. Jesus said, "Where have you laid him?" They said to him, "Lord, come and see." Jesus began to weep. So the Jews said, "See how he loved him!" But some of them said, "Could not he who opened the eyes of the blind man have kept this man from dying?"

Then Jesus, again greatly disturbed, came to the tomb. It was a cave, and a stone was lying against it. Jesus said, "Take away the stone." Martha, the sister of the dead man, said to him, "Lord, already there is a stench because he has been dead four days." Jesus said to her, "Did I not tell you that if you believed, you would see the glory of God?" So they took away the stone. And Jesus looked upward and said, "Father, I thank you for having heard me. I knew that you always hear me, but I have said this for the sake of the crowd standing here, so that they may believe that you sent me."

When he had said this, he cried with a loud voice, "Lazarus, come out!" The dead man came out, his hands and feet bound with strips of cloth, and his face wrapped in a cloth. Jesus said to them, "Unbind him, and let him go."

Many of the Jews therefore, who had come with Mary and had seen what Jesus did, believed in him.

The gospel of the Lord. **Praise to you, Lord Jesus Christ.**

PROFESSION OF FAITH *(Creed, pp. 11-12)*

PRAYER OF THE FAITHFUL *(p. 219)*

PREPARATION OF THE GIFTS *(p. 13)*

PRAYER OVER THE GIFTS

Almighty God, hear our prayers for these men and women who have begun to learn the Christian faith, and by this sacrifice prepare them for baptism. We ask this in the name of Jesus the Lord.

PREFACE *(Fifth Sunday of Lent, p. 25)*

COMMUNION ANTIPHON *(John 11:26)*

He who lives and believes in me will not die for ever, says the Lord.

PRAYER AFTER COMMUNION

Lord, may your people be one in spirit and serve you with all their heart. Free them from all fear. Give them joy in your gifts and love for those who are reborn as your children. We ask this through Christ our Lord.

BLESSING AND DISMISSAL *(p. 65)*

We are always impressed with great achievers. Every day, the media pay homage to those whose achievements impress us most: superstar athletes, sexy models, famous actors and musicians, powerful executives, influential politicians, generous benefactors, and so on. Indeed, it is human nature to be impressed by those who are strong, or beautiful, or famous, or accomplished.

When Jesus arrived in Jerusalem, people were impressed by how strong, famous and accomplished he had become. Three short years ago, he had been virtually unknown; now he was the leader of the most significant peace and justice movement in Israel, entering the heart of the nation as a real folk hero. As people lined the streets to greet him, they must have marvelled that he was truly on the verge of establishing the kingdom he had been proclaiming and would soon be able to stand as an equal beside kings and other political leaders.

As it turned out, they weren't entirely wrong. Jesus was, in fact, near to his mission of establishing a new kingdom, a new order. However, to do this he had to go beyond living on the surface of life with the strong, the famous and the accomplished; he had to enter into the very heart of a suffering humanity. So instead of becoming merely the king of a nation, he became, through his Passion, the King of Suffering. And in his kingdom he now stands not beside kings and princes, but beside the poor and the outcast. In his kingdom, it is not the strong, the famous and the accomplished who matter, but the weak, the lowly and the discouraged whom he has lifted up.

John O'Donnell, Halifax, NS

COMMEMORATION OF THE LORD'S ENTRANCE INTO JERUSALEM

FIRST FORM: THE PROCESSION

INTRODUCTION

The people, carrying palm branches, gather in a suitable place distinct from the church to which the procession will move. As they gather, they may sing #120 Hosanna!

Dear friends in Christ, for five weeks of Lent we have been preparing, by works of charity and self-sacrifice, for the celebration of our Lord's paschal mystery. Today we come together to begin this solemn celebration in union with the whole Church throughout the world. Christ entered in triumph into his own city, to complete his work as our Messiah: to suffer, to die, and to rise again. Let us remember with devotion this entry which began his saving work and follow him with a lively faith. United with him in his suffering on the cross, may we share his resurrection and new life.

Let us pray.

Almighty God, we pray you, bless these branches and make them holy. Today we joyfully acclaim Jesus, our Messiah and King.

May we reach one day the happiness of the new and everlasting Jerusalem by faithfully following him who lives and reigns for ever and ever.

or

Lord, increase the faith of your people and listen to our prayers. Today we honour Christ our triumphant King by carrying these branches. May we honour you every day by living always in him, for he is Lord for ever and ever.

GOSPEL *(Luke 19:28-40)*

A reading from the holy gospel according to Luke.
Glory to you, Lord.

Jesus went on ahead, going up to Jerusalem. When he had come near Bethphage and Bethany, at the place called the Mount of Olives, he sent two of the disciples, saying, "Go into the village ahead of you, and as you enter it you will find tied there a colt that has never been ridden. Untie it and bring it here. If anyone asks you, 'Why are you untying it?' just say this, 'The Lord needs it.' "

So those who were sent departed and found it as Jesus had told them. As they were untying the colt, its owners asked them, "Why are you untying the colt?" They said, "The Lord needs it."

Then they brought the colt to Jesus; and after throwing their cloaks on the colt, they set Jesus on it.

As he rode along, people kept spreading their cloaks on the road. As he was now approaching the path down from the Mount of Olives, the whole multitude of the disciples began to praise

God joyfully, and with a loud voice, for all the deeds of power that they had seen, saying, "Blessed is the king who comes in the name of the Lord! Peace in heaven, and glory in the highest heaven!"

Some of the Pharisees in the crowd said to him, "Teacher, order your disciples to stop."

Jesus answered, "I tell you, if these were silent, the stones would shout out."

The gospel of the Lord. **Praise to you, Lord Jesus Christ.**

PROCESSION

Let us go forth in peace, praising Jesus our Messiah, as did the crowds who welcomed him to Jerusalem.

All process to the church singing a hymn in honour of Christ the King.

Mass continues with the Opening Prayer, *p. 231.*

SECOND FORM: THE SOLEMN ENTRANCE

The blessing of branches and proclamation of the gospel take place, as above, but in the church. After the gospel, the celebrant moves solemnly through the church to the sanctuary, while all sing.

Mass continues with the Opening Prayer, *p. 231 .*

THIRD FORM: THE SIMPLE ENTRANCE

The people gather in the church as usual. While the celebrant goes to the altar, the following entrance antiphon or a suitable hymn is sung.

ENTRANCE ANTIPHON *(See Psalm 24)*

Six days before the solemn Passover, the Lord came to Jerusalem, and children waving palm

branches ran out to welcome him. They loudly praised the Lord:

Blessed are you who have come to us
So rich in love and mercy.

Open wide the doors and gates.
Lift high the ancient portals.
The King of glory enters.

Who is this King of glory?
He is God the mighty Lord.

Hosanna in the highest.
Blessed are you who have come to us
So rich in love and mercy.

INTRODUCTORY RITES (p. 5)

OPENING PRAYER

Almighty, ever-living God, you have given the human race Jesus Christ our Saviour as a model of humility. He fulfilled your will by becoming man and giving his life on the cross. Help us to bear witness to you by following his example of suffering and make us worthy to share in his resurrection.

FIRST READING (Isaiah 50:4-7)

The servant of the Lord said: "The Lord God has given me the tongue of a teacher, that I may know how to sustain the weary with a word. Morning by morning he wakens—wakens my ear to listen as those who are taught. The Lord God has opened my ear, and I was not rebellious, I did not turn backward.

231

"I gave my back to those who struck me, and my cheeks to those who pulled out the beard; I did not hide my face from insult and spitting.

"The Lord God helps me; therefore I have not been disgraced; therefore I have set my face like flint, and I know that I shall not be put to shame."

The word of the Lord. **Thanks be to God.**

RESPONSORIAL PSALM *(Psalm 22)*

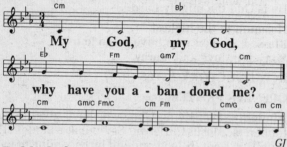

GJ

℟. **My God, my God,**
  why have you abandoned me?

All who see me • **mock_at_me;**
they make mouths at me,
    they shake • **their** heads;
"Commit your cause to the Lord;
    let him de•-**liver;**
let him rescue the one in whom
    he • **de**-lights!" ℟.

For dogs are all a•-**round_me;**
a company of evildoers • **en**-circles_me.
My hands and feet have • **shrivelled;**
I can count all • **my** bones. ℟.

They divide my clothes among them•-**selves,**
and for my clothing they • **cast** lots.
But you, O Lord, do not be far a•-**way!**
O my help, come quickly to • **my** aid! ℞.

I will tell of your name
  to my brothers and sisters;
in the midst of the congregation
  I will • **praise_you;**
You who fear the • **Lord,** praise_him!
All you offspring of Jacob, • **glorify_him;**
stand in awe of him,
  all you offspring • **of** Israel! ℞.

SECOND READING *(Philippians 2:6-11)*

Let the same mind be in you that was in Christ
Jesus, who, though he was in the form of God, did
not regard equality with God as something to be
exploited, but emptied himself, taking the form of
a slave, being born in human likeness. And being
found in human form, he humbled himself and
became obedient to the point of death, even death
on a cross.

Therefore God highly exalted him and gave him
the name that is above every name, so that at the
name of Jesus every knee should bend, in heaven
and on earth and under the earth, and every
tongue should confess that Jesus Christ is Lord, to
the glory of God the Father.

The word of the Lord. **Thanks be to God.**

GOSPEL ACCLAMATION *(Philippians 2:8-9)*

If not sung, this acclamation is omitted.

Christ became obedient for us even to death, dying on the cross. Therefore God raised him on high and gave him a name above all other names.

GOSPEL *(Luke 22:14–23:56)*

Several readers may proclaim the passion narrative today. (N) indicates the narrator, (J) the words of Jesus, and (S) the words of other speakers. The shorter version begins (p. 239) and ends (p. 245) at the asterisks.

(N) The Passion of our Lord Jesus Christ according to Luke.

When the hour came, Jesus took his place at the table, and the apostles with him. He said to them,

(J) *I have eagerly desired to eat this Passover with you before I suffer; for I tell you, I will not eat it until it is fulfilled in the kingdom of God.*

(N) Then he took a cup, and after giving thanks he said,

(J) *Take this and divide it among yourselves; for I tell you that from now on I will not drink of the fruit of the vine until the kingdom of God comes.*

(N) Then Jesus took a loaf of bread, and when he had given thanks, he broke it and gave it to them, saying,

(J) *This is my body, which is given for you. Do this in remembrance of me.*

(N) And he did the same with the cup after supper, saying,

(J) *This cup that is poured out for you is the new covenant in my blood.*

But see, the one who betrays me is with me, and his hand is on the table. For the Son of Man is going as it has been determined, but woe to that one by whom he is betrayed!

(N) Then they began to ask one another, which one of them it could be who would do this. A dispute also arose among them as to which one of them was to be regarded as the greatest. But Jesus said to them,

(J) *The kings of the Gentiles lord it over them; and those in authority over them are called benefactors.*

But not so with you; rather the greatest among you must become like the youngest, and the leader like one who serves. For who is greater, the one who is at the table or the one who serves? Is it not the one at the table? But I am among you as one who serves.

You are those who have stood by me in my trials; and I confer on you, just as my Father has conferred on me, a kingdom, so that you may eat and drink at my table in my kingdom, and you will sit on thrones judging the twelve tribes of Israel.

Simon, Simon, listen! Satan has demanded to sift all of you like wheat, but I have prayed for you that your own faith may not fail; and you, when once you have turned back, strengthen your brothers.

(N) And Peter said to Jesus,

(S1) **Lord, I am ready to go with you to prison and to death!**

(J) *I tell you, Peter, the cock will not crow this day, until you have denied three times that you know me.*

(N) Then Jesus said to the disciples,

(J) *When I sent you out without a purse, bag, or sandals, did you lack anything?*

(S1) **No, not a thing.**

(J) *But now, the one who has a purse must take it, and likewise a bag. And the one who has no sword must sell his cloak and buy one. For I tell you, this scripture must be fulfilled in me, "And he was counted among the lawless"; and indeed what is written about me is being fulfilled.*

(S1) **Lord, look, here are two swords.**

(J) *It is enough.*

At this point all may join in singing an appropriate acclamation.

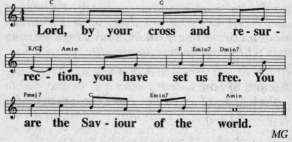

Lord, by your cross and re-sur-rec-tion, you have set us free. You are the Sav-iour of the world.

MG

(N) Jesus came out and went, as was his custom, to the Mount of Olives; and the disciples followed him. When he reached the place, he said to his disciples,

(J) *Pray that you may not come into the time of trial.*

(N) Then Jesus withdrew from them about a stone's throw, knelt down, and prayed,

(J) *Father, if you are willing, remove this cup from me; yet, not my will but yours be done.*

(N) Then an angel from heaven appeared to Jesus and gave him strength. In his anguish he prayed more earnestly, and his sweat became like great drops of blood falling down on the ground.

When Jesus got up from prayer, he came to the disciples and found them sleeping because of grief, and he said to them,

(J) *Why are you sleeping? Get up and pray that you may not come into the time of trial.*

(N) While Jesus was still speaking, suddenly a crowd came, and the one called Judas, one of the twelve, was leading them. He approached Jesus to kiss him; but Jesus said to him,

(J) *Judas, is it with a kiss that you are betraying the Son of Man?*

(N) When those who were around Jesus saw what was coming, they asked,

(S1) **Lord, should we strike with the sword?**

(N) Then one of the disciples struck the slave of the high priest and cut off his right ear. But Jesus said,

(J) *No more of this!*

(N) And Jesus touched the slave's ear and healed him. Then Jesus said to the chief priests, the officers of the temple police, and the elders who had come for him,

(J) *Have you come out with swords and clubs as if I were a bandit? When I was with you day after day in the temple, you did not lay hands on me. But this is your hour, and the power of darkness!*

(N) Then they seized Jesus and led him away, bringing him into the high priest's house. But Peter was following at a distance. When they had kindled a fire in the middle of the courtyard and sat down together, Peter sat among them. Then a servant girl, seeing him in the firelight, stared at him and said,

(S3) **This man also was with him.**

(N) But Peter denied it, saying,

(S1) **Woman, I do not know him.**

(N) A little later someone else, on seeing him, said,

(S3) **You also are one of them.**

(N) But Peter said,

(S1) **Man, I am not!**

(N) Then about an hour later still another kept insisting,

3) **Surely this man also was with him; for he is
Galilean.**

N) But Peter said,

1) **Man, I do not know what you are talking
out!**

N) At that moment, while he was still speaking,
e cock crowed. The Lord turned and looked at
eter. Then Peter remembered the word of the
ord, how he had said to him, "Before the cock
ows today, you will deny me three times." And
eter went out and wept bitterly.

ow the men who were holding Jesus began to
ock him and beat him; they also blindfolded
im and kept asking him,

2) **Prophesy! Who is it that struck you?**

N) They kept heaping many other insults on him.

* * *

N) When day came, the assembly of the elders of
e people, both chief priests and scribes,
athered together, and they brought Jesus to their
uncil. They said,

2) **If you are the Messiah, tell us.**

) *If I tell you, you will not believe; and if I
uestion you, you will not answer. But from now
n the Son of Man will be seated at the right
and of the power of God.*

N) All of them asked,

2) **Are you, then, the Son of God?**

) *You say that I am.*

(S2) **What further testimony do we need? W**
have heard it ourselves from his own lips!

At this point all may join in singir
an appropriate acclamatio.

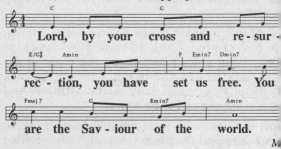

(N) Then the assembly rose as a body and broug!
Jesus before Pilate. They began to accuse hir
saying,

(S2) **We found this man perverting our natio!**
forbidding us to pay taxes to the emperor, ar
saying that he himself is the Messiah, a king.

(N) Then Pilate asked Jesus,

(S3) **Are you the king of the Jews?**

(J) *You say so.*

(N) Then Pilate said to the chief priests and th
crowds,

(S3) **I find no basis for an accusation against th:**
man.

(N) But they were insistent and said,

(S2) **He stirs up the people by teaching through-out all Judea, from Galilee where he began even to this place.**

(N) When Pilate heard this, he asked whether the man was a Galilean. And when he learned that he was under Herod's jurisdiction, he sent him off to Herod, who was himself in Jerusalem at that time.

When Herod saw Jesus, he was very glad, for he had been wanting to see him for a long time, because he had heard about him and was hoping to see Jesus perform some sign.

Herod questioned him at some length, but Jesus gave him no answer. The chief priests and the scribes stood by, vehemently accusing him. Even Herod with his soldiers treated him with contempt and mocked him; then he put an elegant robe on him, and sent him back to Pilate. That same day Herod and Pilate became friends with each other; before this they had been enemies.

Pilate then called together the chief priests, the leaders, and the people, and said to them,

(S3) **You brought me this man as one who was perverting the people; and here I have examined him in your presence and have not found this man guilty of any of your charges against him. Neither has Herod, for he sent him back to us. Indeed, he has done nothing to deserve death. I will therefore have him flogged and release him.**

(N) Now Pilate was obliged to release someone for them at the festival. Then they all shouted out together,

241

(S2) **Away with this fellow! Release Barabbas for us.**

(N) This was a man who had been put in prison for an insurrection that had taken place in the city, and for murder.

Pilate, wanting to release Jesus, addressed them again; but they kept shouting,

(S2) **Crucify, crucify him!**

(N) A third time Pilate said to them,

(S3) **Why, what evil has he done? I have found in him no ground for the sentence of death; I will therefore have him flogged and then release him.**

(N) But they kept urgently demanding with loud shouts that he should be crucified; and their voices prevailed. So Pilate gave his verdict that their demand should be granted. He released the man they asked for, the one who had been put in prison for insurrection and murder, and he handed Jesus over as they wished.

As they led Jesus away, they seized a man, Simon of Cyrene, who was coming from the country, and they laid the cross on him, and made him carry it behind Jesus.

A great number of the people followed him, and among them were women who were beating their breasts and wailing for him. But Jesus turned to them and said,

(J) *Daughters of Jerusalem, do not weep for me, but weep for yourselves and for your children. For the days are surely coming when they will say, "Blessed are the barren, and the wombs that never bore, and the breasts that never nursed." Then they will begin to say to the mountains, "Fall on us," and to the hills, "Cover us." For if they do this when the wood is green, what will happen when it is dry?*

At this point all may join in singing an appropriate acclamation.

Lord, by your cross and re - sur - rec - tion, you have set us free. You are the Sav - iour of the world.

MG

(N) Two others also, who were criminals, were led away to be put to death with Jesus. When they came to the place that is called The Skull, they crucified Jesus there with the criminals, one on his right and one on his left. Then Jesus said,

(J) *Father, forgive them; for they do not know what they are doing.*

(N) And they cast lots to divide his clothing. And the people stood by, watching; but the leaders scoffed at him, saying,

(S2) **He saved others; let him save himself if he is the Messiah of God, his chosen one!**

(N) The soldiers also mocked Jesus, coming up and offering him sour wine, and saying,

(S3) **If you are the King of the Jews, save yourself!**

(N) There was also an inscription over him, "This is the King of the Jews."

One of the criminals who were hanged there kept deriding him and saying,

(S2) **Are you not the Messiah? Save yourself and us!**

(N) But the other criminal rebuked the first, saying,

(S3) **Do you not fear God, since you are under the same sentence of condemnation? And we indeed have been condemned justly, for we are getting what we deserve for our deeds, but this man has done nothing wrong.**

(N) Then he said,

(S3) **Jesus, remember me when you come into your kingdom.**

(J) *Truly I tell you, today you will be with me in Paradise.*

(N) It was now about noon, and darkness came over the whole land until three in the afternoon, while the sun's light failed; and the curtain of the temple was torn in two.

Then Jesus, crying with a loud voice, said,

(J) *Father, into your hands I commend my spirit.*

(N) Having said this, he breathed his last.

> *All may kneel (or stand where customary)*
> *for a period of silence.*

244

(N) When the centurion saw what had taken place, he praised God and said,

(S3) **Certainly this man was innocent.**

(N) And when all the crowds who had gathered there for this spectacle saw what had taken place, they returned home, beating their breasts.

But all his acquaintances, including the women who had followed him from Galilee, stood at a distance, watching these things.

* * *

(N) Now there was a good and righteous man named Joseph, who, though a member of the council, had not agreed to their plan and action. He came from the Jewish town of Arimathea, and he was waiting expectantly for the kingdom of God. This man went to Pilate and asked for the body of Jesus. Then he took it down, wrapped it in a linen cloth, and laid it in a rock-hewn tomb where no one had ever been laid.

It was the day of Preparation, and the sabbath was beginning. The women who had come with Jesus from Galilee followed, and they saw the tomb and how his body was laid. Then they returned, and prepared spices and ointments. On the sabbath these women rested according to the commandment.

The readers return to their places in silence.

PROFESSION OF FAITH *(Creed, pp. 11-12)*

PRAYER OF THE FAITHFUL

The following intentions are suggestions only.

℞: **Lord, hear our prayer.**

For the Church, community of Christ, manifesting his solidarity with the poor and oppressed, we pray to the Lord: ℞.

For leaders of nations and peoples, struggling to implement policies that promote development, justice and peace, we pray to the Lord: ℞.

For those we, as church or society, have rejected, we pray to the Lord: ℞.

For us, God's people, struggling to see the world through the eyes of the crucified Christ, we pray to the Lord: ℞.

PREPARATION OF THE GIFTS *(p. 13)*

PRAYER OVER THE GIFTS

Lord, may the suffering and death of Jesus, your only Son, make us pleasing to you. Alone we can do nothing, but may this perfect sacrifice win us your mercy and love.

PREFACE *(Passion Sunday, p. 25)*

COMMUNION ANTIPHON *(Matthew 26:42)*

Father, if this cup may not pass, but I must drink it, then your will be done.

PRAYER AFTER COMMUNION

Lord, you have satisfied our hunger with this eucharistic food. The death of your Son gives us hope and strengthens our faith. May his resurrection give us perseverance and lead us to salvation.

SOLEMN BLESSING *(Optional)*

Bow your heads and pray for God's blessing.

The Father of mercies has given us an example of unselfish love in the sufferings of his only Son. Through your service of God and neighbour may you receive his countless blessings. **Amen.**

You believe that by his dying Christ destroyed death for ever. May he give you everlasting life. **Amen.**

He humbled himself for our sakes. May you follow his example and share in his resurrection. **Amen.**

May almighty God bless you, the Father, and the Son, and the Holy Spirit. **Amen.**

DISMISSAL *(p. 65)*

Tonight is a night of very mixed emotions: joy, horror, sorrow, expectation... and embarrassment. Especially embarrassment! Why feet? Of all the things that could have been washed, Jesus settled on old, tired—probably less than fragrant—feet. We, like Peter, have an instinctive and powerful reaction: No, thank you!

But, oh, what we miss if we refuse to participate! This is the night we celebrate a multitude of mysteries:

God frees us. Just as God delivered the Israelites from their miserable oppression under Pharaoh, so God rescues us from the powerful bonds of sin, the evil which destroys us and our world.

God loves us. Just as a mother wipes her child's nose or a father changes his baby's diaper with no thought of humiliation, so Jesus washes the feet of his disciples, and goes to his death, to raise them up because he loves them.

God unifies us. The new relationship Jesus gives us to himself by washing our feet, he continues to nourish in the eucharist and through the service of the ministerial priesthood. However, each of us, in our treatment of others, must have this unfailing, tender love as our goal.

May the eucharist, sacrament of union, conform us all to this joyful, reconciled, loving service.

—————————————— *Christine Mader, Toronto, ON*

ENTRANCE ANTIPHON *(Galatians 6:14)*

We should glory in the cross of our Lord Jesus Christ, for he is our salvation, our life and our resurrection; through him we are saved and made free.

INTRODUCTORY RITES *(p. 5)*

OPENING PRAYER

God our Father, we are gathered here to share in the supper which your only Son left to his Church to reveal his love. He gave it to us when he was about to die and commanded us to celebrate it as the new and eternal sacrifice. We pray that in this eucharist we may find the fullness of love and life.

FIRST READING *(Exodus 12:1-8, 11-14)*

The Lord said to Moses and Aaron in the land of Egypt: This month shall mark for you the beginning of months; it shall be the first month of the year for you. Tell the whole congregation of Israel that on the tenth of this month they are to take a lamb for each family, a lamb for each household. If a household is too small for a whole lamb, it shall join its closest neighbour in obtaining one; the lamb shall be divided in proportion to the number of people who eat of it.

Your lamb shall be without blemish, a year-old male; you may take it from the sheep or from the goats. You shall keep it until the fourteenth day of this month; then the whole assembled congregation of Israel shall slaughter it at twilight. They shall take some of the blood and put it on the two doorposts and the lintel of the houses in which they eat it. They shall eat the lamb that same

249

night; they shall eat it roasted over the fire with unleavened bread and bitter herbs.

This is how you shall eat it: your loins girded, your sandals on your feet, and your staff in your hand; and you shall eat it hurriedly. It is the Passover of the Lord.

For I will pass through the land of Egypt that night, and I will strike down every firstborn in the land of Egypt, both human beings and animals; on all the gods of Egypt I will execute judgments: I am the Lord.

The blood shall be a sign for you on the houses where you live: when I see the blood, I will pass over you, and no plague shall destroy you when I strike the land of Egypt.

This day shall be a day of remembrance for you. You shall celebrate it as a festival to the Lord; throughout your generations you shall observe it as a perpetual ordinance.

The word of the Lord. **Thanks be to God.**

RESPONSORIAL PSALM *(Psalm 116)*

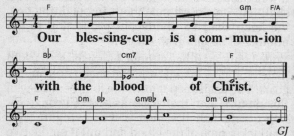

℞. **Our blessing-cup is a communion with the blood of Christ.**

What shall I return to the • **Lord**
for all his bounty to • **me?**
I will lift up the cup of sal•**-vation,**
and call on the name of • **the** Lord. ℞.

Precious in the sight of the Lord is the death
    of his • **faithful_ones.**
O Lord, I am your • **servant;**
I am your servant, the child
    of your • **serving_girl.**
You have loosed • **my** bonds. ℞.

I will offer to you a thanksgiving • **sacrifice**
and call on the name of the • **Lord.**
I will pay my vows to the • **Lord**
in the presence of all • **his** people. ℞.

SECOND READING *(1 Corinthians 11:23-26)*

Beloved: I received from the Lord what I also
handed on to you, that the Lord Jesus on the night
when he was betrayed took a loaf of bread, and
when he had given thanks, he broke it and said,
"This is my body that is for you. Do this in
remembrance of me."

In the same way he took the cup also, after supper,
saying, "This cup is the new covenant in my
blood. Do this, as often as you drink it, in remembrance of me." For as often as you eat this bread
and drink the cup, you proclaim the Lord's death
until he comes.

The word of the Lord. **Thanks be to God.**

GOSPEL ACCLAMATION *(John 13:34)*

If not sung, this acclamation is omitted.

I give you a new commandment: love one another as I have loved you.

GOSPEL *(John 13:1-15)*

A reading from the holy gospel according to John.
Glory to you, Lord.

Now before the festival of the Passover, Jesus knew that his hour had come to depart from this world and go to the Father. Having loved his own who were in the world, he loved them to the end.

The devil had already put it into the heart of Judas, son of Simon Iscariot, to betray him. And during supper Jesus, knowing that the Father had given all things into his hands, and that he had come from God and was going to God, got up from the table, took off his outer robe, and tied a towel around himself. Then he poured water into a basin and began to wash the disciples' feet and to wipe them with the towel that was tied around him.

He came to Simon Peter, who said to him, "Lord, are you going to wash my feet?" Jesus answered, "You do not know now what I am doing, but later you will understand." Peter said to him, "You will never wash my feet." Jesus answered, "Unless I wash you, you have no share with me." Simon Peter said to him, "Lord, not my feet only but also my hands and my head!" Jesus said to him, "One who has bathed does not need to wash, except for the feet, but is entirely clean. And you are clean, though not all of you." For he knew who was to betray him; for this reason he said, "Not all of you are clean."

After he had washed their feet, put on his robe, and returned to the table, Jesus said to them, "Do you know what I have done to you? You call me Teacher and Lord—and you are right, for that is what I am. So if I, your Lord and Teacher, have washed your feet, you also ought to wash one another's feet. For I have set you an example, that you also should do as I have done to you."

The gospel of the Lord. **Praise to you, Lord Jesus Christ.**

The Profession of Faith *is omitted tonight.*

THE WASHING OF THE FEET

During the washing of the feet, the assembly may sing an appropriate song.

PRAYER OF THE FAITHFUL

The following intentions are suggestions only.

℟: **Lord, hear our prayer.**

For the Church, witness to true love and service in Christ, we pray to the Lord: ℟.

For world leaders, called to promote justice and human dignity through true service to their people, we pray to the Lord: ℟.

For those among us whose greed and selfishness cause suffering, and for all those who suffer, we pray to the Lord: ℟.

For us, the Body of Christ, called to pour out our lives for others as Jesus did for us, we pray to the Lord: ℞.

PREPARATION OF THE GIFTS *(p. 13)*

PRAYER OVER THE GIFTS

Lord, make us worthy to celebrate these mysteries. Each time we offer this memorial sacrifice, the work of our redemption is accomplished.

PREFACE *(Holy Eucharist I, p. 29)*

COMMUNION ANTIPHON *(1 Corinthians 11)*

This body will be given for you. This is the cup of the new covenant in my blood; whenever you receive them, do so in remembrance of me.

PRAYER AFTER COMMUNION

Almighty God, we receive new life from the supper your Son gave us in this world. May we find full contentment in the meal we hope to share in your eternal kingdom.

The Blessing and Dismissal *are omitted tonight.*

TRANSFER OF THE HOLY EUCHARIST

The Blessed Sacrament is carried through the church in procession to the place of reposition. During the procession the hymn Pange lingua *(stanzas 1-4) or some other eucharistic song is sung. When the procession reaches the place of reposition, the celebrant incenses the Blessed Sacrament, while* Tantum ergo (Pange lingua, *stanzas 5-6) is sung. The tabernacle of repose is then closed.*

Pange lingua (Sing, my tongue)

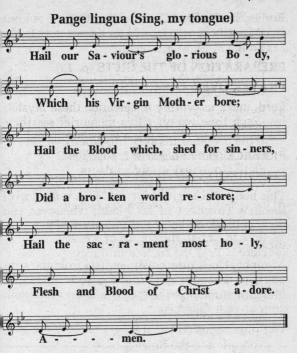

Hail our Saviour's glorious Body,

Which his Virgin Mother bore;

Hail the Blood which, shed for sinners,

Did a broken world restore;

Hail the sacrament most holy,

Flesh and Blood of Christ adore.

A - - - - men.

2. To the Virgin, for our healing,
   His own Son the Father sends;
   From the Father's love proceeding
   Sower, seed and word descends;
   Wondrous life of Word incarnate
   With his greatest wonder ends.

3. On that paschal evening see him
   With the chosen twelve recline,
   To the old law still obedient
   In its feast of love divine;
   Love divine, the new law giving,
   Gives himself as Bread and Wine.

4. By his word the Word almighty
   Makes of bread his flesh indeed;
   Wine becomes his very life-blood;
   Faith God's living Word must heed!
   Faith alone may safely guide us
   Where the senses cannot lead!

At the incensing of the Blessed Sacrament

5. Come, adore this wondrous presence;
   Bow to Christ, the source of grace!
   Here is kept the ancient promise
   Of God's earthly dwelling place!
   Sight is blind before God's glory,
   Faith alone may see God's face.

6. Glory be to God the Father,
   Praise to his co-equal Son,
   Adoration to the Spirit,
   Bond of love in God-head one!
   Blest be God by all creation
   Joyously while ages run! Amen.

Trans: © James Quinn, SJ, b. 1919. Used by permission of Geoffrey Chapman. A division of Cassell PLC, London, England.

After a few moments of silent adoration, the priests and ministers of the altar retire. The faithful are encouraged to continue adoration before the Blessed Sacrament for a suitable period of time through the evening and night. There should be no solemn adoration after midnight.

We need to grasp the cross, to believe. Disturbed by too much violence before our eyes, we sometimes hesitate to consider the cross. Or perhaps we have trivialized the cross so much that it has become a mere magical amulet.

In the prayer of Christians, the cross is the central symbol. Christians believe that the life, death and resurrection of Jesus are all one piece, accepted as something special done for us by God. The cross is part of it. This is a powerful and empowering message. If only we could grasp the cross!

Like other Jews, Jesus believed suffering, death and martyrdom had the power of salvation for the people. On the cross, Jesus accepted the evil and pain inflicted on him by human sinfulness. In Jesus, on the cross, God shared in the suffering and injustice of the human experience.

If we can embrace the cross, God who cares will embrace us. How he loves us!

John Walsh, Scarborough, ON

PRAYER

Lord, by shedding his blood for us, your Son, Jesus Christ, established the paschal mystery. In your goodness, make us holy and watch over us always.

LITURGY OF THE WORD

FIRST READING *(Isaiah 52:13–53:12)*

See, my servant shall prosper; he shall be exalted and lifted up, and shall be very high.

Just as there were many who were astonished at him—so marred was his appearance, beyond human semblance, and his form beyond that of mortals—so he shall startle many nations; kings shall shut their mouths because of him; for that which had not been told them they shall see, and that which they had not heard they shall contemplate. Who has believed what we have heard? And to whom has the arm of the Lord been revealed?

For he grew up before the Lord like a young plant, and like a root out of dry ground; he had no form or majesty that we should look at him, nothing in his appearance that we should desire him. He was despised and rejected by others; a man of suffering and acquainted with infirmity; and as one from whom others hide their faces he was despised, and we held him of no account.

Surely he has borne our infirmities and carried our diseases; yet we accounted him stricken, struck down by God, and afflicted. But he was wounded for our transgressions, crushed for our iniquities; upon him was the punishment that made us whole, and by his bruises we are healed.

All we like sheep have gone astray; we have all turned to our own way, and the Lord has laid on him the iniquity of us all.

He was oppressed, and he was afflicted, yet he did not open his mouth; like a lamb that is led to the slaughter, and like a sheep that before its shearers is silent, so he did not open his mouth.

By a perversion of justice he was taken away. Who could have imagined his future? For he was cut off from the land of the living, stricken for the transgression of my people. They made his grave with the wicked and his tomb with the rich, although he had done no violence, and there was no deceit in his mouth.

Yet it was the will of the Lord to crush him with pain. When you make his life an offering for sin, he shall see his offspring, and shall prolong his days; through him the will of the Lord shall prosper. Out of his anguish he shall see light; he shall find satisfaction through his knowledge. The righteous one, my servant, shall make many righteous, and he shall bear their iniquities.

Therefore I will allot him a portion with the great, and he shall divide the spoil with the strong; because he poured out himself to death, and was numbered with the transgressors; yet he bore the sin of many, and made intercession for the transgressors.

The word of the Lord. **Thanks be to God.**

RESPONSORIAL PSALM *(Psalm 31)*

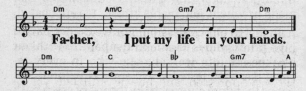

GJ

℞. **Father, I put my life in your hands.**

In you, O Lord, I • **seek** refuge;
do not let me ever be put • **to** shame;
in your righteousness • **de**-liver_me.
Into your hand I commit my spirit;
you have redeemed me,
    O Lord, • **faith**-ful God. ℞.

I am the scorn of all my adversaries,
    a horror to • **my** neighbours,
an object of dread to my • **ac**-quaintances.
Those who see me in the street flee • **from** me.
I have passed out of mind like one who is dead;
I have become like a • **bro**-ken vessel. ℞.

But I trust in you, • **O** Lord;
I say, "You are • **my** God."
My times are in • **your** hand;
deliver me from the hand
    of my • **enemies** and persecutors. ℞.

Let your face shine upon • **your** servant;
save me in your stead •-**fast** love.
Be strong, and let your heart • **take** courage,
all you who wait • **for** the Lord. ℞.

SECOND READING *(Hebrews 4:14-16; 5:7-9)*

Since we have a great high priest who has passed through the heavens, Jesus, the Son of God, let us hold fast to our confession. For we do not have a high priest who is unable to sympathize with our weaknesses, but we have one who in every respect has been tested as we are, yet without sin. Let us therefore approach the throne of grace with boldness, so that we may receive mercy and find grace to help in time of need.

In the days of his flesh, Jesus offered up prayers and supplications, with loud cries and tears, to the one who was able to save him from death, and he was heard because of his reverent submission. Although he was a Son, he learned obedience through what he suffered; and having been made perfect, he became the source of eternal salvation for all who obey him.

The word of the Lord. **Thanks be to God.**

GOSPEL ACCLAMATION *(Philippians 2:8-9)*

If not sung, this acclamation is omitted.

Christ became obedient for us even to death, dying on the cross. Therefore God raised him on high and gave him a name above all other names.

GOSPEL *(John 18:1–19:42)*

Several readers may proclaim the passion narrative today. (N) indicates the narrator, (J) the words of Jesus, and (S) the words of other speakers.

(N) The Passion of our Lord Jesus Christ according to John.

After they had eaten the supper, Jesus went out with his disciples across the Kidron valley to a place where there was a garden, which he and his disciples entered. Now Judas, who betrayed him, also knew the place, because Jesus often met there with his disciples. So Judas brought a detachment of soldiers together with police from the chief priests and the Pharisees, and they came there with lanterns and torches and weapons.

Then Jesus, knowing all that was to happen to him, came forward and asked them,

(J) *Whom are you looking for?*

(N) They answered,

(S2) **Jesus of Nazareth.**

(J) *I am he.*

(N) Judas, who betrayed him, was standing with them. When Jesus said to them, "I am he," they stepped back and fell to the ground. Again he asked them,

(J) *Whom are you looking for?*

(S2) **Jesus of Nazareth.**

(J) *I told you that I am he. So if you are looking for me, let these men go.*

(N) This was to fulfil the word that he had spoken, "I did not lose a single one of those whom you gave me."

Then Simon Peter, who had a sword, drew it, struck the high priest's slave, and cut off his right ear. The slave's name was Malchus. Jesus said to Peter,

(J) *Put your sword back into its sheath. Am I not to drink the cup that the Father has given me?*

(N) So the soldiers, their officer, and the Jewish police arrested Jesus and bound him. First they took him to Annas, who was the father-in-law of Caiaphas, the high priest that year. Caiaphas was the one who had advised the Jewish leaders that it was better to have one person die for the people.

Simon Peter and another disciple followed Jesus. Since that disciple was known to the high priest, he went with Jesus into the courtyard of the high priest, but Peter was standing outside at the gate. So the other disciple, who was known to the high priest, went out, spoke to the woman who guarded the gate, and brought Peter in. The woman said to Peter,

(S3) **You are not also one of this man's disciples, are you?**

(N) Peter said,

(S1) **I am not.**

(N) Now the slaves and the police had made a charcoal fire because it was cold, and they were standing around it and warming themselves. Peter also was standing with them and warming himself.

Then the high priest questioned Jesus about his disciples and about his teaching. Jesus answered,

(J) *I have spoken openly to the world; I have always taught in synagogues and in the temple, where all the Jews come together. I have said nothing in secret. Why do you ask me? Ask those who heard what I said to them; they know what I said.*

(N) When he had said this, one of the police standing nearby struck Jesus on the face, saying,

(S3) **Is that how you answer the high priest?**

(J) *If I have spoken wrongly, testify to the wrong. But if I have spoken rightly, why do you strike me?*

(N) Then Annas sent him bound to Caiaphas the high priest.

Now Simon Peter was standing and warming himself. They asked him,

(S2) **You are not also one of his disciples, are you?**

(N) He denied it and said,

(S1) **I am not.**

(N) One of the slaves of the high priest, a relative of the man whose ear Peter had cut off, asked,

(S2) **Did I not see you in the garden with him?**

(N) Again Peter denied it, and at that moment the cock crowed.

*At this point all may join in singing
an appropriate acclamation.*

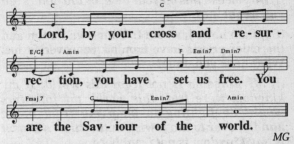

Lord, by your cross and re-sur-rec-tion, you have set us free. You are the Sav-iour of the world.

MG

(N) Then they took Jesus from Caiaphas to Pilate's headquarters. It was early in the morning. They themselves did not enter the headquarters, so as to avoid ritual defilement and to be able to eat the Passover. So Pilate went out to them and said,

(S3) **What accusation do you bring against this man?**

(N) They answered,

(S2) **If this man were not a criminal, we would not have handed him over to you.**

(N) Pilate said to them,

(S3) **Take him yourselves and judge him according to your law.**

(N) They replied,

(S2) **We are not permitted to put anyone to death.**

(N) This was to fulfil what Jesus had said when he indicated the kind of death he was to die.

Then Pilate entered the headquarters again, summoned Jesus, and asked him,

(S3) **Are you the King of the Jews?**

(J) *Do you ask this on your own, or did others tell you about me?*

(S3) **I am not a Jew, am I? Your own nation and the chief priests have handed you over to me. What have you done?**

(J) *My kingdom is not from this world. If my kingdom were from this world, my followers would be fighting to keep me from being handed over to the Jewish authorities. But as it is, my kingdom is not from here.*

(S3) **So you are a king?**

(J) *You say that I am a king. For this I was born, and for this I came into the world, to testify to the truth. Everyone who belongs to the truth listens to my voice.*

(S3) **What is truth?**

(N) After he had said this, Pilate went out to the Jewish leaders again and told them,

(S3) **I find no case against him. But you have a custom that I release someone for you at the Passover. Do you want me to release for you the King of the Jews?**

(N) They shouted in reply,

(S2) **Not this man, but Barabbas!**

(N) Now Barabbas was a bandit. Then Pilate took Jesus and had him flogged. And the soldiers wove a crown of thorns and put it on his head, and they dressed him in a purple robe. They kept coming up to him, saying,

(S2) **Hail, King of the Jews!**

(N) and they struck him on the face.

Pilate went out again and said to them,

(S3) **Look, I am bringing him out to you to let you know that I find no case against him.**

(N) So Jesus came out, wearing the crown of thorns and the purple robe. Pilate said to them,

(S3) **Here is the man!**

(N) When the chief priests and the police saw him, they shouted,

(S2) **Crucify him! Crucify him!**

(N) Pilate said to them,

(S3) **Take him yourselves and crucify him; I find no case against him.**

(N) They answered him,

(S2) **We have a law, and according to that law he ought to die because he has claimed to be the Son of God.**

(N) Now when Pilate heard this, he was more afraid than ever. He entered his headquarters again and asked Jesus,

(S3) **Where are you from?**

(N) But Jesus gave him no answer. Pilate therefore said to him,

(S3) **Do you refuse to speak to me? Do you not know that I have power to release you, and power to crucify you?**

(J) *You would have no power over me unless it had been given you from above; therefore the one who handed me over to you is guilty of a greater sin.*

(N) From then on Pilate tried to release him, but the Jewish leaders cried out,

(S2) **If you release this man, you are no friend of the emperor. Everyone who claims to be a king sets himself against the emperor.**

(N) When Pilate heard these words, he brought Jesus outside and sat on the judge's bench at a place called "The Stone Pavement," or in Hebrew "Gabbatha."

Now it was the day of Preparation for the Passover; and it was about noon. Pilate said to the Jewish leaders,

(S3) **Here is your King!**

(N) They cried out,

(S2) **Away with him! Away with him! Crucify him!**

(N) Pilate asked them,

(S3) **Shall I crucify your King?**

(N) The chief priests answered,

(S2) **We have no king but the emperor.**

*At this point all may join in singing
an appropriate acclamation.*

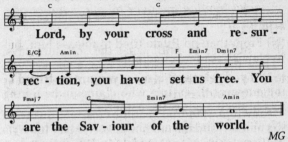

Lord, by your cross and re-sur-rec-tion, you have set us free. You are the Sav-iour of the world.

MG

(N) Then Pilate handed Jesus over to them to be crucified. So they took Jesus; and carrying the cross by himself, he went out to what is called The Place of the Skull, which in Hebrew is called Golgotha. There they crucified him, and with him two others, one on either side, with Jesus between them.

Pilate also had an inscription written and put on the cross. It read, "Jesus of Nazareth, the King of the Jews." Many of the people read this inscription, because the place where Jesus was crucified was near the city; and it was written in Hebrew, in Latin, and in Greek. Then the chief priests of the Jews said to Pilate,

(S2) **Do not write, "The King of the Jews," but, "This man said, I am King of the Jews."**

(N) Pilate answered,

(S3) **What I have written I have written.**

(N) When the soldiers had crucified Jesus, they took his clothes and divided them into four parts, one for each soldier. They also took his tunic;

now the tunic was seamless, woven in one piece from the top. So they said to one another,

(S2) **Let us not tear it, but cast lots for it to see who will get it.**

(N) This was to fulfil what the scripture says, "They divided my clothes among themselves, and for my clothing they cast lots." And that is what the soldiers did.

Meanwhile, standing near the cross of Jesus were his mother, and his mother's sister, Mary the wife of Clopas, and Mary Magdalene. When Jesus saw his mother and the disciple whom he loved standing beside her, he said to his mother,

(J) *Woman, here is your son.*

(N) Then he said to the disciple,

(J) *Here is your mother.*

(N) And from that hour the disciple took her into his own home.

After this, when Jesus knew that all was now finished, in order to fulfil the scripture, he said,

(J) *I am thirsty.*

(N) A jar full of sour wine was standing there. So they put a sponge full of the wine on a branch of hyssop and held it to his mouth. When Jesus had received the wine, he said,

(J) *It is finished.*

(N) Then he bowed his head and gave up his spirit.

> *All may kneel (or stand, where customary)*
> *for a period of silence.*

(N) Since it was the day of Preparation, the Jewish leaders did not want the bodies left on the cross during the sabbath, especially because that sabbath was a day of great solemnity. So they asked Pilate to have the legs of the crucified men broken and the bodies removed.

Then the soldiers came and broke the legs of the first and of the other who had been crucified with him. But when they came to Jesus and saw that he was already dead, they did not break his legs. Instead, one of the soldiers pierced his side with a spear, and at once blood and water came out.

He who saw this has testified so that you also may believe. His testimony is true, and he knows that he tells the truth. These things occurred so that the scripture might be fulfilled, "None of his bones shall be broken." And again another passage of scripture says, "They will look on the one whom they have pierced."

After these things, Joseph of Arimathea, who was a disciple of Jesus, though a secret one because of his fear of the Jewish authorities, asked Pilate to let him take away the body of Jesus. Pilate gave him permission; so he came and removed his body.

Nicodemus, who had at first come to Jesus by night, also came, bringing a mixture of myrrh and aloes, weighing about a hundred pounds. They took the body of Jesus and wrapped it with the spices in linen cloths, according to the burial custom of the Jews. Now there was a garden in the place where he was crucified, and in the garden there was a new tomb in which no one had ever been laid. And so, because it was the Jewish day of Preparation, and the tomb was nearby, they laid Jesus there.

The readers return to their places in silence.

PRAYER OF THE FAITHFUL

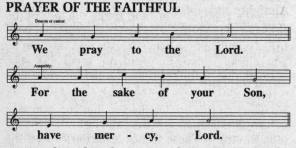

Deacon or cantor:

We pray to the Lord.

Assembly:

For the sake of your Son,

have mer - cy, Lord.

℟: **For the sake of your Son, have mercy, Lord.**

For the Church

Let us pray, dear friends, for the holy Church of God throughout the world, that God the almighty Father guide it and gather it together so that it may worship him in peace and tranquillity. We pray to the Lord: ℟.

Almighty and eternal God, you have shown your glory to all nations in Christ, your Son. Guide the work of your Church. Help it to persevere in faith, proclaim your name and bring your salvation to people everywhere. We ask this through Christ our Lord. **Amen.**

For the Pope

Let us pray for our Holy Father, Pope N., that God who chose him to be bishop may give him health and strength to guide and govern God's holy people. We pray to the Lord: ℟.

Almighty and eternal God, you guide all things by your word, you govern all Christian people. In your love protect the Pope you have chosen for us. Under his leadership deepen our faith and make us better Christians. We ask this through Christ our Lord. **Amen.**

For the clergy and laity of the Church

Let us pray for N., our bishop; for all bishops, priests, and deacons; for all who have a special ministry in the Church; and for all God's people. We pray to the Lord: ℟.

Almighty and eternal God, your Spirit guides the Church and makes it holy. Listen to our prayers and help each of us in his own vocation to do your work more faithfully. We ask this through Christ our Lord. **Amen.**

For those preparing for baptism

Let us pray for those (among us) preparing for baptism, that God in his mercy make them responsive to his love, forgive their sins through the waters of new birth, and give them life in Jesus Christ our Lord. We pray to the Lord: ℟.

Almighty and eternal God, you continually bless your Church with new members. Increase the faith and understanding of those (among us) preparing for baptism. Give them a new birth in these

273

living waters and make them members of your chosen family. We ask this through Christ our Lord. **Amen.**

For the unity of Christians

Let us pray for all our brothers and sisters who share our faith in Jesus Christ, that God may gather and keep together in one church all those who seek the truth with sincerity. We pray to the Lord: ℞.

Almighty and eternal God, you keep together those you have united. Look kindly on all who follow Jesus your Son. We are all consecrated to you by our common baptism. Make us one in the fullness of faith, and keep us in the fellowship of love. We ask this through Christ our Lord. **Amen.**

For the Jewish people

Let us pray for the Jewish people, the first to hear the word of God, that they may continue to grow in the love of his name and in faithfulness to his covenant. We pray to the Lord: ℞.

Almighty and eternal God, long ago you gave your promise to Abraham and his posterity. Listen to your Church as we pray that the people you first made your own may arrive at the fullness of redemption. We ask this through Christ our Lord. **Amen.**

For those who do not believe in Christ

Let us pray for those who do not believe in Christ, that the light of the Holy Spirit may show them the way to salvation. We pray to the Lord: ℞.

Almighty and eternal God, enable those who do not acknowledge Christ to find the truth as they walk before you in sincerity of heart. Help us to grow in love for one another, to grasp more fully the mystery of your godhead, and to become more perfect witnesses of your love in the sight of men. We ask this through Christ our Lord. **Amen.**

For those who do not believe in God

Let us pray for those who do not believe in God, that they may find him by sincerely following all that is right. We pray to the Lord: ℟.

Almighty and eternal God, you created mankind so that all might long to find you and have peace when you are found. Grant that, in spite of the hurtful things that stand in their way, they may all recognize in the lives of Christians the tokens of your love and mercy, and gladly acknowledge you as the one true God and Father of us all. We ask this through Christ our Lord. **Amen.**

For all in public office

Let us pray for those who serve us in public office, that God may guide their minds and hearts, so that all men may live in true peace and freedom. We pray to the Lord: ℟.

Almighty and eternal God, you know the longings of men's hearts and you protect their rights. In your goodness, watch over those in authority, so that your people everywhere may enjoy religious freedom, security, and peace. We ask this through Christ our Lord. **Amen.**

For those in special need

Let us pray, dear friends, that God the almighty Father may heal the sick, comfort the dying, give safety to travellers, free those unjustly deprived of liberty, and rid the world of falsehood, hunger, and disease. We pray to the Lord: ℞.

Almighty, ever-living God, you give strength to the weary and new courage to those who have lost heart. Hear the prayers of all who call on you in any trouble that they may have the joy of receiving your help in their need.
We ask this through Christ our Lord. **Amen.**

VENERATION OF THE CROSS

Three times, the celebrant invites the assembly to proclaim its faith:

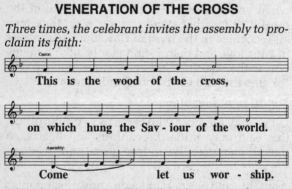

Cantor:
This is the wood of the cross,

on which hung the Sav - iour of the world.

Assembly:
Come let us wor - ship.

After each response all kneel and venerate the cross briefly in silence. After the third response, the cross and the candles are placed at the entrance to the sanctuary, and the people approach to venerate the cross. They may make a simple genuflection or perform some other appropriate sign of reverence according to local custom.

During the veneration, We Adore You, O Christ or other suitable songs are sung. All who have venerated the cross return to their places and sit. Where large numbers of people make individual veneration difficult, the celebrant may raise the cross briefly for all to venerate in silence.

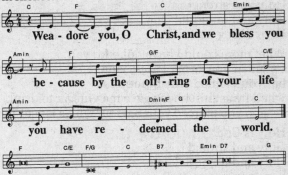

© *Michel Guimont*

℟. **We adore you, O Christ, and we bless you because by the offering of your life you have redeemed the world.**

Reproaches I:

My people, what have I <u>done</u> to you?
How have I offended you? An<u>sw</u>er me!
I led you out of Egypt, from slavery <u>to</u> freedom,
but you led your Saviour <u>to</u> the cross. ℟.

Ho<u>ly</u> is God!
Holy <u>and</u> strong!
Holy and im<u>mor</u>tal One,
have mer<u>cy</u> on us! ℟.

For forty years I led you safely <u>through</u> the desert.
I fed you with manna <u>from</u> heaven
and brought you to a <u>land</u> of plenty;
but you led your Saviour <u>to</u> the cross. ℟.

Ho<u>ly</u> is God!
Holy <u>and</u> strong!
Holy and im<u>mor</u>tal One,
have mer<u>cy</u> on us! ℟.

What more could I have <u>done</u> for you?
I planted you as my fair<u>est</u> vine,
but you yielded only <u>bit</u>terness:
when I was thirsty you gave me vinegar to drink,
    and you pierced your Saviour <u>with</u> a lance. ℟.

Ho<u>ly</u> is God!
Holy <u>and</u> strong!
Holy and im<u>mor</u>tal One,
have mer<u>cy</u> on us! ℟.

Reproaches II:
For your sake I scourged your captors
    and their <u>first</u> born sons,
but you brought your scourges down <u>on</u> me.

℟. **My people, what have I done to you?**
    How have I offended you? Answer me!

I led you from slavery <u>to</u> freedom
and drowned your captors in <u>the</u> sea,
but you hand<u>ed</u> me
over to <u>your</u> high priests. ℟.

I opened the <u>sea</u> before you,
but you opened my side <u>with</u> a spear. ℟.

I led you on your way in a <u>pillar</u> of cloud,
but you led me to <u>Pilate's</u> court. ℟.

I bore you up with manna <u>in</u> the desert,
but you struck me down <u>and</u> scourged me. ℞.

I gave you saving water <u>from</u> the rock,
but you gave me gall and vine<u>gar</u> to drink. ℞.

For you I struck down the <u>kings</u> of Canaan,
but you struck my head wi<u>th</u> a reed. ℞.

I gave you a <u>royal</u> sceptre,
but you gave me a <u>crown</u> of thorns. ℞.

I raised you to the height of <u>maj</u>esty,
but you have raised me high <u>on</u> a cross. ℞.

COMMUNION RITE

LORD'S PRAYER *(p. 63)*

PRAYER AFTER COMMUNION

Let us pray. Almighty and eternal God, you have restored us to life by the triumphant death and resurrection of Christ. Continue this healing work within us. May we who participate in this mystery never cease to serve you. We ask this through Christ our Lord. **Amen.**

PRAYER OVER THE PEOPLE and DISMISSAL

Lord, send down your abundant blessing upon your people who have devoutly recalled the death of your Son in the sure hope of the resurrection. Grant them pardon; bring them comfort. May their faith grow stronger and their eternal salvation be assured. We ask this through Christ our Lord. **Amen.**

All depart in silence.

There is no liturgical action on Holy Saturday. The very absence of celebration is the Church's way of expressing that it waits at the Lord's tomb, meditating on his suffering and death.

Holy Saturday is also a day of hope. We know that Jesus did not remain in the tomb. We anticipate his resurrection during this holy night when the joy of Easter will burst forth and overflow into the 50 days of celebration of the Easter Season.

On this the holiest of nights, we come together to hear our story as the people of God. Since the very beginning, God has been in relationship with his chosen people, calling us forward, preparing us for the coming of his Son who would be our Messiah. This is the story we retell tonight, a story of covenant, of fidelity and of everlasting love.

At first the apostles, like their ancestors before, had expected a Messiah who would lead them to victory, who would be invincible against the enemies of Israel. But Jesus spoke of a new way of love for God who is father, for our neighbour and for our enemy. And he spoke of his own death, a death that was necessary for the realization of new life, the resurrection. He even invited his followers to be baptized into his death and resurrection in order that they may have new life.

Tonight, we are invited anew into this same death and resurrection so that we also may share in this new life, life in the kingdom of God. The story draws us in and prepares us once again to reaffirm our desire to follow Jesus through death and into a resurrected people. Alleluia!

Connie Paré, Chatham, ON

THE SERVICE OF LIGHT

BLESSING OF THE FIRE

Dear friends in Christ, on this most holy night, when our Lord Jesus Christ passed from death to life, the Church invites her children throughout the world to come together in vigil and prayer. This is the passover of the Lord: if we honour the memory of his death and resurrection by hearing his word and celebrating his mysteries, then we may be confident that we shall share his victory over death and live with him for ever in God.

Let us pray. Father, we share in the light of your glory through your Son, the light of the world. Make this new fire holy, and inflame us with new hope. Purify our minds by this Easter celebration, and bring us one day to the feast of eternal light. We ask this through Christ our Lord. **Amen.**

PREPARATION OF THE CANDLE *(Optional)*

The celebrant cuts a cross in the wax of the Easter candle and traces the Greek letters alpha (A) and omega (Ω) and the numerals of the current year on the candle, saying:

Christ yesterday and today, the beginning and the end, Alpha and Omega; all time belongs to him, and all the ages; to him be glory and power through every age and for ever. **Amen.**

When the cross and other marks have been made, the celebrant may insert five grains of incense in the candle.

By his holy and glorious wounds may Christ our Lord guard us and keep us. **Amen.**

LIGHTING OF THE CANDLE

The celebrant lights the Easter candle from the new fire, saying:

May the light of Christ, rising in glory, dispel the darkness of our hearts and minds.

PROCESSION WITH THE EASTER CANDLE

The priest or deacon takes the Easter candle and, three times during the procession to the altar, lifts it high and sings alone. The people respond.

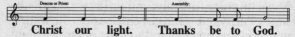

Christ our light. **Thanks be to God.**

Christ our Light. **Thanks be to God.**

After the second such response all the people light their candles with a flame taken from the Easter candle.

EASTER PROCLAMATION (EXSULTET)

For the shorter version, omit the indented parts.

Rejoice, heavenly powers! Sing, choirs of angels!
Exult, all creation around God's throne!
Jesus Christ, our King, is risen!
Sound the trumpet of salvation!
Rejoice, O earth, in shining splendour,
radiant in the brightness of your King!
Christ has conquered! Glory fills you!
Darkness vanishes for ever!
Rejoice, O Mother Church! Exult in glory!
The risen Saviour shines upon you!
Let this place resound with joy,
echoing the mighty song of all God's people!

> My dearest friends, standing with me in this
> holy light, join me in asking God for mercy,
> that he may give his unworthy minister grace
> to sing his Easter praises.

The Lord be with you. **And also with you.**

Lift up your hearts. **We lift them up to the Lord.**

Let us give thanks to the Lord our God.
It is right to give him thanks and praise.

It is truly right
that with full hearts and minds and voices
we should praise the unseen God,
the all-powerful Father,
and his only Son, our Lord Jesus Christ.
For Christ has ransomed us with his blood,
and paid for us the price of Adam's sin
to our eternal Father!

This is our passover feast,
when Christ, the true Lamb, is slain,
whose blood consecrates the homes
of all believers.

This is the night when first you saved our fathers
you freed the people of Israel from their slavery
and led them dry-shod through the sea.

> This is the night when the pillar of fire
> destroyed the darkness of sin!

This is the night when Christians everywhere,
washed clean of sin
and freed from all defilement,
are restored to grace
and grow together in holiness.

This is the night when Jesus Christ
broke the chains of death
and rose triumphant from the grave.

> What good would life have been to us,
> had Christ not come as our Redeemer?

Father, how wonderful your care for us!
How boundless your merciful love!
To ransom a slave you gave away your Son.

O happy fault, O necessary sin of Adam,
which gained for us so great a Redeemer!

> Most blessed of all nights, chosen by God
> to see Christ rising from the dead!

> Of this night scripture says:
> "The night will be as clear as day:
> it will become my light, my joy."

The power of this holy night
dispels all evil, washes guilt away,
restores lost innocence, brings mourners joy;

it casts out hatred, brings us peace,
and humbles earthly pride.

Night truly blessed
when heaven is wedded to earth
and man is reconciled with God!

Therefore, heavenly Father,
in the joy of this night,
receive our evening sacrifice of praise,
your Church's solemn offering.

---

longer version:

Accept this Easter candle, a flame divided but undimmed, a pillar of fire that glows to the honour of God.

Let it mingle with the lights of heaven and continue bravely burning to dispel the darkness of this night!

shorter version:

Accept this Easter candle. May it always dispel the darkness of this night!

May the Morning Star which never sets
find this flame still burning:
Christ, that Morning Star,
who came back from the dead,
and shed his peaceful light on all mankind,
your Son who lives and reigns for ever and ever.
Amen.

LITURGY OF THE WORD

Dear friends in Christ, we have begun our solem
vigil. Let us now listen attentively to the word o
God, recalling how he saved his people through
out history and, in the fullness of time, sent hi
own Son to be our Redeemer. Through this Easte
celebration, may God bring to perfection the sav
ing work he has begun in us.

FIRST READING *(Genesis 1:1–2:2)*

For the shorter version, omit the indented parts.

In the beginning when God created the heaven
and the earth,

> the earth was a formless void and darknes
> covered the face of the deep, while the spirit o
> God swept over the face of the waters. The
> God said, "Let there be light"; and there wa
> light. And God saw that the light was good
> and God separated the light from the darknes
> God called the light "Day," and the darknes
> he called "Night." And there was evening an
> there was morning, the first day.
>
> And God said, "Let there be a dome in th
> midst of the waters, and let it separate th
> waters from the waters." So God made th
> dome and separated the waters that were un
> der the dome from the waters that were abov
> the dome. And it was so. God called the dom
> "Sky." And there was evening and there wa
> morning, the second day.
>
> And God said, "Let the waters under the sk
> be gathered together into one place, and let th

dry land appear." And it was so. God called the dry land "Earth," and the waters that were gathered together he called "Seas." And God saw that it was good.

Then God said, "Let the earth put forth vegetation: plants yielding seed, and fruit trees of every kind on earth that bear fruit with the seed in it." And it was so. The earth brought forth vegetation: plants yielding seed of every kind, and trees of every kind bearing fruit with the seed in it. And God saw that it was good. And there was evening and there was morning, the third day.

And God said, "Let there be lights in the dome of the sky to separate the day from the night; and let them be for signs and for seasons and for days and years, and let them be lights in the dome of the sky to give light upon the earth." And it was so.

God made the two great lights—the greater light to rule the day and the lesser light to rule the night—and the stars. God set them in the dome of the sky to give light upon the earth, to rule over the day and over the night, and to separate the light from the darkness. And God saw that it was good. And there was evening and there was morning, the fourth day.

And God said, "Let the waters bring forth swarms of living creatures, and let birds fly above the earth across the dome of the sky." So God created the great sea monsters and every living creature that moves, of every kind, with which the waters swarm, and every winged bird of every kind. And God saw that it wa good. God blessed them, saying, "Be fruitfu and multiply and fill the waters in the sea and let birds multiply on the earth." And ther was evening and there was morning, the fift day.

And God said, "Let the earth bring forth livin creatures of every kind: cattle and creepin things and wild animals of the earth of ever kind." And it was so. God made the wil animals of the earth of every kind, and th cattle of every kind, and everything tha creeps upon the ground of every kind. An God saw that it was good. Then

God said, "Let us make human beings in ou image, according to our likeness; and let ther have dominion over the fish of the sea, and ove the birds of the air, and over the cattle, and ove all the wild animals of the earth, and over ever creeping thing that creeps upon the earth." S God created human beings in his image, in th image of God he created them; male and female h created them.

God blessed them, and God said to them, "B fruitful and multiply, and fill the earth and sub due it; and have dominion over the fish of the se and over the birds of the air and over every livin thing that moves upon the earth."

God said, "See, I have given you every plar yielding seed that is upon the face of all the eartl and every tree with seed in its fruit; you sha have them for food. And to every beast of th earth, and to every bird of the air, and to every

hing that creeps on the earth, everything that has
he breath of life, I have given every green plant
for food." And it was so.

God saw everything that he had made, and indeed, it was very good. And there was evening
and there was morning, the sixth day.

Thus the heavens and the earth were finished,
and all their multitude. And on the seventh
day God finished the work that he had done,
and he rested on the seventh day from all the
work that he had done.

The word of the Lord. **Thanks be to God.**

RESPONSORIAL PSALM *(Psalm 104)*

℟. **Lord, send out your Spirit,
and renew the face of the earth.**

Bless the Lord, O • **my** soul.
O Lord my God, you are very • **great.**
You are clothed with • **honour** and majesty,
wrapped in light as with • **a** garment. ℟.

You set the earth on its • **found**-ations,
so that it shall never be • **shaken,**
You cover it with the deep as • **with** a garment;
the waters stood above • **the** mountains. ℟.

You make springs gush forth in • **the** valleys
they flow between the • **hills.**
By the streams the birds of the air
    have their • **ha**-bit-ation;
they sing among • **the** branches. ℟.

From your lofty abode
    you water • **the** mountains;
the earth is satisfied with the fruit of
    your • **work.**
You cause the grass to • **grow_for** the cattle,
and plants for people to use, to bring forth
    food from • **the** earth. ℟.

O Lord, how manifold are • **your** works!
In wisdom you have made them • **all;**
the earth is • **full_of** your creatures.
Bless the Lord, O • **my** soul. ℟.

or

RESPONSORIAL PSALM *(Psalm 33)*

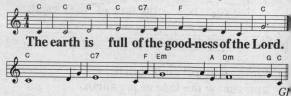

℟. **The earth is full of the goodness of the Lord.**

The word of the Lord • **is** upright,
and all his work is done • **in** faithfulness.
He loves righteousness • **and** justice;
the earth is full of the steadfast love
    of • **the** Lord. ℟.

By the word of the Lord the heavens • **were** made,
and all their host by the breath of • **his** mouth.
He gathered the waters of the sea as in • **a** bottle;
he put the deeps • **in** storehouses. ℞.

Happy is the nation whose God is • **the** Lord,
the people whom he has chosen
    as • **his** heritage.
The Lord looks down • **from** heaven;
he sees all hu•-**man** beings. ℞.

Our soul waits for • **the** Lord;
he is our help • **and** shield.
Let your steadfast love, O Lord, be • **up**_on us,
even as we hope • **in** you. ℞.

PRAYER

Let us pray. Almighty and eternal God, you created all things in wonderful beauty and order. Help us now to perceive how still more wonderful is the new creation by which in the fullness of time you redeemed your people through the sacrifice of our passover, Jesus Christ, who lives and reigns for ever and ever. **Amen.**

SECOND READING *(Genesis 22:1-18)*

For the shorter version, omit the indented parts.

God tested Abraham. He said to him, "Abraham!" And Abraham said, "Here I am." God said, "Take your son, your only son Isaac, whom you love, and go to the land of Moriah, and offer him there as a burnt offering on one of the mountains that I shall show you."

> So Abraham rose early in the morning, saddled his donkey, and took two of his young

men with him, and his son Isaac; he cut the wood for the burnt offering, and set out and went to the place in the distance that God had shown him.

On the third day Abraham looked up and saw the place far away. Then Abraham said to his young men, "Stay here with the donkey; the boy and I will go over there; we will worship and then we will come back to you." Abraham took the wood of the burnt offering and laid it on his son Isaac, and he himself carried the fire and the knife. So the two of them walked on together.

Isaac said to his father Abraham, "Father!" And Abraham said, "Here I am, my son." Isaac said, "The fire and the wood are here, but where is the lamb for a burnt offering?" Abraham said, "God himself will provide the lamb for a burnt offering, my son." So the two of them walked on together.

When Abraham and Isaac came to the place that God had shown him, Abraham built an altar there and laid the wood in order. He bound his son Isaac, and laid him on the altar, on top of the wood. Then Abraham reached out his hand and took the knife to kill his son.

But the angel of the Lord called to him from heaven, and said, "Abraham, Abraham!" And he said, "Here I am." The angel said, "Do not lay your hand on the boy or do anything to him; for now I know that you fear God, since you have not withheld your son, your only son, from me." And Abraham looked up and saw a ram, caught in a

hicket by its horns. Abraham went and took the
ram and offered it up as a burnt offering instead of
his son.

So Abraham called that place "The Lord will
provide"; as it is said to this day, "On the
mount of the Lord it shall be provided."

The angel of the Lord called to Abraham a second
time from heaven, and said, "By myself I have
sworn, says the Lord: Because you have done this,
and have not withheld your son, your only son, I
will indeed bless you, and I will make your offspring as numerous as the stars of heaven and as
the sand that is on the seashore. And your offspring shall possess the gate of their enemies, and
by your offspring shall all the nations of the earth
gain blessing for themselves, because you have
obeyed my voice."

The word of the Lord. **Thanks be to God.**

RESPONSORIAL PSALM *(Psalm 16)*

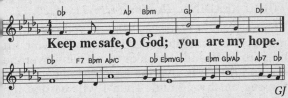

Keep me safe, O God; you are my hope.

℟. **Keep me safe O God; you are my hope.**

The Lord is my chosen portion and • **my** cup;
you hold • **my** lot.
I keep the Lord always • **be**-fore_me;
because he is at my right hand,
 I shall • **not** be moved. ℟.

Therefore my heart is glad,
   and my soul • **re**-joices;
my body also rests • **se**-cure.
For you do not give me up • **to** Sheol,
or let your faithful one • **see** the Pit. ℟.

You show me the path • **of** life.
In your presence there is fullness • **of** joy;
in your right hand • **are** pleasures
for•-**ev**-er-more. ℟.

PRAYER

Let us pray. God and Father of all who believe in you, you promised Abraham that he would become the father of all nations, and through the death and resurrection of Christ you fulfil that promise: everywhere throughout the world you increase your chosen people. May we respond to your call by joyfully accepting your invitation to the new life of grace. We ask this in the name of Jesus the Lord. **Amen.**

THIRD READING *(Exodus 14:15-31; 15:20, 1)*

The Lord said to Moses, "Why do you cry out to me? Tell the Israelites to go forward. But you, lift up your staff, and stretch out your hand over the sea and divide it, that the Israelites may go into the sea on dry ground. Then I will harden the hearts of the Egyptians so that they will go in after them; and so I will gain glory for myself over Pharaoh and all his army, his chariots, and his chariot drivers. And the Egyptians shall know that I am the Lord, when I have gained glory for myself over Pharaoh, his chariots, and his chariot drivers."

The angel of God who was going before the Israelite army moved and went behind them; and the pillar of cloud moved from in front of them and took its place behind them. It came between the army of Egypt and the army of Israel. And so the cloud was there with the darkness, and it lit up the night; one did not come near the other all night. Then Moses stretched out his hand over the sea. The Lord drove the sea back by a strong east wind all night, and turned the sea into dry land; and the waters were divided. The Israelites went into the sea on dry ground, the waters forming a wall for them on their right and on their left.

The Egyptians pursued, and went into the sea after them, all of Pharaoh's horses, chariots, and chariot drivers. At the morning watch, the Lord in the pillar of fire and cloud looked down upon the Egyptian army, and threw the Egyptian army into panic. He clogged their chariot wheels so that they turned with difficulty. The Egyptians said, "Let us flee from the Israelites, for the Lord is fighting for them against Egypt."

Then the Lord said to Moses, "Stretch out your hand over the sea, so that the water may come back upon the Egyptians, upon their chariots and chariot drivers." So Moses stretched out his hand over the sea, and at dawn the sea returned to its normal depth. As the Egyptians fled before it, the Lord tossed the Egyptians into the sea. The waters returned and covered the chariots and the chariot drivers, the entire army of Pharaoh that had followed them into the sea; not one of them remained.

But the Israelites walked on dry ground through the sea, the waters forming a wall for them on their right and on their left. Thus the Lord saved Israel that day from the Egyptians; and Israel saw the Egyptians dead on the seashore. Israel saw the great work that the Lord did against the Egyptians. So the people feared the Lord and believed in the Lord and in his servant Moses.

The prophet Miriam, Aaron's sister, took a tambourine in her hand; and all the women went out after her with tambourines and with dancing. Moses and the Israelites sang this song to the Lord:

RESPONSORIAL CANTICLE (*Exodus 15*)

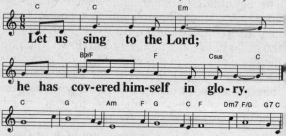

Let us sing to the Lord;
he has cov-ered him-self in glo-ry.

℟. **Let us sing to the Lord;**
   he has covered himself in glory.

I will sing to the Lord,
    for he has triumphed • **gloriously;**
horse and rider he has thrown into • **the** sea.
The Lord is my strength and my • **might,**
and he has become my • **sal**-vation;
this is my God, and I will • **praise_him,**
my father's God, and I will • **ex**-alt_him. ℟.

The Lord is a • **warrior;**
the Lord is • **his** name.
Pharaoh's chariots and his army
    he cast into the • **sea;**
his picked officers were sunk in the • **Red** Sea.
The floods • **covered_them;**
they went down into the depths like • **a** stone. ℞.

Your right hand, O Lord, glorious in • **power;**
your right hand, O Lord, shattered • **the** enemy.
In the greatness of your • **majesty**
you overthrew • **your** adversaries;
you sent out your • **fury,**
it consumed them • **like** stubble. ℞.

You brought your people • **in**
and plant•**-ed** them
on the mountain of your own pos•**-session,**
the place, O Lord, that you made your • **a-**bode,
the sanctuary, O Lord, that your hands
    have es•**-tablished.**
The Lord will reign forever • **and** ever. ℞.

PRAYER

Let us pray. Lord God, in the new covenant you shed light on the miracles you worked in ancient times: the Red Sea is a symbol of our baptism, and the nation you freed from slavery is a sign of your Christian people. May every nation share the faith and privilege of Israel and come to new birth in the Holy Spirit. Grant this through Christ our Lord. **Amen.**

297

FOURTH READING *(Isaiah 54:5-14)*

Thus says the Lord, the God of hosts. Your Maker is your husband, the Lord of hosts is his name; the Holy One of Israel is your Redeemer, the God of the whole earth he is called. For the Lord has called you like a wife forsaken and grieved in spirit, like the wife of a man's youth when she is cast off, says your God.

For a brief moment I abandoned you, but with great compassion I will gather you. In overflowing wrath for a moment I hid my face from you but with everlasting love I will have compassion on you, says the Lord, your Redeemer.

This is like the days of Noah to me: Just as I swore that the waters of Noah would never again go over the earth, so I have sworn that I will not be angry with you and will not rebuke you. For the mountains may depart and the hills be removed, but my steadfast love shall not depart from you, and my covenant of peace shall not be removed, says the Lord, who has compassion on you.

O afflicted one, storm-tossed, and not comforted, I am about to set your stones in antimony, and lay your foundations with sapphires. I will make your pinnacles of rubies, your gates of jewels, and all your wall of precious stones.

All your children shall be taught by the Lord, and great shall be the prosperity of your children. In righteousness you shall be established; you shall be far from oppression, for you shall not fear; and from terror, for it shall not come near you.

The word of the Lord. **Thanks be to God.**

RESPONSORIAL PSALM *(Psalm 30)*

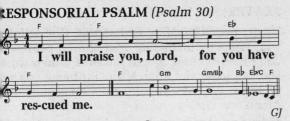

I will praise you, Lord, for you have res-cued me.

GJ

℟. **I will praise you, Lord,
for you have rescued me.**

I will extol you, O Lord,
    for you have drawn me • **up,**
and did not let my foes rejoice over • **me.**
O Lord, you brought up my soul from • **Sheol,**
restored me to life from among those
    gone down to • **the** Pit. ℟.

Sing praises to the Lord,
    O you his • **faithful_ones,**
and give thanks to his holy • **name.**
For his anger is but for a moment;
    his favour is for a • **lifetime.**
Weeping may linger for the night,
    but joy comes with • **the** morning. ℟.

Hear, O Lord, and be gracious to • **me!**
O Lord, be my • **helper!**
You have turned my mourning into • **dancing.**
O Lord my God, I will give thanks
    to you • **for**-ever. ℟.

PRAYER

Let us pray. Almighty and eternal God, glorify your name by increasing your chosen people as you promised long ago. In reward for their trust may we see in the Church the fulfilment of your promise. We ask this through Christ our Lord **Amen.**

FIFTH READING *(Isaiah 55:1-11)*

Everyone who thirsts, come to the waters; and you that have no money, come, buy and eat Come, buy wine and milk without money and without price. Why do you spend your money for that which is not bread, and your labour for that which does not satisfy? Listen carefully to me, and eat what is good, and delight yourselves in rich food. Incline your ear, and come to me; listen, so that you may live. I will make with you an everlasting covenant, my steadfast, sure love for David.

See, I made him a witness to the peoples, a leader and commander for the peoples. See, you shall call nations that you do not know, and nations that do not know you shall run to you, because of the Lord your God, the Holy One of Israel, for he has glorified you.

Seek the Lord while he may be found, call upon him while he is near; let the wicked forsake their way, and the unrighteous their thoughts; let them return to the Lord, that he may have mercy on them, and to our God, for he will abundantly pardon.

For my thoughts are not your thoughts, nor are your ways my ways, says the Lord. For as the heavens are

higher than the earth, so are my ways higher than
your ways and my thoughts than your thoughts.

For as the rain and the snow come down from
heaven, and do not return there until they have
watered the earth, making it bring forth and
sprout, giving seed to the sower and bread to the
eater, so shall my word be that goes out from my
mouth; it shall not return to me empty, but it shall
accomplish that which I purpose, and succeed in
the thing for which I sent it.

The word of the Lord. **Thanks be to God.**

RESPONSORIAL CANTICLE *(Isaiah 12)*

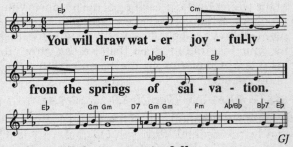

You will draw water joyfully
from the springs of salvation.

GJ

℟. **You will draw water joyfully**
   from the springs of salvation.

Surely God is my salvation; I will trust,
   and will not • **be** a-fraid,
for the Lord God is my strength • **and** my might;
he has become • **my** sal-vation.
With joy you will draw water
   from the • **wells_of** sal-vation. ℟.

301

Give thanks • **to** the Lord,
call • **on** his name;
make known his deeds a•-**mong** the nations;
proclaim that his name • **is** ex-alted. ℟.

Sing praises to the Lord,
    for he • **has** done gloriously;
let this be known in • **all** the earth.
Shout aloud and sing for joy, O • **roy**-al Zion,
for great in your midst is
    the • **Holy_One** of Israel. ℟.

PRAYER

Let us pray. Almighty, ever-living God, only hope of the world, by the preaching of the prophets you proclaimed the mysteries we are celebrating to-night. Help us to be your faithful people, for it is by your inspiration alone that we can grow in goodness. Grant this in the name of Jesus the Lord. **Amen.**

SIXTH READING *(Baruch 3:9-15, 32–4:4)*

Hear the commandments of life, O Israel; give ear, and learn wisdom! Why is it, O Israel, why is it that you are in the land of your enemies, that you are growing old in a foreign country, that you are defiled with the dead, that you are counted among those in Hades? You have forsaken the fountain of wisdom. If you had walked in the way of God, you would be living in peace forever.

Learn where there is wisdom, where there is strength, where there is understanding, so that you may at the same time discern where there is length of days, and life, where there is light for the eyes, and peace. Who has found her place? And who has entered her storehouses?

But the one who knows all things knows her, he found her by his understanding. The one who prepared the earth for all time filled it with four-footed creatures; the one who sends forth the light, and it goes; he called it, and it obeyed him, trembling; the stars shone in their watches, and were glad; he called them, and they said, "Here we are!" They shone with gladness for him who made them.

This is our God; no other can be compared to him. He found the whole way to knowledge, and gave her to his servant Jacob and to Israel, whom he loved. Afterward she appeared on earth and lived with humanity.

She is the book of the commandments of God, the law that endures forever. All who hold her fast will live, and those who forsake her will die.

Turn, O Jacob, and take her; walk toward the shining of her light. Do not give your glory to another, or your advantages to an alien people.

Happy are we, O Israel, for we know what is pleasing to God.

The word of the Lord. **Thanks be to God.**

RESPONSORIAL PSALM *(Psalm 19)*

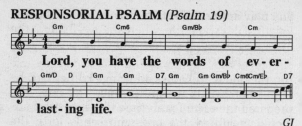

GJ

℞. **Lord, you have the words of everlasting life.**

The law of the Lord is • **perfect,**
reviving the • **soul;**
the decrees of the Lord are • **sure,**
making • **wise** the simple. ℞.

The precepts of the Lord are • **right,**
rejoicing the • **heart;**
the commandment of the Lord is • **clear,**
enlighten•**-ing** the eyes. ℞.

The fear of the Lord is • **pure,**
enduring for•**-ever;**
the ordinances of the Lord are • **true**
and righteous • **al**-to-gether. ℞.

More to be desired are they than • **gold,**
even much fine • **gold;**
sweeter also than • **honey,**
and drippings • **of** the honeycomb. ℞.

PRAYER

Let us pray. Father, you increase your Church by continuing to call all people to salvation. Listen to our prayers and always watch over those you cleanse in baptism. We ask this through Christ our Lord. **Amen.**

SEVENTH READING *(Ezekiel 36:16-17, 18-28)*

The word of the Lord came to me: Mortal, when the house of Israel lived on their own soil, they defiled it with their ways and their deeds; their conduct in my sight was unclean. So I poured out my wrath upon them for the blood that they had shed upon the land, and for the idols with which they had defiled it. I scattered them among the nations, and they were dispersed through the countries; in accordance with their conduct and their deeds I judged them.

But when they came to the nations, wherever they came, they profaned my holy name, in that it was said of them, "These are the people of the Lord, and yet they had to go out of his land."

But I had concern for my holy name, which the house of Israel had profaned among the nations to which they came. Therefore say to the house of Israel, Thus says the Lord God: It is not for your sake, O house of Israel, that I am about to act, but for the sake of my holy name, which you have profaned among the nations to which you came.

I will sanctify my great name, which has been profaned among the nations, and which you have profaned among them; and the nations shall know that I am the Lord, says the Lord God, when through you I display my holiness before their eyes.

I will take you from the nations, and gather you from all the countries, and bring you into your own land.

I will sprinkle clean water upon you, and you shall be clean from all your uncleanness, and from all your idols I will cleanse you.

A new heart I will give you, and a new spirit I will put within you; and I will remove from your body the heart of stone and give you a heart of flesh. I will put my spirit within you, and make you follow my statutes and be careful to observe my ordinances. Then you shall live in the land that I gave to your ancestors; and you shall be my people, and I will be your God.

The word of the Lord. **Thanks be to God.**

RESPONSORIAL PSALM *(Psalm 42)*

(Or, when baptism is celebrated, Isaiah 12, p. 301.)

Like a deer that longs for run - ning streams, my soul longs for you, my God.

GJ

℟. **Like a deer that longs for running streams, my soul longs for you, my God.**

My soul thirsts for • **God,**
for the living • **God.**
When shall I • **come**
and behold the face • **of** God? ℟.

I went with the • **throng,**
and led them in procession to the house
    of • **God,**
with glad shouts and songs of thanks•**-giving,**
a multitude • **keeping** festival. ℟.

O send out your light and your • **truth;**
let them • **lead_me;**
let them bring me to your holy • **mountain**
and to • **your** dwelling. ℟.

Then I will go to the altar of • **God,**
to God my exceeding • **joy;**
and I will praise you with the • **harp,**
O God, • **my** God. ℟.

or

RESPONSORIAL PSALM *(Psalm 51)*

℟. **Create a clean heart in me, O God.**

Create in me a clean heart, • **O God,**
and put a new and steadfast spirit • **with-in_me.**
Do not cast me away from • **your** presence,
and do not take your holy • **spirit** from me. ℟.

Restore to me the joy of your • **sal-vation,**
and sustain in me a will•**-ing** spirit.
Then I will teach transgressors • **your** ways,
and sinners will re•**-turn** to you. ℟.

For you have no delight • **in** sacrifice;
if I were to give a burnt offering,
    you would not • **be** pleased.
The sacrifice acceptable to God is
    a bro•**-ken** spirit;
a broken and contrite heart, O God,
    you will • **not** de-spise. ℟.

307

PRAYER

Let us pray. Father, you teach us in both the Old and the New Testament to celebrate this passover mystery. Help us to understand your great love for us. May the goodness you now show us confirm our hope in your future mercy. We ask this in the name of Jesus the Lord. **Amen.**

Or, if there are candidates to be baptized:

Let us pray. Almighty and eternal God, be present in this sacrament of your love. Send your Spirit of adoption on those to be born again in baptism. And may the work of our humble ministry be brought to perfection by your mighty power. We ask this in the name of Jesus the Lord. **Amen.**

GLORY TO GOD *(p. 10)*

OPENING PRAYER

Lord God, you have brightened this night with the radiance of the risen Christ. Quicken the spirit of sonship in your Church; renew us in mind and body to give you whole-hearted service.

EPISTLE *(Romans 6:3-11)*

Do you not know that all of us who have been baptized into Christ Jesus were baptized into his death? Therefore we have been buried with him by baptism into death, so that, just as Christ was raised from the dead by the glory of the Father, so we too might walk in newness of life. For if we have been united with him in a death like his, we will certainly be united with him in a resurrection like his.

We know that our old self was crucified with him so that the body of sin might be destroyed, and we might no longer be enslaved to sin. For whoever has died is freed from sin. But if we have died with Christ, we believe that we will also live with him.

We know that Christ, being raised from the dead, will never die again; death no longer has dominion over him. The death he died, he died to sin, once for all; but the life he lives, he lives to God. So you also must consider yourselves dead to sin and alive to God in Christ Jesus.

The word of the Lord. **Thanks be to God.**

SOLEMN ALLELUIA *(Psalm 118)*

GJ

℟. **Alleluia!**

O give thanks to the Lord, for he is • **good;**
his steadfast love endures • **for-**ever.
Let Israel say, "His steadfast love
endures • **for-**ever." ℟.

"The right hand of the Lord is ex•**-alted;**
the right hand of the Lord • **does** valiantly."
I shall not die, but I shall live, and recount
the deeds of • **the** Lord. ℟.

The stone that the builders rejected
has become the chief • **cornerstone.**
This is the • **Lord's** doing;
it is marvellous in • **our** eyes. ℟.

GOSPEL *(Luke 24:1-12)*

A reading from the holy gospel according to Luke.
Glory to you, Lord.

On the first day of the week, at early dawn, the women who had accompanied Jesus from Galilee came to the tomb, taking the spices that they had prepared. They found the stone rolled away from the tomb, but when they went in, they did not find the body.

While they were perplexed about this, suddenly two men in dazzling clothes stood beside them. The women were terrified and bowed their faces to the ground, but the men said to them, "Why do you look for the living among the dead? He is not here, but has risen. Remember how he told you, while he was still in Galilee, that the Son of Man must be handed over to sinners, and be crucified, and on the third day rise again."

Then the women remembered Jesus' words, and returning from the tomb, they told all this to the eleven and to all the rest. Now it was Mary Magdalene, Joanna, Mary the mother of James, and the other women with them who told this to the apostles.

These words seemed to the apostles an idle tale, and they did not believe the women. But Peter got up and ran to the tomb; stooping and looking in, he saw the linen cloths by themselves; then he went home, amazed at what had happened.

The gospel of the Lord. **Praise to you, Lord Jesus Christ.**

CELEBRATION OF THE SACRAMENTS OF INITIATION AND THE RITE OF RECEPTION

The outline for this celebration follows the Rite of Christian Initiation of Adults *(CCCB, 1987). If there is no baptism, proceed to the* BLESSING OF THE WATER, *p. 317.*

CELEBRATION OF BAPTISM

INVITATION

Dear friends, let us pray to almighty God for our brothers and sisters, N. and N., who are asking for baptism. He has called them and brought them to this moment; may he grant them light and strength to follow Christ with resolute hearts and to profess the faith of the Church. May he give them the new life of the Holy Spirit, whom we are about to call down on this water.

LITANY OF THE SAINTS

Lord, have mercy. **Lord, have mercy.**
Christ, have mercy. **Christ, have mercy.**
Lord, have mercy. **Lord, have mercy.**

Holy Mary, Mother of <u>God</u>, **pray for us.**
Saint <u>Mi</u>chael
Holy angels of <u>God</u>
Abraham, Moses and E<u>li</u>jah
Saint Joachim and Saint <u>Anne</u>

Saint Joseph
Saint John the Baptist
Saint Peter and Saint Paul
Saint Andrew
Saint John
Saint Mary Magdalene
Saint Stephen
Saint Ignatius
Saint Lawrence
Saint John de Brébeuf and the holy Canadian Martyrs
Saint Perpetua and Saint Felicity
Saint Agnes
Saint Gregory
Saint Augustine
Saint Athanasius
Saint Basil
Saint Catherine of Siena
Saint Teresa of Avila
Saint Martin
Blessed François de Laval
Saint Benedict
Saint Francis and Saint Dominic
Saint Francis Xavier
Saint John Vianney
Saint Marguerite Bourgeoys
Saint Marguerite d'Youville
Saint Monica
Saint Louis
Blessed Kateri Tekakwitha
(other saints)
All holy men and women

Lord, be merciful. **Lord, save your people.**
From all harm
From ev'ry sin
From all temptations
From everlasting death
By your coming among us
By your death and rising to new life
By your gift of the Holy Spirit

Be merciful to us sinners. **Lord, hear our prayer.**
Give new life to these chosen ones by the grace of baptism
Jesus, Son of the living God

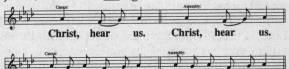

Christ, hear us. **Christ, hear us.**
Lord Jesus, hear our prayer.
Lord Jesus, hear our prayer.

BLESSING OF THE WATER

Father, you give us grace through sacramental signs, which tell us of the wonders of your unseen power. In baptism we use your gift of water,

313

which you have made a rich symbol of the grace you give us in this sacrament.

At the very dawn of creation your Spirit breathed on the waters, making them the wellspring of all holiness. The waters of the great flood you made a sign of the waters of baptism, that make an end of sin and a new beginning of goodness. Through the waters of the Red Sea you led Israel out of slavery, to be an image of God's holy people, set free from sin by baptism.

In the waters of the Jordan your Son was baptized by John and anointed with the Spirit. Your Son willed that water and blood should flow from his side as he hung upon the cross. After his resurrection he told his disciples: "Go out and teach all nations, baptizing them in the name of the Father and of the Son and of the Holy Spirit."

Father, look now with love upon your Church, and unseal for her the fountain of baptism. By the power of the Holy Spirit give to this water the grace of your Son, so that in the sacrament of baptism all those whom you have created in your likeness may be cleansed from sin and rise to a new birth of innocence by water and the Holy Spirit.

We ask you, Father, with your Son to send the Holy Spirit upon the waters of this font. May all who are buried with Christ in the death of baptism rise also with him to newness of life. We ask this through Christ our Lord. **Amen.**

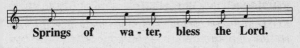

Springs of wa - ter, bless the Lord.

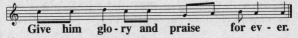

Give him glo - ry and praise for ev - er.

Springs of water, bless the Lord.
Give him glory and praise for ever.

RENUNCIATION OF SIN

Using one of the following formularies, the celebrant questions all the candidates together or individually.

1   Do you reject sin so as to live in the freedom of God's children? **I do.**

Do you reject the glamour of evil, and refuse to be mastered by sin? **I do.**

Do you reject Satan, father of sin and prince of darkness? **I do.**

2   Do you reject Satan, and all his works, and all his empty promises? **I do.**

3   Do you reject Satan? **I do.**
And all his works? **I do.**
And all his empty promises? **I do.**

ANOINTING WITH THE OIL OF CATECHUMENS

We anoint you with the oil of salvation in the name of Christ our Saviour. May he strengthen you with his power, who lives and reigns for ever and ever. **Amen.**

PROFESSION OF FAITH

Each candidate is baptized immediately after this profession of faith.

N., do you believe in God, the Father almighty, creator of heaven and earth? **I do.**

Do you believe in Jesus Christ, his only Son, our Lord, who was born of the Virgin Mary, was crucified, died, and was buried, rose from the dead, and is now seated at the right hand of the Father? **I do.**

Do you believe in the Holy Spirit, the holy catholic Church, the communion of saints, the forgiveness of sins, the resurrection of the body, and the life everlasting? **I do.**

BAPTISM

The celebrant baptizes each candidate either by immersion or by the pouring of water.

N., I baptize you in the name of the Father, and of the Son, and of the Holy Spirit.

ANOINTING AFTER BAPTISM

The newly baptized who will be confirmed at another time are anointed now with chrism.

The God of power and Father of our Lord Jesus Christ has freed you from sin and brought you to new life through water and the Holy Spirit.

He now anoints you with the chrism of salvation, so that, united with his people, you may remain for ever a member of Christ who is Priest, Prophet, and King. **Amen.**

CLOTHING WITH A BAPTISMAL GARMENT

N. and N., you have become a new creation and have clothed yourselves in Christ. Receive this baptismal garment and bring it unstained to the judgment seat of our Lord Jesus Christ, so that you may have everlasting life. **Amen.**

PRESENTATION OF A LIGHTED CANDLE

Godparents, please come forward to give to the newly baptized the light of Christ.

A godparent of each of the newly baptized lights a candle from the Easter candle and presents it to the newly baptized.

You have been enlightened by Christ. Walk always as children of the light and keep the flame of faith alive in your hearts. When the Lord comes, may you go out to meet him with all the saints in the heavenly kingdom. **Amen.**

BLESSING OF THE WATER *(without baptism)*

My brothers and sisters, let us ask the Lord our God to bless this water he has created, which we shall use to recall our baptism. May he renew us and keep us faithful to the Spirit we have all received.

Lord our God, this night your people keep prayerful vigil. Be with us as we recall the wonder of our creation and the greater wonder of our redemption. Bless this water: it makes the seed grow, it refreshes us and makes us clean. You have made of it a servant of your loving kindness: through water you set your people free, and quenched their thirst in the desert. With water the prophets announced a new covenant that you would make with humankind. By water, made holy by Christ in the Jordan, you made our sinful nature new in the bath that gives rebirth. Let this water remind us of our baptism; let us share the joys of our brothers and sisters who are baptized this Easter. We ask this through Christ our Lord. **Amen.**

RENEWAL OF BAPTISMAL PROMISES

INVITATION

The celebrant addresses the community inviting those present to the renewal of their baptismal promises. The candidates for reception into full communion join the rest of the community in this renunciation of sin and profession of faith.

Dear friends, through the paschal mystery we have been buried with Christ in baptism, so that we may rise with him to newness of life. Now that we have completed our Lenten observance, let us renew the promises we made in baptism, when we rejected Satan and his works and promised to serve God faithfully in his holy catholic Church.

RENUNCIATION OF SIN

The celebrant uses one of these formularies:

1   Do you reject sin so as to live in the freedom of God's children? **I do.**

Do you reject the glamour of evil, and refuse to be mastered by sin? **I do.**

Do you reject Satan, father of sin and prince of darkness? **I do.**

2   Do you reject Satan? **I do.**
And all his works? **I do.**
And all his empty promises? **I do.**

PROFESSION OF FAITH

Do you believe in God, the Father almighty, creator of heaven and earth? **I do.**

Do you believe in Jesus Christ, his only Son, our Lord, who was born of the Virgin Mary, was crucified, died, and was buried, rose from the dead, and is now seated at the right hand of the Father? **I do.**

Do you believe in the Holy Spirit, the holy catholic Church, the communion of saints, the forgiveness of sins, the resurrection of the body, and the life everlasting? **I do.**

SPRINKLING WITH BAPTISMAL WATER

The celebrant sprinkles all the people with the blessed baptismal water, while all sing the following or another appropriate song.

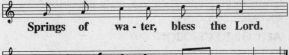

Springs of wa - ter, bless the Lord.

Give him glo - ry and praise for ev - er.

God, the all-powerful Father of our Lord Jesus Christ, has given us a new birth by water and the Holy Spirit and forgiven all our sins. May he also keep us faithful to our Lord Jesus Christ for ever and ever. **Amen.**

If there are no candidates for reception or confirmation, proceed to the PRAYER OF THE FAITHFUL, *p. 322.*

CELEBRATION OF RECEPTION

INVITATION

The celebrant invites the candidates for reception, along with their sponsors, to come into the sanctuary and join the newly baptized and their godparents.

N. and N., of your own free will you have asked to be received into the full communion of the Catholic Church. You have made your decision after careful thought under the guidance of the Holy Spirit. I now invite you to come forward with your sponsors and in the presence of this community to profess the Catholic faith. In this faith you will be one with us for the first time at the eucharistic table of the Lord Jesus, the sign of the Church's unity.

PROFESSION BY THE CANDIDATES

The celebrant asks the candidates to make the following profession of faith. The candidates say:

I believe and profess all that the holy Catholic Church believes, teaches and proclaims to be revealed by God.

ACT OF RECEPTION

Then the candidates with their sponsors go individually to the celebrant, who says to each candidate:

N., the Lord receives you into the Catholic Church. His loving kindness has led you here, so that in the unity of the Holy Spirit you may have full communion with us in the faith that you have professed in the presence of his family.

CELEBRATION OF CONFIRMATION

INVITATION

The newly baptized with their godparents and, if they have not received the sacrament of confirmation, the newly received with their sponsors stand before the celebrant.

My dear candidates for confirmation, by your baptism you have been born again in Christ and you have become members of Christ and of his priestly people. Now you are to share in the outpouring of the Holy Spirit among us, the Spirit sent by the Lord upon his apostles at Pentecost and given by them and their successors to the baptized.

The promised strength of the Holy Spirit, which you are to receive, will make you more like Christ and help you to be witnesses to his suffering, death, and resurrection. It will strengthen you to be active members of the Church and to build up the Body of Christ in faith and love.

My dear friends, let us pray to God our Father, that he will pour out the Holy Spirit on these candidates for confirmation to strengthen them with his gifts and anoint them to be more like Christ, the Son of God.

LAYING ON OF HANDS

All-powerful God, Father of our Lord Jesus Christ, by water and the Holy Spirit you freed your sons and daughters from sin and gave them new life.

Send your Holy Spirit upon them to be their helper and guide.

Give them the spirit of wisdom and understanding, the spirit of right judgment and courage, the spirit of knowledge and reverence. Fill them with the spirit of wonder and awe in your presence.

We ask this through Christ our Lord. **Amen.**

ANOINTING WITH CHRISM

During the conferral of the sacrament an appropriate song may be sung.

The minister of the sacrament dips his right thumb in the chrism and makes the sign of the cross on the forehead of the candidate, saying:

N., be sealed with the Gift of the Holy Spirit. **Amen.**

Peace be with you. **And also with you.**

PRAYER OF THE FAITHFUL

The following intentions are suggestions only.

℟: **Lord, hear our prayer.**

For the Church, joyful witness to the resurrection of its Lord, we pray to the Lord: ℟.

For the peoples of the world, to whom Christ's resurrection offers the fullness of salvation, we pray to the Lord: ℟.

For those baptized this night into Christ's death and resurrection, called as Christ's body to witness to the Good News, we pray to the Lord: ℟.

For Christian communities everywhere, embodying the triumph of life over death, we pray to the Lord: ℟.

LITURGY OF THE EUCHARIST

PREPARATION OF THE GIFTS *(p. 13)*

PRAYER OVER THE GIFTS

Lord, accept the prayers and offerings of your people. With your help may this Easter mystery of our redemption bring to perfection the saving work you have begun in us.

PREFACE *(Easter I, p. 25)*

COMMUNION ANTIPHON *(1 Corinthians 5:7-8)*

Christ has become our paschal sacrifice; let us feast with the unleavened bread of sincerity and truth, alleluia.

PRAYER AFTER COMMUNION

Lord, you have nourished us with your Easter sacraments. Fill us with your Spirit, and make us one in peace and love.

SOLEMN BLESSING— Easter *(Optional)*

Bow your heads and pray for God's blessing.

May almighty God bless you on this solemn feast of Easter, and may he protect you against all sin. **Amen.**

Through the resurrection of his Son, God has granted us healing. May he fulfil his promises, and bless you with eternal life. **Amen.**

You have mourned for Christ's sufferings; now you celebrate the joy of his resurrection. May you come with joy to the feast which lasts for ever. **Amen.**

May almighty God bless you, the Father, and the Son, and the Holy Spirit. **Amen.**

DISMISSAL

Go in the peace of Christ, alleluia, alleluia!

or: The Mass is ended, go in peace, alleluia, alleluia!

or: Go in peace to love and serve the Lord, alleluia, alleluia!

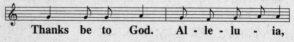
Thanks be to God. Al - le - lu - ia,

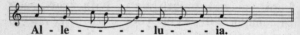
Al - le - - - - lu - - ia.

Thanks be to God, alleluia, alleluia!

Most of us can recall in vivid detail personal or public moments which overwhelmed us. I still shudder at the pain in my mother's voice waking me at 7:20 on a foggy morning five days after Christmas, "Dad won't wake up; I've called Father Doyle." On another occasion I remember the mixture of disbelief and delight at learning that the Berlin Wall was coming down. Significant moments etch their accompanying details in our memory, as though to insist they really happened.

Such details fill John's account of Jesus' resurrection. Mary Magdalene remembers going to the tomb early, it was still dark, and running back to tell Peter and the "other disciple" of the empty tomb. The "other disciple" remembers outrunning Peter to the empty tomb, then waiting for Peter to go in first. Simon Peter remembers seeing that the cloth which had been on Jesus' head was rolled up in a place separate from the other linen wrappings. Mary remembers recognizing Jesus when he called her by name, and announcing to the disciples, "I have seen the Lord."

These details preserve the overwhelming moments for Mary, Peter and the "other disciple" in their realization that Jesus has risen from the dead. Jesus' resurrection transforms the details of our lives into times and places where we, like Mary, can recognize Jesus calling us by name and announce that we "have seen the Lord."

—————— *John Thompson, Saskatoon, SK*

ENTRANCE ANTIPHON *(Psalm 139:18, 5-6)*

I have risen: I am with you once more; you placed your hand on me to keep me safe. How great is the depth of your wisdom, alleluia.

INTRODUCTORY RITES *(p. 5)*

OPENING PRAYER

God our Father, by raising Christ your Son you conquered the power of death and opened for us the way to eternal life. Let our celebration today raise us up and renew our lives by the Spirit that is within us.

FIRST READING *(Acts 10:34, 36-43)*

Peter began to speak to those assembled in the house of Cornelius. "You know the message God sent to the people of Israel, preaching peace by Jesus Christ—he is Lord of all. That message spread throughout Judea, beginning in Galilee after the baptism that John announced: how God anointed Jesus of Nazareth with the Holy Spirit and with power; how he went about doing good and healing all who were oppressed by the devil, for God was with him.

"We are witnesses to all that he did both in Judea and in Jerusalem. They put him to death by hanging him on a tree; but God raised him on the third day and allowed him to appear, not to all the people but to us who were chosen by God as witnesses, and who ate and drank with him after he rose from the dead.

"He commanded us to preach to the people and to testify that he is the one ordained by God as judge of the living and the dead. All the prophets testify about him that everyone who believes in him receives forgiveness of sins through his name."

The word of the Lord. **Thanks be to God.**

RESPONSORIAL PSALM *(Psalm 118)*

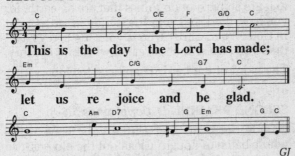

℞. **This is the day the Lord has made;
let us rejoice and be glad.**

O give thanks to the Lord, for he is • **good**;
his steadfast love endures • **for**-ever.
Let Israel say, "His steadfast love
        endures • **for**-ever." ℞.

"The right hand of the Lord is ex•-**alted**;
the right hand of the Lord • **does** valiantly."
I shall not die, but I shall live, and recount
        the deeds of • **the** Lord. ℞.

The stone that the builders rejected
        has become the chief • **cornerstone.**
This is the • **Lord's** doing;
it is marvellous in • **our** eyes. ℞.

An alternate reading follows.

SECOND READING *(Colossians 3:1-4)*

If you have been raised with Christ, seek the things that are above, where Christ is, seated at the right hand of God. Set your minds on things that are above, not on things that are on earth, for you have died, and your life is hidden with Christ in God. When Christ who is your life is revealed, then you also will be revealed with him in glory.

The word of the Lord. **Thanks be to God.**

or

SECOND READING *(1 Corinthians 5:6-8)*

Do you not know that a little yeast leavens the whole batch of dough? Clean out the old yeast so that you may be a new batch, as you really are unleavened. For our paschal lamb, Christ, has been sacrificed. Therefore, let us celebrate the festival, not with the old yeast, the yeast of malice and evil, but with the unleavened bread of sincerity and truth.

The word of the Lord. **Thanks be to God.**

EASTER SEQUENCE *(To be sung)*

1. O Christians on this first of days,
   The Paschal Victim let us praise;
   Our sacrifice of thanks we raise. Alleluia!

℞. **Alleluia, alleluia, alleluia!**

2. To save the sheep, the Lamb did die;
   The sinless Christ did reconcile
   All sinners to our God on high. Alleluia! ℞.

3. In mortal fray now death is slain;
   Life conquered death in brave campaign.
   The Lord of life o'er all does reign. Alleluia! ℞.

4. O Mary, tell the wondrous sight,
   What you did see in morning light.
   "The living Lord in glory bright. Alleluia! ℞.

5. To testify, the angels bright
   Stood at the tomb, all dressed in white,
   Only the grave cloth was in sight. Alleluia! ℞.

6. Christ is our hope, for all to see,
   To him who rose, all glory be:
   Christ is alive in Galilee. Alleluia! ℞.

7. Christ rose indeed: Good News we sing
   Of Jesus Christ, our Victor-King,
   O Lord of life, your mercy bring. Alleluia! ℞.

Text: VICTIMAE PASCHALI LAUDES
Trans: © 1993 John G. Hibbard
Tune: O FILII ET FILIAE 8.8.8.4. with Alleluias; VICTORY or VULPIUS,
8.8.8. with Alleluias. For music, see *CBW II* or *III*.

GOSPEL ACCLAMATION *(1 Corinthians 5:7-8)*

If not sung, this acclamation is omitted.

GJ

Christ has become our paschal • **sacrifice;**
let us feast • **with** joy
in • **the** Lord.

The gospel from the Easter Vigil (p. 310) may be read instead. For an afternoon or evening Mass, see p. 331.

GOSPEL *(John 20:1-18)*

The shorter version ends at the asterisks.

A reading from the holy gospel according to John.
Glory to you, Lord.

Early on the first day of the week, while it was still dark, Mary Magdalene came to the tomb and saw that the stone had been removed from the tomb. So she ran and went to Simon Peter and the other disciple, the one whom Jesus loved, and said to them, "They have taken the Lord out of the tomb, and we do not know where they have laid him."

Then Peter and the other disciple set out and went toward the tomb. The two were running together, but the other disciple outran Peter and reached the tomb first. He bent down to look in and saw the linen wrappings lying there, but he did not go in.

Then Simon Peter came, following him, and went into the tomb. He saw the linen wrappings lying there, and the cloth that had been on Jesus' head, not lying with the linen wrappings but rolled up in a place by itself. Then the other disciple, who reached the tomb first, also went in, and he saw and believed; for as yet they did not understand the scripture, that he must rise from the dead.

******

Then the disciples returned to their homes. But Mary Magdalene stood weeping outside the tomb. As she wept, she bent over to look into the tomb; and she saw two angels in white, sitting where the body of Jesus had been lying, one at the head and the other at the feet. They said to her, "Woman, why are you weeping?" She said to them, "They have taken away my Lord, and I do not know where they have laid him."

When she had said this, she turned around and saw Jesus standing there, but she did not know that it was Jesus. Jesus said to her, "Woman, why are you weeping? Whom are you looking for?" Supposing him to be the gardener, she said to him, "Sir, if you have carried him away, tell me where you have laid him, and I will take him away."

Jesus said to her, "Mary!" She turned and said to him in Hebrew, "Rabbouni!" which means Teacher. Jesus said to her, "Do not hold on to me, because I have not yet ascended to the Father. But go to my brothers and say to them, 'I am ascending to my Father and your Father, to my God and your God.' "

Mary Magdalene went and announced to the disciples, "I have seen the Lord," and she told them that he had said these things to her.

The gospel of the Lord. **Praise to you, Lord Jesus Christ.**

Alternative gospel for an afternoon or evening Mass:

GOSPEL *(Luke 24:13-35)*

A reading from the holy gospel according to Luke. **Glory to you, Lord.**

On the first day of the week, two of the disciples were going to a village called Emmaus, about

331

eleven kilometres from Jerusalem, and talking with each other about all these things that had happened. While they were talking and discussing, Jesus himself came near and went with them, but their eyes were kept from recognizing him.

And Jesus said to them, "What are you discussing with each other while you walk along?" They stood still, looking sad. Then one of them, whose name was Cleopas, answered him, "Are you the only stranger in Jerusalem who does not know the things that have taken place there in these days?"

Jesus asked them, "What things?" They replied, "The things about Jesus of Nazareth, who was a prophet mighty in deed and word before God and all the people, and how our chief priests and leaders handed him over to be condemned to death and crucified him. But we had hoped that he was the one to redeem Israel. Yes, and besides all this, it is now the third day since these things took place. Moreover, some women of our group astounded us. They were at the tomb early this morning, and when they did not find his body there, they came back and told us that they had indeed seen a vision of angels who said that Jesus was alive. Some of those who were with us went to the tomb and found it just as the women had said; but they did not see Jesus."

Then Jesus said to them, "Oh, how foolish you are, and how slow of heart to believe all that the prophets have declared! Was it not necessary that the Messiah should suffer these things and then enter into his glory?"

Then beginning with Moses and all the prophets, Jesus interpreted to them the things about himself in all the scriptures. As they came near the village to which they were going, Jesus walked ahead as if he were going on. But they urged him strongly, saying, "Stay with us, because it is almost evening and the day is now nearly over." So Jesus went in to stay with them.

When he was at the table with them, he took bread, blessed and broke it, and gave it to them. Then their eyes were opened, and they recognized Jesus; and he vanished from their sight.

The two disciples said to each other, "Were not our hearts burning within us while he was talking to us on the road, while he was opening the scriptures to us?"

That same hour they got up and returned to Jerusalem; and they found the eleven and their companions gathered together. These were saying, "The Lord has risen indeed, and he has appeared to Simon!"

Then the two disciples told what had happened on the road, and how the Lord had been made known to them in the breaking of the bread.

The gospel of the Lord. **Praise to you, Lord Jesus Christ.**

RENEWAL OF BAPTISMAL PROMISES *(p. 318)*

As at the Vigil, this rite replaces the Creed.

PRAYER OF THE FAITHFUL

The following intentions are suggestions only.

℟:   **Lord, hear our prayer.**

For the Church, witness to Jesus risen and present in the details of our lives, we pray to the Lord: ℟.

For peace among nations and peoples, for the innocent victims of conflict, we pray to the Lord: ℟.

For those among us who lack caring and compassion, and for those who reach out to us, we pray to the Lord: ℟.

For us, God's people gathered here, called to recognize and celebrate the presence of the risen Jesus, we pray to the Lord: ℟.

PREPARATION OF THE GIFTS *(p. 13)*

PRAYER OVER THE GIFTS

Lord, with Easter joy we offer you the sacrifice by which your Church is reborn and nourished through Christ our Lord.

PREFACE *(Easter I, p. 25)*

COMMUNION ANTIPHON *(1 Corinthians 5:7-8)*

Christ has become our paschal sacrifice; let us celebrate the feast with the unleavened bread of sincerity and truth, alleluia.

PRAYER AFTER COMMUNION

Father of love, watch over your Church and bring us to the glory of the resurrection promised by this Easter sacrament.

SOLEMN BLESSING AND DISMISSAL *(p. 324)*

After the resurrection, Jesus appeared to his frightened apostles and brought them the gift of peace. When Thomas returned he found them exuberant and yet he refused to believe; he wanted to touch and to feel. Eight days later the Lord gave him the opportunity. And Thomas believed!

Like the apostle Thomas, we too, if we are to go on believing, need to 'touch' the Lord. We touch him in our relations with others. The Lord touches others in our relations with them.

To paraphrase the late Thomas Merton, the need today is not so much to go out and preach Christ as it is to let him live in us in such a way that others may find him in us.

If others are going to find Christ in us, then we must relate to them the way Jesus himself related to people: with kindness, gentleness and understanding, with forgiveness, compassion and caring.

Let us never underestimate the cost of treating others as Jesus treated them. It often represents the cross that Jesus told us we must pick up daily.

Thomas believed in the risen Lord after he had touched him. How many will believe in him because they touch him in us?

Iris Kendall, St. John's, NF

ENTRANCE ANTIPHON *(1 Peter 2:2)*

Like newborn children you should thirst for milk, on which your spirit can grow to strength, alleluia.

or

Rejoice to the full in the glory that is yours, and give thanks to God who called you to his kingdom, alleluia.

INTRODUCTORY RITES *(p. 5)*

OPENING PRAYER

God of mercy, you wash away our sins in water, you give us new birth in the Spirit, and redeem us in the blood of Christ. As we celebrate Christ's resurrection increase our awareness of these blessings, and renew your gift of life within us.

FIRST READING *(Acts 5:12-16)*

Many signs and wonders were done among the people through the apostles. And the believers were all together in Solomon's Portico. None of the rest dared to join them, but the people held them in high esteem.

Yet more than ever believers were added to the Lord, great numbers of both men and women, so that they even carried out the sick into the streets, and laid them on cots and mats, in order that Peter's shadow might fall on some of them as he came by.

A great number of people would also gather from the towns around Jerusalem, bringing the sick and those tormented by unclean spirits, and they were all cured.

The word of the Lord. **Thanks be to God.**

RESPONSORIAL PSALM *(Psalm 118)*

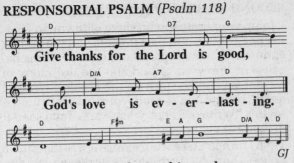

Give thanks for the Lord is good,

God's love is ev - er - last - ing.

GJ

℟. Give thanks, for the Lord is good,
God's love is everlasting.

Let Israel say,
"His steadfast love endures • **for**-ever."
Let the house of Aaron say,
"His steadfast love endures • **for**-ever."
Let those who fear the Lord say,
"His steadfast • **love_en**-dures for-ever." ℟.

The stone that the builders rejected
has become the • **chief** cornerstone.
This is the Lord's doing;
it is marvellous in • **our** eyes.
This is the day that the Lord has made;
let us re•-**joice_and_be** glad in it. ℟.

Save us, we beseech you, O Lord!
O Lord, we beseech you, give us • **suc**-cess!
Blessed is the one who comes in the name
of • **the** Lord.
We bless you from the house of the Lord. The
Lord is God, and • **he_has** given us light. ℟.

SECOND READING *(Rev 1:9-11, 12-13, 17-19)*

I, John, your brother who share with you in Jesus the persecution and the kingdom and the patient endurance, was on the island called Patmos because of the word of God and the testimony of Jesus. I was in the spirit on the Lord's day, and I heard behind me a loud voice like a trumpet saying, "Write in a book what you see and send it to the seven churches."

Then I turned to see whose voice it was that spoke to me, and on turning I saw seven golden lampstands, and in the midst of the lampstands I saw one like the Son of Man, clothed with a long robe and with a golden sash across his chest.

When I saw him, I fell at his feet as though dead. But he placed his right hand on me, saying, "Do not be afraid; I am the first and the last, and the living one. I was dead, but now, I am alive forever and ever; and I have the keys of Death and of Hades. Now write what you have seen, what is, and what is to take place after this."

The word of the Lord. **Thanks be to God.**

GOSPEL ACCLAMATION *(See John 20:29)*

If not sung, this acclamation is omitted.

You believed in me, Thomas, because you have seen me; happy those who have not seen me, but still believe!

GOSPEL *(John 20:19-31)*

A reading from the holy gospel according to John. **Glory to you, Lord.**

It was evening on the day Jesus rose from the dead, the first day of the week, and the doors of

338

he house where the disciples had met were ocked for fear of the authorities. Jesus came and tood among them and said, "Peace be with you." After he said this, he showed them his hands and his side. Then the disciples rejoiced when they saw the Lord. Jesus said to them again, "Peace be with you. As the Father has sent me, so I send you."

When he had said this, he breathed on them and said to them, "Receive the Holy Spirit. If you forgive the sins of any, they are forgiven them; if you retain the sins of any, they are retained."

But Thomas, who was called the Twin, one of the twelve, was not with them when Jesus came. So the other disciples told him, "We have seen the Lord." But he said to them, "Unless I see the mark of the nails in his hands, and put my finger in the mark of the nails and my hand in his side, I will not believe."

A week later his disciples were again in the house, and Thomas was with them. Although the doors were shut, Jesus came and stood among them and said, "Peace be with you." Then he said to Thomas, "Put your finger here and see my hands. Reach out your hand and put it in my side. Do not doubt but believe." Thomas answered him, "My Lord and my God!"

Jesus said to him, "Have you believed because you have seen me? Blessed are those who have not seen and yet have come to believe."

Now Jesus did many other signs in the presence of his disciples, which are not written in this book. But these are written so that you may come to believe that Jesus is the Messiah, the Son of God and that through believing you may have life in his name.

The gospel of the Lord. **Praise to you, Lord Jesus Christ.**

PROFESSION OF FAITH *(Creed, pp. 11-12)*

PRAYER OF THE FAITHFUL

The following intentions are suggestions only.

℞: **Lord, hear our prayer.**

For the Church throughout the world, witness to God's kingdom in daily life, we pray to the Lord: ℞.

For elected officials and leaders of nations, to whom their peoples look for justice, we pray to the Lord: ℞.

For those who are hungry, lonely, abused, sick and dying, especially those who are abandoned or destitute, we pray to the Lord: ℞.

For us, God's people gathered here, fed from your table and called to feed all God's children, we pray to the Lord: ℞.

PREPARATION OF THE GIFTS *(p. 13)*

PRAYER OVER THE GIFTS

Lord, through faith and baptism we have become a new creation. Accept the offerings of your people (and of those born again in baptism) and bring us to eternal happiness.

PREFACE *(Easter I, p. 25)*

COMMUNION ANTIPHON *(See John 20:27)*

Jesus spoke to Thomas: Put your hand here, and see the place of the nails. Doubt no longer, but believe, alleluia.

PRAYER AFTER COMMUNION

Almighty God, may the Easter sacraments we have received live for ever in our minds and hearts.

SOLEMN BLESSING—Easter Season *(Optional)*

Bow your heads and pray for God's blessing.

Through the resurrection of his Son God has redeemed you and made you his children. May he bless you with joy. **Amen.**

The Redeemer has given you lasting freedom. May you inherit his everlasting life. **Amen.**

By faith you rose with him in baptism. May your lives be holy, so that you will be united with him for ever. **Amen.**

May almighty God bless you, the Father, and the Son, and the Holy Spirit. **Amen.**

DISMISSAL *(p. 324)*

Just over two weeks ago, remember. It was early in the morning. Jesus was under arrest. Most of the apostles were hiding. Peter, when confronted, denied him. Today Peter is called again. Jesus says, "Feed my sheep" and "Follow me."

We have denied him also. We have turned our backs on him for less reason than Peter—after all he feared arrest. Still, like Peter, we are called over and over again.

Sometimes our calls are clear. I remember a priest visiting my high school thirty years ago. The late Father John Brayley called us to really live our faith and by doing so transform our world. He pushed us for commitment. Pointing to the door Father John challenged us, "If Jesus were to walk through that door right now and say 'Come follow me' would you?" Only a few heard and joined his Project Christopher.

Most often our calls come amidst the crush of many everyday voices and demands. Maybe today it will be to make more time for your family or to grasp the hand reaching out for yours.

Small steps or large ones, we are all on a journey. Peter said yes to his call and over the next thirty years he served the first Christian communities from Antioch to Rome. He was given the strength to answer his call. So are we.

Michael Dougherty, Whitehorse, YT

ENTRANCE ANTIPHON *(Psalm 66:1-2)*

Let all the earth cry out to God with joy; praise the glory of his name; proclaim his glorious praise, alleluia.

INTRODUCTORY RITES *(p. 5)*

OPENING PRAYER

God our Father, may we look forward with hope to our resurrection, for you have made us your sons and daughters, and restored the joy of our youth.

FIRST READING *(Acts 5:27-32, 40-41)*

The captain went with the temple police and brought the apostles, who were teaching in the temple, and had them stand before the council. The high priest questioned the apostles, saying, 'We gave you strict orders not to teach in this name, yet here you have filled Jerusalem with your teaching and you are determined to bring this man's blood on us."

But Peter and the apostles answered, "We must obey God rather than any human authority. The God of our ancestors raised up Jesus, whom you had killed by hanging him on a tree. God exalted him at his right hand as Leader and Saviour that he might give repentance to Israel and forgiveness of sins. And we are witnesses to these things, and so is the Holy Spirit whom God has given to those who obey him."

Then the council ordered the apostles not to speak in the name of Jesus, and let them go. As they left the council, they rejoiced that they were

considered worthy to suffer dishonour for th
sake of the name.

The word of the Lord. **Thanks be to God.**

RESPONSORIAL PSALM *(Psalm 30)*

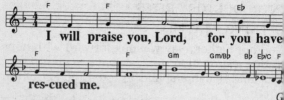

I will praise you, Lord,   for you have

res-cued me.

℞. **I will praise you, Lord,**
for you have rescued me.

I will extol you, O Lord,
    for you have drawn me • **up,**
and did not let my foes rejoice over • **me.**
O Lord, you brought up my soul from • **Sheol**
restored me to life from among those
    gone down to • **the** Pit. ℞.

Sing praises to the Lord,
    O you his • **faithful_ones,**
and give thanks to his holy • **name.**
For his anger is but for a moment;
    his favour is for a • **lifetime.**
Weeping may linger for the night,
    but joy comes with • **the** morning. ℞.

Hear, O Lord, and be gracious to • **me!**
O Lord, be my • **helper!**
You have turned my mourning into • **dancing.**
O Lord my God, I will give thanks
    to you • **for-ever.** ℞.

SECOND READING *(Revelation 5:11-14)*

I, John, looked, and I heard the voice of many angels surrounding the throne and the living creatures and the elders; they numbered myriads of myriads and thousands of thousands, singing with full voice, "Worthy is the Lamb that was slaughtered to receive power and wealth and wisdom and might and honour and glory and blessing!"

Then I heard every creature in heaven and on earth and under the earth and in the sea, and all that is in them, singing, "To the one seated on the throne and to the Lamb be blessing and honour and glory and might forever and ever!" And the four living creatures said, "Amen!" And the elders fell down and worshipped.

The word of the Lord. **Thanks be to God.**

GOSPEL ACCLAMATION

If not sung, this acclamation is omitted.

Christ is risen, the Lord of all creation; he has shown pity on all people.

GOSPEL *(John 21:1-19)*

A reading from the holy gospel according to John. **Glory to you, Lord.**

Jesus showed himself again to the disciples by the Sea of Tiberias; and he showed himself in this way. Gathered there together were Simon Peter, Thomas called the Twin, Nathanael of Cana in Galilee, the sons of Zebedee, and two others of his disciples. Simon Peter said to them, "I am going fishing." They said to him, "We will go with you."

They went out and got into the boat, but that nigh they caught nothing.

Just after daybreak, Jesus stood on the beach; bu the disciples did not know that it was Jesus. Jesu said to them, "Children, you have no fish, hav you?" They answered him, "No." He said to them "Cast the net to the right side of the boat, and yo will find some." So they cast it, and now the were not able to haul it in because there were s many fish.

That disciple whom Jesus loved said to Peter, " is the Lord!" When Simon Peter heard that it wa the Lord, he put on some clothes, for he wa naked, and jumped into the sea. But the othe disciples came in the boat, dragging the net full c fish, for they were not far from the land, onl about ninety metres off.

When they had gone ashore, they saw a charcoa fire there, with fish on it, and bread. Jesus said t them, "Bring some of the fish that you have jus caught." So Simon Peter went aboard and haule the net ashore, full of large fish, a hundred fifty three of them; and though there were so many, th net was not torn. Jesus said to them, "Come an have breakfast." Now none of the disciples dare to ask him, "Who are you?" because they knew i was the Lord. Jesus came and took the bread an gave it to them, and did the same with the fish This was now the third time that Jesus appeare to the disciples after he was raised from the dead

When they had finished breakfast, Jesus said t Simon Peter, "Simon son of John, do you love m more than these?" He said to him, "Yes, Lord; you know that I love you." Jesus said to him, "Feed my lambs."

A second time he said to him, "Simon son of John, do you love me?" He said to him, "Yes, Lord; you know that I love you." Jesus said to him, "Tend my sheep."

He said to him the third time, "Simon son of John, do you love me?" Peter felt hurt because he said to him the third time, "Do you love me?" And he said to him, "Lord, you know everything; you know that I love you." Jesus said to him, "Feed my sheep. Very truly, I tell you, when you were younger, you used to fasten your own belt and go wherever you wished. But when you grow old, you will stretch out your hands, and someone else will fasten a belt around you and take you where you do not wish to go."

He said this to indicate the kind of death by which he would glorify God. After this he said to him, "Follow me."

The gospel of the Lord. **Praise to you, Lord Jesus Christ.**

PROFESSION OF FAITH *(Creed, pp. 11-12)*

PRAYER OF THE FAITHFUL

The following intentions are suggestions only.

℟: **Lord, hear our prayer.**

For the Church, sacrament of Christ in the midst of the world's struggles, we pray to the Lord: ℟.

For an end to ethnic and religious hatreds, and for the birth of understanding and peace among nations and peoples, we pray to the Lord: ℞.

For those among us who are poor, lonely, sick and dying, we pray to the Lord: ℞.

For us, God's holy people, embracing those nearing the end of life's journey, and supporting young people as they discover their life's direction, we pray to the Lord: ℞.

PREPARATION OF THE GIFTS *(p. 13)*

PRAYER OVER THE GIFTS

Lord, receive these gifts from your Church. May the great joy you give us come to perfection in heaven.

PREFACE *(Easter II-V, p. 26)*

COMMUNION ANTIPHON *(See John 21:12-13)*

Jesus said to his disciples: Come and eat. And he took the bread, and gave it to them, alleluia.

PRAYER AFTER COMMUNION

Lord, look on your people with kindness and by these Easter mysteries bring us to the glory of the resurrection.

SOLEMN BLESSING *(p. 341)*

DISMISSAL *(p. 65)*

World Day of Prayer for Vocations

Images of sheep in today's readings may evoke a ripple of nostalgia for the religion of our childhood. At first glance, the gospel seems to be something of a 'warm fuzzy': Jesus' words sound comforting, consoling, reassuring.

On the other hand, to be referred to as "sheep" has a pejorative ring to our ears. In a society which emphasizes individual effort, independence and self-reliance, to be called "sheep" suggests unthinking conformity and indecisiveness. In this sense the image jars with our modern concept of self.

Jesus' pledge of unfailing care for the sheep does not release us from personal and communal responsibility. On the contrary, to get some idea of the challenges presented to the sheep we need only look at Paul and Barnabas. Preaching in Antioch, they are persecuted and driven out by the jealous authorities. Not only do they respond courageously and with renewed determination, but they are "filled with joy and with the Holy Spirit." No passive sheep, these disciples!

Today as we pray for vocations, let us consider our own vocation of discipleship. Trusting in the care of the Lamb who is himself the Shepherd, may we respond courageously and with joy to his call.

Krystyna Higgins, Kitchener, ON

ENTRANCE ANTIPHON *(Psalm 33:5-6)*

The earth is full of the goodness of the Lord; by the word of the Lord the heavens were made, alleluia.

INTRODUCTORY RITES *(p. 5)*

OPENING PRAYER

Almighty and ever-living God, give us new strength from the courage of Christ our shepherd, and lead us to join the saints in heaven.

FIRST READING *(Acts 13:14, 43-52)*

Paul and Barnabas went on from Perga and came to Antioch in Pisidia. On the sabbath day they went into the synagogue and sat down.

When the meeting of the synagogue broke up, many Jews and devout converts to Judaism followed Paul and Barnabas, who spoke to them and urged them to continue in the grace of God.

The next sabbath almost the whole city gathered to hear the word of the Lord. But when the Jewish officials saw the crowds, they were filled with jealousy; and blaspheming, they contradicted what was spoken by Paul.

Then both Paul and Barnabas spoke out boldly, saying, "It was necessary that the word of God should be spoken first to you. Since you reject it and judge yourselves to be unworthy of eternal life, we are now turning to the Gentiles. For so the Lord has commanded us, saying, 'I have set you to be a light for the Gentiles, so that you may bring salvation to the ends of the earth.' " When the Gentiles heard this, they were glad and praised the word of the Lord; and as many as had been destined for eternal life became believers.

Thus the word of the Lord spread throughout the region. But the officials incited the devout women of high standing and the leading men of the city, and stirred up persecution against Paul and Barnabas, and drove them out of their region. So they shook the dust off their feet in protest against them, and went to Iconium. And the disciples were filled with joy and with the Holy Spirit.

The word of the Lord. **Thanks be to God.**

RESPONSORIAL PSALM *(Psalm 100)*

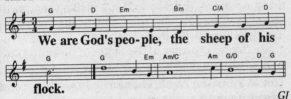

We are God's peo-ple, the sheep of his flock.

GJ

℟. **We are God's people, the sheep of his flock.**

Make a joyful noise to the Lord, all • **the** earth.
Worship the Lord with • **gladness;**
come into his presence • **with** singing. ℟.

Know that the Lord • **is** God.
It is he that made us, and we are • **his;**
we are his people, and the sheep
of • **his** pasture. ℟.

For the Lord • **is** good;
his steadfast love endures for•-**ever,**
and his faithfulness to all • **gener**-ations. ℟.

SECOND READING *(Revelation 7:9, 14-17)*

After this I, John, looked, and there was a great multitude that no one could count, from every nation, from all tribes and peoples and languages, standing before the throne and before the Lamb, robed in white, with palm branches in their hands.

And one of the elders then said to me, "These are they who have come out of the great ordeal; they have washed their robes and made them white in the blood of the Lamb.

"For this reason they are before the throne of God, and worship him day and night within his temple, and the one who is seated on the throne will shelter them. They will hunger no more, and thirst no more; the sun will not strike them, nor any scorching heat; for the Lamb at the centre of the throne will be their shepherd, and he will guide them to springs of the water of life, and God will wipe away every tear from their eyes."

The word of the Lord. **Thanks be to God.**

GOSPEL ACCLAMATION *(John 10:14)*

If not sung, this acclamation is omitted.

I am the good shepherd, says the Lord; I know my sheep, and mine know me.

GOSPEL *(John 10:27-30)*

A reading from the holy gospel according to John. **Glory to you, Lord.**

Jesus said: "My sheep hear my voice. I know them, and they follow me. I give them eternal life, and they will never perish. No one will snatch them out of my hand. What my Father has given me is greater than all else, and no one can snatch it out of the Father's hand. The Father and I are one."

The gospel of the Lord. **Praise to you, Lord Jesus Christ.**

PROFESSION OF FAITH *(Creed, pp. 11-12)*

PRAYER OF THE FAITHFUL

The following intentions are suggestions only.

℞: **Lord, hear our prayer.**

For all who hold positions of authority in the Church, called to model their leadership on that of the Good Shepherd, we pray to the Lord: ℞.

For political leaders whose influence bears fruit in justice for all, we pray to the Lord: ℞.

For those among us struggling to resist peer pressure, we pray to the Lord: ℞.

For us, God's holy people, striving to live out the challenges of our vocations in courage and joy, we pray to the Lord: ℞.

PREPARATION OF THE GIFTS *(p. 13)*

PRAYER OVER THE GIFTS

Lord, restore us by these Easter mysteries. May the continuing work of our redeemer bring us eternal joy.

PREFACE *(Easter II-V, p. 26)*

COMMUNION ANTIPHON

The Good Shepherd is risen! He who laid down his life for his sheep, who died for his flock, he is risen, alleluia.

PRAYER AFTER COMMUNION

Father, eternal shepherd, watch over the flock redeemed by the blood of Christ and lead us to the promised land.

SOLEMN BLESSING *(p. 341)*

DISMISSAL *(p. 65)*

Jesus gives his disciples a new commandment. The newness is not that they are to love one another; rather, it is that they are to love one another *just as Christ loved them*. This command comes the day before the disciples experience the dreadful loss of their teacher. Jesus' physical presence must be replaced by the concrete love that the disciples have for each other. Thus, Jesus' glory will be made manifest to the world.

The building up of Christian communities in Acts reveals another manifestation of God's glory among us despite huge obstacles of persecution. God opened a door of faith for the Gentiles, and the love and encouragement they received from Paul and Barnabas strengthened their hearts to remain firm in the faith.

This is the tremendous tension within which Christians of all times live: the tension between the past (Jesus on earth) and the future (the new Jerusalem). Paradoxically, within this very tension, the glory of God is shown because love is revealed in Christ's love for "his own who were in the world" and in the love that the disciples have for one another. That Christ had "to depart from this world" was difficult for the disciples to understand and accept. That they love one another just as Christ loved them is the response which opens the way to a new heaven and a new earth.

—— *Christine Jamieson, Ottawa, ON*

ENTRANCE ANTIPHON *(Psalm 98:1-2)*

Sing to the Lord a new song, for he has done marvellous deeds; he has revealed to the nations his saving power, alleluia.

INTRODUCTORY RITES *(p. 5)*

OPENING PRAYER

God our Father, look upon us with love. You redeem us and make us your children in Christ. Give us true freedom and bring us to the inheritance you promised.

FIRST READING *(Acts 14:21-27)*

Paul and Barnabas returned to Lystra, then on to Iconium and Antioch. There they strengthened the souls of the disciples and encouraged them to continue in the faith, saying, "It is through many persecutions that we must enter the kingdom of God." And after they had appointed elders for them in each church, with prayer and fasting they entrusted them to the Lord in whom they had come to believe.

Then they passed through Pisidia and came to Pamphylia. When they had spoken the word in Perga, they went down to Attalia. From there they sailed back to Antioch, where they had been commended to the grace of God for the work that they had completed.

When they arrived, they called the church together and related all that God had done with them, and how he had opened a door of faith for the Gentiles.

The word of the Lord. **Thanks be to God.**

RESPONSORIAL PSALM *(Psalm 145)*

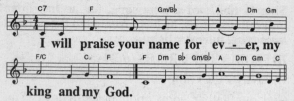

I will praise your name for ev—er, my

king and my God.

GJ

℞. **I will praise your name for ever,**
my king and my God.

The Lord is gracious and • **merciful,**
slow to anger and abounding in steadfast • **love.**
The Lord is good to • **all,**
and his compassion is over all
    that he • **has** made. ℞.

All your works shall give thanks to you,
    O • **Lord,**
and all your faithful shall • **bless you.**
They shall speak of the glory
    of your • **kingdom,**
and tell of • **your** power. ℞.

To make known to all people
    your mighty • **deeds,**
and the glorious splendour of your • **kingdom.**
Your kingdom is an everlasting • **kingdom,**
and your dominion endures
    throughout all • **gener-**ations. ℞.

SECOND READING *(Revelation 21:1-5)*

Then I, John, saw a new heaven and a new earth; for the first heaven and the first earth had passed away, and the sea was no more.

And I saw the holy city, the new Jerusalem, coming down out of heaven from God, prepared as a bride adorned for her husband.

And I heard a loud voice from the throne saying, "See, the home of God is among mortals. He will dwell with them as their God; they will be his peoples, and God himself will be with them; he will wipe every tear from their eyes. Death will be no more; mourning and crying and pain will be no more, for the first things have passed away." And the one who was seated on the throne said, "See, I am making all things new."

The word of the Lord. **Thanks be to God.**

GOSPEL ACCLAMATION *(See John 13:34)*

If not sung, this acclamation is omitted.

I give you a new commandment: love one another as I have loved you.

GOSPEL *(John 13:1, 31-35)*

A reading from the holy gospel according to John. **Glory to you, Lord.**

Before the festival of the Passover, Jesus knew that his hour had come to depart from this world and go to the Father. Having loved his own who were in the world, he loved them to the end.

During the supper, when Judas had gone out, Jesus said, "Now the Son of Man has been glorified, and God has been glorified in him. If God has been glorified in him, God will also glorify him in himself and will glorify him at once.

"Little children, I am with you only a little longer. I give you a new commandment, that you love one another. Just as I have loved you, you also should love one another. By this everyone will know that you are my disciples, if you have love for one another."

The gospel of the Lord. **Praise to you, Lord Jesus Christ.**

PROFESSION OF FAITH *(Creed, pp. 11-12)*

PRAYER OF THE FAITHFUL

The following intentions are suggestions only.

℞: **Lord, hear our prayer.**

For the Church, community of brothers and sisters, called to firm faith and enduring love, we pray to the Lord: ℞.

For the abolition of persecution among nations and between peoples, we pray to the Lord: ℞.

For those among us who are lonely and seeking God's consolation, we pray to the Lord: ℞.

For mothers in our community and everywhere, signs of God's love for his children, we pray to the Lord: ℞.

For us, God's people, called to manifest our discipleship by the love we have for one another, we pray to the Lord: ℞.

PREPARATION OF THE GIFTS *(p. 13)*

PRAYER OVER THE GIFTS

Lord God, by this holy exchange of gifts you share with us your divine life. Grant that everything we do may be directed by the knowledge of your truth.

PREFACE *(Easter II-V, p. 26)*

COMMUNION ANTIPHON *(John 15:1, 5)*

I am the vine and you are the branches, says the Lord; he who lives in me, and I in him, will bear much fruit, alleluia.

PRAYER AFTER COMMUNION

Merciful Father, may these mysteries give us new purpose and bring us to a new life in you.

SOLEMN BLESSING *(p. 341)*

DISMISSAL *(p. 65)*

Pope's Pastoral Works

Today's gospel message was addressed to the apostles shortly before Jesus was arrested and condemned to death. It is as filled with promise and meaning today as it was two thousand years ago.

Jesus reminds us that he and his Father will dwell in the hearts of all who love him and are true to his word. If we truly live our faith, we become a sanctuary wherein the Lord resides. An awesome thought!

Jesus says, "My peace I give to you." These are liberating words, for we live in a world torn by political strife, in which poverty, hunger and disease run rampant. But Jesus does not promise everyday living which is free from turmoil. He offers the gift of inner peace and serenity which allow us to carry on, no matter what.

"Do not be afraid," Jesus counsels. How often our words and actions are governed by fear! The fear of ridicule, the fear of being 'put down,' the fear of rejection—all of these rear up when our values conflict with those of the world. Jesus liberates us from every fear.

Let us live in faith and love, open to the words of the Spirit, in the freedom of God's children.

Barbara K. d'Artois, Pierrefonds, QC

ENTRANCE ANTIPHON *(See Isaiah 48:20)*

Speak out with a voice of joy; let it be heard to the ends of the earth: The Lord has set his people free, alleluia.

INTRODUCTORY RITES *(p. 5)*

OPENING PRAYER

Ever-living God, help us to celebrate our joy in the resurrection of the Lord and to express in our lives the love we celebrate.

FIRST READING *(Acts 15:1-2, 22-29)*

Certain individuals came down from Judea and were teaching the brothers, "Unless you are circumcised according to the custom of Moses, you cannot be saved." And after Paul and Barnabas had no small dissension and debate with them, Paul and Barnabas and some of the others were appointed to go up to Jerusalem to discuss this question with the apostles and the elders.

Then the apostles and the elders, with the consent of the whole church, decided to choose men from among their members and to send them to Antioch with Paul and Barnabas.

They sent Judas called Barsabbas, and Silas, leaders among the brothers, with the following letter:

"The brothers, both the apostles and the elders, to the believers of Gentile origin in Antioch and Syria and Cilicia, greetings. Since we have heard that certain persons who have gone out from us, though with no instructions from us, have said things to disturb you and have unsettled your minds, we have decided unanimously to choose representatives and send them to you, along with our beloved Barnabas and Paul, who have risked their lives for the sake of our Lord Jesus Christ. We have therefore sent Judas and Silas, who themselves will tell you the same things by word of mouth.

"For it has seemed good to the Holy Spirit and to us to impose on you no further burden than these essentials: that you abstain from what has been sacrificed to idols, and from blood and from what is strangled, and from fornication. If you keep yourselves from these, you will do well. Farewell."

The word of the Lord. **Thanks be to God.**

RESPONSORIAL PSALM *(Psalm 67)*

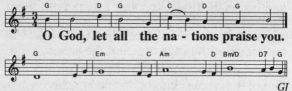

O God, let all the na - tions praise you.

GJ

℟. **O God, let all the nations praise you!**

May God be gracious to us • **and** bless_us
and make his face to shine • **up**-on_us,
that your way may be known up•**-on** earth,
your saving power a•**-mong** all nations. ℟.

Let the nations be glad and sing • **for** joy,
for you judge the peoples with equity
    and guide the nations up•**-on** earth.
Let the peoples praise you, • **O** God;
let all the • **peo**-ples praise_you. ℟.

The earth has yielded • **its** increase;
God, our God, • **has** blessed_us.
May God continue • **to** bless_us;
let all the ends of the • **earth** re-vere_him. ℟.

SECOND READING *(Revelation 21:10-14, 22-23)*

In the spirit the angel carried me away to a great, high mountain and showed me the holy city Jerusalem coming down out of heaven from God. It has the glory of God and a radiance like a very rare jewel, like jasper, clear as crystal.

It has a great, high wall with twelve gates, and at the gates twelve angels, and on the gates are inscribed the names of the twelve tribes of the Israelites; on the east there were three gates, on the north three gates, on the south three gates, and on the west three gates. And the wall of the city has twelve foundations, and on them are the twelve names of the twelve apostles of the Lamb.

I saw no temple in the city, for its temple is the Lord God the Almighty and the Lamb. And the city has no need of sun or moon to shine on it, for the glory of God is its light, and its lamp is the Lamb.

The word of the Lord. **Thanks be to God.**

GOSPEL ACCLAMATION *(John 14:23)*

If not sung, this acclamation is omitted.

All who love me will keep my words, and my Father will love them, and we will come to them.

GOSPEL *(John 14:23-29)*

A reading from the holy gospel according to John. **Glory to you, Lord.**

Jesus said to his disciples: "Those who love me will keep my word, and my Father will love them, and we will come to them and make our home with them. Whoever does not love me does not keep my words; and the word that you hear is not mine, but is from the Father who sent me.

"I have said these things to you while I am still with you. But the Advocate, the Holy Spirit, whom the Father will send in my name, will teach you everything, and remind you of all that I have said to you.

"Peace I leave with you; my peace I give to you. I do not give to you as the world gives. Do not let your hearts be troubled, and do not let them be afraid.

"You heard me say to you, 'I am going away, and I am coming to you.' If you loved me, you would rejoice that I am going to the Father, because the Father is greater than I. And now I have told you this before it occurs, so that when it does occur, you may believe."

The gospel of the Lord. **Praise to you, Lord Jesus Christ.**

PROFESSION OF FAITH *(Creed, pp. 11-12)*

PRAYER OF THE FAITHFUL

The following intentions are suggestions only.

℟: **Lord, hear our prayer.**

For the Church, living temple of God's word, we pray to the Lord: ℟.

For those who strive to make peace and justice part of life in all nations, we pray to the Lord: ℞.

For those who do not recognize their worth as precious creatures fashioned in God's image, we pray to the Lord: ℞.

For us, the Body of Christ, as we minister to the sick, the lonely and those in any kind of need, we pray to the Lord: ℞.

PREPARATION OF THE GIFTS *(p. 13)*

PRAYER OVER THE GIFTS

Lord, accept our prayers and offerings. Make us worthy of your sacraments of love by granting us your forgiveness.

PREFACE *(Easter II-V, p. 26)*

COMMUNION ANTIPHON *(John 14:15-16)*

If you love me, keep my commandments, says the Lord. The Father will send you the Holy Spirit, to be with you for ever, alleluia.

PRAYER AFTER COMMUNION

Almighty and ever-living Lord, you restored us to life by raising Christ from death. Strengthen us by this Easter sacrament; may we feel its saving power in our daily life.

SOLEMN BLESSING *(p. 341)*

DISMISSAL *(p. 65)*

Helen will never be forgotten by the many men and women she taught during her nearly forty years in the classroom. As one former student stated, "she opened our minds and taught us not only by her words but also by her actions."

In addition to her school and family activities, Helen was a tireless parish worker and community leader. She was also a friend to anyone who was sick or in trouble.

On the day of her funeral, the country church was filled with family, friends and former students who had come to bid farewell to a dedicated teacher. In spite of the deep sense of loss, there was a celebration for a woman who had devoted her entire life to the service of others and who was now in heaven.

In today's gospel, we see another group of friends and students who have assembled to say goodbye to a great teacher, Jesus. After the Ascension, Jesus' followers rejoiced in the temple every day and carried out his words.

As followers of Jesus we are called to be disciples, like Helen, and by our words and actions to carry the good news of God's kingdom to our world today. We know that Jesus sent the Holy Spirit to empower and guide us in this mission.

Jim McSheffrey, St. John's, NF

ENTRANCE ANTIPHON *(Acts 1:11)*

Men of Galilee, why do you stand looking into the sky? The Lord will return, just as you have seen him ascend, alleluia.

INTRODUCTORY RITES *(p. 5)*

OPENING PRAYER

God our Father, make us joyful in the ascension of your Son Jesus Christ. May we follow him into the new creation, for his ascension is our glory and our hope.

FIRST READING *(Acts 1:1-11)*

In the first book, Theophilus, I wrote about all that Jesus did and taught from the beginning until the day when he was taken up to heaven, after giving instructions through the Holy Spirit to the apostles whom he had chosen. After his suffering he presented himself alive to them by many convincing proofs, appearing to them during forty days and speaking about the kingdom of God.

While staying with them, he ordered them not to leave Jerusalem, but to wait there for the promise of the Father. "This," he said, "is what you have heard from me; for John baptized with water, but you will be baptized with the Holy Spirit not many days from now."

So when they had come together, they asked him, "Lord, is this the time when you will restore the kingdom to Israel?" He replied, "It is not for you to know the times or periods that the Father has set by his own authority. But you will receive power when the Holy Spirit has come upon you;

and you will be my witnesses in Jerusalem, in all Judea and Samaria, and to the ends of the earth."

When he had said this, as they were watching, he was lifted up, and a cloud took him out of their sight. While he was going and they were gazing up toward heaven, suddenly two men in white robes stood by them. They said, "Men of Galilee, why do you stand looking up toward heaven? This Jesus, who has been taken up from you into heaven, will come in the same way as you saw him go into heaven."

The word of the Lord. **Thanks be to God.**

RESPONSORIAL PSALM *(Psalm 47)*

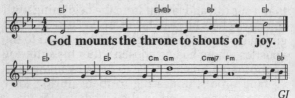

God mounts the throne to shouts of joy.

GJ

℟. **God mounts the throne to shouts of joy: a blare of trumpets for the Lord.**

Clap your hands, all • **you** peoples;
shout to God with loud songs • **of** joy.
For the Lord, the Most High, • **is** awesome,
a great king over • **all** the earth. ℟.

God has gone up with • **a** shout,
the Lord with the sound of • **a** trumpet.
Sing praises to God, • **sing** praises;
sing praises to our • **King,** sing praises. ℟.

For God is the king of all • **the** earth;
sing praises with • **a** psalm.
God is king over • **the** nations;
God sits on his • **ho**-ly throne. ℟.

SECOND READING *(Hebrews 9:24-28; 10:19-23)*

Christ did not enter a sanctuary made by human hands, a mere copy of the true one, but he entered into heaven itself, to appear in the presence of God on our behalf. Nor was it to offer himself again and again, as the high priest enters the Holy Place year after year with blood that is not his own; for then he would have had to suffer again and again since the foundation of the world. But as it is, he has appeared once for all at the end of the age to remove sin by the sacrifice of himself.

Just as it is appointed for mortals to die once, and after that comes the judgment, so Christ, having been offered once to bear the sins of many, will appear a second time, not to deal with sin, but to save those who are eagerly waiting for him.

Therefore, my friends, since we have confidence to enter the sanctuary by the blood of Jesus, by the new and living way that he opened for us through the curtain, that is, through his flesh, and since we have a great priest over the house of God, let us approach with a true heart in full assurance of faith, with our hearts sprinkled clean from an evil conscience and our bodies washed with pure water. Let us hold fast to the confession of our hope without wavering, for he who has promised is faithful.

The word of the Lord. **Thanks be to God.**

GOSPEL ACCLAMATION *(Matthew 28:19, 20)*

If not sung, this acclamation is omitted.

Go and teach all people my gospel; I am with you always, until the end of the world.

GOSPEL *(Luke 24:46-53)*

The conclusion of the holy gospel according to Luke. **Glory to you, Lord.**

Jesus said to the disciples, "These are my words that I spoke to you while I was still with you—that everything written about me in the law of Moses, the prophets, and the psalms must be fulfilled."

Then he opened their minds to understand the scriptures, and he said to them, "Thus it is written, that the Messiah is to suffer and to rise from the dead on the third day, and that repentance and forgiveness of sins is to be proclaimed in his name to all nations, beginning from Jerusalem. You are witnesses of these things.

"And see, I am sending upon you what my Father promised; so stay here in the city until you have been clothed with power from on high."

Then he led them out as far as Bethany, and, lifting up his hands, he blessed them. While he was blessing them, he withdrew from them and was carried up into heaven. And they worshipped him, and returned to Jerusalem with great joy; and they were continually in the temple blessing God.

The gospel of the Lord. **Praise to you, Lord Jesus Christ.**

PROFESSION OF FAITH *(Creed, pp. 11-12)*

PRAYER OF THE FAITHFUL

The following intentions are suggestions only.

℞. **Lord, hear our prayer.**

For the Church, community of disciples entrusted with authority and power to witness to the name of Jesus, we pray to the Lord: ℞.

For all leaders and teachers in the Church, we pray to the Lord: ℞.

For the poor and unemployed, at home and abroad, who seek the support of our words and actions, we pray to the Lord: ℞.

For our parish community, called to speak and act courageously as we spread the good news, we pray to the Lord: ℞.

PREPARATION OF THE GIFTS *(p. 13)*

PRAYER OVER THE GIFTS

Lord, receive our offering as we celebrate the ascension of Christ your Son. May his gifts help us rise with him to the joys of heaven.

PREFACE *(Ascension I-II, p. 28)*

COMMUNION ANTIPHON *(Matthew 28:20)*

I, the Lord, am with you always, until the end of the world, alleluia.

PRAYER AFTER COMMUNION

Father, in this eucharist we touch the divine life you give to the world. Help us to follow Christ with love to eternal life where he is Lord for ever and ever.

SOLEMN BLESSING *(Optional)*

Bow your heads and pray for God's blessing.

May almighty God bless you on this day when his only Son ascended into heaven to prepare a place for you. **Amen.**

After his resurrection, Christ was seen by his disciples. When he appears as judge may you be pleasing for ever in his sight. **Amen.**

You believe that Jesus has taken his seat in majesty at the right hand of the Father. May you have the joy of experiencing that he is also with you to the end of time, according to his promise. **Amen.**

May almighty God bless you, the Father, and the Son, and the Holy Spirit. **Amen.**

DISMISSAL *(p. 65)*

Wasn't early Christianity something! House-shaking winds, tongues of fire and inspired people spreading good news of new hope, new life!

Christian Pentecost was and continues to be God's work—God fulfilling promises, re-creating human society through his life-giving spirit, and bringing to fullness all creation.

What was previously hidden mystery is now wide-open invitation, broadcast to all: God, the Creator of the universe, through the life, death and resurrection of his eternal Son, Jesus of Nazareth, by the power of their Holy Spirit, is freely loving his own personal life into all who accept it. God is fashioning human children, God's own people, heirs of all God owns.

The psalm response today sounds the theme and celebrates this work of God. Acts recounts that astonishing, life-changing, first Christian Pentecost. Paul reassures us that the Holy Spirit continues to divinize and energize us. And the gospel reminds us that Jesus fulfilled his promise by sending us the Holy Spirit.

Amazing! All who gratefully welcome in faith God's gift of his own eternal life and nurture it by sacramental celebrations and loving service of others, all those enjoy that life forever!

Armand Nigro, Malawi

ENTRANCE ANTIPHON *(Wisdom 1:7)*

The Spirit of the Lord fills the whole world. It holds all things together and knows every word spoken by man, alleluia.

INTRODUCTORY RITES *(p. 5)*

OPENING PRAYER

God our Father, let the Spirit you sent on your Church to begin the teaching of the gospel continue to work in the world through the hearts of all who believe.

FIRST READING *(Acts 2:1-11)*

When the day of Pentecost had come, they were all together in one place. And suddenly from heaven there came a sound like the rush of a violent wind, and it filled the entire house where they were sitting. Divided tongues, as of fire, appeared among them, and a tongue rested on each of them. All of them were filled with the Holy Spirit and began to speak in other languages, as the Spirit gave them ability.

Now there were devout Jews from every nation under heaven living in Jerusalem. And at this sound the crowd gathered and was bewildered, because all heard them speaking in their own languages. Amazed and astonished, they asked, "Are not all these who are speaking Galileans? And how is it that we hear, each of us, in our own language? Parthians, Medes, Elamites, and residents of Mesopotamia, Judea and Cappadocia, Pontus and Asia, Phrygia and Pamphylia, Egypt and the parts of Libya belonging to Cyrene, and visitors from Rome, both Jews and converts, Cretans and Arabs—in our own languages we hear them speaking about God's deeds of power."

The word of the Lord. **Thanks be to God.**

RESPONSORIAL PSALM *(Psalm 104)*

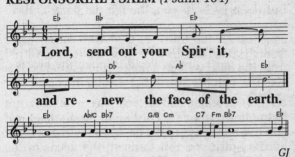

GJ

℞. **Lord send out your Spirit,**
and renew the face of the earth.

Bless the Lord, O • **my** soul.
O Lord my God, you are very • **great.**
O Lord, how manifold • **are** your works!
The earth is full of • **your** creatures. ℞.

When you take away their breath, • **they** die
and return to their • **dust.**
When you send forth your spirit,
    they • **are** cre-ated;
and you renew the face of • **the** earth. ℞.

May the glory of the Lord endure • **for**-ever;
may the Lord rejoice in his • **works.**
May my meditation be • **pleasing** to him,
for I rejoice in • **the** Lord. ℞.

SECOND READING *(Romans 8:8-17)*

Those who are in the flesh cannot please God. But you are not in the flesh; you are in the Spirit, since the Spirit of God dwells in you. Anyone who does not have the Spirit of Christ does not belong to him.

But if Christ is in you, though the body is dead because of sin, the Spirit is life because of righteousness. If the Spirit of God who raised Jesus from the dead dwells in you, he who raised Christ from the dead will give life to your mortal bodies also through his Spirit that dwells in you.

So then, brothers and sisters, we are debtors, not to the flesh, to live according to the flesh—for if you live according to the flesh, you will die; but if by the Spirit you put to death the deeds of the body, you will live. For all who are led by the Spirit of God are children of God. For you did not receive a spirit of slavery to fall back into fear, but you have received a spirit of adoption. When we cry, "Abba! Father!" it is that very Spirit bearing witness with our spirit that we are children of God, and if children, then heirs, heirs of God and joint heirs with Christ—if, in fact, we suffer with him so that we may also be glorified with him.

The word of the Lord. **Thanks be to God.**

SEQUENCE

1. Holy Spirit, Lord Divine,
   Come, from heights of heav'n and shine,
   Come with blessed radiance bright!

2. Come, O Father of the poor,
   Come, whose treasured gifts ensure,
   Come, our heart's unfailing light!

3. Of consolers, wisest, best,
   And our soul's most welcome guest,
   Sweet refreshment, sweet repose.

4. In our labour rest most sweet,
   Pleasant coolness in the heat,
   Consolation in our woes.

5. Light most blessed, shine with grace
   In our heart's most secret place,
   Fill your faithful through and through.

6. Left without your presence here,
   Life itself would disappear,
   Nothing thrives apart from you!

7. Cleanse our soiled hearts of sin,
   Arid souls refresh within,
   Wounded lives to health restore.

8. Bend the stubborn heart and will,
   Melt the frozen, warm the chill,
   Guide the wayward home once more!

9. On the faithful who are true
   and profess their faith in you,
   In your sev'nfold gift descend!

10 Give us virtue's sure reward,
   Give us your salvation, Lord,
   Give us joys that never end!

Text: *Veni, Sancte Spiritus*, 13th century
Trans: © Peter J. Scagnelli (1949-)

GOSPEL ACCLAMATION

If not sung, this acclamation is omitted.

Come, Holy Spirit, fill the hearts of your faithful
and kindle in them the fire of your love.

GOSPEL *(John 14:15-16, 23-26)*

A reading from the holy gospel according to John.
Glory to you, Lord.

Jesus spoke to the disciples: "If you love me, you
will keep my commandments. And I will ask the
Father, and he will give you another Advocate, to
be with you forever.

"Those who love me will keep my word, and my
Father will love them, and we will come to them
and make our home with them. Whoever does not
love me does not keep my words; and the word
that you hear is not mine, but is from the Father
who sent me.

"I have said these things to you while I am still
with you. But the Advocate, the Holy Spirit,
whom the Father will send in my name, will
teach you everything, and remind you of all that I
have said to you."

The gospel of the Lord. **Praise to you, Lord Jesus
Christ.**

PROFESSION OF FAITH *(Nicene Creed, p. 12)*

PRAYER OF THE FAITHFUL

The following intentions are suggestions only.

℟: **Lord, hear our prayer.**

For the Church, carrying on the ministry of Jesus by mediating the mercy and compassion of God, we pray to the Lord: ℟.

For the world, longing for God's peace and justice that end violence against the person, we pray to the Lord. ℟.

For those who are sick, homeless, hungry, unemployed, needy or suffering in any way, we pray to the Lord: ℟.

For the outpouring of God's Spirit on our parish community as we love and serve God and each other, we pray to the Lord: ℟.

PREPARATION OF THE GIFTS *(p. 13)*

PRAYER OVER THE GIFTS

Lord, may the Spirit you promised lead us into all truth and reveal to us the full meaning of this sacrifice.

PREFACE *(Pentecost, p. 28)*

COMMUNION ANTIPHON *(Acts 2:4, 11)*

They were all filled with the Holy Spirit, and they spoke of the great things God had done, alleluia.

PRAYER AFTER COMMUNION

Father, may the food we receive in the eucharist help our eternal redemption. Keep within us the vigour of your Spirit and protect the gifts you have given to your Church.

SOLEMN BLESSING—Pentecost *(Optional)*

Bow your heads and pray for God's blessing

(This day) the Father of light has enlightened the minds of the disciples by the outpouring of the Holy Spirit. May he bless you and give the gifts of the Spirit for ever. **Amen.**

May that fire which hovered over the disciples as tongues of flame burn out all evil from your hearts and make them glow with pure light. **Amen.**

God inspired speech in different tongues to proclaim one faith. May he strengthen your faith and fulfill your hope of seeing him face to face. **Amen.**

May almighty God bless you, the Father, and the Son, and the Holy Spirit. **Amen.**

DISMISSAL *(p. 324)*

Have you ever wrestled with the question 'Who is God?' If so, were you confused and frustrated?—it's a normal reaction. It is impossible for our finite minds ever to fathom the totality that is God. The ancient Hebrews had the right idea: they would never name God because that meant putting limits on God. They knew that no human being could possibly comprehend God.

Jesus understood this. He knew that he could not simply give his disciples a description of God and expect that to last a lifetime. Knowing their limitations and frailties, Jesus reassured the disciples of the gift of the Spirit who would guide them "into all the truth." In other words, Jesus tells us that we are to grow in our understanding of God. And that means that we cannot despair or give up in frustration—because we will never be finished. Growing in our understanding of God will take a lifetime.

So how do we grow in our understanding of God? Certainly not just by being told about God. We can be told a million times about the love of God, but only if we experience that love will it become a reality for us. Doctrines and dogmas can help us on our way, but it is only by experiencing God in our own lives that we will ever truly come to know who God is. Our challenge, then, is to recognize the myriad little ways that God enters our lives every day: the friend who takes the time to listen, the helpful stranger on the street, the child who loves us unconditionally. We need to recognize these for what they really are—stirrings of the Divine. Only then will be begin to answer the question: 'Who is God?'

Teresa Whalen, Regina, SK

ENTRANCE ANTIPHON

Blessed be God the Father and his only-begotten Son and the Holy Spirit: for he has shown that he loves us.

INTRODUCTORY RITES *(p. 5)*

OPENING PRAYER

Father, you sent your Word to bring us truth and your Spirit to make us holy. Through them we come to know the mystery of your life. Help us to worship you, one God in three Persons, by proclaiming and living our faith in you.

FIRST READING *(Proverbs 8:22-31)*

Thus says the wisdom of God:
"The Lord created me at the beginning of his work,
the first of his acts of long ago.
Ages ago I was set up,
at the first, before the beginning of the earth.
When there were no depths I was brought forth,
when there were no springs abounding with water.

"Before the mountains had been shaped,
before the hills, I was brought forth—
when he had not yet made earth and fields,
or the world's first bits of soil.

"When he established the heavens, I was there,
when he drew a circle on the face of the deep,
when he made firm the skies above,
when he established the fountains of the deep,
when he assigned to the sea its limit, so that
    the waters might not transgress his command,
when he marked out the foundations of the earth,
then I was beside him, like a master worker;
and I was daily his delight,
rejoicing before him always,
rejoicing in his inhabited world
and delighting in the human race."

The word of the Lord. **Thanks be to God.**

RESPONSORIAL PSALM *(Psalm 8)*

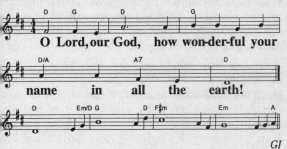

O Lord, our God,   how won-der-ful your

name   in   all   the   earth!

GJ

℟. **O Lord, our God,
how wonderful your name in all the earth!**

When I look at your heavens,
    the work of • **your** fingers,
the moon and the stars
    that you have • **es**-tablished;
what are human beings
    that you • **are** mindful_of_them,
mortals • **that** you care_for_them? ℟.

383

Yet you have made them
    a little lower • **than** God,
and crowned them with glory • **and** honour.
You have given them dominion
    over the works of • **your** hands;
you have put all things un•**-der** their feet. ℞.

All sheep • **and** oxen,
and also the beasts of • **the** field,
the birds of the air, and the fish of • **the** sea,
    whatever passes along
        the paths • **of** the seas. ℞.

SECOND READING *(Romans 5:1-5)*

Since we are justified by faith, we have peace
with God through our Lord Jesus Christ, through
whom we have obtained access to this grace in
which we stand; and we boast in our hope of
sharing the glory of God.

And not only that, but we also boast in our
sufferings, knowing that suffering produces endurance, and endurance produces character, and
character produces hope, and hope does not disappoint us, because God's love has been poured
into our hearts through the Holy Spirit that has
been given to us.

The word of the Lord. **Thanks be to God.**

GOSPEL ACCLAMATION *(See Revelation 1:8)*

If not sung, this acclamation is omitted.

Glory to the Father, the Son, and the Holy Spirit
to God who is, who was, and who is to come.

GOSPEL *(John 16:12-15)*

A reading from the holy gospel according to John.
Glory to you, Lord.

Jesus said to his disciples: "I still have many
things to say to you, but you cannot bear them
now. When the Spirit of truth comes, he will
guide you into all the truth; for he will not speak
on his own, but will speak whatever he hears, and
he will declare to you the things that are to come.
He will glorify me, because he will take what is
mine and declare it to you. All that the Father has
is mine. For this reason I said that he will take
what is mine and declare it to you."

The gospel of the Lord. **Praise to you, Lord Jesus
Christ.**

PROFESSION OF FAITH *(Creed, pp. 11-12)*

PRAYER OF THE FAITHFUL

The following intentions are suggestions only.

℟: **Lord, hear our prayer.**

For the Church, called to deepen its understanding of the mystery of God, we pray to the Lord: ℟.

For our nation's leaders, seeking to learn the ways
of peace and gentleness, we pray to the Lord: ℟.

For all who are oppressed because of race, gender
or religion, and for their oppressors, we pray to
the Lord: ℟.

For the young people of our parish, in whose lives
the Divine is working, often unrecognized, we
pray to the Lord: ℟.

PREPARATION OF THE GIFTS *(p. 13)*

PRAYER OVER THE GIFTS

Lord our God, make these gifts holy, and through them make us a perfect offering to you.

PREFACE *(Trinity, p. 29)*

COMMUNION ANTIPHON *(Galatians 4:6)*

You are the sons of God, so God has given you the Spirit of his Son to form your hearts and make you cry out: Abba, Father.

PRAYER AFTER COMMUNION

Lord God, we worship you, a Trinity of Persons, one eternal God. May our faith and the sacrament we receive bring us health of mind and body.

BLESSING AND DISMISSAL *(p. 65)*

June 18   Body and Blood of Christ

Imagine the scene: the apostles have just returned from their first mission of healing and proclamation. It was a successful mission though they took nothing with them but the clothes on their backs and the conviction that God would somehow be present in their ministry. Now they withdraw with Jesus to a deserted place. However, the crowds find them and begin to gather.

Obviously, their message has had a powerful impact on people. Over five thousand have come to a remote part of the countryside without any provisions but the clothes on their backs and the conviction that God is somehow present in a powerful way. Jesus welcomes them, speaks to them about the kingdom of God, and heals the sick. The day draws on, and yet the people remain, seemingly unaware of their own hunger. They are free to go in search of lodging and provisions, and yet the apostles sense that the people will not go unless Jesus sends them away.

Had the story ended there, it would have been amazing enough. What a miracle that someone could have such an impact on any group of people! What a miracle that poor and rich alike would put aside their daily work to follow (uninvited) a poor preacher and his simple band of disciples to some remote part of the countryside! What a miracle that people could be so captivated by someone and his teachings that they would forget their need for food and shelter!

But, of course, the story doesn't end there. The apostles urge Jesus to send the people away. He responds, "You give them something to eat"—as if to say "Haven't you recognized that I have been feeding them?" Then taking five loaves and two fish, he looks up to heaven, blesses and breaks them, and feeds the people... again.

———————————— *John O'Donnell, Halifax, NS*

ENTRANCE ANTIPHON *(Psalm 81:16)*

The Lord fed his people with the finest wheat and honey; their hunger was satisfied.

INTRODUCTORY RITES *(p. 5)*

OPENING PRAYER

Lord Jesus Christ, you gave us the eucharist as the memorial of your suffering and death. May our worship of this sacrament of your body and blood help us to experience the salvation you won for us and the peace of the kingdom.

FIRST READING *(Genesis 14:18-20)*

When Abram heard that his nephew, Lot, had been taken captive, he led forth his trained men, and routed the abductors.

After Abram's return King Melchizedek of Salem brought out bread and wine; he was priest of God Most High. He blessed Abram and said, "Blessed be Abram by God Most High, maker of heaven and earth; and blessed be God Most High, who has delivered your enemies into your hand!"

And Abram gave him one tenth of everything.

The word of the Lord. **Thanks be to God.**

RESPONSORIAL PSALM *(Psalm 110)*

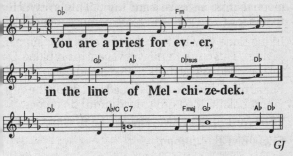

You are a priest for ev - er,

in the line of Mel - chi - ze - dek.

GJ

℟. **You are a priest for ever,
in the line of Melchizedek.**

The Lord says to • **my** lord,
"Sit at my • **right** hand
until I make your enemies • **your** footstool." ℟.

The Lord sends out • **from** Zion
your might•**-y** sceptre.
Rule in the midst of • **your** foes. ℟.

Your people will offer them•**-selves** willingly
on the day you lead your forces
on the ho•**-ly** mountains.
From the womb of the morning, like dew,
your youth will come • **to** you. ℟.

The Lord has sworn and will
not change • **his** mind,
"You are a priest • **for-**ever
according to the order of • **Mel-**chizedek." ℟.

SECOND READING *(1 Corinthians 11:23-26)*

Beloved, I received from the Lord what I also handed
on to you, that the Lord Jesus on the night when he

389

Body and Blood of Christ

was betrayed took a loaf of bread, and when he had given thanks, he broke it and said, "This is my body that is for you. Do this in remembrance of me."

In the same way he took the cup also, after supper, saying, "This cup is the new covenant in my blood. Do this, as often as you drink it, in remembrance of me."

For as often as you eat this bread and drink the cup, you proclaim the Lord's death until he comes.

The word of the Lord. **Thanks be to God.**

SEQUENCE *(Optional)*

This sequence is intended to be sung; otherwise, it is better omitted. The shorter version (Ecce Panis) begins at the asterisks.

1. Praise, O Zion, Christ our glory;
   To the Shepherd let us sing,
   Tell to all the world the story;
   Laud with all our might the King.
   Bread of life and source of living!
   Lacking, still our praises ring.

2. This our special theme for singing,
   Christ the Lamb for us was slain.
   At the paschal meal he taught us,
   To the twelve he made it plain:
   Flesh as food for us was giving,
   Therefore let your faith not wane.

3. On this day of Christian feasting,
   With full voices we delight:
   Instituting our salvation,
   In the sacred meal that night,
   Christ the ancient law fulfilling,
   Fills all people with new sight.

4. To obey the call of Jesus,
   Gathered we as chosen band.
   Bread and wine Christ is transforming,
   Flesh and blood are now at hand.
   From his words and actions learning,
   Love we share at his command.

5. Gathered at this solemn table,
   Darkness now has taken flight.
   In the bread and wine partaking,
   Christ is for each one the light,
   Then as food to us disciples,
   Gives our souls a new delight.

6. To all people Christ is giving
   Truth in word and sacrament.
   By the sacrifice redeeming
   All into one covenant.
   One in Jesus' name assembling:
   Faith and love our testament.

7. To our minds these signs disclosing,
   To our senses must unfold:
   Bread is broken, blood outpouring;
   Christ the myst'ry, awe untold!
   Flesh and blood to sight revealing:
   This the story to be told.

8. Undivided is his body,
   Yet Christ gives himself to all.
   Word made flesh with us abiding,
   For without him we must fall.
   Christ the Pasch we are consuming,
   One in spirit is our call.

9. Good and evil are all sharing,
   Seeds of destiny are sown.
   To new life our Saviour guides us;
   Death prevails when on our own.
   Life immortal for those seeking,
   Is fulfilled in Christ alone.

10. When the sacred bread is broken,
    All receive the Christ as one.
    By his love Christ is transforming,
    Though so many we are one;
    All the scattered are united,
    All the lonely welcomed home.

* * * * * *

11. Come, behold, the bread of angels,
    This our strength on pilgrims' way.
    For the children God is giving,
    Manna for our bread each day.
    Now the sign of Isaac telling:
    Christ has conquered on this day.

12. Hear our prayers, O kindly Shepherd,
    Be for us true living bread.
    Grant us peace in all our doings,
    To our resting place be led,
    Forth with all the saints now dwelling,
    We the body, you the Head.

Text: *Lauda Sion*
Trans: John G. Hibbard, © *1992 Concanan, Inc.*
Tune: REGENT SQUARE *or* ST. THOMAS; 87.87.87.
Music: *CBW II* 528, 582; *CBW III* 456, 688

GOSPEL ACCLAMATION *(John 6:51-52)*

If not sung, this acclamation is omitted.

I am the living bread from heaven, says the Lord;
whoever eats this bread will live forever.

GOSPEL *(Luke 9:11-17)*

A reading from the holy gospel according to Luke.
Glory to you, Lord.

Jesus spoke to the crowds about the kingdom of God, and healed those who needed to be cured. The day was drawing to a close, and the twelve came to him and said, "Send the crowd away, so that they may go into the surrounding villages and countryside, to lodge and get provisions; for we are here in a deserted place."

But Jesus said to them, "You give them something to eat." They said, "We have no more than five loaves and two fish—unless we are to go and buy food for all these people." For there were about five thousand men.

And Jesus said to his disciples, "Make the people sit down in groups of about fifty each." They did so and made them all sit down. And taking the five loaves and the two fish, he looked up to heaven, and blessed and broke them, and gave them to the disciples to set before the crowd.

And all ate and were filled. What was left over was gathered up, twelve baskets of broken pieces.

The gospel of the Lord. **Praise to you, Lord Jesus Christ.**

PROFESSION OF FAITH *(Creed, pp. 11-12)*

PRAYER OF THE FAITHFUL

The following intentions are suggestions only.

℟: **Lord, hear our prayer.**

For the Church, people of God, nourished by the word and the eucharist we share, we pray to the Lord: ℟.

For governments searching for ways to ensure fair and equitable distribution of food and other resources, we pray to the Lord: ℞.

For the children of this country who live in poverty, and for all the world's children whose parents struggle to nourish them, we pray to the Lord: ℞.

For fathers in our community, called by God to care for their children, we pray to the Lord: ℞.

For us, God's people, called to put God's word of love into action every day, we pray to the Lord: ℞.

PREPARATION OF THE GIFTS *(p. 13)*

PRAYER OVER THE GIFTS

Lord, may the bread and cup we offer bring your Church the unity and peace they signify.

PREFACE *(Holy Eucharist I-II, p. 29)*

COMMUNION ANTIPHON *(John 6:57)*

Whoever eats my flesh and drinks my blood will live in me and I in him, says the Lord.

PRAYER AFTER COMMUNION

Lord Jesus Christ, you give us your body and blood in the eucharist as a sign that even now we share your life. May we come to possess it completely in the kingdom where you live for ever and ever.

BLESSING AND DISMISSAL *(p. 65)*

I sometimes wonder what event or circumstance would cause me to risk my life. Would I put my life on the line for the safety of those I love? Certainly! Without a doubt. No hesitation. Would I risk my life to save someone I did not know personally? I think I would. Many people have done so in courageous acts of rescuing or defending others. Would I put my life on the line for a belief? My conviction wavers at this point. I am not sure.

Yet this is precisely what today's gospel calls us to do. We are not asked to lay down our lives to save a 'person,' but we are called to risk our lives to defend what Jesus stands for and what we, as Christians, profess to believe in: justice, compassion, right relationships.

Throughout the world today people are not only risking but *losing* their lives in the defence of human rights, in the struggle for freedom, in the fight to ensure that all people have their basic needs met. They are martyrs in the ongoing battle for a world order that puts people before profits.

So where do I stand? How far am I willing to go? How clearly will I speak out against policies and practices that contradict my beliefs? I don't know. But it would be a whole lot easier if we could take our stand together.

Susan Eaton, Toronto, ON

ENTRANCE ANTIPHON *(Psalm 28:8-9)*

God is the strength of his people. In him, we his chosen live in safety. Save us, Lord, who share in your life, and give us your blessing; be our shepherd for ever.

INTRODUCTORY RITES *(p. 5)*

OPENING PRAYER

Father, guide and protector of your people, grant us an unfailing respect for your name, and keep us always in your love.

FIRST READING *(Zechariah 12:10-11)*

The Lord says this: "I will pour out a spirit of compassion and supplication on the house of David and the inhabitants of Jerusalem, so that, when they look on the one whom they have pierced, they shall mourn for him, as one mourns for an only child, and weep bitterly over him, as one weeps over a firstborn.

"On that day the mourning in Jerusalem will be as great as the mourning for Hadad-rimmon in the plain of Megiddo."

The word of the Lord. **Thanks be to God.**

RESPONSORIAL PSALM *(Psalm 63)*

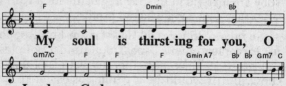

GJ

℟. **My soul is thirsting for you, O Lord my God.**

O God, you are my God, I • **seek_you,**
my soul thirsts for • **you;**
my flesh faints for • **you,**
as in a dry and weary land
    where there • **is** no water. ℞.

So I have looked upon you in the • **sanctuary,**
beholding your power and • **glory.**
Because your steadfast love is better
    than • **life,**
my • **lips** will praise_you. ℞.

So I will bless you as long as I • **live;**
I will lift up my hands and call on
    your • **name.**
My soul is satisfied as with a rich • **feast,**
and my mouth praises you with • **joy**-ful lips. ℞.

For you have been my • **help,**
and in the shadow of your wings I sing for • **joy.**
My soul clings to • **you;**
your • **right_hand** up-holds_me. ℞.

SECOND READING *(Galatians 3:26-29)*

My brothers and sisters, in Christ Jesus you are all children of God through faith. As many of you as were baptized into Christ have clothed yourselves with Christ.

There is no longer Jew or Greek, there is no longer slave or free, there is no longer male and female; for all of you are one in Christ Jesus.

And if you belong to Christ, then you are Abraham's offspring, heirs according to the promise.

The word of the Lord. **Thanks be to God.**

GOSPEL ACCLAMATION *(John 10:27)*

If not sung, this acclamation is omitted.

My sheep listen to my voice, says the Lord; I know them, and they follow me.

GOSPEL *(Luke 9:18-24)*

A reading from the holy gospel according to Luke. **Glory to you, Lord.**

One day when Jesus was praying alone, with only the disciples near him, he asked them, "Who do the crowds say that I am?"

They answered, "John the Baptist; but others, Elijah; and still others, that one of the ancient prophets has arisen." Jesus said to them, "But who do you say that I am?" Peter answered, "The Messiah of God."

Jesus sternly ordered and commanded the disciples not to tell anyone, saying, "The Son of Man must undergo great suffering, and be rejected by the elders, chief priests, and scribes, and be killed, and on the third day be raised."

Then Jesus said to them all, "If any want to become my followers, let them deny themselves and take up their cross daily and follow me. For those who want to save their life will lose it, and those who lose their life for my sake will save it."

The gospel of the Lord. **Praise to you, Lord Jesus Christ.**

PROFESSION OF FAITH *(Creed, pp. 11-12)*

PRAYER OF THE FAITHFUL

The following intentions are suggestions only.

℟: **Lord, hear our prayer.**

For the Church, gifted with a rich tradition of social teaching for the common good, we pray to the Lord: ℟.

For all leaders, invited to root their policies and decisions in a commitment to the dignity of all people and the integrity of creation, we pray to the Lord: ℟.

For our sisters and brothers throughout the world who risk their lives in the struggle for justice, we pray to the Lord: ℟.

For us, God's people, needing strength and courage to defend values, we pray to the Lord: ℟.

PREPARATION OF THE GIFTS *(p. 13)*

PRAYER OVER THE GIFTS

Lord, receive our offering, and may this sacrifice of praise purify us in mind and heart and make us always eager to serve you.

PREFACE *(Sundays in Ord. Time, p. 18)*

COMMUNION ANTIPHON *(Psalm 145:15)*

The eyes of all look to you, O Lord, and you give them food in due season.

PRAYER AFTER COMMUNION

Lord, you give us the body and blood of your Son to renew your life within us. In your mercy, assure our redemption and bring us to the eternal life we celebrate in this eucharist.

BLESSING AND DISMISSAL *(p. 65)*

Three people are called to follow Jesus. Three people are rejected. One because he did not count the cost, a second because he wanted to bury his father, a third because he wanted to say goodbye to his family. No one can say that Jesus was not honest in making clear the requirements of discipleship. What is bothersome though is that the demands seem too high. What could be more human, more understandable, more responsible than fulfilling family obligations?

To grasp the meaning of these passages we must see that Jesus doesn't weigh family against service to God. Those invited to follow him do. Jesus is saying that when the spirit quickens within us, when we come spiritually alive, the moment is decisive. It is time to act. But these people who feel the spirit quickening within them ask for delay when the decisiveness of the moment is so fragile and so quickly past. In these passages, family becomes an excuse to wait, to withdraw, to allow the moment of fervour to pass.

Not long ago, just before going to sleep, I remembered that I needed to write a letter. I felt badly for not having written; I wanted to write the letter. But, comfortable in a warm bed and ready for sleep, I put it off. The next morning the letter did not seem quite so important or urgent. Failing to act had allowed good feelings and intentions to remain just good feelings and intentions. The letter is still not written.

Following Jesus is a matter of urgency. His call is a call to life. It is a call to life in the spirit and joy of his kingdom. But to follow I must act, not just wish to act. To act decisively so that nothing can come between me and Jesus' call.

James B. Sauer, San Antonio, TX

ENTRANCE ANTIPHON *(Psalm 47:1)*

All nations, clap your hands. Shout with a voice of joy to God.

INTRODUCTORY RITES *(p. 5)*

OPENING PRAYER

Father, you call your children to walk in the light of Christ. Free us from darkness and keep us in the radiance of your truth.

FIRST READING *(1 Kings 19:16, 19-21)*

The Lord spoke to the prophet Elijah and said, "You shall anoint Elisha, son of Shaphat, as prophet in your place."

So Elijah set out from there, and found Elisha, who was ploughing. There were twelve yoke of oxen ahead of him, and he was with the twelfth.

Elijah passed by Elisha and threw his mantle over him. Elisha left the oxen, ran after Elijah, and said, "Let me kiss my father and my mother, and then I will follow you."

Then Elijah said to him, "Go back again; for what have I done to you?" Elisha returned from following Elijah, took the yoke of oxen, and slaughtered them; using the equipment from the oxen, he boiled their flesh, and gave it to the people, and they ate. Then Elisha set out and followed Elijah, and became his servant.

The word of the Lord. **Thanks be to God.**

RESPONSORIAL PSALM *(Psalm 16)*

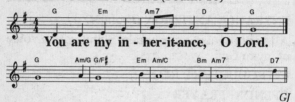

GJ

℟. **You are my inheritance, O Lord.**

Protect me, O God, for in you I take • **refuge.**
I say to the Lord, "You are my • **Lord;**
I have no good apart from • **you.**"
The Lord is my chosen portion and my cup;
    you hold my • **lot.** ℟.

I bless the Lord who gives me • **counsel;**
in the night also my heart in•-**structs_me.**
I keep the Lord always be•-**fore_me;**
because he is at my right hand,
    I shall not be • **moved.** ℟.

Therefore my heart is glad,
    and my soul re•-**joices;**
my body also rests se•-**cure.**
For you do not give me up to • **Sheol,**
or let your faithful one see the • **Pit.** ℟.

* You show me the path of • **life.**
 In your presence there is fullness of • **joy;**
 in your right hand are pleasures
   forever•-**more.** ℞.

* Omit the third bar of the psalm tone.

SECOND READING *(Galatians 5:1, 13-18)*

For freedom Christ has set us free. Stand firm, therefore, and do not submit again to a yoke of slavery. For you were called to freedom, brothers and sisters; only do not use your freedom as an opportunity for self-indulgence, but through love become slaves to one another.

For the whole law is summed up in a single commandment, "You shall love your neighbour as yourself." If, however, you bite and devour one another, take care that you are not consumed by one another.

Live by the Spirit, I say, and do not gratify the desires of the flesh. For what the flesh desires is opposed to the Spirit, and what the Spirit desires is opposed to the flesh; for these are opposed to each other, to prevent you from doing what you want. But if you are led by the Spirit, you are not subject to the law.

The word of the Lord. **Thanks be to God.**

GOSPEL ACCLAMATION *(1 Sam 3:9; John 6:69)*

If not sung, this acclamation is omitted.

Speak, O Lord, your servant is listening; you have the words of everlasting life.

GOSPEL *(Luke 9:51-62)*

A reading from the holy gospel according to Luke. **Glory to you, Lord.**

When the days drew near for him to be taken up, Jesus set his face to go to Jerusalem.

And he sent messengers ahead of him. On their way they entered a village of the Samaritans to make ready for Jesus; but the Samaritans did not receive him, because his face was set toward Jerusalem.

When his disciples James and John saw it, they said, "Lord, do you want us to command fire to come down from heaven and consume them?" But Jesus turned and rebuked them. Then they went on to another village.

As they were going along the road, someone said to him, "I will follow you wherever you go." And Jesus said to him, "Foxes have holes, and birds of the air have nests; but the Son of Man has nowhere to lay his head."

To another Jesus said, "Follow me." But he replied, "Lord, first let me go and bury my father." But Jesus said to him, "Let the dead bury their own dead; but as for you, go and proclaim the kingdom of God."

Another said, "I will follow you, Lord; but let me first say farewell to those at my home." Jesus said to him, "No one who puts a hand to the plough and looks back is fit for the kingdom of God."

The gospel of the Lord. **Praise to you, Lord Jesus Christ.**

PROFESSION OF FAITH *(Creed, pp. 11-12)*

PRAYER OF THE FAITHFUL

The following intentions are suggestions only.

℞: **Lord, hear our prayer.**

For the Church, always learning, always teaching the ways of God's salvation, we pray to the Lord: ℞.

For our country and our leaders in this time of national celebration, we pray to the Lord: ℞.

For those who suffer loneliness, depression, hunger, sickness or grief, and for those who minister to them, we pray to the Lord: ℞.

For us, God's people gathered in this parish, witnesses to the living Christ, we pray to the Lord: ℞.

PREPARATION OF THE GIFTS *(p. 13)*

PRAYER OVER THE GIFTS

Lord God, through your sacraments you give us the power of your grace. May this eucharist help us to serve you faithfully.

PREFACE *(Sundays in Ord. Time, p. 18)*

COMMUNION ANTIPHON *(Psalm 103:1)*

O, bless the Lord, my soul, and all that is within me bless his holy name.

PRAYER AFTER COMMUNION

Lord, may this sacrifice and communion give us a share in your life and help us bring your love to the world.

BLESSING AND DISMISSAL *(p. 65)*

Welcome the long, lazy days of summer—days of different routines, longlasting light and, hopefully, time to relax and reflect. It is a good time to take a walk with a friend and share deep thoughts.

Jesus sends the disciples out in two's to every town where he intends to go. This wise decision to send them in pairs provides the disciples with opportunity for support and reflection on experiences. It is good to discuss the events of the day with someone. The disciples are instructed to proceed in simplicity—not to be weighed down by things, but to carry a message of peace.

The gospel speaks of the need to proclaim and the need to receive. One must be open to receive the message that is offered; it is up to each person to adopt a welcoming attitude. Those who are open to peace and newness have good things happen to them: strangers come with the word of God, the sick are healed, there is a glimpse of God's realm. We read of abundance, simplicity, peace, hospitality, shared meals, healing... all signs of community centred around the good news of Jesus... all signs that God's realm is very near.

As I reflect on these signs, I wonder how I can come to that simplicity that carries only peace? What do I need to leave behind? Deep thoughts for a summer Sunday!

Sandra Barrett, Saint John, NB

ENTRANCE ANTIPHON *(Psalm 48:9-10)*

Within your temple, we ponder your loving kindness, O God. As your name, so also your praise reaches to the ends of the earth; your right hand is filled with justice.

INTRODUCTORY RITES *(p. 5)*

OPENING PRAYER

Father, through the obedience of Jesus, your servant and your Son, you raised a fallen world. Free us from sin and bring us the joy that lasts for ever.

FIRST READING *(Isaiah 66:10-14)*

Rejoice with Jerusalem,
and be glad for her,
all you who love her;
rejoice with her in joy,
all you who mourn over her—
that you may nurse and be satisfied
from her consoling breast;
that you may drink deeply with delight
from her glorious bosom.

For thus says the Lord:
"I will extend prosperity to her like a river,
and the wealth of the nations
        like an overflowing stream;
and you shall nurse and be carried on her arm,
and dandled on her knees.
As a mother comforts her child,
so I will comfort you;
you shall be comforted in Jerusalem.

"You shall see, and your heart shall rejoice;
your bodies shall flourish like the grass;
and it shall be known
that the hand of the Lord is with his servants."

The word of the Lord. **Thanks be to God.**

RESPONSORIAL PSALM *(Psalm 66)*

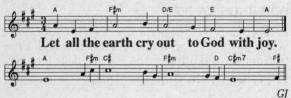

GJ

℟. **Let all the earth cry out to God with joy.**

Make a joyful noise to God, all • **the** earth;
sing the glory of • **his** name;
give to him glori•**-ous** praise.
Say to God, "How awesome are your • **deeds!**" ℟.

"All the earth wor•**-ships** you;
they sing praises to you, sing praises
to • **your** name."
Come and see what God • **has** done:
he is awesome in his deeds among • **mortals.** ℟.

He turned the sea into • **dry** land;
they passed through the river • **on** foot.
There we rejoiced • **in** him,
who rules by his might for•**-ever.** ℟.

Come and hear, all you who • **fear** God,
and I will tell what he has done • **for** me.
Blessed be God, because he has not
rejected • **my** prayer
or removed his steadfast love from • **me.** ℟.

SECOND READING *(Galatians 6:14-18)*

May I never boast of anything except the cross of our Lord Jesus Christ, by which the world has been crucified to me, and I to the world. For neither circumcision nor uncircumcision is anything; but a new creation is everything!

As for those who will follow this rule—peace be upon them, and mercy, and upon the Israel of God. From now on, let no one make trouble for me; for I carry the marks of Jesus branded on my body.

May the grace of our Lord Jesus Christ be with your spirit, brothers and sisters. Amen.

The word of the Lord. **Thanks be to God.**

GOSPEL ACCLAMATION *(Colossians 3:15, 16)*

If not sung, this acclamation is omitted.

May the peace of Christ rule in your hearts, and the fullness of his message live within you.

GOSPEL *(Luke 10:1-12, 17-20)*

The shorter version ends at the asterisks.

A reading from the holy gospel according to Luke. **Glory to you, Lord.**

The Lord appointed seventy others and sent them on ahead of him in pairs to every town and place where he himself intended to go.

He said to them, "The harvest is plentiful, but the labourers are few; therefore ask the Lord of the harvest to send out labourers into his harvest. Go on your way. See, I am sending you out like lambs into the midst of wolves. Carry no purse, no bag, no sandals; and greet no one on the road.

"Whatever house you enter, first say, 'Peace to this house!' And if anyone is there who shares in peace, your peace will rest on that person; but if not, it will return to you. Remain in the same house, eating and drinking whatever they provide, for the labourer deserves to be paid. Do not move about from house to house.

"Whenever you enter a town and its people welcome you, eat what is set before you; cure the sick who are there, and say to them, 'The kingdom of God has come near to you.'

* * *

"But whenever you enter a town and they do not welcome you, go out into its streets and say, 'Even the dust of your town that clings to our feet, we wipe off in protest against you. Yet know this: the kingdom of God has come near.' I tell you, on that day it will be more tolerable for Sodom than for that town."

The seventy returned with joy, saying, "Lord, in your name even the demons submit to us!" Jesus said to them, "I watched Satan fall from heaven like a flash of lightning. See, I have given you authority to tread on snakes and scorpions, and over all the power of the enemy; and nothing will hurt you.

"Nevertheless, do not rejoice at this, that the spirits submit to you, but rejoice that your names are written in heaven."

The gospel of the Lord. **Praise to you, Lord Jesus Christ.**

PROFESSION OF FAITH *(Creed, pp. 11-12)*

PRAYER OF THE FAITHFUL

The following intentions are suggestions only.

℞: **Lord, hear our prayer.**

For Pope N., and all in the Church who lead in simplicity and peace, we pray to the Lord: ℞.

For leaders of nations, from whom people expect words and deeds of peace, we pray to the Lord: ℞.

For those whose lives lack peace, and for those who reach out to them, we pray to the Lord: ℞.

For us, God's people, called to bring peace to the lives of others, we pray to the Lord: ℞.

PREPARATION OF THE GIFTS *(p. 13)*

PRAYER OVER THE GIFTS

Lord, let this offering to the glory of your name purify us and bring us closer to eternal life.

PREFACE *(Sundays in Ord. Time, p. 18)*

COMMUNION ANTIPHON *(Psalm 34:8)*

Taste and see the goodness of the Lord; blessed is he who hopes in God.

PRAYER AFTER COMMUNION

Lord, may we never fail to praise you for the fullness of life and salvation you give us in this eucharist.

BLESSING AND DISMISSAL *(p. 65)*

Today's readings speak of unconditional love. It's the way of love to which we are called in every encounter, in all relationships. A tall order! Yet we are assured in Deuteronomy that the commandment of love is neither too high nor too far... in fact, very near. Here and now it can be spoken through our mouths and from our hearts. We *can* put the command into practice.

The Samaritan's reaction reveals a vivid insight into the elements of love: awareness, compassion, intimacy, responsiveness, self-sacrifice and efficient help. While such loving action has the spark of spontaneity, we know that this generosity is the result of years of self-discipline.

What happens when we are called to action in the often complex situations that confront us? Do we seek the letter or the spirit of the law? Do we get paralyzed when we count up our material resources before the enormous need? Do we take a long, loving look at 'neighbours' and see in each our own poverty? Do we take another deeper look inside ourselves and find God's love engraved on our hearts?

If we still fearfully waver, then let us take heart from the words of the psalm: "seek God, let your hearts revive." Revived in love, we will restore life in our neighbours. We *can* do it!

Esther Jedynak, Victoria, BC

ENTRANCE ANTIPHON *(Psalm 17:15)*

In my justice I shall see your face, O Lord; when your glory appears, my joy will be full.

INTRODUCTORY RITES *(p. 5)*

OPENING PRAYER

God our Father, your light of truth guides us to the way of Christ. May all who follow him reject what is contrary to the gospel.

FIRST READING *(Deuteronomy 30:10-14)*

Moses spoke to the people, saying, "Obey the Lord your God by observing his commandments and decrees that are written in this book of the law; turn to the Lord your God with all your heart and with all your soul.

"Surely this commandment that I am commanding you today is not too hard for you, nor is it too far away. It is not in heaven, that you should say, 'Who will go up to heaven for us, and get it for us so that we may hear it and observe it?'

"Neither is it beyond the sea, that you should say, 'Who will cross to the other side of the sea for us, and get it for us so that we may hear it and observe it?'

"No, the word is very near to you; it is in your mouth and in your heart for you to observe."

The word of the Lord. **Thanks be to God.**

RESPONSORIAL PSALM *(Psalm 69)*

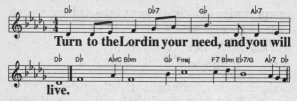

GJ

℞. **Turn to the Lord in your need,
and you will live.**

As for me, my prayer is to you, O • **Lord.**
At an acceptable time, O God,
 in the abundance of your steadfast love,
 • **answer_me.**
With your steadfast • **help,** rescue_me.
Answer me, O Lord,
 for your steadfast love is good;
 according to your abundant mercy,
 • **turn** to me. ℞.

But I am lowly and in • **pain;**
let your salvation, O God, pro•-**tect_me.**
I will praise the name of God • **with_a** song;
I will magnify him • **with** thanks-giving. ℞.

Let the oppressed see it and be • **glad;**
you who seek God, let your hearts re•-**vive.**
For the Lord hears the • **needy,**
and does not despise his own
 that • **are** in bonds. ℞.

For God will save • **Zion**
and rebuild the cities of • **Judah;**
the children of his servants shall • **in**-herit_it,
those who love his name shall • **live** in it. ℞.

414

or

RESPONSORIAL PSALM *(Psalm 19)*

The pre-cepts of the Lord give joy to the heart.

GJ

℟. **The precepts of the Lord give joy to the heart.**

The law of the Lord is • **perfect,**
reviving the • **soul;**
the decrees of the Lord are • **sure,**
making wise • **the** simple. ℟.

The precepts of the Lord are • **right,**
rejoicing the • **heart;**
the commandment of the Lord is • **clear,**
enlightening • **the** eyes. ℟.

The fear of the Lord is • **pure,**
enduring for • **-ever;**
the ordinances of the Lord are • **true**
and righteous • **alto-**gether. ℟.

More to be desired are they than • **gold,**
even much fine • **gold;**
sweeter also than • **honey,**
and drippings of • **the** honeycomb. ℟.

SECOND READING *(Colossians 1:15-20)*

Christ is the image of the invisible God, the firstborn of all creation; for in him all things in heaven and on earth were created, things visible and invisible, whether thrones or dominions or

415

rulers or powers—all things have been created through him and for him.

Christ is before all things, and in him all things hold together. He is the head of the body, the church; he is the beginning, the firstborn from the dead, so that he might come to have first place in everything.

For in Christ all the fullness of God was pleased to dwell, and through him God was pleased to reconcile to himself all things, whether on earth or in heaven, by making peace through the blood of his cross.

The word of the Lord. **Thanks be to God.**

GOSPEL ACCLAMATION *(John 6:63, 68)*

If not sung, this acclamation is omitted.

Your words, Lord, are spirit and life; you have the words of everlasting life.

GOSPEL *(Luke 10:25-37)*

A reading from the holy gospel according to Luke. **Glory to you, Lord.**

A lawyer stood up to test Jesus. "Teacher," he said, "what must I do to inherit eternal life?"

Jesus said to him, "What is written in the law? What do you read there?" The lawyer answered, "You shall love the Lord your God with all your heart, and with all your soul, and with all your strength, and with all your mind; and your neighbour as yourself."

And Jesus said to him, "You have given the right answer; do this, and you will live." But wanting to justify himself, the lawyer asked Jesus, "And who is my neighbour?"

Jesus replied, "A man was going down from Jerusalem to Jericho, and fell into the hands of robbers, who stripped him, beat him, and went away, leaving him half dead. Now by chance a priest was going down that road; and when he saw him, he passed by on the other side. So likewise a Levite, when he came to the place and saw him, passed by on the other side.

"But a Samaritan while travelling came near him; and when he saw him, he was moved with pity. He went to him and bandaged his wounds, having poured oil and wine on them. Then he put him on his own animal, brought him to an inn, and took care of him.

"The next day the Samaritan took out two denarii, gave them to the innkeeper, and said, 'Take care of him; and when I come back, I will repay you whatever more you spend.' "

Jesus asked, "Which of these three, do you think, was a neighbour to the man who fell into the hands of the robbers?" The lawyer said, "The one who showed him mercy." Jesus said to him, "Go and do likewise."

The gospel of the Lord. **Praise to you, Lord Jesus Christ.**

PROFESSION OF FAITH *(Creed, pp. 11-12)*

PRAYER OF THE FAITHFUL

The following intentions are suggestions only.

℞: **Lord, hear our prayer.**

For the Church, healer and refuge as Jesus was, we pray to the Lord: ℞.

For leaders of nations who respond to cries for help, locally and globally, we pray to the Lord: ℟.

For the wounded, the alienated, the hungry who turn to us for help, we pray to the Lord: ℟.

For us, God's people, needy and wounded, looking to each other for support, we pray to the Lord: ℟.

PREPARATION OF THE GIFTS *(p. 13)*

PRAYER OVER THE GIFTS

Lord, accept the gifts of your Church. May this eucharist help us grow in holiness and faith.

PREFACE *(Sundays in Ord. Time, p. 18)*

COMMUNION ANTIPHON *(Psalm 84:3-4)*

The sparrow even finds a home, the swallow finds a nest wherein to place her young, near to your altars, Lord of hosts, my King, my God! How happy they who dwell in your house! For ever they are praising you.

PRAYER AFTER COMMUNION

Lord, by our sharing in the mystery of this eucharist, let your saving love grow within us.

BLESSING AND DISMISSAL *(p. 65)*

In reflecting on today's readings I was struck by the notion of *welcome* — first, of Abraham and Sarah's welcome to the three strangers and, second, of Martha and Mary's welcome to Jesus.

It may come as a bit of a surprise to hear Jesus say, "Martha, Martha, you are worried and distracted by many things; there is need of only one thing. Mary has chosen the better part." But, we might ask, what about the meal, the house, the dishes?

What is that "one thing" to which Jesus refers? Time and time again Jesus invites us to hear the word of God and to welcome it in our lives. In our busy-ness, we are reminded to be still, to listen with our hearts to God's word, and to let it speak in our lives.

Are we a welcoming people? Is our parish a welcoming community? Too often we are distracted by questions of belonging. Today's psalm asks: "Who may dwell on your holy hill?" The response is those who "speak the truth from their heart." We need to take the time to listen, to listen to one another's stories of God's love acting in our lives and to celebrate that word of God living among us!

Caryl Green, Chelsea, QC

ENTRANCE ANTIPHON *(Psalm 54:4, 6)*

God himself is my help. The Lord upholds my life. I will offer you a willing sacrifice; I will praise your name, O Lord, for its goodness.

INTRODUCTORY RITES *(p. 5)*

OPENING PRAYER

Lord, be merciful to your people. Fill us with your gifts and make us always eager to serve you in faith, hope and love.

FIRST READING *(Genesis 18:1-10)*

The Lord appeared to Abraham by the oaks of Mamre, as Abraham sat at the entrance of his tent in the heat of the day. Abraham looked up and saw three men standing near him. When he saw them, he ran from the tent entrance to meet them, and bowed down to the ground.

He said, "My lord, if I find favour with you, do not pass by your servant. Let a little water be brought, and wash your feet, and rest yourselves under the tree. Let me bring a little bread, that you may refresh yourselves, and after that you may pass on—since you have come to your servant." So they said, "Do as you have said."

And Abraham hastened into the tent to Sarah, and said, "Make ready quickly three measures of choice flour, knead it, and make cakes." Abraham ran to the herd, and took a calf, tender and good, and gave it to the servant, who hastened to prepare it. Then he took curds and milk and the calf that he had prepared, and set it before them; and he stood by them under the tree while they ate.

They said to Abraham, "Where is your wife Sarah?" And he said, "There, in the tent."

Then one said, "I will surely return to you in due season, and your wife Sarah shall have a son."

The word of the Lord. **Thanks be to God.**

RESPONSORIAL PSALM *(Psalm 15)*

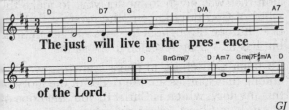

GJ

℞. **The just will live in the presence of the Lord.**

O Lord, who may dwell on your holy • **hill?**
Those who walk blamelessly,
    and do what is • **right,**
and speak the truth from their • **heart;**
who do not slander with • **their** tongue. ℞.

Those who do no evil to their • **friends,**
nor take up a reproach against
    their • **neighbours;**
in whose eyes the wicked are de•-**spised,**
but who honour those who fear • **the** Lord. ℞.

Those who stand by their oath
    even to their • **hurt;**
who do not lend money at • **interest,**
and do not take a bribe against the • **innocent.**
Those who do these things
    shall never • **be** moved. ℞.

SECOND READING *(Colossians 1:24-28)*

I am now rejoicing in my sufferings for your sake and in my flesh I am completing what is lacking in Christ's afflictions for the sake of his body, that is, the church.

I became its servant according to God's commission that was given to me for you, to make the word of God fully known, the mystery that has been hidden throughout the ages and generations but has now been revealed to his saints.

To them God chose to make known how great among the Gentiles are the riches of the glory of this mystery, which is Christ in you, the hope of glory. It is Christ whom we proclaim, warning everyone and teaching everyone in all wisdom, so that we may present everyone mature in Christ.

The word of the Lord. **Thanks be to God.**

GOSPEL ACCLAMATION *(See Luke 8:15)*

If not sung, this acclamation is omitted.

Blessed are they who have kept the word with a generous heart and yield a harvest through perseverance.

GOSPEL *(Luke 10:38-42)*

A reading from the holy gospel according to Luke. **Glory to you, Lord.**

Now as Jesus and his disciples went on their way, he entered a certain village, where a woman named Martha welcomed him into her home. She had a sister named Mary, who sat at the Lord's feet and listened to what he was saying.

But Martha was distracted by her many tasks; so she came to Jesus and asked, "Lord, do you not care that my sister has left me to do all the work by myself? Tell her then to help me."

But the Lord answered her, "Martha, Martha, you are worried and distracted by many things; there is need of only one thing. Mary has chosen the better part, which will not be taken away from her."

The gospel of the Lord. **Praise to you, Lord Jesus Christ.**

PROFESSION OF FAITH *(Creed, pp. 11-12)*

PRAYER OF THE FAITHFUL

The following intentions are suggestions only.

℟: **Lord, hear our prayer.**

For the Church, striving to live in openness to God's word revealed in our day, we pray to the Lord: ℟.

For our world, in need of structures that welcome and respect the stranger, we pray to the Lord: ℟.

For busy people seeking stillness to listen to God and their own hearts, we pray to the Lord: ℟.

For this Christian community, called to put God's word of love into action every day, we pray to the Lord: ℟.

PREPARATION OF THE GIFTS *(p. 13)*

PRAYER OVER THE GIFTS

Lord, bring us closer to salvation through thes
gifts which we bring in your honour. Accept th
perfect sacrifice you have given us, bless it as yo
blessed the gifts of Abel.

PREFACE *(Sundays in Ord. Time, p. 18)*

COMMUNION ANTIPHON *(Psalm 111:4-5)*

**The Lord keeps in our minds the wonderfu
things he has done. He is compassion and love
he always provides for his faithful.**

PRAYER AFTER COMMUNION

Merciful Father, may these mysteries give us new
purpose and bring us to a new life in you.

BLESSING AND DISMISSAL *(p. 65)*

Last June, I was blessed to be with my mother for three weeks while she was dying. She asked me how it was that when she was sick or depressed—at the time that she most needed it—she was not able to pray. She was a woman who prayed fervently throughout her life. When it came near the end, I found myself repeating the rote prayers of my childhood for her and for myself: the Our Father, the Hail Mary and the Glory Be. They swelled up spontaneously to my lips; I knew they were her familiar prayers.

Many of us feel we fall short when we compare our faith with the faith of our parents or grandparents. They were such people of faith! Our society makes this kind of simple faith so difficult to practise. It is hard for us to identify deeply with the words of today's epistle, "live your lives in him, rooted and built up in him." How can we experience that? We are driven to ask, "Am I really Christian?"... especially if we cannot seem to pray as our ancestors in the faith did, as Abraham did, in his haggling with God.

This disaffection which many of us feel is also felt by many of the great spiritual writers of our time. The monk, Thomas Merton, prayed, "I believe that the desire to please you does in fact please you." Isn't Merton's prayer similar to the disciples' "Lord, teach us to pray..."? The disciples' request, made at a specific moment in time 2,000 years ago, has become a timeless cry, our own deepest prayer, "Lord, teach us to pray..."

John Walsh, Scarborough, ON

ENTRANCE ANTIPHON *(Psalm 68:5-6, 35)*

God is in his holy dwelling; he will give a home to the lonely, he gives power and strength to his people.

INTRODUCTORY RITES *(p. 5)*

OPENING PRAYER

God our Father and protector, without you nothing is holy, nothing has value. Guide us to everlasting life by helping us to use wisely the blessings you have given to the world.

FIRST READING *(Genesis 18:20-32)*

The Lord appeared to Abraham by the oaks of Mamre and said, "How great is the outcry against Sodom and Gomorrah and how very grave their sin! I must go down and see whether they have done altogether according to the outcry that has come to me; and if not, I will know."

Then Abraham came near and said, "Will you indeed sweep away the righteous with the wicked? Suppose there are fifty righteous within the city; will you then sweep away the place and not forgive it for the fifty righteous who are in it?

Far be it from you to do such a thing, to slay the righteous with the wicked, so that the righteous fare as the wicked! Far be that from you! Shall not the Judge of all the earth do what is just?" And the Lord said, "If I find at Sodom fifty righteous in the city, I will forgive the whole place for their sake."

Abraham answered, "Let me take it upon myself to speak to the Lord, I who am but dust and ashes. Suppose five of the fifty righteous are lacking? Will you destroy the whole city for lack of five?" And the Lord said, "I will not destroy it if I find forty-five there."

Again Abraham spoke to the Lord, "Suppose forty are found there." He answered, "For the sake of forty I will not do it."

Then Abraham said, "Oh do not let the Lord be angry if I speak. Suppose thirty are found there." The Lord answered, "I will not do it, if I find thirty there."

Abraham said, "Let me take it upon myself to speak to the Lord. Suppose twenty are found there." The Lord answered, "For the sake of twenty I will not destroy it."

Then Abraham said, "Oh do not let the Lord be angry if I speak just once more. Suppose ten are found there." The Lord answered, "For the sake of ten I will not destroy it."

The word of the Lord. **Thanks be to God.**

RESPONSORIAL PSALM *(Psalm 138)*

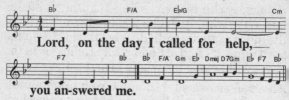

GJ

℟. **Lord, on the day I called for help,
you answered me.**

I give you thanks, O Lord,
   with my whole • **heart,**
before the gods I sing your • **praise;**
I bow down toward your ho•**-ly** temple.
I give thanks to your name for your
    steadfast love • **and** your faithfulness. ℟.

For you have exalted your • **name**
and your word above • **everything.**
On the day I called, • **you** answered_me;
you increased my • **strength** of soul. ℟.

For though the Lord is high,
   he regards the • **lowly;**
but the haughty he perceives from far a•**-way.**
Though I walk in the midst • **of** trouble,
you preserve me against
   the • **wrath_of** my enemies. ℟.

You stretch out your hand
   and your right hand de•**-livers_me.**
The Lord will fulfil his purpose for • **me;**
your steadfast love, O Lord,
   endures • **for-**ever.
Do not forsake the • **work_of** your hands. ℟.

428

SECOND READING *(Colossians 2:6-14)*

Brothers and sisters, as you have received Christ Jesus the Lord, continue to live your lives in him, rooted and built up in him and established in the faith, just as you were taught, abounding in thanksgiving. For in him the whole fullness of deity dwells bodily, and you have come to fullness in him, who is the head of every ruler and authority.

In him also you were circumcised with a spiritual circumcision, by putting off the body of flesh in the circumcision of Christ. When you were buried with Christ in baptism, you were also raised with him through faith in the power of God, who raised Christ from the dead.

And when you were dead in trespasses and the uncircumcision of your flesh, God made you alive together with him, when he forgave us all our trespasses, erasing the record that stood against us with its legal demands. He set this aside, nailing it to the cross.

The word of the Lord. **Thanks be to God.**

GOSPEL ACCLAMATION *(Romans 8:15)*

If not sung, this acclamation is omitted.

You have received the Spirit which makes us God's children, and in that Spirit we call God our Father.

GOSPEL *(Luke 11:1-13)*

A reading from the holy gospel according to Luke.
Glory to you, Lord.

Jesus was praying in a certain place, and after he had finished, one of his disciples said to him, "Lord, teach us to pray, as John taught his disciples."

He said to them, "When you pray, say: 'Father, hallowed be your name. Your kingdom come. Give us each day our daily bread. And forgive us our sins, for we ourselves forgive everyone indebted to us. And do not bring us to the time of trial.' "

And Jesus said to the disciples, "Suppose one of you has a friend, and you go to him at midnight and say to him, 'Friend, lend me three loaves of bread; for a friend of mine has arrived, and I have nothing to set before him.' And your friend answers from within, 'Do not bother me; the door has already been locked, and my children are with me in bed; I cannot get up and give you anything.'

"I tell you, even though he will not get up and give him anything because he is his friend, at least because of his persistence he will get up and give him whatever he needs.

"So I say to you: Ask, and it will be given you; search, and you will find; knock, and the door will be opened for you. For everyone who asks receives, and everyone who searches finds, and for everyone who knocks, the door will be opened.

"Is there anyone among you who, if your child asks for a fish, will give a snake instead of a fish? Or if the child asks for an egg, will give a scorpion?

"If you then, who are evil, know how to give good gifts to your children, how much more will the heavenly Father give the Holy Spirit to those who ask him!"

The gospel of the Lord. **Praise to you, Lord Jesus Christ.**

PROFESSION OF FAITH *(Creed, pp. 11-12)*

PRAYER OF THE FAITHFUL

The following intentions are suggestions only.

℟: **Lord, hear our prayer.**

For the Church, people of prayer and praise, we pray to the Lord: ℟.

For the healing of nations and for peace and justice in lands torn by strife, we pray to the Lord: ℟.

For the poor and the suffering and for those who are hurt and wounded, we pray to the Lord: ℟.

For us, God's people, seeking strength in our common prayer and our desire to do God's will, we pray to the Lord: ℟.

PREPARATION OF THE GIFTS *(p. 13)*

PRAYER OVER THE GIFTS

Lord, receive these offerings chosen from your many gifts. May these mysteries make us holy and lead us to eternal joy.

PREFACE *(Sundays in Ord. Time, p. 18)*

COMMUNION ANTIPHON *(Psalm 103:2)*

O bless the Lord, my soul, and remember all his kindness.

PRAYER AFTER COMMUNION

Lord, we receive the sacrament which celebrates the memory of the death and resurrection of Christ your Son. May this gift bring us closer to our eternal salvation.

BLESSING AND DISMISSAL *(p. 65)*

The readings on the transfiguration of Jesus show him to be the one foretold, revealing the glory and majesty bestowed on him by God. But putting this account into perspective with all the later actions of Peter, it also reveals much of the compassion, love and forgiveness of God.

Peter, John and James are given something rare in the spiritual life: a sign from God that the master they follow is the Chosen One. Peter speaks of it again when he says in his letter, "we had been eyewitnesses of his majesty."

Even so, the Peter who has had this sign is the same one who later denies knowing Jesus when he is betrayed to the power of the chief priests—not once, but three times.

Yet Peter is forgiven, not only forgiven but given the responsibility of caring for those who believe in Jesus. In our worldly way of looking at things, Peter should never be trusted again if he could deny his master. Yet once forgiven, he is reinstated in the circle of Jesus' friends, restored to Jesus' love. This is a very reassuring thought. Although we are sinners, yet when we turn to ask forgiveness we can be absolutely sure of God's mercy and love.

Barbara Green, Albany, PEI

ENTRANCE ANTIPHON *(See Matthew 17:5)*

In the shining cloud the Spirit is seen; from it th
voice of the Father is heard: This is my Son, m
beloved, in whom is all my delight. Listen to him

INTRODUCTORY RITES *(p. 5)*

OPENING PRAYER

God our Father, in the transfigured glory of Chris
your Son, you strengthen our faith by confirmin
the witness of your prophets, and show us th
splendour of your beloved sons and daughters
As we listen to the voice of your Son, help us t
become heirs to eternal life with him.

FIRST READING *(Daniel 7:9-10, 13-14)*

As I watched, thrones were set in place, and a
Ancient One took his throne. His clothing wa
white as snow, and the hair of his head like pur
wool. His throne was fiery flames, and its wheel
were burning fire. A stream of fire issued an
flowed out from his presence. A thousand thou
sands served him, and ten thousand times te
thousand stood attending him. The court sat i
judgment, and the books were opened.

As I watched visions in the night, I saw one like
human being coming with the clouds of heaven
And he came to the Ancient One and was pre
sented before him.

To him was given dominion and glory and king
ship, that all peoples, nations, and language
should serve him. His dominion is an everlasting
dominion that shall not pass away, and his king
ship is one that shall never be destroyed.

The word of the Lord. **Thanks be to God.**

RESPONSORIAL PSALM *(Psalm 97)*

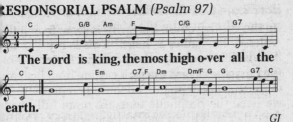

The Lord is king, the most high o-ver all the earth.

GJ

℟. **The Lord is king, the most high
over all the earth.**

The Lord is king! Let the earth re•-**joice**;
let the many coastlands • **be** glad!
Clouds and thick darkness
    are • **all** a-round him;
righteousness and justice
    are the foundation • **of** his throne. ℟.

The mountains melt like wax
    before the • **Lord,**
before the Lord of all • **the** earth.
The heavens pro•-**claim** his righteousness;
and all the peoples be•-**hold** his glory. ℟.

For you, O Lord, are most high
    over all the • **earth;**
you are exalted far above • **all** gods.
Rejoice in the Lord, • **O** you righteous,
and give thanks to his •**ho**-ly name. ℟.

SECOND READING *(2 Peter 1:16-19)*

We did not follow cleverly devised myths when
we made known to you the power and coming of
our Lord Jesus Christ, but we had been eyewitnesses of his majesty. For he received honour and

glory from God the Father when that voice was conveyed to him by the Majestic Glory, saying "This is my Son, my Beloved, with whom I am well pleased."

We ourselves heard this voice come from heaven while we were with him on the holy mountain. So we have the prophetic message more fully confirmed. You will do well to be attentive to this as to a lamp shining in a dark place, until the day dawns and the morning star rises in your hearts.

The word of the Lord. **Thanks be to God.**

GOSPEL ACCLAMATION *(Matthew 17:5)*

If not sung, this acclamation is omitted.

This is my beloved Son, in whom is all my delight, hear him.

GOSPEL *(Luke 9:28-36)*

A reading from the holy gospel according to Luke. **Glory to you, Lord.**

Jesus took with him Peter and John and James, and went up on the mountain to pray. And while he was praying, the appearance of his face changed, and his clothes became dazzling white.

Suddenly they saw two men, Moses and Elijah, talking to Jesus. They appeared in glory and were speaking of his departure, which he was about to accomplish at Jerusalem.

Now Peter and his companions were weighed down with sleep; but since they had stayed awake, they saw his glory and the two men who stood with him.

ust as they were leaving him, Peter said to Jesus, Master, it is good for us to be here; let us make hree tents, one for you, one for Moses, and one or Elijah," but Peter did not know what he said.

Vhile he was saying this, a cloud came and vershadowed them; and they were terrified as hey entered the cloud. Then from the cloud came voice that said, "This is my Son, my Chosen; isten to him!"

Vhen the voice had spoken, Jesus was found lone. The disciples kept silent and in those days old no one any of the things they had seen.

The gospel of the Lord. **Praise to you, Lord Jesus Christ.**

PROFESSION OF FAITH *(Creed, pp. 11-12)*

PRAYER OF THE FAITHFUL

The following intentions are suggestions only.

℟. **Lord, hear our prayer.**

For the Church, called to learn from Peter the path of forgiveness and reconciliation, we pray to the Lord: ℟.

For peace in our broken world and for leaders who work tirelessly for peace, we pray to the Lord: ℟.

For those who are lonely, or sick or in prison, we pray to the Lord: ℟.

For us, God's people gathered here, tasting at the Lord's table the feast of the kingdom, we pray to the Lord: ℟.

PREPARATION OF THE GIFTS *(p. 13)*

PRAYER OVER THE GIFTS

Lord, by the transfiguration of your Son make our gifts holy, and by his radiant glory free us from our sins.

PREFACE *(Transfiguration, p. 18)*

COMMUNION ANTIPHON *(1 John 3:2)*

When Christ is revealed we shall be like him, for we shall see him as he is.

PRAYER AFTER COMMUNION

Lord, you revealed the true radiance of Christ in the glory of his transfiguration. May the food we receive from heaven change us into his image.

BLESSING AND DISMISSAL *(p. 65)*

Is Christian life worth living? Do disturbing newscasts suggest to you that good may not triumph over evil after all? Do the prosperity of the unscrupulous and the greed of officials—both secular and religious—make you wonder if you too should live for yourself alone? If you are short of hope, today's readings offer this: persevere in faith because you know Jesus Christ.

The people of Israel were able to find in the Exodus event proof of God's justice—the righteous were delivered and the wicked destroyed—and assurance that their trust in God had not been misplaced. They could remain hopeful and consoled even in times of severe adversity.

In the gospel story, the cost of disobedience is more than just physical punishment; there is also the possibility of a permanent rupture in the relationship between the slave and his master.

Through Jesus Christ we have a new relationship to God which we cannot ignore: a relationship of love, gratitude and trust. Rejection of this loving relationship with God leaves us enslaved to greed, selfishness, fear, aggression, and so on.

Our true treasure is one-ness with God and we must not substitute any other wealth or idol in its place. Let us persevere in faith and trust, looking forward in hope to union with God.

— *Christine Mader, Toronto, ON*

ENTRANCE ANTIPHON *(Psalm 74:19-23)*

Lord, be true to your covenant, forget not the life of your poor ones for ever. Rise up, O God, and defend your cause; do not ignore the shouts of your enemies.

INTRODUCTORY RITES *(p. 5)*

OPENING PRAYER

Almighty and ever-living God, your Spirit made us your children, confident to call you Father. Increase your Spirit within us and bring us to our promised inheritance.

FIRST READING *(Wisdom 18:6-9)*

The night of the deliverance from Egypt was made known beforehand to our ancestors, so that they might rejoice in sure knowledge of the oaths in which they trusted.

The deliverance of the righteous and the destruction of their enemies were expected by your people. For by the same means by which you punished our enemies you called us to yourself and glorified us.

For in secret the holy children of good people offered sacrifices, and with one accord agreed to the divine law, so that the saints would share alike the same things, both blessings and dangers; and already they were singing the praises of the ancestors.

The word of the Lord. **Thanks be to God.**

RESPONSORIAL PSALM *(Psalm 33)*

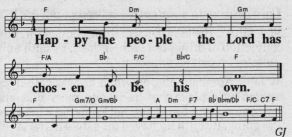

Hap - py the peo - ple the Lord has chos - en to be his own.

GJ

℞. **Happy the people the Lord has chosen
to be his own.**

Rejoice in the Lord, • **O** you righteous.
Praise be•-**fits** the upright.
Happy is the nation whose • **God_is** the Lord,
the people whom
   he has • **chosen_as** his heritage. ℞.

Truly the eye of the Lord
   is on • **those** who fear_him,
on those who hope in his • **stead**-fast love,
to deliver their • **soul** from death,
and to keep them a•-**live** in famine. ℞.

Our soul waits • **for** the Lord;
he is our • **help** and shield.
Let your steadfast love, O Lord, • **be** up-on_us,
even as we • **hope** in you. ℞.

SECOND READING *(Hebrews 11:1-2, 8-19)*

The shorter version ends at the asterisks.

Now faith is the assurance of things hoped for, the conviction of things not seen. Indeed, by faith our ancestors received approval.

By faith Abraham obeyed when he was called to set out for a place that he was to receive as an inheritance; and he set out, not knowing where he was going. By faith he stayed for a time in the land he had been promised, as in a foreign land, living in tents, as did Isaac and Jacob, who were heirs with him of the same promise.

For Abraham looked forward to the city that has foundations, whose architect and builder is God. By faith Sarah herself, though barren, received power to conceive, even when she was too old, because she considered him faithful who had promised.

Therefore from one person, and this one as good as dead, descendants were born, "as many as the stars of heaven and as the innumerable grains of sand by the seashore."

* * *

All of these died in faith without having received the promises, but from a distance they saw and greeted them. They confessed that they were strangers and foreigners on the earth, for people who speak in this way make it clear that they are seeking a homeland. If they had been thinking of the land that they had left behind, they would have had opportunity to return.

But as it is, they desire a better country, that is, a heavenly one. Therefore God is not ashamed to be called their God; indeed, he has prepared a city for them.

By faith Abraham, when put to the test, offered up Isaac. He who had received the promises was ready to offer up his only son, of whom he had been told, "It is through Isaac that descendants shall be named for you." Abraham considered the fact that God is able even to raise someone from the dead—and figuratively speaking, he did receive Isaac back.

The word of the Lord. **Thanks be to God.**

GOSPEL ACCLAMATION *(Matthew 24:42, 44)*

If not sung, this acclamation is omitted.

Be watchful and ready: you know not when the Son of Man is coming.

GOSPEL *(Luke 12:32-48)*

For the shorter version, omit the indented parts.

A reading from the holy gospel according to Luke. **Glory to you, Lord.**

> Jesus said to his disciples, "Do not be afraid, little flock, for it is your Father's good pleasure to give you the kingdom. Sell your possessions, and give alms. Make purses for yourselves that do not wear out, an unfailing treasure in heaven, where no thief comes near and no moth destroys. For where your treasure is, there your heart will be also.

"Be dressed for action and have your lamps lit; be like those who are waiting for their master to return from the wedding banquet, so that they may open the door for him as soon as he comes and knocks. Blessed are those slaves whom the master finds alert when he comes; truly I tell you, he will fasten his belt and have them sit down to eat, and he will come and serve them. If he comes during the middle of the night, or near dawn, and finds them so, blessed are those slaves.

"But know this: if the owner of the house had known at what hour the thief was coming, he would not have let his house be broken into. You also must be ready, for the Son of Man is coming at an unexpected hour."

Peter said, "Lord, are you telling this parable for us or for everyone?" And the Lord said, "Who then is the faithful and prudent manager whom his master will put in charge of his slaves, to give them their allowance of food at the proper time? Blessed is that slave whom his master will find at work when he arrives. Truly I tell you, he will put that one in charge of all his possessions. But if that slave says to himself, 'My master is delayed in coming,' and if he begins to beat the other slaves, men and women, and to eat and drink and get drunk, the master of that slave will come on a day when he does not expect him and at an hour that he does not know, and will cut him in pieces, and put him with the unfaithful.

"That slave who knew what his master wanted, but did not prepare himself or do what was wanted, will receive a severe beating. But the one who did not know and did what deserved a beating will receive a light beating.

"From everyone to whom much has been given, much will be required; and from the one to whom much has been entrusted, even more will be demanded."

The gospel of the Lord. **Praise to you, Lord Jesus Christ.**

PROFESSION OF FAITH *(Creed, pp. 11-12)*

PRAYER OF THE FAITHFUL

The following intentions are suggestions only.

℞: **Lord, hear our prayer.**

For the Church, faithful and steadfast sign of the love and trust between God and humanity, we pray to the Lord: ℞.

For world leaders, called to be just and caring stewards of the world's material wealth, we pray to the Lord: ℞.

For the poor and all who search in hope for relief from their troubles, we pray to the Lord: ℞.

For this parish community, striving to live as God's holy people, we pray to the Lord: ℞.

PREPARATION OF THE GIFTS *(p. 13)*

PRAYER OVER THE GIFTS

God of power, giver of the gifts we bring, accept the offering of your Church and make it the sacrament of our salvation.

PREFACE *(Sundays in Ord. Time, p. 18)*

COMMUNION ANTIPHON *(Psalm 147:12, 14)*

Praise the Lord, Jerusalem; he feeds you with the finest wheat.

PRAYER AFTER COMMUNION

Lord, may the eucharist you give us bring us to salvation and keep us faithful to the light of your truth.

BLESSING AND DISMISSAL *(p. 65)*

Prophets never win popularity contests. More often than not, they suffer immensely for their beliefs and faithfulness. They are the heroes of faith.

All the readings today are prophetic: they call us to conversion, and the journey of conversion will be very demanding.

Like Jeremiah, Jesus calls the people to conversion, to change. The fire he brings to us is the fire of his love. He is eager to have his love burning within us.

The gospel words of Jesus seem harsh. Jesus does not want to cause division, especially among families, but it will happen. His message and mission will convince some people to respond to his call, while others will mock those who become followers.

Jesus calls us to heed his prophetic words. Are we open to the call of Jesus? Does fear prevent us from choosing a life rooted in Jesus? Jesus calls us to strip away everything that hinders us, to be converted and to become prophets ourselves. Who says we cannot be prophets? Listen to the Good News and let the Spirit of Jesus set you on fire with his love.

Murray Hanowski, Neudorf, SK

ENTRANCE ANTIPHON *(Psalm 84:10-11)*

God, our protector, keep us in mind; always give strength to your people. For if we can be with you even one day, it is better than a thousand without you.

INTRODUCTORY RITES *(p. 5)*

OPENING PRAYER

God our Father, may we love you in all things and above all things and reach the joy you have prepared for us beyond all our imagining.

FIRST READING *(Jeremiah 38:1-2, 4-6, 8-10)*

The officials of King Zedekiah heard the words that Jeremiah was saying to all the people: "Thus says the Lord: 'Those who stay in the city shall die; but those who go out to the Chaldeans shall live.' "

Then the officials said to the king, "This man ought to be put to death, because he is discouraging the soldiers who are left in this city, and all the people, by speaking such words to them. For this man is not seeking the welfare of this people, but their harm."

King Zedekiah said, "Here he is; he is in your hands; for the king is powerless against you."

So they took Jeremiah and threw him into the cistern of Malchiah, the king's son, which was in the court of the guard, letting Jeremiah down by ropes. Now there was no water in the cistern, but only mud, and Jeremiah sank in the mud.

So Ebed-melech the Ethiopian, an officer in the king's house, left the king's house and spoke to the king, "My lord king, these men have acted wickedly in all they did to the prophet Jeremiah by throwing him into the cistern to die there of hunger, for there is no bread left in the city." Then the king commanded Ebed-melech the Ethiopian, "Take three men with you from here, and pull the prophet Jeremiah up from the cistern before he dies."

The word of the Lord. **Thanks be to God.**

RESPONSORIAL PSALM *(Psalm 40)*

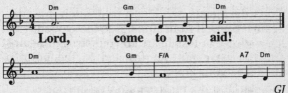

Lord, come to my aid!

GJ

℟. **Lord, come to my aid!**

I waited patiently for the • **Lord;**
he inclined to me and heard • **my** cry. ℟.

He drew me up from the desolate pit,
   out of the miry • **bog,**
and set my feet upon a rock,
   making my steps • **se**-cure. ℟.

He put a new song in my mouth,
   a song of praise to our • **God.**
Many will see and fear, and put their trust
   in • **the** Lord. ℟.

As for me, I am poor and needy,
   but the Lord takes thought for • **me.**
You are my help and my deliverer;
   do not delay, O • **my** God. ℟.

SECOND READING *(Hebrews 12:1-4)*

Since we are surrounded by so great a cloud of witnesses, let us also lay aside every weight and the sin that clings so closely, and let us run with perseverance the race that is set before us, looking to Jesus the pioneer and perfecter of our faith, who for the sake of the joy that was set before him endured the cross, disregarding its shame, and has taken his seat at the right hand of the throne of God.

Consider Jesus who endured such hostility against himself from sinners, so that you may not grow weary or lose heart. In your struggle against sin you have not yet resisted to the point of shedding your blood.

The word of the Lord. **Thanks be to God.**

GOSPEL ACCLAMATION *(John 10:27)*

If not sung, this acclamation is omitted.

My sheep listen to my voice, says the Lord; I know them, and they follow me.

GOSPEL *(Luke 12:49-53)*

A reading from the holy gospel according to Luke. **Glory to you, Lord.**

Jesus said to his disciples: "I came to bring fire to the earth, and how I wish it were already kindled! I have a baptism with which to be baptized, and what stress I am under until it is completed!

"Do you think that I have come to bring peace to the earth? No, I tell you, but rather division! From now on five in one household will be divided, three against two and two against three; they will be divided: father against son and son against father, mother against daughter and daughter against mother, mother-in-law against her daughter-in-law and daughter-in-law against mother-in-law."

The gospel of the Lord. **Praise to you, Lord Jesus Christ.**

PROFESSION OF FAITH *(Creed, pp. 11-12)*

PRAYER OF THE FAITHFUL

The following intentions are suggestions only.

℟: **Lord, hear our prayer.**

For the Church and its leaders, called to hear and to proclaim the words of the prophets, we pray to the Lord: ℟.

For national leaders willing to risk the prophetic task of establishing peace and justice, we pray to the Lord: ℟.

For those among us who are poor, sick and persecuted, and for all who minister to them, we pray to the Lord: ℟.

For us, called in baptism to be a people of prophetic words and actions, we pray to the Lord: ℟.

PREPARATION OF THE GIFTS *(p. 13)*

PRAYER OVER THE GIFTS

Lord, accept our sacrifice as a holy exchange of gifts. By offering what you have given us may we receive the gift of yourself.

PREFACE *(Sundays in Ord. Time, p. 18)*

COMMUNION ANTIPHON *(Psalm 130:7)*

With the Lord there is mercy, and fullness of redemption.

PRAYER AFTER COMMUNION

God of mercy, by this sacrament you make us one with Christ. By becoming more like him on earth, may we come to share his glory in heaven.

BLESSING AND DISMISSAL *(p. 65)*

Summer is drawing to a close once again. Many of us have enjoyed some vacation time, or at least become attuned to the different rhythms imposed by heat and sunshine, longer days and more flexible schedules. Now we look forward—with varying degrees of anticipation or reluctance!—to resuming the tasks and timetables that autumn brings.

Today's gospel, with its talk of closed doors and weeping and gnashing of teeth, seems a harsh one to digest in these last lazy summer days. We are somewhat taken aback by Jesus' uncompromising words which offer little in the way of encouragement or consolation.

Perhaps what is being offered is a warning against complacency. We are reminded that the reign of God is neither an automatic right nor an exclusive possession. Rather, God's invitation is extended to all people and to all nations, and in particular to those who are 'last' in the eyes of society.

Sobering food for thought as summer ends!

Krystyna Higgins, Kitchener, ON

ENTRANCE ANTIPHON *(Psalm 86:1-3)*

Listen, Lord, and answer me. Save your servant who trusts in you. I call to you all day long, have mercy on me, O Lord.

INTRODUCTORY RITES *(p. 5)*

OPENING PRAYER

Father, help us to seek the values that will bring us lasting joy in this changing world. In our desire for what you promise make us one in mind and heart.

FIRST READING *(Isaiah 66:18-21)*

Thus says the Lord: "For I know their works and their thoughts, and I am coming to gather all nations and tongues; and they shall come and shall see my glory, and I will set a sign among them.

"From them I will send survivors to the nations, to Tarshish, Put, and Lud—which draw the bow—to Tubal and Javan, to the coastlands far away that have not heard of my fame or seen my glory; and they shall declare my glory among the nations.

"They shall bring all your kindred from all the nations as an offering to the Lord, on horses, and in chariots, and in litters, and on mules, and on dromedaries, to my holy mountain Jerusalem," says the Lord, "just as the Israelites bring a grain offering in a clean vessel to the house of the Lord.

"And I will also take some of them as priests and as Levites," says the Lord.

The word of the Lord. **Thanks be to God.**

RESPONSORIAL PSALM *(Psalm 117)*

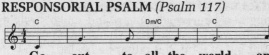

Go out to all the world and

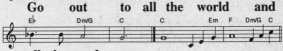

tell the good news.

GJ

℟. **Go out to all the world and tell the good news.**

Praise the Lord, • **all** you nations!
Extol him, • **all** you peoples! ℟.

For great is his steadfast • **love** toward us,
and the faithfulness of the Lord
en•**-dures** for-ever. ℟.

SECOND READING *(Hebrews 12:5-7, 11-13)*

And you have forgotten the exhortation that addresses you as children—"My child, do not regard lightly the discipline of the Lord, or lose heart when you are punished by him; for the Lord disciplines those whom he loves, and chastises every child whom he accepts."

Endure trials for the sake of discipline. God is treating you as children; for what child is there whom a parent does not discipline?

Now, discipline always seems painful rather than pleasant at the time, but later it yields the peaceful fruit of righteousness to those who have been trained by it.

Therefore lift your drooping hands and strengthen your weak knees, and make straight paths for your feet, so that what is lame may not be put out of joint, but rather be healed.

The word of the Lord. **Thanks be to God.**

GOSPEL ACCLAMATION *(John 14:6)*

If not sung, this acclamation is omitted.

I am the way, the truth, and the life, says the Lord; no one comes to the Father, except through me.

GOSPEL *(Luke 13:22-30)*

A reading from the holy gospel according to Luke. **Glory to you, Lord.**

Jesus went through one town and village after another, teaching as he made his way to Jerusalem. Someone asked him, "Lord, will only a few be saved?"

Jesus said to them, "Strive to enter through the narrow door; for many, I tell you, will try to enter and will not be able.

"When once the owner of the house has got up and shut the door, and you begin to stand outside and to knock at the door, saying, 'Lord, open to us,' then in reply he will say to you, 'I do not know where you come from.'

"Then you will begin to say, 'We ate and drank with you, and you taught in our streets.' But the Lord will say, 'I do not know where you come from; go away from me, all you evildoers!'

"There will be weeping and gnashing of teeth when you see Abraham and Isaac and Jacob and all the prophets in the kingdom of God, and you yourselves thrown out. Then people will come from east and west, from north and south, and will eat in the kingdom of God.

"Indeed, some are last who will be first, and some are first who will be last."

The gospel of the Lord. **Praise to you, Lord Jesus Christ.**

PROFESSION OF FAITH *(Creed, pp. 11-12)*

PRAYER OF THE FAITHFUL

The following intentions are suggestions only.

℞: **Lord, hear our prayer.**

For all people of faith, sharers in the work of building up the reign of God, we pray to the Lord: ℞.

For those who work, publicly and privately, to end unjust structures that oppress the poor and the powerless, we pray to the Lord: ℞.

For those who feel excluded or unwelcome in our communities, we pray to the Lord: ℞.

For us, called in baptism to welcome all in God's name, we pray to the Lord: ℞.

PREPARATION OF THE GIFTS *(p. 13)*

PRAYER OVER THE GIFTS

Merciful God, the perfect sacrifice of Jesus Christ made us your people. In your love, grant peace and unity to your Church.

PREFACE *(Sundays in Ord. Time, p. 18)*

COMMUNION ANTIPHON *(Psalm 104:13-15)*

Lord, the earth is filled with your gift from heaven; man grows bread from earth, and wine to cheer his heart.

PRAYER AFTER COMMUNION

Lord, may this eucharist increase within us the healing power of your love. May it guide and direct our efforts to please you in all things.

BLESSING AND DISMISSAL *(p. 65)*

September 3 Twenty-second Sunday in Ordinary Time

The most prestigious banquet I have ever attended took place when Nelson Mandela came to Canada, shortly after his release from over 20 years in a South African prison. The Prime Minister was there, along with a host of dignitaries, business leaders and people from community groups. Our tables were pre-assigned. Mine was at the very back of the hall, next to a serving station. To my surprise, a prominent politician was also seated there. Just before Mandela's arrival, the politician and his companion were inexplicably moved to the front of the room. Two young black women from a small community organization were steered into the vacated chairs.

Few of the 2,000 people at the banquet could actually *see* Mandela. Between the head table and the rest of us were a raised platform and a long string of television cameras. We ate our meals while watching his image on two huge video monitors.

After the speeches, my tablemates and I stepped out into the foyer—just as Mandela, surrounded by security guards, was being whisked away. He stopped to speak to us. He took the hand of the young woman next to me and tears of joy and admiration rolled down her face. It was a touching moment.

I sometimes think about the people who had 'places of honour' at the front of that room but never actually met Nelson Mandela. And I think about the long struggle for justice and the rewards that come to those who are 'last.'

Susan Eaton, Toronto, ON

ENTRANCE ANTIPHON *(Psalm 86:3, 5)*

I call to you all day long, have mercy on me, O Lord. You are good and forgiving, full of love for all who call to you.

INTRODUCTORY RITES *(p. 5)*

OPENING PRAYER

Almighty God, every good thing comes from you. Fill our hearts with love for you, increase our faith, and by your constant care protect the good you have given us.

FIRST READING *(Sirach 3:17-20, 28-29)*

My child, perform your tasks with humility; then you will be loved by those whom God accepts. The greater you are, the more you must humble yourself; so you will find favour in the sight of the Lord. Many are lofty and renowned, but to the humble the Lord reveals his secrets. For great is the might of the Lord; but by the humble he is glorified.

When calamity befalls the proud, there is no healing, for an evil plant has taken root in them.

The mind of the intelligent appreciates proverbs, and an attentive ear is the desire of the wise.

The word of the Lord. **Thanks be to God.**

RESPONSORIAL PSALM *(Psalm 68)*

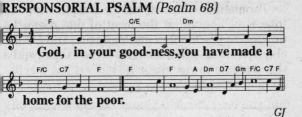

God, in your good-ness, you have made a

home for the poor.

GJ

℟. **God, in your goodness,
you have made a home for the poor.**

Let the righteous be • **joyful;**
let them exult before God;
  let them be jubilant • **with** joy.
Sing to God, sing praises • **to** his name;
his name is the Lord,
  be exultant • **be**-fore_him. ℟.

Father of orphans and protector of • **widows**
is God in his holy hab•**-i**-tation.
God gives the desolate a • **home** to live_in;
he leads out the prisoners • **to_pros**-perity. ℟.

Rain in abundance, O God,
  you showered a•**-broad;**
you restored your heritage
  when • **it** languished;
your flock found a • **dwelling** in it;
in your goodness, O God,
  you provided • **for_the** needy. ℟.

SECOND READING *(Hebrews 12:18-19, 22-24)*

You have not come to something that can be touched, a blazing fire, and darkness, and gloom, and a tempest, and the sound of a trumpet, and a voice whose words made the hearers beg that not another word be spoken to them.

But you have come to Mount Zion and to the city of the living God, the heavenly Jerusalem, and to innumerable angels in festal gathering, and to the assembly of the firstborn who are enroled in heaven, and to God the judge of all, and to the spirits of the righteous made perfect, and to Jesus, the mediator of a new covenant.

The word of the Lord. **Thanks be to God.**

GOSPEL ACCLAMATION *(Matthew 11:29)*

If not sung, this acclamation is omitted.

Take my yoke upon you; learn from me, for I am gentle and humble of heart.

GOSPEL *(Luke 14:1, 7-14)*

A reading from the holy gospel according to Luke. **Glory to you, Lord.**

On one occasion when Jesus was going to the house of a leader of the Pharisees to eat a meal on the sabbath, the lawyers and Pharisees were watching him closely. When Jesus noticed how the guests chose the places of honour, he told them a parable.

"When you are invited by someone to a wedding banquet, do not sit down at the place of honour, in case someone more distinguished than you has been invited by your host; and the host who invited both of you may come and say to you, 'Give this person your place,' and then in disgrace you would start to take the lowest place.

"But when you are invited, go and sit down at the lowest place, so that when your host comes, he may say to you, 'Friend, move up higher'; then you will be honoured in the presence of all who sit at the table with you. For all who exalt themselves will be humbled, and those who humble themselves will be exalted."

Jesus said also to the Pharisee who had invited him, "When you give a luncheon or a dinner, do not invite your friends or your brothers or sisters or your relatives or rich neighbours, in case they may invite you in return, and you would be repaid. But when you give a banquet, invite the poor, the crippled, the lame, and the blind. And you will be blessed, because they cannot repay you, for you will be repaid at the resurrection of the righteous."

The gospel of the Lord. **Praise to you, Lord Jesus Christ.**

PROFESSION OF FAITH *(Creed, pp. 11-12)*

PRAYER OF THE FAITHFUL

The following intentions are suggestions only.

℞: **Lord, hear our prayer.**

For the Church, witness in Christ's name to the dignity and equality of all people, we pray to the Lord: ℞.

For leaders of countries who work together to protect the fragile gift of God's creation, we pray to the Lord: ℞.

For those among us excluded from society because of race, gender, ethnic origin, religion, or disability, we pray to the Lord: ℞.

For us, called in baptism to make room at God's table for all people, we pray to the Lord: ℞.

PREPARATION OF THE GIFTS *(p. 13)*

PRAYER OVER THE GIFTS

Lord, may this holy offering bring us your blessing and accomplish within us its promise of salvation.

PREFACE *(Sundays in Ord. Time, p. 18)*

COMMUNION ANTIPHON *(Psalm 31:19)*

O Lord, how great is the depth of the kindness which you have shown to those who love you.

PRAYER AFTER COMMUNION

Lord, you renew us at your table with the bread of life. May this food strengthen us in love and help us to serve you in each other.

BLESSING AND DISMISSAL *(p. 65)*

My ethnic roots are in southern Italy, a Mediterranean culture like the Hebrews' in which practical wisdom is prized and wise sayings help us cope with life.

Today's readings are slices of biblical wisdom literature. "In every age, O Lord, you have been our refuge," says Psalm 90. As for coping with life, the psalmist prays, "Satisfy us in the morning with your steadfast love, so that we may rejoice and be glad all our days."

The first reading from the Book of Wisdom reminds us, "Who has learned your counsel (O, Lord), unless you have given wisdom and sent your holy spirit from on high?"

Paul's letter, a masterful bit of affectionate blackmail, pleads for the freedom of a newly baptized slave. The reasoning is a gem of Christian wisdom: Onesimus is no longer Philemon's slave, but a cherished brother of us all.

Luke records Jesus saying that God must be first in our lives. He warns us that discipleship involves cross-bearing, too. The advice to calculate needs, risks and consequences before beginning to build towers or wage war is a reminder to exercise our gift of practical wisdom (prudence) as we journey home to God.

Armand Nigro, Spokane, WA

ENTRANCE ANTIPHON *(Psalm 119:137, 124)*

Lord, you are just, and the judgments you make are right. Show mercy when you judge me, your servant.

INTRODUCTORY RITES *(p. 5)*

OPENING PRAYER

God our Father, you redeem us and make us your children in Christ. Look upon us, give us true freedom and bring us to the inheritance you promised.

FIRST READING *(Wisdom 9:13-18)*

For who can learn the counsel of God?
Or who can discern what the Lord wills?
For the reasoning of mortals is worthless,
and our designs are likely to fail;
for a perishable body weighs down the soul,
and this earthy tent burdens the thoughtful mind.

We can hardly guess at what is on earth,
and what is at hand we find with labour;
but who has traced out what is in the heavens?
Who has learned your counsel,
unless you have given wisdom
and sent your holy spirit from on high?

And thus the paths of those on earth
    were set right,
and people were taught what pleases you,
and were saved by wisdom.

The word of the Lord. **Thanks be to God.**

RESPONSORIAL PSALM *(Psalm 90)*

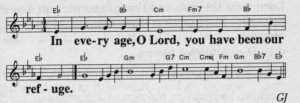

In eve-ry age, O Lord, you have been our ref - uge.

GJ

℟. **In every age, O Lord,
you have been our refuge.**

You turn us back to dust, and say,
　　"Turn • **back**, you mortals."
For a thousand years • **in** your sight
are like yesterday when • **it** is past,
or like a watch • **in** the night. ℟.

You sweep them away;
　　they are • **like** a dream,
like grass that is renewed • **in** the morning;
in the morning it flourishes and • **is** re-newed;
in the evening it • **fades** and withers. ℟.

So teach us to • **count** our days
that we may gain • **a** wise heart.
Turn, O • **Lord**! How long?
Have compassion • **on** your servants! ℟.

Satisfy us in the morning
　　with your • **stead**-fast love,
so that we may rejoice
　　and be glad • **all** our days.
Let the favour of the Lord
　　our • **God_be** up-on_us,
and prosper for us
　　the • **work_of** our hands. ℟.

SECOND READING *(Philemon 9-10, 12-17)*

I, Paul, do this as an old man, and now also as a prisoner of Christ Jesus. I am appealing to you for my child, Onesimus, whose father I have become during my imprisonment.

I am sending him, that is, my own heart, back to you. I wanted to keep him with me, so that he might be of service to me in your place during my imprisonment for the gospel; but I preferred to do nothing without your consent, in order that your good deed might be voluntary and not something forced.

Perhaps this is the reason he was separated from you for a while, so that you might have him back forever, no longer as a slave but more than a slave, a beloved brother—especially to me but how much more to you, both in the flesh and in the Lord.

So if you consider me your partner, welcome him as you would welcome me.

The word of the Lord. **Thanks be to God.**

GOSPEL ACCLAMATION *(Psalm 118:135)*

If not sung, this acclamation is omitted.

Let your face shine on your servant, and teach me your laws.

GOSPEL *(Luke 14:25-33)*

A reading from the holy gospel according to Luke.
Glory to you, Lord.

Large crowds were travelling with Jesus; and he turned and said to them, "Whoever comes to me and does not hate father and mother, spouse and children, brothers and sisters, yes, and even life itself, cannot be my disciple. Whoever does not carry the cross and follow me cannot be my disciple.

For which of you, intending to build a tower, does not first sit down and estimate the cost, to see whether he has enough to complete it? Otherwise, when he has laid a foundation and is not able to finish, all who see it will begin to ridicule him, saying, 'This fellow began to build and was not able to finish.'

Or what king, going out to wage war against another king, will not sit down first and consider whether he is able with ten thousand to oppose the one who comes against him with twenty thousand? If he cannot, then, while the other is still far away, he sends a delegation and asks for the terms of peace.

So therefore, none of you can become my disciple if you do not give up all your possessions."

The gospel of the Lord. **Praise to you, Lord Jesus Christ.**

PROFESSION OF FAITH *(Creed, pp. 11-12)*

PRAYER OF THE FAITHFUL

The following intentions are suggestions only.

℞: **Lord, hear our prayer.**

For the Church and all her ministers, on whom the Spirit pours out the gift of wisdom, we pray to the Lord: ℞.

For world leaders, standing in need of wisdom compassion, prudence and a passion for justice we pray to the Lord: ℞.

For the needy and suffering, reaching out fo God's healing strength, peace and joy, we pray t the Lord: ℞.

For us, God's people gathered here, on whom Go pours out wisdom and love, we pray to the Lord: ℞

PREPARATION OF THE GIFTS *(p. 13)*

PRAYER OVER THE GIFTS

God of peace and love, may our offering bring yo true worship and make us one with you.

PREFACE *(Sundays in Ord. Time, p. 18)*

COMMUNION ANTIPHON *(Psalm 42:1-2)*

Like a deer that longs for running streams, m soul longs for you, my God. My soul is thirstin for the living God.

PRAYER AFTER COMMUNION

Lord, your word and your sacrament give us foo and life. May this gift of your Son lead us to shar his life for ever.

BLESSING AND DISMISSAL *(p. 65)*

September 17   Twenty-fourth Sunday in Ordinary Time

In today's gospel, Jesus speaks about the joy of recovering something precious which had been lost: a sheep, a coin, a child. Most especially, he tells about his Father's joy over the repentance of a single sinner.

The parable of the prodigal son evokes deep soul searching. Are we, like the younger son, rebellious, arrogant, selfish, and easy prey to the pleasures of the world? Or are we, like the elder son, models of good behaviour, concealing a heart filled with anger, resentment and jealousy because our rigid obedience to the call of duty seems to be neither acknowledged nor rewarded?

Whether we brazenly flaunt our disregard for God's law or self-righteously follow it to the letter, our soul is not at peace. We are denying the voice which speaks to us from the depths of our being. We have left home for "a distant country"—lost, lonely and bitter.

Only God, who is tender and compassionate, can rescue us. We have but to surrender to his love and be willing to accept the gift of his forgiveness.

Then, grace-filled and with a new sense of self-worth, we can reach out to others in a spirit of compassion and forgiveness.

Barbara K. d'Artois, Pierrefonds, QC

ENTRANCE ANTIPHON *(See Sirach 36:21-22)*

Give peace, Lord, to those who wait for you an◄ your prophets will proclaim you as you deserve Hear the prayers of your servant and of you▸ people Israel.

INTRODUCTORY RITES *(p. 5)*

OPENING PRAYER

Almighty God, our creator and guide, may w◄ serve you with all our heart and know your for giveness in our lives.

FIRST READING *(Exodus 32:7-11, 13-14)*

At the top of Mount Sinai, the Lord said to Moses "Go down at once! Your people, whom yo▸ brought up out of the land of Egypt, have acted perversely; they have been quick to turn aside from the way that I commanded them; they have cast for themselves an image of a calf, and have worshipped it and sacrificed to it, and said 'These are your gods, O Israel, who brought yo▸ up out of the land of Egypt!' "

The Lord said to Moses, "I have seen this people how stiff-necked they are. Now let me alone, s◄ that my wrath may burn hot against them and ▸ may consume them; and of you I will make a grea nation."

But Moses implored the Lord his God, and said "O Lord, why does your wrath burn hot agains your people, whom you brought out of the land o Egypt with great power and with a mighty hand Remember Abraham, Isaac, and Israel, your serv ants, how you swore to them by your own self

472

saying to them, 'I will multiply your descendants like the stars of heaven, and all this land that I have promised I will give to your descendants, and they shall inherit it forever.' "

And the Lord changed his mind about the disaster that he planned to bring on his people.

The word of the Lord. **Thanks be to God.**

RESPONSORIAL PSALM *(Psalm 51)*

GJ

℟. **I will rise and go to my father.**

Have mercy on me, O God,
    according to your stead•-**fast** love;
according to your abundant mercy
    blot out my • **trans**-gressions.
Wash me thoroughly from my • **in**-iquity,
and cleanse me • **from** my sin. ℟.

Create in me a clean heart, • **O** God,
and put a new and right spirit • **with**-in _me.
Do not cast me away from • **your** presence,
and do not take your holy • **spirit** from me. ℟.

O Lord, open • **my** lips,
and my mouth will declare • **your** praise.
The sacrifice acceptable to God
    is a bro•-**ken** spirit;
a broken and contrite heart, O God,
    you will • **not** de-spise. ℟.

473

SECOND READING *(1 Timothy 1:12-17)*

I am grateful to Christ Jesus our Lord, who has strengthened me, because he judged me faithful and appointed me to his service, even though I was formerly a blasphemer, a persecutor, and a man of violence.

But I received mercy because I had acted ignorantly in unbelief, and the grace of our Lord overflowed for me with the faith and love that are in Christ Jesus.

The saying is sure and worthy of full acceptance, that Christ Jesus came into the world to save sinners—of whom I am the foremost.

But for that very reason I received mercy, so that in me, as the foremost, Jesus Christ might display the utmost patience, making me an example to those who would come to believe in him for eternal life.

To the King of the ages, immortal, invisible, the only God, be honour and glory forever and ever. Amen.

The word of the Lord. **Thanks be to God.**

GOSPEL ACCLAMATION *(2 Corinthians 5:19)*

If not sung, this acclamation is omitted.

God was in Christ, to reconcile the world to himself; and the good news of reconciliation he has entrusted to us.

GOSPEL *(Luke 15:1-32)*

The shorter version ends at the asterisks.

A reading from the holy gospel according to Luke.
Glory to you, Lord.

All the tax collectors and sinners were coming near to listen to Jesus. And the Pharisees and the scribes were grumbling and saying, "This fellow welcomes sinners and eats with them."

So Jesus told them a parable: "Which one of you, having a hundred sheep and losing one of them, does not leave the ninety-nine in the wilderness and go after the one that is lost until he finds it? When he has found it, he lays it on his shoulders and rejoices. And when he comes home, he calls together his friends and neighbours, saying to them, 'Rejoice with me, for I have found my sheep that was lost.' Just so, I tell you, there will be more joy in heaven over one sinner who repents than over ninety-nine righteous persons who need no repentance.

'Or what woman having ten silver coins, if she loses one of them, does not light a lamp, sweep the house, and search carefully until she finds it? When she has found it, she calls together her friends and neighbours, saying, 'Rejoice with me, for I have found the coin that I had lost.' Just so, I tell you, there is joy in the presence of the angels of God over one sinner who repents."

* * *

Then Jesus said, "There was a man who had two sons. The younger of them said to his father,

'Father, give me the share of the property that wil belong to me.' So the father divided his property between them.

"A few days later the younger son gathered all h had and travelled to a distant country, and ther he squandered his property in dissolute living When he had spent everything, a severe famin took place throughout that country, and he begar to be in need. So he went and hired himself out t one of the citizens of that country, who sent him to his fields to feed the pigs. The young mar would gladly have filled himself with the pod that the pigs were eating; and no one gave him anything.

"But when he came to himself he said, 'How many of my father's hired hands have brea enough and to spare, but here I am dying o hunger! I will get up and go to my father, and will say to him, "Father, I have sinned agains heaven and before you; I am no longer worthy t be called your son; treat me like one of your hire hands." '

"So he set off and went to his father. But while h was still far off, his father saw him and was fille with compassion; he ran and put his arms aroun him and kissed him. Then the son said to him 'Father, I have sinned against heaven and befor you; I am no longer worthy to be called your son.

"But the father said to his slaves, 'Quickly, brin out a robe—the best one—and put it on him; pu a ring on his finger and sandals on his feet. An get the fatted calf and kill it, and let us eat and celebrate; for this son of mine was dead and is alive again; he was lost and is found!' And they began to celebrate.

'Now his elder son was in the field; and when he came and approached the house, he heard music and dancing. He called one of the slaves and asked what was going on. The slave replied, 'Your brother has come, and your father has killed the fatted calf, because he has got him back safe and sound.'

Then the elder son became angry and refused to go in. His father came out and began to plead with him. But he answered his father, 'Listen! For all these years I have been working like a slave for you, and I have never disobeyed your command; yet you have never given me even a young goat so that I might celebrate with my friends. But when this son of yours came back, who has devoured your property with prostitutes, you killed the fatted calf for him!'

"Then the father said to him, 'Son, you are always with me, and all that is mine is yours. But we had to celebrate and rejoice, because this brother of yours was dead and has come to life; he was lost and has been found.' "

The gospel of the Lord. **Praise to you, Lord Jesus Christ.**

PROFESSION OF FAITH (*Creed, pp. 11-12*)

PRAYER OF THE FAITHFUL

The following intentions are suggestions only.

℟: **Lord, hear our prayer.**

For the reconciliation of all Christians, called to be signs of God's unconditional love and infinite compassion, we pray to the Lord: ℟.

For the leaders of all nations and their peoples, entrusted as stewards of God's creation, we pray to the Lord: ℟.

For those whose anger, resentment and bitterness have caused them to withdraw to "a distant country," and for those who await their return, we pray to the Lord: ℟.

For us, God's people, called to open our arms to all, we pray to the Lord: ℟.

PREPARATION OF THE GIFTS *(p. 13)*

PRAYER OVER THE GIFTS

Lord, hear the prayers of your people and receive our gifts. May the worship of each one here bring salvation to all.

PREFACE *(Sundays in Ord. Time, p. 18)*

COMMUNION ANTIPHON *(See 1 Cor 10:16)*

When we break the bread, we share in the body of the Lord; when we bless the cup, we share in the blood of Christ.

PRAYER AFTER COMMUNION

Lord, may the eucharist you have given us influence our thoughts and actions. May your Spirit guide and direct us in your way.

BLESSING AND DISMISSAL *(p. 65)*

The message in today's first reading demonstrates the link that the prophets made between religion and ethics. The Hebrews practised virtue as a way of doing God's will. Social justice—safeguarding the rights of the poor and needy, championing the cause of the weak and disadvantaged—is clearly the message of the prophet Amos.

The perplexing parable from the gospel presents a figure who is unworthy and unlovable and creates a situation where he, in a seemingly dishonest manner, ultimately wins the approval of his master. Even Jesus praises the manager's shrewdness in dealing with the world.

Placing Amos alongside the gospel, one wonders how to relate the ethics of the prophets to the parable of the "dishonest" manager. Was he dishonest or was he only trying to save himself from dismissal? This parable has much more to say to us than merely to promote the virtue of prudence or the wise use of money. It forces the reader to wrestle with what it means to be just and unjust or honest and dishonest. It is not as clear cut as we would like to think. The hazy arena of blurred boundaries forces Christians to continue to explore ever more deeply the paradoxes of our faith.

Christine Jamieson, Ottawa, ON

ENTRANCE ANTIPHON

I am the Saviour of all people, says the Lord. Whatever their troubles, I will answer their cry, and l will always be their Lord.

INTRODUCTORY RITES *(p. 5)*

OPENING PRAYER

Father, guide us as you guide creation according to your law of love. May we love one another and come to perfection in the eternal life prepared for us.

FIRST READING *(Amos 8:4-7)*

Hear this, you that trample on the needy,
and bring to ruin the poor of the land,
saying, "When will the new moon be over
so that we may sell grain;
and the sabbath,
so that we may offer wheat for sale?
We will measure out less and charge more,
and tamper with the scales,
buying the poor for silver
and the needy for a pair of sandals,
and selling the sweepings of the wheat."

The Lord has sworn by the pride of Jacob:
"Surely I will never forget any of their deeds."

The word of the Lord. **Thanks be to God.**

ESPONSORIAL PSALM *(Psalm 113)*

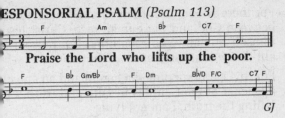

Praise the Lord who lifts up the poor.

GJ

. **Praise the Lord who lifts up the poor.**

Praise, O servants of the • **Lord;**
praise the name of the • **Lord.**
Blessed be the name of the • **Lord**
from this time on and forev•-er-more. ℟.

The Lord is high above all • **nations,**
and his glory above the • **heavens.**
Who is like the Lord our God,
    who is seated on • **high,**
who looks far down on the heavens
    and • **the** earth? ℟.

The Lord raises the poor from the • **dust,**
and lifts the needy from the • **ash_heap,**
to make them sit with • **princes,**
with the princes of • **his** people. ℟.

ECOND READING *(1 Timothy 2:1-7)*

[M]y dearly beloved, I urge that supplications,
[p]rayers, intercessions, and thanksgivings be
[m]ade for everyone, for kings and all who are in
[hi]gh positions, so that we may lead a quiet and
[p]eaceable life in all godliness and dignity. This is
[ri]ght and is acceptable in the sight of God our
[S]aviour, who desires everyone to be saved and to
[c]ome to the knowledge of the truth.

481

For there is one God; there is also one mediat
between God and the human race. Christ Jesu
himself human, who gave himself a ransom f
all; this was attested at the right time.

For this I was appointed a herald and an apostl
a teacher of the Gentiles in faith and truth. I a
telling the truth, I am not lying.

The word of the Lord. **Thanks be to God.**

GOSPEL ACCLAMATION *(2 Corinthians 8:9)*

If not sung, this acclamation is omitted.

Jesus Christ was rich but he became poor, to mal
you rich out of his poverty.

GOSPEL *(Luke 16:1-13)*

The shorter version begins at the asterisks.

A reading from the holy gospel according to Luk
Glory to you, Lord.

Jesus said to the disciples, "There was a rich ma
who had a manager, and charges were brought
him that the manager was squandering his pro
erty. So the rich man summoned him and said
him, 'What is this that I hear about you? Give n
an accounting of your management, because yc
cannot be my manager any longer.'

"Then the manager said to himself, 'What wil
do, now that my master is taking the positic
away from me? I am not strong enough to dig, ar
I am ashamed to beg. I have decided what to do :
that, when I am dismissed as manager, peop
may welcome me into their homes.'

So, summoning his master's debtors one by one, he asked the first, 'How much do you owe my master?' He answered, 'A hundred jugs of olive oil.' He said to him, 'Take your bill, sit down quickly, and make it fifty.' Then he asked another, 'And how much do you owe?' He replied, 'A hundred containers of wheat.' He said to him, 'Take your bill and make it eighty.'

And his master commended the dishonest manager because he had acted shrewdly; for the children of this age are more shrewd in dealing with their own generation than are the children of light.

And I tell you, make friends for yourselves by means of dishonest wealth so that when it is gone, they may welcome you into the eternal homes.

* * *

Whoever is faithful in a very little is faithful also in much; and whoever is dishonest in a very little is dishonest also in much. If then you have not been faithful with the dishonest wealth, who will entrust to you the true riches? And if you have not been faithful with what belongs to another, who will give you what is your own?

No slave can serve two masters; for a slave will either hate the one and love the other, or be devoted to the one and despise the other. You cannot serve God and wealth."

The gospel of the Lord. **Praise to you, Lord Jesus Christ.**

PROFESSION OF FAITH (*Creed, pp. 11-12*)

PRAYER OF THE FAITHFUL

The following intentions are suggestions only.

℟: **Lord, hear our prayer.**

For the Church, entrusted with the riches of the gospel of life, we pray to the Lord: ℟.

For those who govern nations and hold offices of authority, called to serve their people and the common good, we pray to the Lord: ℟.

For the poor and needy of our world, defenceless against those who oppress them, we pray to the Lord: ℟.

For us, God's people gathered here today, called to nurture true justice, we pray to the Lord: ℟.

PREPARATION OF THE GIFTS *(p. 13)*

PRAYER OVER THE GIFTS

Lord, may these gifts which we now offer to show our belief and our love be pleasing to you. May they become for us the eucharist of Jesus Christ your Son.

PREFACE *(Sundays in Ord. Time, p. 18)*

COMMUNION ANTIPHON *(Psalm 119:4-5)*

You have laid down your precepts to be faithfully kept. May my footsteps be firm in keeping your commands.

PRAYER AFTER COMMUNION

Lord, help us with your kindness. Make us strong through the eucharist. May we put into action the saving mystery we celebrate.

BLESSING AND DISMISSAL *(p. 65)*

484

Twenty-sixth Sunday in Ordinary Time

We are daily exposed to the crying needs of others. Unlike the rich man in today's gospel, we cannot fail to notice. If our global vision is blinded, then local concerns open our eyes. Our awareness and response to what we see are initial steps to filling in that gap that separates us from poor and rich alike. It is not wealth which validates our humanity, but service.

Lazarus is the only character in the parables who has a name; translated, it means "God has helped." To be called by name is a humanizing experience. We could fill the gap even more if we came close enough, not just spatially, but in a loving gesture of friendship to those we know are 'there' but are afraid to notice, let alone name.

If we recognize our fear and search out the root of it, we might be surprised by the Spirit. Will we be diminished by giving more of ourselves to another? What might we gain interiorly?

Jesus isn't trying to make us feel guilty; guilt can push us into destructive action or paralyze us into inaction. Always, his message is love. Can we who are poor in our own way love those who are poor in other ways? Can we call them by name? Share our space, our life? Love goes the whole way in filling the gap. Barriers must be broken down *now*. Later is too late.

— Esther Jedynak, Victoria, BC

ENTRANCE ANTIPHON *(Daniel 3)*

O Lord, you had just cause to judge us as you di
because we sinned against you and disobeye
your will. But now show us your greatness (
heart, and treat us with your unbounded kin
ness.

INTRODUCTORY RITES *(p. 5)*

OPENING PRAYER

Father, you show your almighty power in you
mercy and forgiveness. Continue to fill us wit
your gifts of love. Help us to hurry toward th
eternal life you promise and come to share in th
joys of your kingdom.

FIRST READING *(Amos 6:1, 4-7)*

Thus says the Lord, the God of hosts: "Alas fo
those who are at ease in Zion, and for those wh
feel secure on Mount Samaria!

"Alas for those who lie on beds of ivory, an
lounge on their couches, and eat lambs from th
flock, and calves from the stall; who sing idl
songs to the sound of the harp, and like Davi
improvise on instruments of music; who drin
wine from bowls, and anoint themselves with th
finest oils, but are not grieved over the ruin (
Joseph!

"Therefore they shall now be the first to go int
exile, and the revelry of those who lie in ease shal
pass away.

The word of the Lord. **Thanks be to God.**

RESPONSORIAL PSALM *(Psalm 146)*

Praise the Lord,⎯⎯ my soul!

GJ

℟. **Praise the Lord, my soul!**

It is the Lord who keeps faith • **forever,**
who executes justice for the op•**-pressed;**
who gives food to the • **hungry.**
The Lord sets the prison•**-ers** free. ℟.

The Lord opens the eyes of the • **blind**
and lifts up those who are bowed • **down;**
the Lord loves the • **righteous**
and watches over • **the** strangers. ℟.

The Lord upholds the orphan and the • **widow,**
but the way of the wicked he brings to • **ruin.**
The Lord will reign for•**-ever,**
your God, O Zion, for all gen•**-er**-ations. ℟.

SECOND READING *(1 Timothy 6:11-16)*

As for you, Timothy, man of God; pursue righteousness, godliness, faith, love, endurance, gentleness. Fight the good fight of the faith; take hold
of the eternal life, to which you were called and
for which you made the good confession in the
presence of many witnesses.

In the presence of God, who gives life to all things,
and of Christ Jesus, who in his testimony before
Pontius Pilate made the good confession, I charge

you to keep the commandment without spot c
blame until the manifestation of our Lord Jesu
Christ, which he will bring about at the right tim
He is the blessed and only Sovereign, the King c
kings and Lord of lords.

It is he alone who has immortality and dwells i
unapproachable light, whom no one has eve
seen or can see; to him be honour and eterna
dominion. Amen.

The word of the Lord. **Thanks be to God.**

GOSPEL ACCLAMATION *(2 Corinthians 8:9)*

If not sung, this acclamation is omitted.

Jesus Christ was rich but he became poor, to mak
you rich out of his poverty.

GOSPEL *(Luke 16:19-31)*

A reading from the holy gospel according to Luke
Glory to you, Lord.

Jesus told this parable to those among the Phari
sees who loved money:

"There was a rich man who was dressed in purpl
and fine linen and who feasted sumptuously ever
day. And at his gate lay a poor man named Lazarus
covered with sores, who longed to satisfy hi
hunger with what fell from the rich man's table
even the dogs would come and lick his sores.

"The poor man died and was carried away by th
angels to be with Abraham. The rich man als
died and was buried. In Hades, where he wa

being tormented, he looked up and saw Abraham far away with Lazarus by his side. He called out, 'Father Abraham, have mercy on me, and send Lazarus to dip the tip of his finger in water and cool my tongue; for I am in agony in these flames.'

'But Abraham said, 'Child, remember that during your lifetime you received your good things, and Lazarus in like manner evil things; but now he is comforted here, and you are in agony. Besides all this, between you and us a great chasm has been fixed, so that those who might want to pass from here to you cannot do so, and no one can cross from there to us.'

"The man who had been rich said, 'Then, father, I beg you to send Lazarus to my father's house— for I have five brothers—that he may warn them, so that they will not also come into this place of torment.'

"Abraham replied, 'They have Moses and the prophets; they should listen to them.' He said, 'No, father Abraham; but if someone goes to them from the dead, they will repent.' Abraham said to him, 'If they do not listen to Moses and the prophets, neither will they be convinced even if someone rises from the dead.' "

The gospel of the Lord. **Praise to you, Lord Jesus Christ.**

PROFESSION OF FAITH *(Creed, pp. 11-12)*

PRAYER OF THE FAITHFUL

The following intentions are suggestions only.

℟: **Lord, hear our prayer.**

For the Church, called to give up everything tha
separates us from each other, we pray to the Lord
℟.

For leaders in Church and society, as they strug
gle to heal our world, we pray to the Lord: ℟.

For those among us whom we have rejected, w
pray to the Lord: ℟.

For young people of our parish community an
everywhere who seek our support in building
world of justice and peace, we pray to the Lord: ℟

PREPARATION OF THE GIFTS *(p. 13)*

PRAYER OVER THE GIFTS

God of mercy, accept our offering and make it
source of blessing for us.

PREFACE *(Sundays in Ord. Time, p. 18)*

COMMUNION ANTIPHON *(Psalm 119:49-50)*

**O Lord, remember the words you spoke to me
your servant, which made me live in hope and
consoled me when I was downcast.**

PRAYER AFTER COMMUNION

Lord, may this eucharist in which we proclaim
the death of Christ bring us salvation and make us
one with him in glory.

BLESSING AND DISMISSAL *(p. 65)*

Have you ever held a mustard seed in the palm of your hand? There's really nothing to it, this inconsequential speck. However, given the right conditions, its potential far exceeds its size. From this smallest seed grows a sturdy plant.

In the gospel today Jesus counters the apostles' request to increase their faith by comparing the amount of faith it takes to move a mulberry tree to the tiny mustard seed. Surely not the response the apostles were expecting. For them it is quantity that is important while for Jesus it is the power that faith can evoke in us. He speaks of a faith that has the power to love. This is the same faith that Paul writes about in his letter to Timothy, the second reading.

Still today, our prayer is often the same as that of the apostles—increase our faith—as if quantity were still the issue. What we need to do is believe in the potential and the power of faith and disregard the quantity. If we believed in the power that is present in the smallest amount of faith, think of some of the 'mulberry trees' in our lives (the hard-heartedness, the selfishness, the violence) that we could move.

Connie Paré, Chatham, ON

ENTRANCE ANTIPHON *(Esther 13:9, 10-11)*

O Lord, you have given everything its place in the world, and no one can make it otherwise. For it is your creation, the heavens and the earth and the stars: you are the Lord of all.

INTRODUCTORY RITES *(p. 5)*

OPENING PRAYER

Father, your love for us surpasses all our hopes and desires. Forgive our failings, keep us in your peace and lead us in the way of salvation.

FIRST READING *(Habakkuk 1:2-3; 2:2-4)*

Habakkuk called out to the Lord:
"O Lord, how long shall I cry for help,
and you will not listen?
Or cry to you 'Violence!'
and you will not save?
Why do you make me see wrongdoing
and look at trouble?
Destruction and violence are before me;
strife and contention arise."

Then the Lord answered me and said:
"Write the vision;
make it plain on tablets,
so that a runner may read it.
For there is still a vision for the appointed time;
it speaks of the end, and does not lie.
If it seems to tarry, wait for it;
it will surely come, it will not delay.
Look at the proud!
Their spirit is not right in them,
but the righteous live by their faith."

The word of the Lord. **Thanks be to God.**

RESPONSORIAL PSALM *(Psalm 95)*

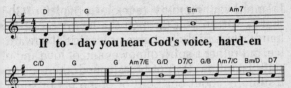

If to-day you hear God's voice, hard-en not your hearts.

GJ

℟. **If today you hear God's voice,**
harden not your hearts.

O come, let us sing to • **the** Lord;
let us make a joyful noise
    to the rock of our • **sal**-vation!
Let us come into his presence
    • **with** thanksgiving;
let us make a joyful noise to him
    with songs • **of** praise! ℟.

O come, let us worship and • **bow** down,
let us kneel before the Lord, • **our** Maker!
For he is our God, and we are the people
    of • **his** pasture,
and the sheep of • **his** hand. ℟.

O that today you would listen to • **his** voice!
Do not harden your hearts, as at Meribah,
    as on the day at Massah in • **the** wilderness,
when your ancestors tested me,
    and put me to • **the** proof,
though they had seen • **my** work. ℟.

SECOND READING *(2 Timothy 1:6-8, 13-14)*

I remind you, Timothy, to rekindle the gift of God that is within you through the laying on of my hands; for God did not give us a spirit of cowardice, but rather a spirit of power and of love and of self-discipline. Do not be ashamed, then, of the testimony about our Lord or of me his prisoner, but join with me in suffering for the gospel, relying on the power of God.

Hold to the standard of sound teaching that you have heard from me, in the faith and love that are in Christ Jesus. Guard the good treasure entrusted to you, with the help of the Holy Spirit living in us.

The word of the Lord. **Thanks be to God.**

GOSPEL ACCLAMATION *(1 Peter 1:25)*

If not sung, this acclamation is omitted.

The word of the Lord stands for ever; it is the word given to you, the good news.

GOSPEL *(Luke 17:5-10)*

A reading from the holy gospel according to Luke. **Glory to you, Lord.**

The apostles said to the Lord, "Increase our faith!" The Lord replied, "If you had faith the size of a mustard seed, you could say to this mulberry tree, 'Be uprooted and planted in the sea,' and it would obey you.

"Who among you would say to your slave who has just come in from ploughing or tending sheep in the field, 'Come here at once and take your place at the table'? Would you not rather say to

494

him, 'Prepare supper for me, put on your apron and serve me while I eat and drink; later you may eat and drink'? Do you thank the slave for doing what was commanded? So you also, when you have done all that you were ordered to do, say, 'We are worthless slaves; we have done only what we ought to have done!' "

The gospel of the Lord. **Praise to you, Lord Jesus Christ.**

PROFESSION OF FAITH *(Creed, pp. 11-12)*

PRAYER OF THE FAITHFUL

The following intentions are suggestions only.

℞: **Lord, hear our prayer.**

For the Church, people of God, entrusted with sharing the gift of faith with the world, we pray to the Lord: ℞.

For leaders everywhere, called to help their people grow to the fullness of their human dignity, we pray to the Lord: ℞.

For those who struggle for a share in the bounty of God's creation, we pray to the Lord: ℞.

For us, God's people gathered here, community of faith called to recognize the power entrusted to us, we pray to the Lord: ℞.

PREPARATION OF THE GIFTS *(p. 13)*

PRAYER OVER THE GIFTS

Father, receive these gifts which our Lord Jesus Christ has asked us to offer in his memory. May our obedient service bring us to the fullness of your redemption.

PREFACE *(Sundays in Ord. Time, p. 18)*

COMMUNION ANTIPHON *(Lamentations 3:25)*

The Lord is good to those who hope in him, to those who are searching for his love.

PRAYER AFTER COMMUNION

Almighty God, let the eucharist we share fill us with your life. May the love of Christ which we celebrate here touch our lives and lead us to you.

BLESSING AND DISMISSAL *(p. 65)*

Bill was an alcoholic for many years. He tried often to stop drinking but each time he failed. His whole life was falling apart and he was about to give up. When all else had failed, Bill turned to Jesus for help.

Eventually, Bill's prayers were answered and he was given the gift of sobriety. Bill was most thankful for this gift. What he soon came to realize, however, was that he could keep this gift of sobriety only if he shared it with other alcoholics.

Bill did share this gift with others. He was a founding member of Alcoholics Anonymous, a world-wide organization which today continues to help millions of alcoholics like himself.

In today's gospel we hear of another remarkable healing story. What is striking is that only one of the ten lepers, a Samaritan considered an outcast from society, came back to thank Jesus.

Each one of us has received much and been healed many times, whether from physical illness, broken relationships, damaged emotions, or false images of God.

Do we, like Bill and the leper, recognize these miracles as gifts from God? Are we always grateful for them? Do we share our gifts with other people in need?

Jim McSheffrey, St. John's, NF

ENTRANCE ANTIPHON *(Psalm 130:3-4)*

If you, O Lord, laid bare our guilt, who could endure it? But you are forgiving, God of Israel.

INTRODUCTORY RITES *(p. 5)*

OPENING PRAYER

Lord, our help and guide, make your love the foundation of our lives. May our love for you express itself in our eagerness to do good for others.

FIRST READING *(2 Kings 5:14-17)*

Naaman, commander of the army of the king of Aram and a mighty warrior, obeyed Elisha: he went down and immersed himself seven times in the Jordan, according to the word of the man of God; his flesh was restored like the flesh of a young boy, and he was clean.

Then he returned to the man of God, he and all his company; Naaman came and stood before Elisha and said, "Now I know that there is no God in all the earth except in Israel; please accept a present from your servant."

But Elisha said, "As the Lord lives, whom I serve, I will accept nothing!" Naaman urged Elisha to accept, but he refused.

Then Naaman said, "If not, please let two mule-loads of earth be given to your servant; for your servant will no longer offer burnt offering or sacrifice to any god except the Lord."

The word of the Lord. **Thanks be to God.**

RESPONSORIAL PSALM *(Psalm 98)*

The Lord has re-vealed to the na-tions___ his sav-ing power.

GJ

℟. **The Lord has revealed to the nations his saving power.**

O sing to the Lord • **a** new song,
for he has done • **marvel**-lous things.
His right hand and his • **ho**-ly arm
have • **brought** him victory. ℟.

The Lord has made • **known** his victory;
he has revealed his vindication
    in the sight • **of** the nations.
He has remembered his • **stead**-fast love
and faithfulness to the • **house** of Israel. ℟.

All the ends of the • **earth** have seen
the victory • **of** our God.
Make a joyful noise to the Lord, • **all** the earth;
break forth into
    joyous • **song_and** sing praises. ℟.

SECOND READING *(2 Timothy 2:8-13)*

Remember Jesus Christ, raised from the dead, a descendant of David—that is my gospel, for which I suffer hardship, even to the point of being chained like a criminal. But the word of God is not chained.

Therefore I endure everything for the sake of the elect, so that they may also obtain the salvation that is in Christ Jesus, with eternal glory.

The saying is sure: If we have died with him, we will also live with him; if we endure, we will also reign with him; if we deny him, he will also deny us; if we are faithless, he remains faithful—for he cannot deny himself.

The word of the Lord. **Thanks be to God.**

GOSPEL ACCLAMATION *(1 Thessalonians 5:18)*

If not sung, this acclamation is omitted.

For all things give thanks to God, because this is what he expects of you in Christ Jesus.

GOSPEL *(Luke 17:11-19)*

A reading from the holy gospel according to Luke. **Glory to you, Lord.**

On the way to Jerusalem Jesus was going through the region between Samaria and Galilee.

As he entered a village, ten lepers approached him. Keeping their distance, they called out, saying, "Jesus, Master, have mercy on us!"

When Jesus saw them, he said to them, "Go and show yourselves to the priests." And as they went, they were made clean. Then one of them, when he saw that he was healed, turned back, praising God with a loud voice. He prostrated himself at Jesus' feet and thanked him. And he was a Samaritan.

Then Jesus asked, "Were not ten made clean? But the other nine, where are they? Was none of them found to return and give praise to God except this foreigner?"

Then Jesus said to the Samaritan, "Get up and go on your way; your faith has made you well."

The gospel of the Lord. **Praise to you, Lord Jesus Christ.**

PROFESSION OF FAITH *(Creed, pp. 11-12)*

PRAYER OF THE FAITHFUL

The following intentions are suggestions only.

℟: **Lord, hear our prayer.**

For the Church, community graced by the blood of martyrs for faith and justice, we pray to the Lord: ℟.

For the leaders of nations, called to effective action on behalf of the poor, we pray to the Lord: ℟.

For those whom our society casts out: alcoholics, drug addicts, people with AIDS, refugees, prisoners, the jobless,... we pray to the Lord: ℟.

For us, God's people gathered here, called as a parish to act justly and lovingly, we pray to the Lord: ℟.

PREPARATION OF THE GIFTS *(p. 13)*

PRAYER OVER THE GIFTS

Lord, accept the prayers and gifts we offer in faith and love. May this eucharist bring us to your glory.

PREFACE *(Sundays in Ord. Time, p. 18)*

COMMUNION ANTIPHON *(Psalm 34:10)*

The rich suffer want and go hungry, but nothing shall be lacking to those who fear the Lord.

PRAYER AFTER COMMUNION

Almighty Father, may the body and blood of your Son give us a share in his life.

BLESSING AND DISMISSAL *(p. 65)*

The woman in today's gospel could not be silenced! Neither can we! But there's a difference between her and us: she had a complaint, whereas we have Good News.

Today we celebrate the fact that we are 'missionary.' That doesn't mean that all of us go to faraway places. It means that, wherever we find ourselves, we witness to Jesus Christ. It cannot be otherwise. Our experience of Jesus communicates itself!

We've all met them: Christians who don't talk about Jesus all the time but who show that they know him. These people radiate peace and joy and impress us with their compassion and kindness. Their lives speak to us and invite us to look for a deeper peace and joy in our own lives.

Perhaps never before have people been searching more consciously—as individuals and as communities—for peace and joy. Never perhaps has the goal seemed more elusive.

As Christians, we carry a message of hope: Jesus Christ is our peace and our joy! At appropriate moments we speak to others about our experience of Jesus and we listen to their experience of the divine. We have something to offer the world; we offer it in a spirit of dialogue.

David Warren, Scarborough, ON

ENTRANCE ANTIPHON *(Psalm 17:6, 8)*

I call upon you, God, for you will answer me; bend your ear and hear my prayer. Guard me as the pupil of your eye; hide me in the shade of your wings.

INTRODUCTORY RITES *(p. 5)*

OPENING PRAYER

Almighty and ever-living God, our source of power and inspiration, give us strength and joy in serving you as followers of Christ.

FIRST READING *(Exodus 17:8-13)*

Amalek came and fought with Israel at Rephidim. Moses said to Joshua, "Choose some men for us and go out, fight with Amalek. Tomorrow I will stand on the top of the hill with the staff of God in my hand."

So Joshua did as Moses told him, and fought with Amalek, while Moses, Aaron, and Hur went up to the top of the hill.

Whenever Moses held up his hands, Israel prevailed; and whenever he lowered his hands, Amalek prevailed. But Moses' hands grew weary; so they took a stone and put it under him, and he sat on it. Aaron and Hur held up his hands, one on one side, and the other on the other side; so his hands were steady until the sun set.

And Joshua defeated Amalek and his people with the sword.

The word of the Lord. **Thanks be to God.**

RESPONSORIAL PSALM *(Psalm 121)*

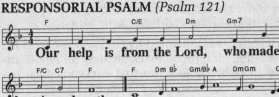

GJ

℞. **Our help is from the Lord,**
   who made heaven and earth.

I lift up my eyes to the • **hills**—
from where will my help • **come?**
My help comes from the • **Lord,**
who made heaven • **and** earth. ℞.

The Lord will not let your foot be • **moved;**
he who keeps you will not • **slumber.**
He who keeps • **Israel**
will neither slumber • **nor** sleep. ℞.

The Lord is your • **keeper;**
the Lord is your shade at your right • **hand.**
The sun shall not strike you by • **day,**
nor the moon • **by** night. ℞.

The Lord will keep you from all • **evil;**
he will keep your • **life.**
The Lord will keep your going out
   and your coming • **in**
from this time on and for•**-ever**-more. ℞.

SECOND READING *(2 Timothy 3:14–4:2)*

Continue in what you have learned and firmly
believed, knowing from whom you learned it,
and how from childhood you have known the

505

sacred writings that are able to instruct you for salvation through faith in Christ Jesus.

All scripture is inspired by God and is useful for teaching, for reproof, for correction, and for training in righteousness, so that everyone who belongs to God may be proficient, equipped for every good work.

In the presence of God and of Christ Jesus, who is to judge the living and the dead, and in view of his appearing and his kingdom, I solemnly urge you: proclaim the message; be persistent whether the time is favourable or unfavourable; convince, rebuke, and encourage, with the utmost patience in teaching.

The word of the Lord. **Thanks be to God.**

GOSPEL ACCLAMATION *(Hebrews 4:12)*

If not sung, this acclamation is omitted.

The word of God is living and active; it probes the thoughts and motives of our heart.

GOSPEL *(Luke 18:1-8)*

A reading from the holy gospel according to Luke. **Glory to you, Lord.**

Jesus told the disciples a parable about their need to pray always and not to lose heart.

He said, "In a certain city there was a judge who neither feared God nor had respect for people. In that city there was a widow who kept coming to him and saying, 'Grant me justice against my opponent.'

'For a while the judge refused; but later he said to himself, 'Though I have no fear of God and no respect for anyone, yet because this widow keeps bothering me, I will grant her justice, so that she may not wear me out by continually coming.' "

And the Lord said, "Listen to what the unjust judge says. Will not God grant justice to his chosen ones who cry to him day and night? Will he delay long in helping them? I tell you, God will quickly grant justice to them. "And yet, when the Son of Man comes, will he find faith on earth?"

The gospel of the Lord. **Praise to you, Lord Jesus Christ.**

PROFESSION OF FAITH *(Creed, pp. 11-12)*

PRAYER OF THE FAITHFUL

The following intentions are suggestions only.

℞: **Lord, hear our prayer.**

For the Church and its leaders, called to proclaim Jesus Christ in today's world, we pray to the Lord: ℞.

For all who seek God, enriching our human community by their spiritual values, we pray to the Lord: ℞.

For those who seek meaning in their lives and those who search for hope, we pray to the Lord: ℞.

For us, community of faith, called in baptism to witness to Jesus Christ, we pray to the Lord: ℞.

PREPARATION OF THE GIFTS *(p. 13)*

PRAYER OVER THE GIFTS

Lord God, may the gifts we offer bring us your love and forgiveness and give us freedom to serve you with our lives.

PREFACE *(Sundays in Ord. Time, p. 18)*

COMMUNION ANTIPHON *(Psalm 33:18-19)*

See how the eyes of the Lord are on those who fear him, on those who hope in his love; that he may rescue them from death and feed them in time of famine.

PRAYER AFTER COMMUNION

Lord, may this eucharist help us to remain faithful. May it teach us the way to eternal life.

BLESSING AND DISMISSAL *(p. 65)*

The parable of the pharisee and the tax collector is one I recall vividly from childhood. The gap I felt between how I strove to appear before others and my failures left me feeling trapped. I desperately wanted others' approval. Even though I recognized that Jesus praised the tax collector standing at the back of the temple who owned up to his sinfulness, how could I admit mine?

I worked hard to justify myself, to be righteous. Like Jesus' contemporaries who held the tax collector in contempt, I looked down on others I judged to be struggling, failing to live up to moral standards. Those with alcohol problems, those whose marriages had failed, even those poorly dressed at Mass. I was, thank God, not like them.

Painfully, I have been forced to watch myself reluctantly move toward the back of the church. My self-justification has fallen apart before my sinfulness. In seeing myself differently, I have lowered my eyes to see others differently. In this parable, Jesus says we do not save ourselves. Paradoxically, I have come to know the gift of God's forgiving love in my sinfulness. Recognizing and accepting God's mercy joins me to others in our shared human condition.

John Thompson, Saskatoon, SK

ENTRANCE ANTIPHON *(Psalm 105:3-4)*

Let hearts rejoice who search for the Lord. Seek the Lord and his strength, seek always the face of the Lord.

INTRODUCTORY RITES *(p. 5)*

OPENING PRAYER

Almighty and ever-living God, strengthen our faith, hope, and love. May we do with loving hearts what you ask of us and come to share the life you promise.

FIRST READING *(Sirach 35:15-17, 20-22)*

The Lord is the judge, and with him there is no partiality. He will not show partiality to the poor, but he will listen to the prayer of one who is wronged. The Lord will not ignore the supplication of the orphan, or the widow when she pours out her complaint.

The one whose service is pleasing to the Lord will be accepted, and the prayer of such a person will reach to the clouds.

The prayer of the humble pierces the clouds, and it will not rest until it reaches its goal; it will not desist until the Most High responds and does justice for the righteous, and executes judgment. Indeed, the Lord will not delay.

The word of the Lord. **Thanks be to God.**

RESPONSORIAL PSALM (*Psalm 34*)

GJ

℟. **The Lord hears the cry of the poor.**

I will bless the Lord at all • **times;**
his praise shall continually be in • **my** mouth.
My soul makes its boast in the • **Lord;**
let the humble hear and • **be** glad. ℟.

The face of the Lord is against evil•**-doers,**
to cut off the remembrance of them
from • **the** earth.
When the righteous cry for help,
the Lord • **hears,**
and rescues them from all • **their** troubles. ℟.

The Lord is near to the broken•**-hearted,**
and saves the crushed • **in** spirit.
The Lord redeems the life of his • **servants;**
none of those who take refuge in him
will be • **con**-demned. ℟.

SECOND READING (*2 Timothy 4:6-8, 16-18*)

As for me, I am already being poured out as a
libation, and the time of my departure has come.
I have fought the good fight, I have finished the
race, I have kept the faith.

From now on there is reserved for me the crown of
righteousness, which the Lord, the righteous

judge, will give me on that day, and not only to m
but also to all who have longed for his appearing

At my first defence no one came to my suppor
but all deserted me. May it not be counted agains
them!

But the Lord stood by me and gave me strength, s
that through me the message might be fully pro
claimed and all the Gentiles might hear it. So
was rescued from the lion's mouth.

The Lord will rescue me from every evil attac
and save me for his heavenly kingdom. To him b
the glory forever and ever. Amen.

The word of the Lord. **Thanks be to God.**

GOSPEL ACCLAMATION *(2 Corinthians 5:19)*

If not sung, this acclamation is omitted.

God was in Christ, to reconcile the world t
himself; and the good news of reconciliation h
has entrusted to us.

GOSPEL *(Luke 18:9-14)*

A reading from the holy gospel according to Luke
Glory to you, Lord.

Jesus told this parable to some who trusted ir
themselves that they were righteous, and re
garded others with contempt:

"Two men went up to the temple to pray, one a
Pharisee and the other a tax collector. The Phari
see, standing by himself, was praying thus, 'God
I thank you that I am not like other people
thieves, rogues, adulterers, or even like this ta

collector. I fast twice a week; I give a tenth of all my income.'

"But the tax collector, standing far off, would not even look up to heaven, but was beating his breast and saying, 'God, be merciful to me, a sinner!'

"I tell you, this man went back home justified rather than the other; for all who exalt themselves will be humbled, but all who humble themselves will be exalted."

The gospel of the Lord. **Praise to you, Lord Jesus Christ.**

PROFESSION OF FAITH *(Creed, pp. 11-12)*

PRAYER OF THE FAITHFUL

The following intentions are suggestions only.

℞: **Lord, hear our prayer.**

For the Church, sacrament of God's forgiveness in word and action, we pray to the Lord: ℞.

For leaders, entrusted with the protection and promotion of the common good, we pray to the Lord: ℞.

For all who search for forgiveness and for those who reach out to them, we pray to the Lord: ℞.

For us, God's holy people, called to offer each other God's mercy and forgiveness, we pray to the Lord: ℞.

PREPARATION OF THE GIFTS *(p. 13)*

PRAYER OVER THE GIFTS

Lord God of power and might, receive the gifts we
offer and let our service give you glory.

PREFACE *(Sundays in Ord. Time, p. 18)*

COMMUNION ANTIPHON *(Psalm 20:5)*

**We will rejoice at the victory of God and make
our boast in his great name.**

PRAYER AFTER COMMUNION

Lord, bring to perfection within us the communion we share in this sacrament. May our celebration have an effect in our lives.

BLESSING AND DISMISSAL *(p. 65)*

Zacchaeus was an important tax collector, a wealthy man, and that is all we know about him until he encountered Jesus. Yet today, almost 2,000 years later, his story is being proclaimed as the "word of the Lord."

In reality Zacchaeus represents every human being who seeks to know more about the Lord. His experience can also be the experience of every Christian, for we are all in need of a visit from the Lord to change our sinful hearts.

Zacchaeus made the effort to overcome the obstacle of height. The Lord responded with an invitation to "Come down; for I must stay at your house today." In that brief encounter Zacchaeus was radically changed to the point where Jesus could say, "Today salvation has come to this house."

Is there some obstacle in our own lives that prevents us from seeking Jesus? perhaps pride, money, addiction? laziness, or unreasonable attachment to material goods, or a sinful lifestyle? Whatever it is, when we make the effort to go to the Lord he will come to us and heal us. He will give us reason to rejoice that change has taken place, that salvation has come to us.

Iris Kendall, St. John's, NF

Thirty-first Sunday in Ordinary Time

ENTRANCE ANTIPHON *(Psalm 38:21-22)*

Do not abandon me, Lord. My God, do not g
away from me! Hurry to help me, Lord, m
Saviour.

INTRODUCTORY RITES *(p. 5)*

OPENING PRAYER

God of power and mercy, only with your help ca
we offer you fitting service and praise. May w
live the faith we profess and trust your promise (
eternal life.

FIRST READING *(Wisdom 11:22–12:2)*

The whole world before you, O Lord, is like
speck that tips the scales, and like a drop (
morning dew that falls on the ground. But you ar
merciful to all, for you can do all things, and yo
overlook people's sins, so that they may repent.

Lord, you love all things that exist, and detes
none of the things that you have made, for yo
would not have made anything if you had hate
it. How would anything have endured if you ha
not willed it? Or how would anything not calle
forth by you have been preserved? You spare al
things, for they are yours, O Lord, you who lov
the living.

For your immortal spirit is in all things. Therefor
you correct little by little those who trespass, an
you remind and warn them of the things throug
which they sin, so that they may be freed fror
wickedness and put their trust in you, O Lord.

The word of the Lord. **Thanks be to God.**

516

RESPONSORIAL PSALM *(Psalm 145)*

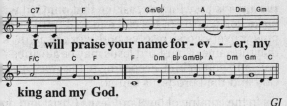

I will praise your name for - ev — er, my

king and my God.

GJ

℟. **I will praise your name for ever,**
my king and my God.

I will extol you, my God and • **King,**
and bless your name forever and • **ever.**
Every day I will • **bless_you,**
and praise your name forever • **and** ever. ℟.

The Lord is gracious and • **merciful,**
slow to anger and abounding in steadfast • **love.**
The Lord is good to • **all,**
and his compassion is over all
    that he • **has** made. ℟.

All your works shall give thanks to you,
    O • **Lord,**
and all your faithful shall • **bless_you.**
They shall speak of the glory of your • **kingdom,**
and tell of • **your** power. ℟.

The Lord is faithful in all his • **words,**
and gracious in all his • **deeds.**
The Lord upholds all who are • **falling,**
and raises up all who are • **bowed** down. ℟.

SECOND READING *(2 Thessalonians 1:11–2:2)*

We always pray for you, asking that our God will make you worthy of his call and will fulfil by his power every good resolve and work of faith, so that the name of our Lord Jesus may be glorified in you, and you in him, according to the grace of our God and the Lord Jesus Christ.

As to the coming of our Lord Jesus Christ and our being gathered together to him, we beg you, brothers and sisters, not to be quickly shaken in mind or alarmed, either by spirit or by word or by letter as though from us, to the effect that the day of the Lord is already here.

The word of the Lord. **Thanks be to God.**

GOSPEL ACCLAMATION *(John 3:16)*

If not sung, this acclamation is omitted.

God loved the world so much, he gave us his only Son, that all who believe in him might have eternal life.

GOSPEL *(Luke 19:1-10)*

A reading from the holy gospel according to Luke. **Glory to you, Lord.**

Jesus entered Jericho and was passing through it. A man was there named Zacchaeus; he was a chief tax collector and was rich. He was trying to see who Jesus was, but on account of the crowd he could not, because he was short in stature.

So he ran ahead and climbed a sycamore tree to see Jesus, because he was going to pass that way. When Jesus came to the place, he looked up and aid to him, "Zacchaeus, hurry and come down; or I must stay at your house today."

So Zacchaeus hurried down and was happy to welcome Jesus. All who saw it began to grumble and said, "He has gone to be the guest of one who is a sinner."

Zacchaeus stood there and said to the Lord, "Look, half of my possessions, Lord, I will give to the poor; and if I have defrauded anyone of anything, I will pay back four times as much."

Then Jesus said of him, "Today salvation has come to this house, because Zacchaeus too is a son of Abraham. For the Son of Man came to seek out and to save the lost."

The gospel of the Lord. **Praise to you, Lord Jesus Christ.**

PROFESSION OF FAITH *(Creed, pp. 11-12)*

PRAYER OF THE FAITHFUL

The following intentions are suggestions only.

℟: **Lord, hear our prayer.**

For the Church, sacrament of Christ's salvation offered to all, we pray to the Lord: ℟.

For wise lawmakers who recognize the value of the world's natural resources, we pray to the Lord: ℟.

For the sick and the elderly who struggle to maintain dignity and for those who care for them, we pray to the Lord: ℟.

For us, God's priestly people, called to seek the Lord daily, we pray to the Lord: ℟.

PREPARATION OF THE GIFTS *(p. 13)*

PRAYER OVER THE GIFTS

God of mercy, may we offer a pure sacrifice for the forgiveness of our sins.

PREFACE *(Sundays in Ord. Time, p. 18)*

COMMUNION ANTIPHON *(Psalm 16:11)*

Lord, you will show me the path of life and fill me with joy in your presence.

PRAYER AFTER COMMUNION

Lord, you give us new hope in this eucharist. May the power of your love continue its saving work among us and bring us to the joy you promise.

BLESSING AND DISMISSAL *(p. 65)*

"If they kill me, I will rise again in the Salvadorean people," said Archbishop Oscar Romero. The bloody war in El Salvador claimed him as a martyr along with thousands of his fellow citizens. In spite of the horrible toll in human suffering, this people's clamour for justice was not silenced.

The Salvadoreans found the strength to continue, much like the family in today's first reading. Facing appalling tortures at the hands of the tyrant Antiochus, this family's faith sustained it. These ancient and modern martyrs held strongly to the justness of their causes but also drew strength from the promise of the resurrection.

We are not living under a despotic regime or suffering through war. Yet a thousand injustices do tear at the fabric of our society, from unchallenged individual acts of racism to our silent acceptance of unfair global trading arrangements that benefit us. Do we have any less grace given us to work for justice? Look around you. What groups in your community are seeking to transform our society into one based on gospel values?

Even in the darkest, most hopeless times or the visionless, complacent ones, voices like Romero's call us on to the more abundant life promised by Jesus. Add your voice to theirs.

Michael Dougherty, Whitehorse, YT

521

ENTRANCE ANTIPHON *(Psalm 88:2)*

Let my prayer come before you, Lord; listen, and answer me.

INTRODUCTORY RITES *(p. 5)*

OPENING PRAYER

God of power and mercy, protect us from all harm. Give us freedom of spirit and health in mind and body to do your work on earth.

FIRST READING *(2 Maccabees 7:1-2, 9-14)*

It happened that seven brothers and their mother were arrested and were being compelled by King Antiochus, under torture with whips and thongs, to partake of unlawful swine's flesh. One of the brothers, speaking for all, said, "What do you intend to ask and learn from us? For we are ready to die rather than transgress the laws of our ancestors."

After the first brother had died, they brought forward the second for their sport. And when he was at his last breath, he said to the King, "You accursed wretch, you dismiss us from this present life, but the King of the universe will raise us up to an everlasting renewal of life, because we have died for his laws."

After him, the third was the victim of their sport. When it was demanded, he quickly put out his tongue and courageously stretched forth his hands, and said nobly, "I got these from Heaven, and because of God's laws I disdain them, and from God I hope to get them back again."

As a result the king himself and those with him were astonished at the young man's spirit, for he regarded his sufferings as nothing.

After the third brother too had died, they maltreated and tortured the fourth in the same way. When he was near death, he said to his torturers, "One cannot but choose to die at the hands of mortals and to cherish the hope God gives of being raised again by him. But for you, there will be no resurrection to life!"

The word of the Lord. **Thanks be to God.**

RESPONSORIAL PSALM *(Psalm 17)*

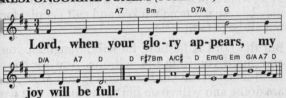

GJ

℟. **Lord, when your glory appears,**
   my joy will be full.

Hear a just cause, • **O** Lord;
attend to • **my** cry;
give ear to • **my** prayer
from lips • **free of** de-ceit. ℟.

My steps have held fast to • **your** paths;
my feet have • **not** slipped.
I call upon you, for you will answer me, • **O** God;
incline your ear to me, • **hear** my words. ℟.

Guard me as the apple of • **the** eye;
hide me in the shadow of • **your** wings,
As for me, I shall behold your face
     • **in** righteousness;
when I awake I shall be satisfied,
     be•-**holding** your likeness. ℟.

523

SECOND READING *(2 Thessalonians 2:16–3:5)*

May our Lord Jesus Christ himself and God our Father, who loved us and through grace gave us eternal comfort and good hope, comfort your hearts and strengthen them in every good work and word.

Brothers and sisters, pray for us, so that the word of the Lord may spread rapidly and be glorified everywhere, just as it is among you, and that we may be rescued from wicked and evil people; for not all have faith.

But the Lord is faithful; he will strengthen you and guard you from the evil one. And we have confidence in the Lord concerning you, that you are doing and will go on doing the things that we command. May the Lord direct your hearts to the love of God and to the steadfastness of Christ.

The word of the Lord. **Thanks be to God.**

GOSPEL ACCLAMATION *(Revelation 1:5-6)*

If not sung, this acclamation is omitted.

Jesus Christ is the firstborn of the dead; glory and kingship be his for ever and ever.

GOSPEL *(Luke 20:27-38)*

For the shorter version omit the indented part.

A reading from the holy gospel according to Luke. **Glory to you, Lord.**

Some Sadducees, those who say there is no resurrection, came to Jesus.

> and asked him a question, "Teacher, Moses wrote for us that if a man's brother dies, leav-

ing a wife but no children, the man shall marry the widow and raise up children for his brother. Now there were seven brothers; the first married, and died childless; then the second and the third married her, and so in the same way all seven died childless. Finally the woman also died. In the resurrection, therefore, whose wife will the woman be?—for the seven had married her."

Jesus said to them, "Those who belong to this age marry and are given in marriage; but those who are considered worthy of a place in that age and in the resurrection from the dead neither marry nor are given in marriage. Indeed they cannot die any more, because they are like angels and are children of God, being children of the resurrection.

'And the fact that the dead are raised Moses himself showed in the story about the bush, where he speaks of the Lord as the God of Abraham, the God of Isaac, and the God of Jacob. Now he is God not of the dead, but of the living; for to him all of them are alive."

The gospel of the Lord. **Praise to you, Lord Jesus Christ.**

PROFESSION OF FAITH *(Creed, pp. 11-12)*

PRAYER OF THE FAITHFUL

The following intentions are suggestions only.

℞: **Lord, hear our prayer.**

For the Church, called to follow Jesus boldly, secure in the promise of the resurrection, we pray to the Lord: ℞.

For all who clamour for justice in our world, we pray to the Lord: ℞.

For the needs of the forgotten in our midst, we pray to the Lord: ℞.

For us, God's people, called as a parish community to recognize and respond to local issues of justice, we pray to the Lord: ℞.

PREPARATION OF THE GIFTS *(p. 13)*

PRAYER OVER THE GIFTS

God of mercy, in this eucharist we proclaim the death of the Lord. Accept the gifts we present and help us follow him with love.

PREFACE *(Sundays in Ord. Time, p. 18)*

COMMUNION ANTIPHON *(Psalm 23:1-2)*

The Lord is my shepherd; there is nothing I shall want. In green pastures he gives me rest, he leads me beside the waters of peace.

PRAYER AFTER COMMUNION

Lord, we thank you for the nourishment you give us through your holy gift. Pour out your Spirit upon us and in the strength of this food from heaven keep us single-minded in your service.

BLESSING AND DISMISSAL *(p. 65)*

How tempting it is, upon hearing today's gospel, to simply throw up our hands in terror and resignation. After all, the signs which Jesus said heralded the coming end are certainly with us today. War, famine and natural disasters are everywhere. No wonder our society is filled with people who have lost hope and just given up.

And yet, Jesus exhorts us to do the exact opposite. "By your endurance," he says, "you will gain your souls." We cannot ignore the reality of suffering in our world by pretending that it doesn't exist; there simply are no quick or easy solutions to the anguish and misery faced by thousands. We can, however, face suffering with hope. We are called to remain steadfast, to endure, to witness to the gospel by proclaiming our belief that God is still at work in our world. As Christians, we live in 'in-between times.' While professing that the kingdom of God has arrived with the coming of Jesus, we also acknowledge that that kingdom has yet to be fulfilled.

As the Body of Christ alive on earth today, it is our responsibility to bring God's kingdom to completion. And we need to begin where we are right now. We needn't think that working for the kingdom of God means going to the ends of the earth to do exceptional deeds in extraordinary circumstances. In fact, we must recognize how

God's kingdom can be proclaimed and brought to fulfilment in our ordinary, everyday lives. By striving to live according to gospel values of love and justice, integrity and peace, both at work and at home, we make vital contributions to the realization of the kingdom. Our challenge, then, lies in making God's kingdom more and more a reality in our own circumstances and our own day.

Teresa Whalen, Regina, SK

ENTRANCE ANTIPHON *(Jeremiah 29:11, 12, 14)*

The Lord says: my plans for you are peace and not disaster; when you call to me, I will listen to you, and I will bring you back to the place from which I exiled you.

INTRODUCTORY RITES *(p. 5)*

OPENING PRAYER

Father of all that is good, keep us faithful in serving you, for to serve you is lasting joy.

FIRST READING *(Malachi 4:1-2)*

The Lord says this: "See, the day is coming, burning like an oven, when all the arrogant and all evildoers will be stubble; the day that comes shall burn them up," says the Lord of hosts, "so that it will leave them neither root nor branch.

"But for you who revere my name the sun of righteousness shall rise, with healing in its wings."

The word of the Lord. **Thanks be to God.**

ESPONSORIAL PSALM *(Psalm 98)*

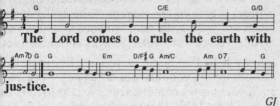

The Lord comes to rule the earth with jus-tice.

GJ

. **The Lord comes to rule the earth with justice.**

Sing praises to the Lord • **with** the lyre,
with the lyre and the • **sound** of melody.
With trumpets and the sound of • **the** horn
make a joyful noise
    before the • **King,** the Lord. ℟.

Let the sea roar, and • **all** that fills_it;
the world and • **those** who live_in_it.
Let the floods clap • **their** hands;
let the hills sing together for joy
    at the presence • **of** the Lord. ℟.

For the • **Lord** is coming,
coming to • **judge** the earth.
He will judge the world • **with** righteousness,
and the • **peoples** with equity. ℟.

ECOND READING *(2 Thessalonians 3:7-12)*

others and sisters, you yourselves know how
ou ought to imitate us; we were not idle when we
ere with you, and we did not eat anyone's bread
ithout paying for it; but with toil and labour we
orked night and day, so that we might not
urden any of you.

This was not because we do not have that right, b
in order to give you an example to imitate. For eve
when we were with you, we gave you this con
mand: "Anyone unwilling to work should not eat

For we hear that some of you are living in idl
ness, mere busybodies, not doing any work. No
such persons we command and exhort in the Lor
Jesus Christ to do their work quietly and to ear
their own living.

The word of the Lord. **Thanks be to God.**

GOSPEL ACCLAMATION *(Luke 21:28)*

If not sung, this acclamation is omitted.

Lift up your heads and see; your redemption
near at hand.

GOSPEL *(Luke 21:5-19)*

A reading from the holy gospel according to Luk
Glory to you, Lord.

When some were speaking about the temple, ho
it was adorned with beautiful stones and gif
dedicated to God, Jesus said, "As for these thin
that you see, the days will come when not or
stone will be left upon another; all will be throw
down."

They asked him, "Teacher, when will this be, ar
what will be the sign that this is about to tal
place?"

And Jesus said, "Beware that you are not le
astray; for many will come in my name and say,
am he!' and, 'The time is near!' Do not go aft
them.

When you hear of wars and insurrections, do not
be terrified; for these things must take place first,
but the end will not follow immediately."

Then Jesus said to them, "Nation will rise against
nation, and kingdom against kingdom; there will
be great earthquakes, and in various places fam-
ines and plagues; and there will be dreadful por-
tents and great signs from heaven.

But before all this occurs, they will arrest you
and persecute you; they will hand you over to
synagogues and prisons, and you will be brought
before kings and governors because of my name.

This will give you an opportunity to testify. So
make up your minds not to prepare your defence
in advance; for I will give you words and a wisdom that none of your opponents will be able to
withstand or contradict.

You will be betrayed even by parents, by brothers and sisters, and by relatives and friends; and
they will put some of you to death. You will be
hated by all because of my name. But not a hair of
your head will perish. By your endurance you
will gain your souls."

The gospel of the Lord. **Praise to you, Lord Jesus
Christ.**

PROFESSION OF FAITH *(Creed, pp. 11-12)*

PRAYER OF THE FAITHFUL

The following intentions are suggestions only.

℞: **Lord, hear our prayer.**

For the Church, partner in establishing peace and justice as we pray for the coming of God's kingdom, we pray to the Lord: ℞.

For world leaders inspired to work together to make peace a reality in our world, we pray to the Lord: ℞.

For those among us who suffer from depression and despair, we pray to the Lord: ℞.

For us, called as God's holy people to witness to God's presence in our daily lives, we pray to the Lord: ℞.

PREPARATION OF THE GIFTS *(p. 13)*

PRAYER OVER THE GIFTS

Lord God, may the gifts we offer increase our love for you and bring us to eternal life.

PREFACE *(Sundays in Ord. Time, p. 18)*

COMMUNION ANTIPHON *(Psalm 73:28)*

It is good for me to be with the Lord and to put my hope in him.

PRAYER AFTER COMMUNION

Father, may we grow in love by the eucharist we have celebrated in memory of the Lord Jesus.

BLESSING AND DISMISSAL *(p. 65)*

Every aspect of a Roman crucifixion was calculated to humiliate the victim. Jesus, though, seems to have been singled out for special humiliation—even down to the signboard that called him "King of the Jews." There is very little doubt that the sign was also calculated to irritate Jewish sensitivities. The Jewish authorities had used the charge of treason to catch Jesus in Roman justice; the Romans' sense of irony turned justice on the accusers. But this double play meant to humiliate Jesus and his accusers carried a truth far beyond its intended humiliation, because Jesus is in fact king of a principality far beyond historical Israel.

One remarkable thing about this gospel is that Christ's regal character shines through even in humiliation. One of the thieves crucified with Jesus asks Jesus to remember him in his kingdom. Jesus tells him, "Today you will be with me in Paradise." The word 'paradise' is a Persian word meaning 'walled garden'; the Persians were renowned for their beautiful gardens. When a Persian monarch wanted to single out a subject for special recognition and honour, the monarch would invite the subject to walk in the garden. Jesus promised the thief a place of honour and privilege in heaven as his special companion.

Jesus didn't reject the thief or give him an off-handed promise of eternal life. His promise is quite specific: he would walk and talk with Jesus in paradise. Even at the height of humiliation feeling deserted by everyone, Jesus understands his nature as heaven's king and the Lord of life.

This is the King we worship. Unwittingly, the Romans acknowledged his kingship and the repentant thief experienced his forgiveness.

James B. Sauer, San Antonio, TX

ENTRANCE ANTIPHON *(Revelation 5:12; 1:6)*

The Lamb who was slain is worthy to receive strength and divinity, wisdom and power and honour: to him be glory and power for ever.

INTRODUCTORY RITES *(p. 5)*

OPENING PRAYER

Almighty and merciful God, you break the power of evil and make all things new in your Son Jesus Christ, the King of the universe. May all in heaven and earth acclaim your glory and never cease to praise you.

FIRST READING *(2 Samuel 5:1-3)*

All the tribes of Israel came to David at Hebron and said, "Look, we are your bone and flesh. For some time, while Saul was king over us, it was you who led out Israel and brought it in. The Lord said to you: 'It is you who shall be shepherd of my people Israel, you who shall be ruler over Israel.'"

So all the elders of Israel came to the king at Hebron; and King David made a covenant with

hem at Hebron before the Lord, and they
nointed David king over Israel.

he word of the Lord. **Thanks be to God.**

RESPONSORIAL PSALM *(Psalm 122)*

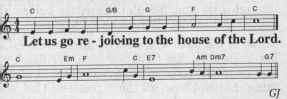

Let us go re - joic-ing to the house of the Lord.

GJ

℟. **Let us go rejoicing to the house of the Lord.**

I was glad when they said • **to** me,
"Let us go to the house of • **the** Lord!"
Our feet • **are** standing
within your gates, O • **Je**-rusalem. ℟.

Jerusalem—built as • **a** city
that is bound firmly • **to**-gether.
To it the tribes • **go** up,
the tribes of • **the** Lord. ℟.

As it was decreed • **for** Israel,
to give thanks to the name of • **the** Lord.
For there the thrones for judgment were • **set** up,
the thrones of the house • **of** David. ℟.

SECOND READING *(Colossians 1:12-20)*

Give thanks to the Father, who has enabled you to
share in the inheritance of the saints in the light.

The Father has rescued us from the power of
darkness and transferred us into the kingdom of
his beloved Son, in whom we have redemption,
the forgiveness of sins.

Christ is the image of the invisible God, the firstborn of all creation; for in him all things in heaven and on earth were created, things visible and invisible, whether thrones or dominions or rulers or powers—all things have been created through him and for him. Christ is before all things, and in him all things hold together.

Christ is the head of the body, the church; he is the beginning, the firstborn from the dead, so that he might come to have first place in every thing. For in Christ all the fullness of God was pleased to dwell, and through him God was pleased to reconcile to himself all things, whether on earth or in heaven, by making peace through the blood of his cross.

The word of the Lord. **Thanks be to God.**

GOSPEL ACCLAMATION *(Mark 11:10)*

If not sung, this acclamation is omitted.

Blessed is the one who inherits the kingdom of David our father; blessed is the one who comes in the name of the Lord.

GOSPEL *(Luke 23:35-43)*

A reading from the holy gospel according to Luke. **Glory to you, Lord.**

When Jesus had been crucified, the people stood by watching; the leaders scoffed at him saying, "He saved others; let him save himself if he is the Messiah of God, his chosen one!" The soldiers also mocked Jesus, coming up and offering him sour wine, and saying, "If you are the King of the ews, save yourself!" There was also an inscription over Jesus, "This is the King of the Jews."

One of the criminals who were hanged there kept deriding Jesus and saying, "Are you not the Messiah? Save yourself and us!"

But the other rebuked him, saying, "Do you not fear God, since you are under the same sentence of condemnation? And we indeed have been condemned justly, for we are getting what we deserve for our deeds, but this man has done nothing wrong." Then he said, "Jesus, remember me when you come into your kingdom." Jesus replied, "Truly I tell you, today you will be with me in Paradise."

The gospel of the Lord. **Praise to you, Lord Jesus Christ.**

PROFESSION OF FAITH *(Nicene Creed, p. 12)*

PRAYER OF THE FAITHFUL

The following intentions are suggestions only.

℣: **Lord, hear our prayer.**

For the Church, instrument of unity and salvation, we pray to the Lord: ℟.

For the triumph of peace, harmony and hope in our world community, we pray to the Lord: ℟.

For those among us who are poor, persecuted or lonely, we pray to the Lord: ℟.

For us, God's people, called as a parish to witness to Christ and his salvation, we pray to the Lord: ℟.

PREPARATION OF THE GIFTS *(p. 13)*

PRAYER OVER THE GIFTS

Lord, we offer you the sacrifice by which your Son reconciles the human family. May it bring unity and peace to the world.

PREFACE *(Christ the King, p. 30)*

COMMUNION ANTIPHON *(Psalm 29:10-11)*

The Lord will reign for ever and will give his people the gift of peace.

PRAYER AFTER COMMUNION

Lord, you give us Christ, the King of all creation, as food for everlasting life. Help us to live by his gospel and bring us to the joy of his kingdom.

BLESSING AND DISMISSAL *(p. 65)*

Note on the Liturgical Calendar

For historical reasons, the civil and liturgical calendars are not identical. The civil calendar always begins on January 1st, while the liturgical calendar always begins on the First Sunday of Advent. *Living with Christ Sunday Missal* follows the liturgical calendar and so spans two civil years: 1994-1995.

Every year, the liturgical seasons follow the same pattern: Advent, Christmas, Lent, Easter, and Ordinary Time. Within each season, the readings reflect suitable themes. There are many readings available on certain liturgical themes and the Church seeks to broaden our experience of the Bible by varying the readings from one year to the next.

> The treasures of the Bible are to be opened up more lavishly, so that richer fare may be provided for the faithful at the table of God's Word. In this way a more representative portion of the holy Scriptures will be read to the people over a set cycle of years (Vatican II, *Constitution on the Sacred Liturgy*, §51).

The Bible is a 'library' of 73 books from which readings have been selected for pastoral purposes and arranged in a book called the *Lectionary*. These readings are "aimed at giving the faithful an ever-deepening perception of the faith they profess and of the history of salvation" (*Introduction to the Lectionary for Mass*, §60).

The preparation of a lectionary takes years of study, consultation, and revision. In 1992 the Canadian Church inaugurated a new Sunday Lectionary based on the New Revised Standard Version of the Bible (NRSV).

The lectionary features a different Synoptic Gospel each year over a three-year cycle. The first year of the cycle, Year A, is the year for the reading of the Gospel of Matthew; in the second and third years, the readings are from the Gospel of Mark (Year B) and the Gospel of Luke (Year C). John's Gospel is featured at other liturgical times, for instance during Lent and the Easter Season. This liturgical year is Year C. Therefore, Luke's Gospel will be emphasized all year.

All this has been planned to develop among the faithful a greater hunger for the word of God... We are fully confident on this account that both priests and faithful will prepare their minds and hearts more devoutly for the Lord's Supper and that, meditating on the Scriptures, they will be nourished more each day by the words of the Lord. In accord with the hopes of Vatican Council II, all will thus regard sacred Scripture as the abiding source of spiritual life, the foundation for Christian instruction and the core of all theological study (Paul VI *Apostolic Constitution on the Roman Missal*)

Morning Offering

Lord Jesus,
I give you my hands to do your work.
I give you my feet to go your way.
I give you my eyes to see as you do.
I give you my tongue to speak your words.
I give you my mind that you may think in me.
I give you my spirit that you may pray in me.
Above all, I give you my heart that you may love in me your Father and all humanity.
I give you my whole self that you may grow in me, so that it is you, Lord Jesus, who live and work and pray in me.

Grail Prayer

Morning Hymn

Breathe on me, breath of God, fill me with life anew, that I may love the things you love, and do what you would do.

Breathe on me, breath of God, until my heart is pure, until with you I have one will to live and to endure.

Breathe on me, breath of God, my soul with grace refine, until this earthly part of me glows with your fire divine.

Breathe on me, breath of God, so I shall never die, but live with you the perfect life in your eternity.

Edwin Hatch, 1835-1889

Dedication

Father, I dedicate this new day to you; as I go about my work, I ask you to bless those with whom I come in contact.

Lord, I pray for all men and women who work to earn their living; give them satisfaction in what they do.

Spirit of God, comfort the unemployed and their families; they are your children and my brothers and sisters. I ask you to help them find work soon.

St. Ignatius Loyola, 1491-1556

Each New Day

Let me pause as I begin this new day to give it to you, Lord. Before the tumult of activities breaks in; before breakfast plates crash through my still sleepy mind; for this last moment in my bed, thank you, Lord.

Let me hold your promise of new life. Keep me from slipping back for I know that what is forgiven is as if it never were. Each new day, your grace gives me a fresh start to walk in your light again.

May the Lord support us all the day long, till the shades lengthen and the evening comes, and the busy world is hushed, and the fever of life is over, and our work is done. Then in his mercy may he give us a safe lodging, and a holy rest, and peace at the last. Amen.

John Henry Cardinal Newman, 1801-1890

Evening Praise

All praise to you, O God, this night
For all the blessings of the light;
Keep us, we pray, O King of kings,
Beneath your own almighty wings.

Forgive us, Lord, through Christ your Son,
Whatever wrong this day we've done;
Your peace give to the world, O Lord,
That we might live in one accord.

Enlighten us, O blessed Light,
and give us rest throughout this night.
O strengthen us, that for your sake,
We all may serve you when we wake.

Thomas Ken, 1673-1711

At Eventide

O radiant Light, O Sun divine
Of God the Father's deathless face,
O image of the light sublime
That fills the heav'nly dwelling place.

Son of God, source of life,
Praise is yours both day and night;
Our happy voice must raise the strain
Of your proclaimed and splendid name.

Lord Jesus Christ, as daylight fades,
As shine the lights of eventide,
We praise the Father with the Son,
The Spirit blest and with them one.

Third century Greek hymn

Night-time

Thank you, God
for the balance of day and night
for the comfort and warmth of our beds;
for unbroken nights in fresh sheets;
for changes in attitudes that refreshing sleep
    brings;
for your care and love continuing through the
    night.

Remind us, Lord, of those
    sleeping in the streets — rejected,
    tossing through hospital nights,
    sitting alone by dying relations;
    insomniacs who dread these dark hours,
    children frightened by drunken fights,
    mothers helplessly watching
        ill or starving children;
    those with fears magnified
        by the intensity of darkness,
    the lonely, the sick, the disturbed,
    the outcasts of society,
    whom in our comfort we easily forget.

Use us, Lord, join our prayers with those of countless others to spread your love and to ease the sufferings beyond our imaginings for which we must share responsibility.

Canticle of Zechariah

Luke 1:68-79

Blessed be the Lord, the God of Israel;
he has come to his people and set them free.
He has raised up for us a mighty saviour,
born of the house of his servant David.
Through his holy prophets he promised of old
that he would save us from our enemies,
from the hands of all who hate us.
He promised to show mercy to our ancestors
and to remember his holy covenant.
This was the oath he swore
to our father Abraham:
to set us free from the hands of our enemies,
free to worship him without fear,
holy and righteous in his sight
all the days of our life.
You, my child, shall be called
the prophet of the Most High;
for you will go before the Lord to prepare his way,
to give his people knowledge of salvation
by the forgiveness of their sins.
In the tender compassion of our God
the dawn from on high shall break upon us,
to shine on those who dwell in darkness
and the shadow of death,
and to guide our feet into the way of peace.

Magnificat

Luke 1:46-55

My soul proclaims the greatness of the Lord,
my spirit exults in God my Saviour;
for he has looked with favour
on his lowly servant.

From this day all generations will call me blessed:
the Almighty has done great things for me,
and holy is his Name.

He has mercy on those who fear him
in every generation.
He has shown the strength of his arm,
he has scattered the proud in their conceit.

He has cast down the mighty from their thrones,
and has lifted up the lowly.
He has filled the hungry with good things,
and the rich he has sent away empty.

He has come to the help of his servant Israel
for he has remembered his promise of mercy,
the promise he made to our ancestors,
to Abraham and his children for ever.

Canticle of Simeon

Luke 2:29-32

Now, Master, you can let your servant go in peace,
just as you promised;
for my eyes have seen the salvation
which you prepared for all peoples to see,
a light to enlighten the nations,
and the glory of your people, Israel.

Beatitudes

Matthew 5:1-12

Blessed are the poor in spirit;
    theirs is the Kingdom of heaven.
Blessed are the gentle;
    they shall inherit the earth.
Blessed are those who mourn;
    they shall be comforted.
Blessed are those who hunger and thirst
    for righteousness;
    they shall be satisfied.
Blessed are the merciful;
    they shall have mercy shown them.
Blessed are the pure in heart;
    they shall see God.
Blessed are the peacemakers;
    they shall be called children of God.
Blessed are those who are persecuted
    in the cause of righteousness;
    theirs is the Kingdom of heaven.
Blessed are you when people abuse you
    and persecute you
    and speak all kinds of calumny against you
    on my account.
Rejoice and be glad,
    for your reward will be great in heaven.

Out of the Depths

Psalm 130

Out of the depths I call to you, Lord.
O Lord, listen to my cry.
Be attentive to the sound of my pleading.

If you, Lord, note all our offences,
who then, O Lord, could stand?
But with you is forgiveness,
for which we revere you.

I wait for the Lord, my soul awaits;
I hope in his word.
My soul waits for the Lord,
more than watchmen wait for dawn,
more than watchmen awaiting the dawn.

Israel, hope in the Lord, for with the Lord
there is mercy and generous redemption.
It is he who redeems Israel from all its sins.

The Lord Forgives

Psalm 32

Happy those whose offence is forgiven,
whose sin is remitted.
happy those to whom the Lord
imputes no guilt,
in whose spirit is no guile.

I kept it secret and my frame was wasted.
I groaned all day long,
for night and day your hand was heavy upon me.
Indeed my strength was dried up
as by the summer's heat.

But now I have acknowledged my sins;
my guilt I did not hide. I said:
"I will confess my offence to the Lord."
And you, Lord, have forgiven
the guilt of my sin.

So let faithful men and women pray to you
in the time of need.
The floods of water may reach high
but they shall stand secure.
You are my hiding place, O Lord;
you save me from distress.

Rejoice, rejoice in the Lord,
exult, you just!
O come, ring out your joy,
all you upright of heart.

Divine Glory and Human Dignity

Psalm 8

How great is your name, O Lord our God,
through all the earth!

When I see the heavens, the work of your hands
the moon and the stars which you arranged,
what are we that you should keep us in mind,
men and women that you care for us?

Yet you have made us little less than gods;
and crowned us with glory and honour,
gave us power over the works of your hands,
put all things under our feet.

How great is your name, O Lord our God
through all the earth!

Praise to God

Psalm 67

God, be gracious and bless us
and let your face shed its light upon us.
So will your ways be known upon earth
and all nations learn your saving help.

Let the peoples praise you, O God;
let all the peoples praise you.

Let the nations be glad and exult
for you rule the world with justice.
With fairness you rule the peoples,
you guide the nations on earth.

Let the peoples praise you, O God;
let all the peoples praise you.

The earth has yielded its fruit
for God, our God, has blessed us.
May God still give us his blessing
till the ends of the earth revere him.

Let the peoples praise you, O God;
let all the peoples praise you.

A Prayer in Desolation

Psalm 143

Lord, listen to my prayer,
turn your ear to my appeal.
You are faithful, you are just; give answer.

Do not call your servant to judgment
for no one is just in your sight.

The enemy pursues my soul;
he has crushed my life to the ground;
he has made me dwell in darkness
like the dead, long forgotten.
Therefore my spirit fails;
my heart is numb within me.

I remember the days that are past;
I ponder all your works.
I muse on what your hand has wrought
and to you I stretch out my hands.
Like a parched land my soul thirsts for you.

Lord, make haste and answer;
for my spirit fails within me.
Do not hide your face
lest I become like those in the grave.

In the morning let me know your love
for I put my trust in you.
Make me know the way I should walk;
to you I lift up my soul.

escue me, Lord, from my enemies;
have fled to you for refuge.
each me to do your will
r you, O Lord, are my God.
et your good spirit guide me
ways that are level and smooth.

or your name's sake, Lord, save my life;
your justice save my soul from distress.

your love make an end of my foes;
estroy all those who oppress me
r I am your servant, O Lord.

TRADITIONAL PRAYERS

The Lord's Prayer

Our Father, who art in heaven, hallowed be th
name; thy kingdom come; thy will be done o
earth as it is in heaven.

Give us this day our daily bread; and forgive u
our trespasses as we forgive those who trespas
against us; and lead us not into temptation, bu
deliver us from evil. Amen.

Hail Mary

Hail Mary, full of grace, the Lord is with thee
Blessed art thou among women and blessed is th
fruit of thy womb, Jesus.

Holy Mary, Mother of God, pray for us sinners
now and the hour of our death. Amen.

Glory Be to the Father

Glory be to the Father, and to the Son, and to the
Holy Spirit. As it was in the beginning, is now,
and ever shall be, world without end. Amen.

Act of Contrition

My God, I am sorry for my sins with all my heart.
In choosing to do wrong and failing to do good, I
have sinned against you whom I should love
above all things. I firmly intend, with your help,
to do penance, to sin no more, and to avoid
whatever leads me to sin.

Our Saviour Jesus Christ suffered and died for us.
In his name, my God, have mercy.

Act of Faith

O my God, I firmly believe that you are one God
three divine Persons, Father, Son, and Ho
Spirit. I believe that your divine Son became ma
died for our sins, and that he will come to judg
the living and the dead. I believe these and all th
truths which the holy Catholic Church teache
because you have revealed them, who can neith
deceive nor be deceived.

Act of Hope

O my God, relying on your almighty power an
infinite mercy and promises, I hope to obtai
pardon of my sins, the help of your grace, and li
everlasting through the merits of Jesus Christ, m
Lord and Redeemer.

Act of Love

O my God, I love you above all things, with m
whole heart and soul, because you are all goo
and worthy of all love. I love my neighbour a
myself for the love of you. I forgive all who hav
injured me, and ask pardon of all whom I hav
injured. Amen.

Angelus

The angel of the Lord declared unto Mary, and she conceived of the Holy Spirit. *Hail Mary...*

Behold, the handmaid of the Lord; be it done to me according to thy word. *Hail Mary...*

And the word was made flesh, and dwelt among us. *Hail Mary...*

Pray for us, O holy Mother of God; that we may be made worthy of the promises of Christ.

Pour forth, we beseech thee, O Lord, thy grace into our hearts, that we to whom the message of thy Son was made known by an angel, may by his passion and death be brought to the glory of his resurrection, through the same Christ our Lord. Amen.

The Rosary

In the Rosary we focus on 15 events or mysteri
in the life and death of Jesus and meditate on ho
we share with Mary in the redemptive work
Christ. The mysteries are arranged in three cycle
the joyful, the sorrowful and the glorious. Ma
today deepen their meditation on a particul
mystery by reading a pertinent passage from t
Bible.

~ Begin the Rosary at the crucifix by praying t
  Apostles' Creed (p. 11)

~ At each large bead, pray the *Lord's Prayer*

~ At each small bead, pray the *Hail Mary*

~ At the first three beads it is customary to pra
  a *Hail Mary* for each of the gifts of faith, hop
  and love

~ For each mystery, begin with the *Lord
  Prayer*, then recite the *Hail Mary* ten time
  and end with *Glory Be to the Father.*

e Five Joyful Mysteries:

The Annunciation (Luke 1:26-38)
The Visitation (John 1:1-14)
The Nativity (Luke 2: 1-20)
The Presentation (Luke 2:22-38)
The Finding in the Temple (Luke 2:41-52)

e Five Sorrowful Mysteries:

The Agony in the Garden (Matthew 26:36-56)
The Scourging at the Pillar (Matthew 27:20-26)
The Crowning with Thorns (Matthew 27:27-30)
The Carrying of the Cross (Matthew 27:31-33)
The Crucifixion (Matthew 27: 34-60)

he Five Glorious Mysteries:

The Resurrection (John 20:1-18)
The Ascension (Acts 1:9-11)
The Descent of the Holy Spirit (John 20:19-23)
The Assumption of Mary (John 11:26)
The Crowning of Mary (Philippians 2:1-11)

Hail, Holy Queen

Hail, holy Queen, mother of mercy, our life, (
sweetness and our hope. To you do we cry, po
banished children of Eve; to you we send up
sighs, mourning and weeping in this valley
tears. Turn then, most gracious advocate, yo
eyes of mercy upon us, and after this, our ex
show unto us the blessed fruit of your wom
Jesus. O clement, O loving, O kind Virgin Mar

Regina Caeli

Queen of heaven, rejoice, alleluia!
For he whom you chose to bear, alleluia!
Is risen as he said, alleluia!
Pray for us to God, alleluia!
Rejoice and be glad, O Virgin Mary, alleluia!
For the Lord is truly risen, alleluia!

O God, by the resurrection of your Son, our Lord,
you were pleased to make glad the whole world;
grant, we beseech you, that through the intercession of the Virgin Mary, his mother, we may attain
the joys of everlasting life, through the same
Christ our Lord. Amen.

Come, Holy Spirit

Come, Holy Spirit, fill the hearts of your faithful
and kindle in them the fire of your love. Send
forth your Spirit, O Lord, and renew the face of
the earth.

O God, on the first Pentecost you instructed the
hearts of those who believed in you by the light of
the Holy Spirit: under the inspiration of the same
Spirit, give us a taste for what is right and true and
a continuing sense of his joy-bringing presence
and power, through Jesus Christ our Lord. Amen.

Anima Christi

Soul of Christ, make me holy.
Body of Christ, save me.
Blood of Christ, inebriate me.
Water from the side of Christ, wash me clean.
Passion of Christ, strengthen me.
Kind Jesus, hear me.
Hide me within your wounds.
Let me never be separated from you.
Defend me from evil.
In the hour of my death call me to yourself,
that with your saints I may praise you
in everlasting life. Amen.

God be in my head, and in my understanding;
God be in my eyes, and in my looking;
God be in my mouth, and in my speaking;
God be in my heart, and in my thinking;
God be at my end, and at my departing.

Sarum Breviary (1085)

The Stations of the Cross

(Traditional version)

Prayer before each station:

> We adore you, O Christ, and we prais
> you, because by your holy cross you hav
> redeemed the world.

1. Jesus is condemned to death

Consider how Jesus, having been
scourged and crowned with thorns, i
unjustly condemned by Pilate to deat
on a cross.

2. Jesus takes up his cross

Consider how Jesus, bearing this cros
on his shoulders, offers his sufferin
to the Father for us.

3. Jesus falls for the first time

Consider this first fall. Jesus, bleed
ing, crowned with thorns, so weak he
can hardly walk, yet forced to carry
this heavy burden. The soldiers strike
him and he falls.

4. Jesus meets his mother

Consider this meeting between
mother and son... their tender love for
one another, their hearts torn asun-
der.

Simon helps Jesus carry the cross

Consider how the torturers force the bystander Simon to carry Jesus' cross. They want Jesus to stay alive long enough to die crucified.

Veronica wipes Jesus' face

Consider how Veronica recognizes Jesus' pain and attempts to lessen his suffering.

Jesus falls for the second time

Consider this second fall. It reopens his wounds, hurts his head, pains his whole body.

*The women of Jerusalem
weep for Jesus*

Consider how these compassionate women wept at the sight of the tortured Jesus.

Jesus falls for the third time

Consider this third fall. Though extremely weak, Jesus is urged on by the soldiers.

10. Jesus is stripped of his garments

Consider the violence with which the soldiers tear off the bloody garments which cling to his broken skin and start the wounds bleeding again.

11. Jesus is nailed to the cross

Consider how Jesus, arms extended on the cross, offers to his Father the ultimate sacrifice for our salvation.

12. Jesus dies on the cross

Consider how Jesus, after hours of agony and anguish on the cross, abandons himself to the Father and dies.

13. Jesus is removed from the cross

Consider how two disciples take the broken body down from the cross and place Jesus in his grieving mother's arms.

14. Jesus is placed in the tomb

Consider how the disciples, filled with grief, carry the body to the burial place. They close the tomb and come away confused and sorrowful.

The Way of the Cross

(Revised version: The Sacred Congregation for Divine Worship recommends that the traditional *Stations* be revised to emphasize that the sufferings and resurrection of Christ are one redemptive mystery.)

Opening Prayer

Lord Jesus, all of your life led up to the Way of the Cross. In this final journey you lay down your life for your friends.

Jesus, you consider us your friends. You walk side by side with us on the journey of life. You know its joys and hopes, its suffering and pain. Today we want to walk side by side with you on our way to the Cross. Your suffering, your death, your rising from the dead give meaning to our lives. The way of the Cross is the way of life.

Lord, as you took the bread, your body, take us, bless us, break us, give us to others, so that in you we may be instruments of salvation for the world. Amen.

1. The Last Supper

Jesus said to them, "I have wanted so much to eat this Passover meal with you before I suffer! For I tell you, I will never eat it until it is given its full meaning in the Kingdom of God."

Then Jesus took a cup, gave thanks to God, and said, "Take this and share it among yourselves. I tell you that from now on I will not drink this wine until the Kingdom of God comes."

Then he took a loaf of bread, gave thanks to Go broke it, and gave it to them, saying, "This is m body, which is given for you. Do this in memory me." In the same way, he gave them the cup aft supper, saying, "This cup is God's new covenar sealed with my blood, which is poured out for you.

(Luke 22:15-2

Jesus, you love us. Make us realize we are covenant people, make our eucharists mo ments when we feel your friendship, so tha we may live this out for all humankind.

2. In the Garden of Gethsemane

Then Jesus went with his disciples to a plac called Gethsemane, and said to them, "Sit her while I go over there and pray." He took with hin Peter and the two sons of Zebedee. Grief and anguish came over him, and he said to them, "Th sorrow in my heart is so great that it almos crushes me. Stay here and keep watch with me."

(Matthew 26:36-38

Jesus, you love us. Comfort us in times of distress. Help us to see beyond ourselves; help us to overcome the feeling of senseless chaos; help us to see the joy and hope of those who truly suffer and who truly believe. Remind us of your covenant of friendship with us.

3. Before the Sanhedrin

Jesus was taken to the High Priest's house, where the chief priests, the elders, and the teachers of the Law were gathering. Peter followed at a distance and went into the courtyard, where he sat down with the guards, keeping himself warm by the fire. The chief priests and the whole Council tried to find some evidence against Jesus in order to put him to death, but they could not find any.

(Mark 14:53-55)

Jesus, you love us. Help us live out your covenant of friendship; give us strength to stand against authorities who exercise power for evil. Make us nonviolent, but strong in this struggle for humankind. Jesus, strengthen us.

4. Before Pontius Pilate

Early in the morning Jesus was taken from Caiaphas' house to the governor's palace. The Jewish authorities did not go inside the palace, for they wanted to keep themselves ritually clean in order to be able to eat the Passover meal. So Pilate went outside to them and asked, "What do you accuse this man of?" Their answer was, "We would not have brought him to you if he had not committed a crime." (John 18:28-30)

Jesus, you love us. You stand with the victims in this world. Is that one meaning of the covenant for us: that we too should side with the oppressed against the oppressor? Lord, this is hard for us, teach us how to side with the oppressed, with the victims.

5. The whipping and crowning with thorns

Then Pilate took Jesus and had him whipped. The soldiers made a crown of thorny branches, put it on his head, then put a purple robe on him. They came to him and said, "Long live the King of the Jews!" and slapped him. (John 19:1-3)

Jesus, you love us. Turn our sympathies to the poor victims of desperate soldiers all over the world. Empower us to stop the sale of arms to ruthless armies. Show us the way to curb senseless attacks by states against their own people. Jesus, teach us how to resist evil.

. The carrying of the cross

>o they took charge of Jesus. He went out, carry-
ng his cross, and came to the 'Place of the Skull,'
s it is called. (In Hebrew it is called 'Golgotha.')

(John 19:16-17)

> Jesus, you love us. Your love for
> us affirms the goodness of our hu-
> manity. We are the friends for
> whom you suffered. Teach us to
> respect others, not to dismiss or
> diminish them as less human.

7. Simon of Cyrene

On the way they met a man named Simon, who
was coming into the city from the country. The
soldiers forced him to carry Jesus' cross.

(Mark 15:21)

> Jesus, you love us. We don't like
> carrying crosses, but many times
> our cross is of our own making. It is
> a self-centred cross. Help us find the
> true cross in the lives of the poor.
> Help us to help carry their burden.
> Jesus, help us!

8. The women of Jerusalem

A large crowd of people followed him; among
them were some women who were weeping and
wailing for him. Jesus turned to them and said,
"Women of Jerusalem! Do not cry for me, but for

yourselves and your children. For the days are
coming when people will say, 'How lucky are the
women who never had children, who never bore
babies, who never nursed them!' "

(Luke 23:27-31)

Jesus, you love us. Allow us to comfort the grieving women of our time.
But even more, enable us to prevent
their grief, which so often could be
avoided. Help us to break down the
human systems which starve and
kill. Jesus, make us angry about this
unnecessary grief and suffering. Teach us to
weep, knowing all the time that tears are
never enough.

9. The stripping and crucifixion

They came to a place called Golgotha, which
means 'Place of the Skull.' There they offered
Jesus wine mixed with a bitter substance; but
after tasting it, he would not drink it.
They crucified him and then divided his clothes
among them by throwing dice.

(Matthew 27:33-35)

Jesus, you love us. Stripped naked,
nailed to the cross, you have given
your all for us. Jesus, help us break
the bonds of our selfishness and
materialism. Show us how we can
give our life for others, in your covenant.

0. The second thief

One of the criminals hanging there hurled insults at him: "Aren't you the Messiah? Save yourself and us!"

The other one, however, rebuked him, saying, "Don't you fear God? You received the same sentence he did. Ours, however, is only right because we are getting what we deserve; but he has done no wrong." And he said to Jesus, "Remember me, Jesus, when you come as King!"

Jesus said to him, "I promise you that today you will be in Paradise with me."

(Luke 23:39-43)

Jesus, you love us. Impress on us that the lives we live, the work we do, have consequences for others. Awaken our awareness to real evil and real faith. Help us honour your covenant of friendship in our lives.

1. Mary and John

Standing close to Jesus' cross were his mother, his mother's sister, Mary the wife of Clopas, and Mary Magdalene. Jesus saw his mother and the disciple he loved standing there; so he said to his mother, "He is your son."

Then he said to the disciple, "She is your mother." From that time the disciple took her to live in his home.   (John 19:25-27)

Jesus, you love us. You gave us your mothe
Mary as our own mother. Touch our heart:
with her sorrow at your death. Lift our eyes so
we may see in her the beauty of your cov
enant; the beauty of her gift of herself to you
and to us.

12. Death on the cross

But when they came to Jesus, they saw that he wa
already dead, so they did not break his legs. On
of the soldiers, however, plunged his spear int
Jesus' side, and at once blood and water poured
out.   (John 19:33-34

 Jesus, you love us. Teach us you
way. Give us the wisdom to recog
nize evil. Give us the courage to con
front it, to struggle against it, so tha
we may truly be your friends.

13. The new sepulchre

When it was evening, a rich man from Arimathe
arrived; his name was Joseph, and he also was
disciple of Jesus. He went to Pilate and asked fo
the body of Jesus. Pilate gave orders for the bod
to be given to Joseph. So Joseph took it, wrappe
it in a new linen sheet, and placed it in his ow
tomb which he had just recently dug out of soli
rock. Then he rolled a large stone across th
entrance to the tomb and went away.

(Matthew 27:57-6(

Jesus, you love us. Help us to distinguish justice and charity. Sometimes it is easier to do charity than to do justice. Let us know which should be our response and when, in our lives. Give us the grace to act charitably and justly.

4. The resurrection

Very early on Sunday morning the women went to the tomb, carrying the spices they had prepared. They found the stone rolled away from the entrance to the tomb, so they went in; but they did not find the body of the Lord Jesus.

(Luke 24:1-3)

Jesus, you love us. You have returned from the dead to be with us. Be our promise, our hope that all evil will be overcome. Bless us with full life for all humankind, under your covenant.

Alleluia!

Final Prayer

We know that Christ has been raised from death and will never die again — death will no longer rule over him. And so, because he died, sin has no power over him; and now he lives his life in fellowship with God. In the same way, you are to think of yourselves as dead, so far as sin is concerned, but living in fellowship with God through Christ Jesus.

(Romans 6:9-11)

Father, your only Son gave up his life for us his friends. Help us understand the meaning of that friendship. Help us grow in that friendship.

We are a weak and distracted people. Often we neglect you, but you never abandon us. You love us. Make us a less selfish and a more caring people. Help us to share the crosses of others, as Simon did. Show us how to live your covenant of friendship day by day with the victims and the poor of this world. Father, we depend on you.

We pray this through Jesus, the Christ, your Son who has risen from the dead. Amen.

PRAYERS AND MEDITATIONS FROM THE SAINTS

Prayer of St. Francis

Lord, make me an instrument of your peace.
Where there is hatred, let me sow love;
where there is injury, pardon;
where there is doubt, faith;
where there is despair, hope;
where there is darkness, light;
and where there is sadness, joy.

Divine Master,
grant that I may not so much seek
to be consoled as to console,
to be understood as to understand,
to be loved as to love.

For it is in giving that we receive,
in pardoning that we are pardoned,
and in dying that we are born to eternal life.

St. Francis of Assisi, ca. 1181-1226

Memorare

Remember, most gracious Virgin Mary, that never was it known that anyone who fled to your protection, implored your help, and sought your intercession, was left unaided.

Inspired with this confidence, I fly to you, O Virgin of virgins, my mother. To you I come, before you I stand, sinful and sorrowful. Mother of the Word Incarnate, despise not my petitions, but in your mercy hear and answer me.

St. Bernard of Clairvaux, 1090-1153

Prayer for Trust

O Christ Jesus, when all is darkness and we feel our weakness and helplessness, give us the sense of your presence, your love, and your strength. Help us to have perfect trust in your protecting love and strengthening power, so that nothing may frighten or worry us, for, living close to you, we shall see your hand, your purpose, your will through all things.

St. Ignatius of Loyola, 1491-1556

Love and Do What You Will

Therefore once for all this short command is given to you: "Love and do what you will." If you keep silent, keep silent by love; if you speak, speak by love; if you correct, correct by love; if you pardon, pardon by love: let love be rooted in you, and from the root nothing but good can grow.

St. Augustine of Hippo, 354-430

Perfect prayer is achieved not with many words but with loving desire.

St. Catherine of Siena, 1347-1380, *The Dialogue*

Lines Written in Her Breviary

Let nothing disturb you, nothing frighten you;
All things are passing, God never changes;
Patient endurance attains to all things;
She whom God possesses wants for nothing.
God alone suffices.

St. Teresa of Avila, 1515-1582

Nothing great was ever done without much enduring.

St. Catherine of Siena, 1347-1380

Patrick's Breastplate

Christ be with me, Christ within me
Christ behind me, Christ before me
Christ beside me, Christ to win me
Christ to comfort and restore me.

Christ beneath me, Christ above me
Christ in quiet, Christ in danger
Christ in hearts of all that love me
Christ in mouth of friend or stranger.

Attributed to St. Patrick, ca. 390-461

Almsgiving

Let us now speak of the *manner* of bestowing alms, for that is necessary more than any other thing, that we may virtuously live and die most happily. First, it is necessary that we give alms with a most *sincere intention* of pleasing God and not for seeking popular praise....

Again, our alms is to be given *readily*, and with facility, that it may not seem to be wrung out by entreaty, nor delayed from day to day when it may presently be dispatched....

Thirdly, it is requisite that our alms be given *cheerfully*, and not with grudging....

Fourthly, it is necessary that our alms be given with *humility*, in such manner as the giver may know himself to receive more than he gives....

Fifthly, it is necessary that we give *abundantly*, according to the proportion or measure of our ability.

St. Robert Bellarmine, 1542-1621,
The Art of Dying Well

On Prayer

My blessed daughter, know now that prayer is more perfect when it is made in the essence of the soul — when the soul prays in the Spirit of God. This is a most profound language, but when God wants to, he can make even stones speak. Allow then this great Good, this immense Good to repose in your spirit. This is a reciprocal rest: God in you, you in God. Oh, what a sweet work! What a divine work!...

Lucy, my daughter in Christ, God wants you to be a saint; he wants you to be holy. So be humble of heart, persevering in the prayer God gives you....

Enter more deeply into that holy desert, into that divine solitude within you, in the very essence of your soul, and there you will be reborn in the divine Word to a new life of love. God rests in you: God fills you and you are all in God. God is transforming you completely in his love.

St. Paul of the Cross, 1694-1775
Letter to Lucy Berlin

On Knowledge

Is knowledge not counted among the seven gifts of the Holy Spirit?... How can a person know if he does not learn? How can he learn without teachers? O stupid and idle gossip of the ignorant! An enemy of nature is the one who despises knowledge: the longing for knowledge lies within human nature....

Are you, without study, able to have a clear idea of faith, hope, and charity, prudence, fortitude, temperance and the other virtues? Of the gifts, of the corporal and spiritual works of mercy?... How shall your light shine before men if you yourselves are obscurantists, hiding in the general darkness?...

Do you not believe that the Lord will demand an account of your ignorance? [... The Lord's] messenger you will not be if you do not announce the truth; and the truth is not made known by one who does not know it; and one cannot know it unless one learns it; and one cannot learn it without a teacher. And you flee from teachers and still feel satisfied. The crafty devil will test your ignorance as he once did Eve's....

The danger lies not in knowledge, but in the abuse of knowledge.

St. John of Capistrano, 1386-1456,
Letter on Study to the Friars of the Observance

The Beauty of Creation
Bears Witness to God

Question the beauty of the earth,
the beauty of the sea,
the beauty of the wide air around you,
the beauty of the sky;
question the order of the stars,
the sun whose brightness lights the day,
the moon whose splendour softens
the gloom of night;
question the living creatures
that move in the waters,
that roam upon the earth,
that fly through the air;
the spirit that lies hidden,
the matter that is manifest;
the visible things that are ruled,
the invisible that rule them;
question all these.
They will answer you:
"Behold and see, we are beautiful."
Their beauty is their confession of God.
Who made these beautiful changing things,
if not one who is beautiful and does not change?

St. Augustine of Hippo, 354-430

On Scripture

Can there be a more fitting pursuit in youth or a more valuable possession in old age than a knowledge of sacred scripture? In the midst of storms it will preserve you from the dangers of shipwreck and guide you to the shore of an enchanting paradise and the everlasting bliss of the angels.... "Wisdom overcomes evil: it stretches from end to end mightily and disposes all things sweetly. Her have I loved from my youth" (Wis 8:1).

St. Boniface, ca. 680-754, *Letter to St. Nithard*

A Spirit To Know You

Gracious and holy Father, please give me:
intellect to understand you,
reason to discern you,
diligence to seek you,
wisdom to find you,
a spirit to know you,
a heart to meditate upon you,
ears to hear you,
eyes to see you,
a tongue to proclaim you,
a way of life pleasing to you,
patience to wait for you
and perseverance to look for you.
Grant me a perfect end,
your holy presence,
a blessed resurrection
and life everlasting.

St. Benedict of Nursia, ca. 480-54

Flood the Path with Light

God of our Life, there are days when the burdens we carry chafe our shoulders and weigh us down; when the road seems dreary and endless, the skies grey and threatening; when our lives have no music in them, and our hearts are lonely, and our souls have lost their courage.

Flood the path with light, turn our eyes to where the skies are full of promise; tune our hearts to brave music; give us the sense of comradeship with heroes and saints of every age; and so quicken our spirits that we may be able to encourage the souls of all who journey with us on the road of life, to your honour and glory.

Attributed to St. Augustine of Hippo, 354-430

You can do nothing about avoiding death, but you can do something about living well.

St. Augustine of Hippo, 354-430

Prayer of Saint Thomas Aquinas

Grant me, O Lord my God, a mind to know you, a
heart to seek you, wisdom to find you, conduct
pleasing to you, faithful perseverance in waiting
for you, and a hope of finally embracing you.
Amen.

St. Thomas Aquinas, 1225-1274

Cling now to nothing save to God alone.

St. Vincent de Paul, ca. 1580-1660

Day by day, O dear Lord, three things I pray: to see
thee more clearly, love thee more dearly, follow
thee more nearly, day by day.

St. Richard of Chichester, ca. 1197-1253

Prayer of Saint Ambrose

Lord Jesus Christ, you stretched out your hands on the cross and redeemed us by your blood: forgive me, a sinner, for none of my thoughts are hidden from you. Pardon I ask, pardon I hope for, pardon I trust to have. You are full of compassion and of mercy: spare me and forgive.

St. Ambrose of Milan, ca. 340-397

To Keep a True Lent

Is this a Fast, to keep
　　The larder lean?
　　　　And clean
From fat of veals and sheep?

Is it to quit the dish
　　Of flesh, yet still
　　　　To fill
The platter high with fish?

Is it to fast an hour,
　　Or ragg'd to go,
　　　　Or show
A down-cast look and sour?

No: 'tis a Fast to dole
　　Thy sheaf of wheat
　　　　And meat
Unto the hungry soul.

It is to fast from strife
　　And old debate,
　　　　And hate;
To circumcise thy life.

To show a heart grief-rent;
　　To starve thy sin,
　　　　Not bin;
And that's to keep thy Lent.

Robert Herrick, 1591-167⸱

596

Dying to Sin

It is useless to recall the sufferings of the martyrs just to give pleasure to your ears. [...]

You then who think that persecution has died down and there is no struggle for you with our enemies, search the intimate hidden place of your heart, and as a careful examiner enter into all the windings of your soul; and see if no opposed forces attack you, if no tyrant wants to dominate in the fortress of your mind.

Make no peace with avarice, and despise the growth of evil gains. Refuse any pact with pride, and fear more to be received in honour than to be walked on in lowliness! Distance yourself from anger, let not the passion for vengeance excite the torment of envy. Renounce the desire for pleasure, turn away from impurity, reject luxury, fly iniquity, resist falsehood; and, when you have seen that you have a battle on many fronts, then, like the martyrs, seek a manifold victory.

For as often as we die to sins, just so often does sin die in us.

St. Leo the Great, †461, *Sermon 97*

Prayer for Courage

Almighty, eternal, just, and merciful God, grant us in our misery the grace to do for you alone what we know you want us to do, and always to desire what pleases you.

Thus, inwardly cleansed, interiorly enlightened, and inflamed by the fire of the Holy Spirit, may we be able to follow in the footprints of your beloved Son, our Lord Jesus Christ.

And, by your grace alone, may we make our way to you, Most High, who live and rule in perfect Trinity and simple Unity, and are glorified God all-powerful forever and ever. Amen.

St. Francis of Assisi, ca. 1181-1226,
Letter to the Order

A Martyr's Prayer

Alas, my dearest Father, when shall I begin at length to serve him and to love him whose love for us has been without any beginning? When shall I begin to give myself entirely to him who has given himself wholly to me and without reserve? Although I am the most miserable of creatures [...], I do not despair in my soul; for I see that he takes care to offer me new opportunities through which I may die to myself and by which I may unite myself to him inseparably.

St. Isaac Jogues, 1607-1646,
Letter to an unnamed Jesuit friend in France

Service

Lord Jesus, teach me to be generous;
teach me to serve you as you deserve,
to give and not to count the cost,
to fight and not to heed the wounds,
to toil and not to seek for rest,
to labour and not to seek reward,
except that of knowing that I do your will.

St. Ignatius Loyola, 1491-1556

Prayer

In all our needs, trials and difficulties, there
remains to us no better and surer means than
prayer and hope that God will provide for us, by
such means as he wills.

St. John of the Cross, 1542-1591,
Ascent of Mount Carmel

Pied Beauty

Glory be to God for dappled things —
    For skies of couple-colour as a brinded cow;
        For rose-moles all in stipple upon trout that
        swim;
Fresh-firecoal chestnut-falls; finches' wings;
    Landscape plotted and pieced — fold, fallow,
        and plough;
        And all trades, their gear and tackle and
        trim.

All things counter, original, spare, strange;
    Whatever is fickle, freckled (who knows
        how?)
        With swift, slow; sweet, sour; adazzle, dim;
He fathers-forth whose beauty is past change:
        Praise him.

                Gerard Manley Hopkins, 1844-1889

The Earth Is Precious

The earth is precious to the Creator and to harm the earth is to heap contempt upon its Creator. Man did not weave the web of life, he is merely a strand of it. Whatever he does to the web, he does to himself. Therefore give the rivers the kindness you would give your brother.

Chief Seattle (1854)

A "Creed" by Pedro Casaldáliga

do not believe in racial or class segregation.

Because there is but one image of God in us,
do not believe in slavery of any kind.

Because all of us have the right and duty to
ive in the freedom to which Christ freed us.

do not believe in progress at any cost.

Because we have been bought at the cost of
Christ's blood.

do not believe in the technology of those who
pray to their mechanical god: "Our Father art
Thou."

Because only the living God is our Father.

I do not believe in the 'consumer society.'

Because only those who hunger and thirst
after justice are blessed.

I do not believe in the so-called order of the status
quo.

Because the kingdom of God is a new heaven
and a new earth.

I do not believe in the heavenly city at the cost of
the earthly city.

Because the earth is the only road which can
lead us to heaven.

I do not believe in the earthly city at the cost of the
heavenly city.

Because we have here no lasting city, but seek
the city that is to come.

I do not believe in the old.

Because I believe in the new.

I believe in the new One who is Jesus Christ risen,
the firstborn of all! Amen, Alleluia!

from *I Believe in Justice and Hope*

Solidarity

Solidarity is not a feeling of vague compassion or shallow distress at the misfortunes of so many people, both near and far. On the contrary, it is a firm and persevering determination to commit oneself to the common good: that is to say, to the good of all and of each individual, because we are all really responsible for all.

Pope John Paul II, 1920-
Concern for the Social Order (1987)

Lead, Kindly Light

Lead, kindly Light, amid the encircling gloom,
Lead thou me on;
The night is dark, and I am far from home,
Lead thou me on.
Keep thou my feet; I do not ask to see
The distant scene; one step enough for me.

I was not ever thus, nor prayed that thou
Shouldst lead me on;
I loved to choose and see my path; but now
Lead thou me on.
I loved the garish day, and, spite of fears,
Pride ruled my will: remember not past years.

So long thy power hath blessed me, sure it still
Will lead me on
O'er moor and fen, o'er crag and torrent, till
The night gone,
And with the morn those Angel faces smile,
Which I have loved long since, and lost awhile.

Cardinal Newman, 1801-1890

The Answer to My Prayers

I asked God for strength, that I might achieve. I was made weak, that I might learn humbly to obey.

I asked for health, that I might do greater things. I was given infirmity, that I might do better things.

I asked for riches, that I might be happy. I was given poverty, that I might be wise.

I asked for all things, that I might enjoy life. I was given life, that I might enjoy all things.

I got nothing that I asked for, but everything I had hoped for. Despite myself, my prayers were answered. I among all people am most richly blessed.

Anonymous Soldier, American Civil War

The Laity

[n the pilgrimage of this life, hidden with Christ
n God and free from enslavement to wealth, they
who have faith] aspire to those riches which
emain forever, and generously dedicate their
ntire selves to spreading God's kingdom and to
ashioning and perfecting the sphere of earthly
hings according to the spirit of Christ....

Laypersons' ... should not cease to earnestly develop the qualities and talents bestowed on them
n accord with their condition of life, and they
hould make use of the gifts which they have
eceived from the Holy Spirit.

Furthermore, the laity ... should also hold in high
esteem professional skill, family and civic spirit,
and the virtues relating to social behaviour,
namely, honesty, justice, sincerity, kindness, and
courage, without which there can be no true
Christian life.

Vatican II, *Decree on the Apostolate of the Laity*

On Vocation

God calls all the souls he has created to love him with their whole being, here and hereafter, which means that he calls all of them to holiness, to perfection, to a close following of him and obedience to his will. But he does not ask all souls to show their love by the same works, to climb to heaven by the same ladder, to achieve goodness in the same way of life. What sort of work, then, must *I* do? Which is *my* road to heaven? In what kind of life am *I* to sanctify myself?...

This question: "What kind of life am I going to undertake?" is the question of *vocation*....

There is therefore a very grave duty for each one of us when we reach a certain age to take the most careful trouble to find out what vocation we have to follow. This vocation is God's call to undertake such-and-such a sort of holy life in preference to all others, his urgent call to each individual soul to sanctify itself in this particular way. There can never be any question of *choosing* a vocation: the word 'choice' is excluded by the word 'vocation,' which means 'calling,' a call from God.

Charles de Foucauld, 1858-1916
Sermons in the Sahara (1938)

Abide with Me

Abide with me; fast falls the eventide;
The darkness deepens; Lord, with me abide;
When other helpers fail, and comforts flee,
Help of the helpless, O abide with me.

Swift to its close ebbs out life's little day;
Earth's joys grow dim, its glories pass away;
Change and decay in all around I see;
O thou who changest not, abide with me.

Hold thou thy Cross before my closing eyes;
Shine through the gloom,
 and point me to the skies;
Heaven's morning breaks,
 and earth's vain shadows flee;
In life, in death, O Lord, abide with me.

Henry Francis Lyte (1847)

Prayer for Peace

Almighty and eternal God, may your grace enkindle in all of us a love for the many unfortunate people whom poverty and misery reduce to a condition of life unworthy of human beings.

Arouse in the hearts of those who call you Father a hunger and thirst for justice and peace and for fraternal charity in deeds and in truth.

Grant, O Lord, peace in our days, peace to souls, peace to families, peace to our country, and peace among nations. Amen.

Pope Pius XII, 1876-1958

Family Prayer

ther, what love you have given us.
ay we love as you would have us love.
ach us to be kind to each other,
atient and gentle with one another.
elp us to bear all things together,
  see in our love, your love,
rough Christ our Lord. Amen.

The Desert

We must have no illusions. We shall not walk on roses. People will not throng to hear us and applaud; we shall not always be aware of divine protection. If we are to be pilgrims for justice and peace, we must expect the desert.

Dom Helder Camara, 1909-
Me llaman el obispo rojo

Christmas Prayer

Moonless darkness stands between.
Past, the Past, no more be seen!
But the Bethlehem star may lead me
To the sight of Him Who freed me
From the self that I have been.
Make me pure, Lord: Thou art Holy;
Make me meek, Lord: Thou wert lowly;
Now beginning, and alway:
Now begin, on Christmas day.

Gerard Manley Hopkins, 1844-1889

On Aging

The passing of the years brings its frailties. You may be forced to give up activities that you once enjoyed. Your limbs may not seem as agile as they used to be. Your memory and your eyesight may refuse to give service. And so the world may cease to be familiar — the world of your family, the world around you, the world you once knew. Even the Church, which you have loved for so long, may seem strange to many of you as she goes forward in this period of renewal. Yet despite changes and any weaknesses you may feel, you are of great value to all. Society needs you and so does the Church. [...]

We need your experience and your insights. We need the faith which has sustained you and continues to be your light. We need your example of patient waiting and trust. We need to see in you that mature love which is yours, that love which is the fruit of your lives lived in both joys and sorrows. And yes, we need your wisdom for you can offer assurance in times of uncertainty. You can be an incentive to live according to the higher values of the spirit.

Pope John Paul II, 1920- (Vancouver, 18 Sept., 1984)

On Christian Formation

cannot be too much underlined: the Christian
rmation of youth is of prime importance.
othing can replace that slow imbuing with
hristian values which is the fruit of teaching
ven by those who have consecrated their lives
› such values. [...]

he work is pressing, and it demands many la-
ourers. All over the world there are developing
oung minds in search of the truth [...]. It is an
dmirable work, worthy to arouse the enthusiasm
f young Catholics, this work of devoting oneself
› the human and supernatural formation of those
ho will be the responsible adults of tomorrow.

Pope John XXIII, 1881-1963 (14 June, 1961)

Character of Mind

It is difficult and rare virtue to mean what we say
to love without dissimulation, to think no evil, to
bear no grudge, to be free from selfishness, to be
innocent and straightforward. This character of
mind [...] is one of the surest marks of Christ's
elect.

Cardinal Newman, 1801-1890
Parochial and Plain Sermons

Listen to the Word

Do whatever he tells you" [John 2:5]. What Jesus tells us – through his life and by his word – has been preserved for us in the gospels, and in the letters of the apostles and of St Paul and transmitted to us by the Church. We must make ourselves familiar with his words [...] by listening to the readings from sacred scripture in the liturgy of the word [...]; by reading the scriptures on our own, in the family, or together with friends; by reflecting on what the Lord tells us when we recite the rosary [...].

Do whatever he tells you." So many different voices assail the Christian in today's wonderful but complicated and demanding world, [voices] that conflict with the word of the Lord, that tell you that truth is less important than personal gain; that comfort, wealth and pleasure are the true aims of life; that the refusal of new life is better than generosity of spirit and the taking up of responsibility; that justice must be achieved but without any personal involvement by the Christian; that violence can be a means to a good end; that unity can be built without giving up hate.

Pope John Paul II, 1920- , *Homily* (30 Sept., 1979)

Love and the Family

The transformation of the world [...] comes about
in the quiet home of all life, the family. It comes
whenever people understand that the true meaning of love is not the will to dominate, to exploit
and to possess; but that it lies in service, generosity, sacrifice, willingness to change and a desire
that others be blessed and brought close to God.
When [people] can emerge from the quiet and
solitude of their homes touched and renewed by
true love, a love that sanctifies us and helps us
find the way to heaven, then our land and our
people will be blessed, and we will have the
strength to face whatever lies ahead.

Alfred Delp, SJ, *On Elizabeth of Hungary* (1985)

The Serenity Prayer

God, give me the serenity
accept the things I cannot change,
e courage to change the things I can,
d the wisdom to know the difference.

                    Reinhold Niebuhr, 1892-1971

Into Your Hands

Father, I abandon myself into your hands; do with
me what you will. Whatever you may do, I thank
you: I am ready for all, I accept all. Let only your
will be done in me, and in all your creatures — I
wish no more than this, O Lord.

Into your hands I commend my soul; I offer it to
you with all the love of my heart, for I love you
Lord, and so need to give myself, to surrender
myself into your hands, without reserve, and
with boundless confidence, for you are my Father.

Charles de Foucauld, 1858-1916

Gems

e best prayers often have more groans than
rds.

John Bunyan, 1628-1688

e disease of mankind is this: that we neglect
r own fields and go and weed the fields of
ers.

Meng K'o, 372-289 BC

rd, give peace to our troubled world, and give
your children security of mind and freedom
m anxiety.

Bidding Prayer

lon't mind dying because my bags are always
cked.

Pope John XXIII, 1881-1963

Scots Gaelic Blessing

Peace between neighbours,
Peace between kindred,
Peace between lovers...
Peace between person and person,
Peace between wife and husband,
Peace between woman and children,
The peace of Christ above all peace.

Irish Blessing

Deep peace of the running wave to you.
Deep peace of the flowing air to you.
Deep peace of the quiet earth to you.
Deep peace of the shining stars to you.
Deep peace of the Son of Peace to you.

Prayer for the Constitutional Process

Lord God,
Creator and Ruler of the universe,
from the beginning of time
you have guided
all nations and peoples to yourself.

In our time of constitutional deliberation
guide our hearts and minds
that in all things we may serve you
in faith and love
and live in justice and mutual respect with all.

Grant that the problems that confront us
may never cause us to lose heart
or to cease working for your kingdom,
but may lead us to a greater understanding
of the diversity of gifts
you have given to the human race.

We ask this through Christ our Lord. Amen.

National Liturgy Offic
Canadian Conference of Catholic Bishop

January

at the faithful distinguish true from fictitious
ues in today's culture.

at catechetical formation in Christian commu-
ies be missionary and ecumenical.

February

at the Oriental Catholic Churches of eastern
rope develop in freedom, justice and charity.

at religious communities live fully the mis-
nary dimension of their charism.

March

r all those who are marginalized by consumer-
n and unjust economic systems.

at the young churches of Africa grow in the
ssionary vitality of their faith.

April

at local communities welcome and integrate
ugees who have had to leave their homelands.

at during the UN Year of Tolerance respect for
 beliefs of others be strengthened among na-
ns and religious groups.

May

That parents contribute to evangelization forming their children in the school of Jesus.

That young people, like Mary, be prompt in th response to a missionary vocation.

June

For the sick, that they may feel united to Christ his cross and resurrection.

That active Christian witness help conquor challenge of AIDS.

July

That men and women recognize the dignity every person as they promote justice in societ

That the God-given rights of women be promot especially in developing countries.

August

That the prayer of all in the Church obtain pea and fraternity for nations in conflict.

That the Church in China strengthen visible co munion with the See of Peter.

September

hat the Catechism of the Catholic Church be
ed in the new evangelization to deepen faith.

or renewed missionary effort in Latin America
llowing the Vth Latin American Congress on
ission.

October

or the elderly who are alone and abandoned,
at they receive help and comfort from others.

hat World Mission Day increase awareness and
nerous sharing in announcing Christ's gospel.

November

hat people who are discouraged and want to die
discover through friendship life's sense and
ernal value.

or an increase in love and respect for human life
d dignity.

December

hat all persons of good will reject the politics of
atred, discrimination and intolerance.

or children who are victims of violence.

MUSIC

These hymns and acclamations offer a limit selection of music for the liturgical season Familiarize yourself with all the selections of fered, since they may be suitable for other ce ebrations as well. The seasonal psalms from t *Lectionary for Sundays and Solemnities* may found beginning on page 638.

We have included words only for many of t metred hymns, along with the metre of the tu (indicated by the numbers following the name the hymn tune) and a recommendation for hymn tune (indicated by the name of the tune block capitals). In this way, a number of differe texts may be used with the same melody. Y may find, however, that one tune seems to "fit' text better than others. Using this simple syste you can match the text provided with a tune th is familiar to your congregation. Most standa hymnals, such as the *Catholic Book of Worsh* *(CBW)*, index their contents both by tune and metre. We refer to numbers in *CBW II* and *CBW I*

Full accompaniment for *The Novalis Mass* Michel Guimont (p. 631) is available fro Novalis–Saint Paul University, 223 Main Stre Ottawa, ON K1S 1C4.

. Church of God

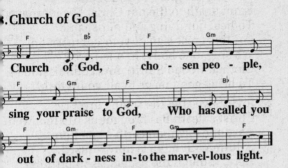

Church of God, cho - sen peo - ple,

sing your praise to God, Who has called you

out of dark - ness in - to the mar-vel-lous light.

r verses, see *CBW III* 581

xt: Pamela Stotter, alt.; ICEL translation of the *Resource
ollection of Hymns and Service Music for the Liturgy,* © 1981
ernational Committee on English in the Liturgy, Inc. All
hts reserved.
ne: Margaret Daly; ICEL translation of the *Resource Collec-
n of Hymns and Service Music for the Liturgy,* © 1981
ernational Committee on English in the Liturgy, Inc. All
hts reserved.
usic: *CBW III* 581

99. Reborn of Water and the Spirit

1. Reborn of water and the Spirit
   We sing the glory of your name.
   From death to life our Christ has journeyed
   To heal our dying and our shame.
   For this great sign of your compassion
   We sing, one body, in one Lord,
   Clothed in one Spirit, now commissioned,
   To bring good news to all your world.

2. Joyful, we sing the saving myst'ry:
   Christ's death has brought us life renewed.
   As at the dawn on earth's creation
   All life with hope is now infused.
   Here, through the waters, as in birthing,
   Your people pass through death to life.
   Here, too, you feed us at your banquet
   With bread and cup that end all strife.

3. O womb of joy and front of mercy,
   O well of life that will not cease,
   Rain on us now your Spirit's power:
   A torrent of your love and peace.
   Transform your people, here assembled,
   Into a sign of your great love:
   A holy, priestly, kingly people,
   A seed on earth of heav'n above.

Text: © 1994 Bernadette Gasslein
Tune: RENDEZ À DIEU
Music: *CBW II* 659, 676; *CBW III* 324, 528

THE NOVALIS MASS

Lord, Have Mercy

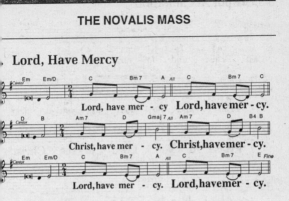

1993 Michel Guimont

Glory to God

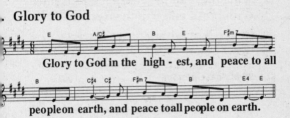

1993 Michel Guimont

3. Gospel Acclamation

Lent: Praise and honour to you!

© 1992 Michel Guimont

Holy, Holy

Ho-ly, ho - ly, ho-ly Lord, God of pow'r and might. Heaven and earth, Heaven and earth are filled with your glo - ry, ho - san-na in the high - est! Ho-san-na in the high - est! Bless-ed is he, bless-ed is he who comes in the name of the Lord. Ho-san-na in the high-est, ho- san - na in the high - est.

5. Memorial Acclamation 1

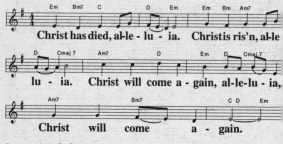

Christ has died, al-le - lu - ia. Christ is ris'n, al-le

lu - ia. Christ will come a - gain, al-le-lu - ia,

Christ will come a - gain.

6. Memorial Acclamation 2

Dy - ing you de - stroyed our death.

Ris - ing you re - stored our life. Lord

Je - sus, come in glo - ry, Lord

Je - sus, come in glo - ry.

Memorial Acclamation 3

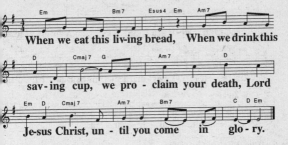

When we eat this liv-ing bread, When we drink this sav-ing cup, we pro - claim your death, Lord Je-sus Christ, un - til you come in glo - ry.

© 1992 Michel Guimont

Memorial Acclamation 4

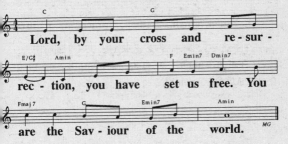

Lord, by your cross and re - sur - rec - tion, you have set us free. You are the Sav - iour of the world.

© 1992 Michel Guimont

9. Great Amen: Easter and Ordinary Time

A-men, al-le-lu-ia! A-men, al-le-lu-ia, for-ev-er, a-men, al-le-lu-ia.
A-men, al-le-lu-ia.

10. Great Amen: Lent

Amen, a-men, a-men, a-men, a-men.
A-men, a-men, a-men, a-men, a-men.

11. Lamb of God

Lamb of God, you take a-way the sin of the world, have mer-cy on us.

world, grant us your peace.

ADVENT
SEASONAL PSALM *(Psalm 25)*

℟. **To you, O Lord, I lift my soul.**

Make me to know your ways, O • **Lord,**
teach me your • **paths.**
Lead me in your truth and • **teach_me,**
for you are the God of my • **sal**-vation. ℟.

Good and upright is the • **Lord,**
therefore he instructs sinners in the • **way.**
He leads the humble in what is • **right,**
and teaches the humble • **his** way. ℟.

All the paths of the Lord are steadfast love
     and • **faithfulness,**
for those who keep his covenant and his • **decrees**
The friendship of the Lord is for those
     who • **fear_him,**
and he makes his covenant known • **to** them. ℟.

Lord, show us your mer - cy and love.

GJ

℟. **Lord, show us your mercy and love.**

Let me hear what God the Lord will • **speak,**
for he will speak peace to his • **people.**
Surely his salvation is at hand for those
      who • **fear_him,**
that his glory may dwell in • **our** land. ℟.

Steadfast love and faithfulness will • **meet;**
righteousness and peace will • **kiss_each_other.**
Faithfulness will spring up from the • **ground,**
and righteousness will look down
      from • **the** sky. ℟.

The Lord will give what is • **good,**
and our land will yield its • **increase.**
Righteousness will go be•**-fore_him,**
and will make a path for • **his** steps. ℟.

ADVENT
SEASONAL PSALM *(Psalm 146)*

Lord, come and save us.

℟. **Lord, come and save us.**

It is the Lord who keeps faith for•-**ever**,
who executes justice for the op•-**pressed**;
who gives food to the • **hungry.**
The Lord sets the prison•-**ers** free. ℟.

The Lord opens the eyes of the • **blind**
and lifts up those who are bowed • **down;**
the Lord loves the • **righteous**
and watches over • **the** strangers. ℟.

The Lord upholds the orphan and the • **widow,**
but the way of the wicked he brings to • **ruin.**
The Lord will reign for•-**ever,**
your God, O Zion, for all • **gener-**ations. ℟.

CHRISTMAS
SEASONAL PSALM *(Psalm 34)*

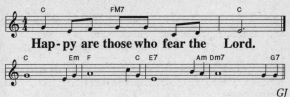

Hap- py are those who fear the   Lord.

GJ

℟. **Happy are those who fear the Lord.**

I will bless the Lord at • **all** times;
his praise shall continually be in • **my** mouth.
My soul makes its boast in • **the** Lord;
let the humble hear and • **be** glad. ℟.

O fear the Lord, you • **his** holy_ones,
for those who fear him have • **no** want.
The young lions suffer want • **and** hunger,
but those who seek the Lord
   lack no • **good** thing. ℟.

Come, O children, listen • **to** me;
I will teach you the fear of • **the** Lord.
Which of you de•-**sires** life,
and covets many days to en•-**joy** good? ℟.

Keep your tongue • **from** evil,
and your lips from speaking • **de**-ceit.
Depart from evil, and • **do** good;
seek peace, and • **pur**-sue_it. ℟.

CHRISTMAS
SEASONAL PSALM *(Psalm 72)*

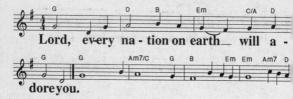

Lord, every nation on earth will adore you.

℞. **Lord, every nation on earth will adore you.**

Give the king your justice, O • **God,**
and your righteousness to a king's • **son.**
May he judge your • **people** with righteousness,
and your • **poor** with justice. ℞.

In his days may righteousness • **flourish**
and peace abound, until the moon is no • **more.**
May he have dominion from • **sea** to sea,
and from the River to the • **ends of** the earth. ℞.

May the kings of Tarshish and of the isles
    render him • **tribute,**
may the kings of Sheba and Seba brings • **gifts.**
May all kings fall • **down** before him,
all nations • **give** him service. ℞.

For he delivers the needy when they • **call,**
the poor and those who have no • **helper.**
He has pity on the • **weak and** the needy,
and saves the • **lives of** the needy. ℞.

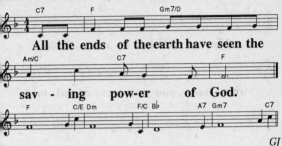

All the ends of the earth have seen the sav - ing pow-er of God.

GJ

℟. **All the ends of the earth
have seen the saving power of God.**

O sing to the Lord a • **new** song,
for he has done marvel • **-lous** things.
His right hand and his holy • **arm**
have brought • **him** victory. ℟.

The Lord has made known • **his** victory;
he has revealed his vindication in the sight
       of • **the** nations.
He has remembered his steadfast • **love**
and faithfulness to the house • **of** Israel. ℟.

All the ends of the earth • **have** seen
the victory of • **our** God.
Make a joyful noise to the Lord, all the • **earth;**
break forth into joyous song and • **sing** praises. ℟.

Sing praises to the Lord with • **the** lyre,
with the lyre and the sound • **of** melody.
With trumpets and the sound of the • **horn**
make a joyful noise before the King, • **the** Lord. ℟.

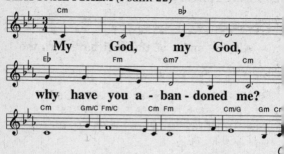

℟. **My God, my God, why have you abandoned me?**

All who see me • **mock_at_me;**
they make mouths at me, they shake • **their** heads
"Commit your cause to the Lord; let him de•-**liver**
let him rescue the one in whom he • **de**-lights!" ℟

For dogs are all a•-**round_me;**
a company of evildoers • **en**-circles_me.
My hands and feet have • **shrivelled;**
I can count all • **my** bones. ℟.

They divide my clothes among them•-**selves,**
and for my clothing they • **cast** lots.
But you, O Lord, do not be far a•-**way!**
O my help, come quickly to • **my** aid! ℟.

I will tell of your name to my brothers and sisters
in the midst of the congregation I will • **praise_you**
You who fear the • **Lord**, praise_him!
All you offspring of Jacob, • **glorify_him;**
stand in awe of him, all you offspring • **of** Israel! ℟

Be mer-ci-ful, O Lord, for we have sinned.

GJ

℟. Be merciful, O Lord, for we have sinned.

Have mercy on me, O God,
   according to your steadfast • **love;**
according to your abundant mercy
   blot out my trans•**-gressions.**
Wash me thoroughly from my in•**-iquity,**
and cleanse me from my • **sin.** ℟.

For I know my trans•**-gressions,**
and my sin is ever be•**-fore_me.**
Against you, you alone, have I • **sinned,**
and done what is evil in your • **sight.** ℟.

Create in me a clean heart, O • **God,**
and put a new and right spirit with•**-in_me.**
Do not cast me away from your • **presence,**
and do not take your holy spirit • **from_me.** ℟.

Restore to me the joy of your sal•**-vation,**
and sustain in me a willing • **spirit.**
O Lord, open my • **lips,**
and my mouth will declare your • **praise.** ℟.

LENT
SEASONAL PSALM *(Psalm 91)*

Be with me, Lord, when I am in trouble.

℞. **Be with me, Lord, when I am in trouble.**

You who live in the shelter of the Most • **High,**
who abide in the shadow of the • **Al**-mighty,
will say to the Lord, "My refuge and my • **fortress;**
my God, in whom • **I** trust." ℞.

No evil shall be•-**fall_you,**
no scourge come near • **your** tent.
For he will command his angels con•-**cerning_you**
to guard you in all • **your** ways. ℞.

On their hands they will bear you • **up,**
so that you will not dash your foot against • **a stone.**
You will tread on the lion and the • **adder,**
the young lion and the serpent you will trample
    un•-**der** foot. ℞.

Those who love me, I will de•-**liver;**
I will protect those who know • **my** name.
When they call to me, I will • **answer_them;**
I will be with them in trouble,
    I will rescue them • **and** honour_them. ℞.

With the Lord there is mer—cy —

and full-ness of re - demp-tion.

GJ

℟. **With the Lord there is mercy
and fullness of redemption.**

Out of the depths I cry to you, O • **Lord.**
Lord, hear • **my** voice!
Let your ears be at • **-tentive**
to the voice of my sup • **-pli**-cations! ℟.

If you, O Lord, should mark in • **-iquities,**
Lord, who • **could** stand?
But there is forgiveness with • **you,**
so that you may be • **re**-vered. ℟.

I wait for the • **Lord,**
my soul waits, and in his word • **I** hope;
my soul waits for the • **Lord**
more than those who watch for • **the** morning. ℟.

For with the Lord there is steadfast • **love,**
and with him is great power to • **re**-deem.
It is he who will redeem • **Israel**
from all its • **in**-iquities. ℟.

EASTER
SEASONAL PSALM *(Psalm 47)*

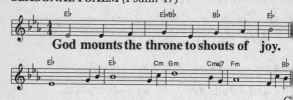

God mounts the throne to shouts of joy.

℞. **God mounts the throne to shouts of joy:**
   a blare of trumpets for the Lord.

Clap your hands, all • **you** peoples;
shout to God with loud songs • **of** joy.
For the Lord, the Most High, • **is** awesome,
a great king over • **all** the earth. ℞.

God has gone up with • **a** shout,
the Lord with the sound of • **a** trumpet.
Sing praises to God, • **sing** praises;
sing praises to our • **King,** sing praises. ℞.

For God is the king of all • **the** earth;
sing praises with • **a** psalm.
God is king over • **the** nations;
God sits on his • **ho**-ly throne. ℞.

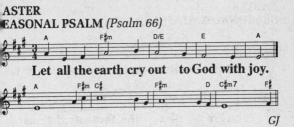

Let all the earth cry out to God with joy.

GJ

℞. **Let all the earth cry out to God with joy.**

Make a joyful noise to God, all • **the** earth;
sing the glory of • **his** name;
give to him glori•**-ous** praise.
Say to God, "How awesome are your • **deeds!**" ℞.

"All the earth wor•**-ships** you;
they sing praises to you, sing praises
    to • **your** name."
Come and see what God • **has** done:
he is awesome in his deeds among • **mortals.** ℞.

He turned the sea into • **dry** land;
they passed through the river • **on** foot.
There we rejoiced • **in** him,
who rules by his might for•**-ever.** ℞.

Come and hear, all you who • **fear** God,
and I will tell what he has done • **for** me.
Blessed be God,
    because he has not rejected • **my** prayer
or removed his steadfast love from • **me.** ℞.

EASTER
SEASONAL PSALM *(Psalm 104)*

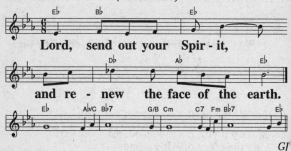

Lord, send out your Spir - it,

and re - new the face of the earth.

GJ

℟. **Lord, send out your Spirit,**
and renew the face of the earth.

Bless the Lord, O • **my** soul.
O Lord my God, you are very • **great.**
O Lord, how manifold • **are** your works!
The earth is full of • **your** creatures. ℟.

When you take away their breath, • **they** die
and return to their • **dust.**
When you send forth your spirit, they • **are** cre-ated;
and you renew the face of • **the** earth. ℟.

May the glory of the Lord endure • **for**-ever;
may the Lord rejoice in his • **works**.
May my meditation be • **pleasing** to him,
for I rejoice in • **the** Lord. ℟.

EASTER
SEASONAL PSALM *(Psalm 118)*

This is the day the Lord has made;

let us re - joice and be glad.

GJ

℟. **This is the day the Lord has made;**
   let us rejoice and be glad.

O give thanks to the Lord, for he is • **good;**
his steadfast love endures • **for-**ever.
Let Israel say, "His steadfast love
   endures • **for-**ever." ℟.

"The right hand of the Lord is ex•**-alted;**
the right hand of the Lord • **does** valiantly."
I shall not die, but I shall live, and recount the deeds
   of • **the** Lord. ℟.

The stone that the builders rejected has become
   the chief • **cornerstone.**
This is the • **Lord's** doing;
it is marvellous in • **our** eyes. ℟.

ORDINARY TIME
SEASONAL PSALM *(Psalm 19)*

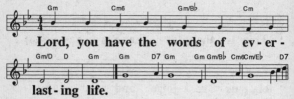

GJ

℞. **Lord, you have the words of everlasting life.**

The law of the Lord is • **perfect,**
reviving the • **soul;**
the decrees of the Lord are • **sure,**
making • **wise** the simple. ℞.

The precepts of the Lord are • **right,**
rejoicing the • **heart;**
the commandment of the Lord is • **clear,**
enlighten•**-ing** the eyes. ℞.

The fear of the Lord is • **pure,**
enduring for•**-ever;**
the ordinances of the Lord are • **true**
and righteous • **al**-to-gether. ℞.

More to be desired are they than • **gold,**
even much fine • **gold;**
sweeter also than • **honey,**
and drippings • **of** the honeycomb. ℞.

The Lord is my light and my sal - va-tion.

GJ

℟. **The Lord is my light and my salvation.**

The Lord is my light and my sal • -**vation**;
whom shall • **I** fear?
The Lord is the stronghold of my • **life**;
of whom shall I be • **a**-fraid? ℟.

One thing I asked of the Lord, that will I • **seek**:
to live in the house of the Lord all the days
    of • **my** life,
to behold the beauty of the • **Lord**,
and to inquire in • **his** temple. ℟.

I believe that I shall see the goodness of the • **Lord**
in the land of • **the** living.
Wait for the Lord; be • **strong**,
and let your heart take courage; wait for • **the** Lord! ℟.

ORDINARY TIME
SEASONAL PSALM *(Psalm 34)*

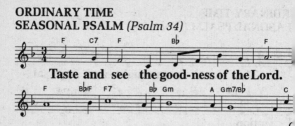

℟. **Taste and see the goodness of the Lord.**

I will bless the Lord at all • **times;**
his praise shall continually be in • **my** mouth.
My soul makes its boast in the • **Lord;**
let the humble hear and • **be glad.** ℟.

O magnify the Lord with • **me,**
and let us exalt his name • **to-**gether.
I sought the Lord, and he • **answered_me,**
and delivered me from all • **my** fears. ℟.

Look to him, and be • **radiant;**
so your faces shall never be • **a-**shamed.
This poor soul cried, and was heard by the • **Lord**
and was saved from eve•-**ry** trouble. ℟.

The angel of the Lord en•-**camps**
around those who fear him, and • **de-**livers_them
O taste and see that the Lord is • **good;**
happy are those who take refuge • **in** him. ℟.

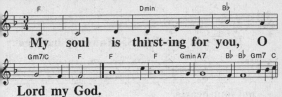

My soul is thirst-ing for you, O

Lord my God.

GJ

℟. **My soul is thirsting for you, O Lord my God.**

O God, you are my God, I • **seek_you,**
my soul thirsts for • **you;**
my flesh faints for • **you,**
as in a dry and weary land where there • **is** no water. ℟.

So I have looked upon you in the • **sanctuary,**
beholding your power and • **glory.**
Because your steadfast love is better than • **life,**
my • **lips** will praise_you. ℟.

So I will bless you as long as I • **live;**
I will lift up my hands and call on your • **name.**
My soul is satisfied as with a rich • **feast,**
and my mouth praises you with • **joy**-ful lips. ℟.

For you have been my • **help,**
and in the shadow of your wings I sing for • **joy.**
My soul clings to • **you;**
your • **right_hand** up-holds_me. ℟.

SEASONAL PSALM *(Psalm 95)*

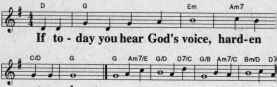

If to - day you hear God's voice, hard-en

not your hearts.

℟. **If today you hear God's voice,
harden not your hearts.**

O come, let us sing to • the Lord;
let us make a joyful noise to the rock
of our • **sal**-vation!
Let us come into his presence • **with** thanksgiving,
let us make a joyful noise to him
with songs • **of** praise! ℟.

O come, let us worship and • **bow** down,
let us kneel before the Lord, • **our** Maker!
For he is our God, and we are the people
of • **his** pasture,
and the sheep of • **his** hand. ℟.

O that today you would listen to • **his** voice!
Do not harden your hearts, as at Meribah,
as on the day at Massah in • **the** wilderness,
when your ancestors tested me, and put me
to • **the** proof,
though they had seen • **my** work. ℟.

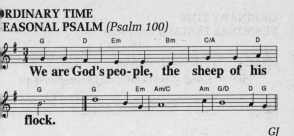

We are God's peo-ple, the sheep of his
flock.

GJ

℟. **We are God's people, the sheep of his flock.**

Make a joyful noise to the Lord, all • **the** earth.
Worship the Lord with • **gladness;**
come into his presence • **with** singing. ℟.

Know that the Lord • **is** God.
It is he that made us, and we are • **his;**
we are his people, and the sheep of • **his** pasture. ℟.

For the Lord • **is** good;
his steadfast love endures for•-**ever,**
and his faithfulness to all • **gener-**ations. ℟.

ORDINARY TIME
SEASONAL PSALM *(Psalm 103)*

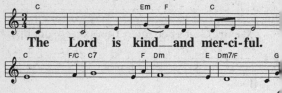

The Lord is kind and mer-ci-ful.

℞. **The Lord is kind and merciful.**

Bless the Lord, O my • **soul,**
and all that is within me, bless his ho•**-ly** name.
Bless the Lord, O my • **soul,**
and do not forget all • **his** benefits. ℞.

It is the Lord who forgives all your in•**-iquity,**
who heals all your • **dis**-eases,
who redeems your life from the • **Pit,**
who crowns you with steadfast love
        • **and** mercy. ℞.

The Lord is merciful and • **gracious,**
slow to anger and abounding in stead•**-fast** love.
He does not deal with us according to our • **sins,**
nor repay us according to our • **in**-iquities. ℞.

As far as the east is from the • **west,**
so far he removes our transgressions • **from** us.
As a father has compassion for his • **children,**
so the Lord has compassion
        for those • **who** fear_him. ℞.

658

ORDINARY TIME
SEASONAL PSALM *(Psalm 122)*

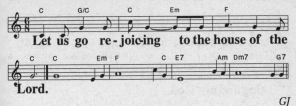

Let us go re - joic-ing   to the house of   the

Lord.

GJ

℟. **Let us go rejoicing to the house of the Lord.**

I was glad when they said • **to** me,
"Let us go to the house of • **the** Lord!"
Our feet • **are** standing
within your gates, O • **Je**-rusalem. ℟.

Jerusalem—built as • **a** city
that is bound firmly • **to**-gether.
To it the tribes • **go** up,
the tribes of • **the** Lord. ℟.

As was decreed • **for** Israel,
to give thanks to the name of • **the** Lord.
For there the thrones for judgment were • **set** up,
the thrones of the house • **of** David. ℟.

Pray for the peace of • **Je**-rusalem:
"May they prosper • **who** love_you.
Peace be within • **your** walls,
and security within • **your** towers." ℟.

For the sake of my relatives • **and** friends
I will say, "Peace be • **with**-in_you."
For the sake of the house of the Lord • **our** God,
I will seek • **your** good. ℟.

SEASONAL PSALM *(Psalm 145)*

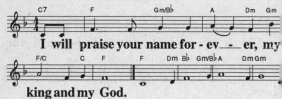

I will praise your name for - ev __ er, my

king and my God.

℟. **I will praise your name for ever,**
   my king and my God.

I will extol you, my God and • **King,**
and bless your name forever and • **ever.**
Every day I will • **bless_you,**
and praise your name forever • **and** ever. ℟.

The Lord is gracious and • **merciful,**
slow to anger and abounding in steadfast • **love.**
The Lord is good to • **all,**
and his compassion is over
     all that he • **has** made. ℟.

All your works shall give thanks to you, O • **Lor**
and all your faithful shall • **bless_you.**
They shall speak of the glory of your • **kingdom**
and tell of • **your** power. ℟.

The Lord is faithful in all his • **words,**
and gracious in all his • **deeds.**
The Lord upholds all who are • **falling,**
and raises up all who are • **bowed** down. ℟.

100. O Come, O Come Emmanuel

1. O come, o come Emmanuel,
    And ransom captive Israel,
    That mourns in lowly exile here,
    Until the son of God appear.

Ref: Rejoice! Rejoice! O Israel
       To thee shall come Emmanuel.

2. O come, thou rod of Jesse, free,
    Thine own from Satan's tyranny,
    From depths of hell thy people save,
    And give them vic'try o'er the grave.

3. O come, thou dayspring, come and cheer
    Our spirits by thine advent here;
    Disperse the gloomy clouds of night
    And death's dark shadows put to flight.

4. O come, thou key of David come,
    And open wide our heav'nly home;
    Make safe the way that leads on high,
    And close the path to misery.

5. O come, O come, thou Lord of might,
    Who to thy tribes, from Sinai's height,
    In ancient times didst give the law
    In cloud, in majesty and awe.

Text: 13th century; tr. John Mason Neale, 1818-66 and others
Tune: VENI EMMANUEL, 88.88.88.
Music: *CBW II* 440; *CBW III* 312

101. O Come, Divine Messiah

1. O come, divine Messiah!
   The world in silence waits the day
   When hope shall sing its triumph,
   And sadness flee away.

Ref: Sweet Saviour, haste;
   Come, come to earth:
   Dispel the night, and show thy face,
   And bid us hail the dawn of grace.
   O come, divine Messiah!
   The world in silence waits the day
   When hope shall sing its triumph,
   And sadness flee away.

2. O thou, whom nations sighed for,
   Whom priests and prophets long foretold,
   Wilt break the captive fetters,
   Redeem the long-lost fold.

3. Shalt come in peace and meekness,
   And lowly will thy cradle be:
   All clothed in human weakness
   Shall we thy Godhead see.

Text: Abbé Pellegrin, 1663-1745; tr. Sr. Mary of St. Philip
Tune: VENEZ DIVIN MESSIE, 78.76.888
Music: *CBW II* 441; *CBW III* 310

02. Hark! A Herald Voice Is Calling

Hark! A herald voice is calling:
"Christ is near," it seems to say,
"Cast away the dreams of darkness,
Waken, children of the day!"

Startled at the solemn warning
Let the earth-bound soul arise;
Christ, her sun, all sloth dispelling,
Shines upon the morning skies.

Lo, the Lamb so long expected
Comes with pardon down from heav'n;
Let us meet him with repentance,
Pray that we may be forgiv'n.

So, when love comes forth in judgment,
Debts and doubts and wrongs to clear,
Faithful may he find his servants
Watching till the dawn appear.

Honour, glory, praise and blessing
To the Father and the Son,
With the everlasting Spirit,
While eternal ages run.

Text: 10th century, tr. Edward Caswall (1814-78) and others
Tune: EN CLARA VOX or STUTTGART, 87.87.
Music: *CBW II* 453, 448; *CBW III* 624, 306

103. On Jordan's Bank

1. On Jordan's bank the Baptist's cry
   Announces that the Lord is nigh;
   Awake and hearken, for he brings
   Glad tidings of the King of kings.

2. Then cleansed be every heart from sin,
   Make straight the way for God within,
   And let each heart prepare a home
   Where such a mighty guest may come.

3. For you are our salvation, Lord,
   Our refuge and our great reward;
   Without your grace we waste away,
   Like flow'rs that wither and decay.

4. To heal the sick, stretch out your hand,
   And bid the fallen sinner stand;
   Shine forth, and let your light restore
   Earth's own true loveliness once more.

5. To God the Son all glory be
   Whose advent sets your people free;
   Whom with the Father we adore
   And Holy Spirit evermore.

Text: Charles Coffin, 1676-1749; tr. John Chandler, 1806-7
Tune: WINCHESTER NEW, L.M.
Music: *CBW II* 443; *CBW III* 350

04. Eternal Son, Creating Word

Eternal Son, creating Word,
Throughout the world good news is heard
Of God the Father's love divine
Embodied as a holy sign.

O Saviour of the human race,
Refreshing dew of God's embrace,
As joyous light dawn on our days
To rouse our hearts to sing God's praise,

In joyful hope the Church does wait
The day when you will recreate
This people in your image true
To reign for evermore with you.

All praise to you, Eternal Son,
Whose advent makes your people one,
Whom with the Father we adore
And Spirit blest for evermore.

Text: © 1992 John G. Hibbard
Tune: CONDITOR ALME SIDERUM or DEUS TUORUM MILITUM
Music: *CBW II* 539, 445; *CBW III* 307, 304

105. Listen, My People

Lis-ten, my peo-ple, your hopes are an-swered. Lis-ten, and hear my voice, your hopes are an-swered, your hopes are an-swered.

1. God waits for his peo-ple to throw off the dark of night and to wel-come the new day, where all is light.

2. God waits for his peo-ple to o-pen wide their eyes, and to mar-vel at the sight of the sun-rise.

3. God waits for his peo-ple to cast off their cloak of fear, and to walk up-on this earth: God is so near.

Text and Music: © Paul-André Durocher
Full accompaniment: *CBW III* 309

06. In Glad Accord

In glad accord let us rejoice
In John, the desert's finest voice;
Revealing in our midst the Son:
The advent of th'Incarnate One.

For John is witness to the Light
Who came to banish sin's dark night;
That we might live in endless day
the power of death his hand does stay.

Good news! The poor in praise rejoice,
The prisoners, too, lift up their voice
That he whose death by tyrant's sword
Prepared the coming of the Lord.

We sing of Christ, God's only Son
Anointed by the Holy One.
Rememb'ring him who did proclaim
The dawning justice of God's reign.

xt: © *1992 Bernadette Gasslein and John Hibbard.* Used by
permission.
ne: WINCHESTER NEW, L.M.
usic: *CBW II* 443; *CBW III* 350, 647

107. Hail to the Lord's Anointed

1. Hail to the Lord's Anointed,
   Great David's greater Son!
   Hail, in the time appointed,
   His reign on earth begun!
   He comes to break oppression,
   To set the captive free;
   To take away transgression
   And rule in equity.

2. He comes with help so speedy
   To those who suffer wrong,
   To help the poor and needy,
   And bid the weak be strong;
   To give them songs for sighing,
   Their darkness turn to light,
   Whose souls, condemned and dying,
   Were precious in his sight.

3. He shall come down like showers
   Upon the fruitful earth,
   And love, joy, hope, like flowers,
   Spring in his path to birth;
   Before him on the mountains
   Shall peace, the herald go;
   And righteousness in fountains
   From hill to valley flow.

. Kings shall bow down before him,
And gold and incense bring;
All nations shall adore him,
His praise, all people sing;
To him shall prayer unceasing
And daily vows ascend;
His kingdom still increasing,
A kingdom without end.

O'er ev'ry foe victorious,
He on his throne shall rest;
From age and age more glorious,
All-blessing and all-blest:
The tide of time shall never
His covenant remove;
His Name shall stand for ever,
His changeless Name of love.

Text: based on Psalm 72, James Montgomery, 1771-1854
Tune: PEARSALL or ELLACOMBE
Music: *CBW II* 619, 732; *CBW III* 455, 593

108. O Come, All Ye Faithful

1. O come, all ye faithful,
     joyful and triumphant,
   O come ye, o come ye to Bethlehem;
   Come and behold him,
     born the King of angels.

Ref: O come, let us adore him,
       O come, let us adore him,
       O come, let us adore him,
       Christ, the Lord.

2. Sing, choirs of angels,
     sing in exultation,
   Sing, all ye citizens of heav'n above.
   Glory to God in the highest.

3. See how the shepherds
     summoned to his cradle,
   Leaving their flocks, draw nigh with lowly fea
   We too will thither, bend our joyful footstep

4. Yea, Lord, we greet thee,
     born this happy morning,
   Jesus, to thee be glory giv'n;
   Word of the Father, now in flesh appearing.

Text: 18th century, tr. Frederick Oakely (1802-80) and othe
Tune: ADESTE FIDELES; Irregular
Music: *CBW II* 458; *CBW III* 329

109. Joy to the World

1. Joy to the world! the Lord is come;
   Let earth receive her King;
   Let every heart prepare him room,
   And heav'n and nature sing,
   And heav'n and nature sing,
   And heav'n and heaven and nature sing.

2. Joy to the world! the Saviour reigns;
   Let men their songs employ,
   While fields and floods, rocks hills and plains
   Repeat the sounding joy,
   Repeat the sounding joy,
   Repeat the sounding joy.

3. He rules the world with truth and grace
   And makes the nations prove
   The glories of his righteousness
   And wonders of his love,
   And wonders of his love,
   And wonders of his love.

Text: Isaac Watts, 1674-1748
Tune: ANTIOCH; C.M.
Music: *CBW II* 454; *CBW III* 328

671

110. Silent Night

1. Silent night! Holy night!
   All is calm, all is bright;
   Round yon virgin mother and child,
   Holy infant so tender and mild,
   Sleep in heavenly peace,
   Sleep in heavenly peace.

2. Silent night! Holy night!
   Shepherds quake at the sight:
   Glories stream from heaven afar,
   Heav'nly hosts sing alleluia,
   Christ, the Saviour is born,
   Christ, the Saviour is born.

3. Silent night! Holy night!
   Son of God, love's pure light
   Radiant beams from thy holy face,
   With the dawn of redeeming grace,
   Jesus, Lord at thy birth,
   Jesus, Lord at thy birth.

Text: J. Mohr, 1792-1848; tr. J. M. Campbell, 1817-78
Tune: STILLE NACHT; Irregular
Music: *CBW II* 455; *CBW III* 332

1. In the Darkness Shines the Splendour

In the darkness shines the splendour
Of the Word who took our flesh,
Welcoming, in love's surrender,
Death's dark shadow at his crèche.
Bearing ev'ry human story,
Word made flesh reveals his glory.

Light of nations, veiled in hist'ry,
Born of woman's flesh and blood,
Calling to the depths of myst'ry
Restless hearts that seek the good.
Healing ev'ry human story,
Word made flesh reveals his glory.

Broken bread, sustaining us in sorrow,
Wine poured out to toast our joy;
Exodus and new tomorrow,
Life's full promise to enjoy!
Gladd'ning ev'ry human story,
Word made flesh reveals his glory.

All God's people, sing in jubilation
Of the birth that sets us free,
Telling of the revelation:
Jesus, God's epiphany.
Celebrate the human story!
Word made flesh reveals our glory.

xt: © 1992 Bernadette Gasslein
ne: IRBY; 87.87.77.
sic: CBW II 473; CBW III 346

112. Before Creation Saw the Light

1. Before creation saw the light,
   before the stars or sun,
   with God there dwelt the Living Word;
   the Word with God was one.
   And through that Word the world was bor
   all space and time began to form,
   marked with his shaping touch,
   pulsing with life, by the power of the Wor

2. For in the Word of God was light
   that in the darkness shone;
   the Word was life and light for us
   and was not overcome.
   The light that glows in ev'ry heart
   was drawing near to take our part,
   and to the world he came,
   came he unknown,
   all unknown into his world.

3. The light that shines on ev'ryone
   appeared before our eyes,
   to make us children of our God
   when him we recognized.
   The Word our human flesh embraced,
   believers with God's glory graced,
   fullness of grace and truth, dwelling with
   Jesus Christ the Word made flesh.

Text: In principio; tr. © *Dominican Friars of Toronto*. Use
   permission.
Tune: JESOUS AHATONHIA; 86.86.88.647
Music: *CBW II* 467; *CBW III* 337

3. In Glory Now Upon the Earth

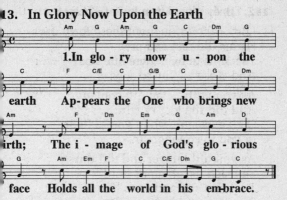

1.In glo - ry now u - pon the earth Ap-pears the One who brings new irth; The i - mage of God's glo - rious face Holds all the world in his em-brace.

Arise! God's people, let us sing,
God's reign of mercy he does bring!
For us who seek our truest home,
He is our peace, God's great shalom.

Rejoice, all desert hearts, rejoice!
To slake our thirst has come a voice,
God's word in human flesh we see;
Belovèd, God's epiphany.

O Lamb of God, we greet your reign,
Awaiting your return again.
Come, feed us with your living bread,
Till earth and heav'n once more are wed.

Text: © 1992 Bernadette Gasslein. Accompaniments for this tune can be found in many standard hymnals and collections of Christmas carols.

Alternative tunes: EISENACH, WINCHESTER NEW, L.M.
Alternative music: CBW II 518, 443; CBW III 464, 647

114. Lord, Who Throughout These Forty Days

1. Lord, who throughout these forty days
   For us did fast and pray,
   Teach us to overcome our sins
   And close by you to stay.

2. As you with Satan did contend
   And did the vict'ry win,
   O give us strength in you to fight,
   In you to conquer sin.

3. As you did hunger and did thirst,
   So teach us, gracious Lord,
   To die to self and so to live
   By your most holy word.

4. And through these days of penitence
   And through your passiontide,
   For evermore, in life and death,
   O Lord, with us abide.

5. Abide with us, that through this life
   Of suff'ring and of pain
   An Easter of unending joy
   We may at last attain.

Text: Claudia F. Hernaman, 1893-98
Tune: ST. FLAVIAN, C.M.
Music: *CBW II* 482; *CBW III* 367

115. O Jealous Lord of Liberty

1. O jealous Lord of liberty,
   who formed us from the dust of earth,
   our heart's first love renew again,
   heal and bind up our wounded worth.

2. As earth's cold sleep gives way to life,
   long dormant root and branch awake;
   so let your Spirit's fire flow,
   our spirits' icy bonds to break.

3. By bitter death and barren wood
   came joy into the universe:
   strengthen our faith to bear the cross,
   breaking the chain of Adam's curse.

4. O Mystery of Threefold Love,
   for whom the human heart is made:
   all praise be yours as we await
   Christ's death-destroying paschal day!

Text: © *Dominican Friars of Toronto.* Used by permission.
Tune: MELCOMBE or ERHALT UNS HERR, L.M.
Music: *CBW II* 484, 481; *CBW III* 369, 352

116. From the Depths

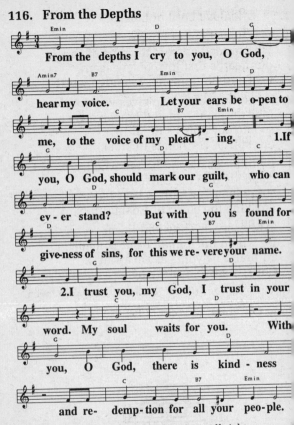

From the depths I cry to you, O God, hear my voice. Let your ears be o-pen to me, to the voice of my plead - ing. 1.If you, O God, should mark our guilt, who can ev - er stand? But with you is found for give-ness of sins, for this we re- vere your name. 2.I trust you, my God, I trust in your word. My soul waits for you. With you, O God, there is kind - ness and re- demp-tion for all your peo-ple.

17. Cold the Earth

Cold, the earth still sleeps in winter,
mantled o'er with chill and night,
yet within her womb's dark chamber
stirs the seedling toward the light.

Timeless Master of the seasons,
as these days' bright sadness grows,
stir the waiting earth within us
as the paschal journey goes.

Cast the Word's own seed among us,
let it root in hungry ground.
Draw out faith from hearts' dull slumber:
Wake us to the Gospel's sound.

By our Lord's long desert journey,
by his days of fast and prayer,
bring us to his third day's glory:
Let him easter in us there!

Text: © *Dominican Friars of Toronto*. Used by permission.
Tune: RUSSIAN SONG, DRAKE'S BROUGHTON, STUTTGART, 87.87.
Music: *CBW II* 487, 533, 448; *CBW III* 465, 577

118. Branches of the One Vine

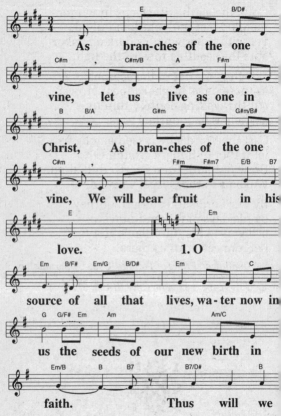

As bran-ches of the one vine, let us live as one in Christ, As bran-ches of the one vine, We will bear fruit in his love.

1. O source of all that lives, wa-ter now in us the seeds of our new birth in faith. Thus will we

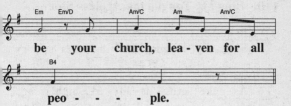

be your church, lea-ven for all

peo - - - - ple.

2. O Source of holiness,
   Give us pow'r today
   To proclaim the gospel's saving message.
   Thus will we be your church,
   Leaven for all people.

3. O Source of unity,
   Bind us all as one
   In communion with all men and women
   Thus will we be your light,
   Shining for all people.

4. O Source of truth and peace
   Use our tongues to speak
   The gospel's words of lasting justice.
   Thus will we be your church,
   Prophets to all people.

5. O Source of God's own life,
   Bring to birth in us
   The hope of life with you in glory.
   Thus will we be your sign,
   Promise for all people.

Text: © 1993 Madeleine Dubé; tr. © 1994 Bernadette Gasslein
Source: "Sarments d'une même vigne," *Mission d'amour*,
   Éd. du Cénacle
Music: © 1993 Madeleine Dubé

119. Sing My Tongue the Ageless Story

Sing, my tongue, the age-less sto - ry

As the cross is lift-ed high!

Tell how Christ our Sav-iour con-quered,

When for us he came to die

As a vic-tim in the bat-tle,

Death's do-min-ion to be-lie.

2. Adam tasted sin and sorrow,
   Eating of the fearful tree;
   All undoing our enchainment,
   By the tree Christ sets us free,
   Crushing hell's own tool of bondage,
   By his great humility.

3. Silence cloaked the earth and heavens
   Round the hill of Calvary;
   Nailed upon the tree of glory,
   Christ endured his agony.
   In his royal blood descending
   Comes our peace, our liberty.

. Cross triumphant! Cross transforming!
Ensign of humanity!
Faithful cross, above all others,
One and only noble tree:
Gracious wood and gracious iron,
Gracious burden borne on thee!

Text: © *Dominican Friars of Toronto*. Used by permission.
Tune: PANGE LINGUA, REGENT SQUARE, PICARDY, 87.87.87.
Music: *CBW II* 583, 528, 571; *CBW III* 381, 456, 596

20. Hosanna!

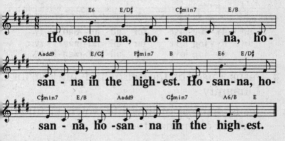

Ho-san-na, ho-san-na, ho-san-na in the high-est. Ho-san-na, ho-san-na, ho-san-na in the high-est.

© *Michel Guimont*

121. Jesus, Word of God, Kyrie!

Try using this piece as a processional during Lent; use th
refrain as the response to the penitential rite, and as th
response to the Prayer of the Faithful.

Ky-ri-e, Chris-te, Ky-ri-e e-le-i-son!

1. Je - sus, God's liv - ing Word of
2. Je - sus, God's hid - den glo - ry,
3. Je - sus, tem - ple of glo-ry built of

un - dy - ing love for all hu-man-i-ty.
un - dy - ing love for all hu-man-i-ty.
un - dy - ing love for all hu-man-i-ty.

4. Jesus, raised on the tree of undying love for al
   humanity.

5. Jesus, harvest of new life, sown in undyin
   love for all humanity.

6. Jesus, God crucified out of undying love for al
   humanity.

7. Jesus, Servant and Lord, you are undying lov
   for all humanity.

8. Jesus, bread born of wheat, food of undyin
   love for all humanity.

9. Jesus, wine from the grape, cup of undyin
   love for all humanity.

0. Jesus, abandoned on the tree in your undying love for all humanity.

Verses for the five Sundays of Lent, Year C:

. Jesus, God's living Word of undying love for all humanity.

. Jesus, God's hidden glory shining forth in love for all humanity.

. Jesus, you have conquered all sin in your undying love for all humanity.

. Jesus, God's beloved Son, you are undying love for all humanity.

. Jesus, Lover and Lord, you are undying love for all humanity.

Text: Didier Rimaud, © *CNPL*; tr., adapt. © *1993 Bernadette Gasslein*
Source: "Jésus, Verbe de Dieu, Kyrie," © *Éditions Musicales Studio SM*, 060794-2
Music: Jacques Berthier

122.   O Sacred Head, Surrounded

1. O sacred Head, surrounded
   By crown of piercing thorn.
   O bleeding Head, so wounded,
   Reviled and put to scorn!
   Death's pallid hue comes o'er you,
   The glow of life decays.
   Yet angel hosts adore thee
   And tremble as they gaze.

2. In this your bitter passion,
   Good Shepherd, think of me
   With your most sweet compassion,
   Unworthy though I be:
   Beneath your cross abiding
   For ever would I rest,
   In your dear love confiding,
   And with your presence blest.

3. Christ Jesus, we adore you,
   Our thorn-crowned Lord and King.
   We bow our hearts before you
   And to your cross we cling.
   Lord, give us strength to bear it
   With patience and with love,
   That we may truly merit
   A glorious crown above.

Text: Bernard of Clairvaux, v. 1 tr. (1861) Henry William
Baker, 1821-77; v. 2 and 3, written (1851) by Arthur Toze
Russell, 1806-74, alt.
Tune : PASSION CHORALE, 76.76.D., Hans Leo Hassler, 1564-161
Music: *CBW II* 491; *CBW III* 377

23. Ye Sons and Daughters

Ref: Alleluia, alleluia, alleluia!

Ye sons and daughters, let us sing!
The King of heav'n, our glorious King,
From death today rose triumphing. Alleluia!

That Easter morn, at break of day,
The faithful women went their way
To seek the tomb where Jesus lay. Alleluia!

An angel clothed in white they see,
Who sat and spoke unto the three,
"Your Lord has gone to Galilee." Alleluia!

That night th'apostles met in fear;
And Christ did in their midst appear,
And said, "My peace be with you here."
    Alleluia!

How blest are they who have not seen,
And yet whose faith has constant been,
For they eternal life shall win. Alleluia!

On this most holy day of days,
To God your hearts and voices raise,
In laud, and jubilee, and praise. Alleluia!

Text: Jean Tisserand, †1494; tr. John Mason Neale, 1818-66, alt.
Tune: O FILII ET FILIAE or VICTORY
Music: *CBW II* 506, 503; *CBW III* 404, 395

124. At the Lamb's High Feast We Sing

1. At the Lamb's high feast we sing
   Praise to our victorious King.
   He has washed us in the tide
   Flowing from his opened side.
   Praise we him, whose love divine
   Gives his sacred blood for wine,
   Gives his body for the feast,
   Christ the victim, Christ the priest.

2. Where the paschal blood is poured,
   Death's dark angel sheathes his sword;
   Israel's hosts triumphant go
   Through the wave that drowns the foe.
   Christ, the Lamb, whose blood was shed,
   Paschal victim, paschal bread!
   With sincerity and love,
   Eat we manna from above.

3. Mighty victim from the sky,
   Pow'rs of hell beneath you lie;
   Death is broken in the fight,
   You have brought us life and light.
   Vict'ry's banner you now wave,
   Conqu'ring Satan and the grave;
   See the prince of darkness quelled,
   Heaven's gates are open held.

4. Easter triumph, Easter joy,
   Sin alone can these destroy;
   From sins' death now set us free:
   Souls reborn, O Lord, we'll be.
   Hymns of glory, songs of praise,
   Father, unto you we raise;
   And to you, our risen King,
   With the Spirit, praise we sing.

Text: *Roman Breviary*, 1632; tr. Robert Campbell, 1814-68
Tune: SALZBURG, 77.77.D.
Music: *CBW II* 563; *CBW III* 348, 375

125. Jesus Christ Is Ris'n Today

1. Jesus Christ is ris'n today, Alleluia!
   Our triumphant holy day, Alleluia!
   Who did once upon the cross, Alleluia!
   Suffer to redeem our loss. Alleluia!

2. Hymns of praise then let us sing, Alleluia!
   Unto Christ our heav'nly King, Alleluia!
   Who endured the cross and grave, Alleluia!
   Sinners to redeem and save. Alleluia!

3. But the pains which he endured, Alleluia!
   Our salvation have procured; Alleluia!
   Now above the sky he's King, Alleluia!
   Where the angels ever sing. Alleluia!

4. Sing we to our God above, Alleluia!
   Praise eternal as his love, Alleluia!
   Praise him, all ye heav'nly host, Alleluia!
   Father, Son and Holy Ghost. Alleluia!

Text: *Lyra Davidica*, 1708 and others
Tune: EASTER HYMN; 77.77. with alleluias
Music: *CBW II* 500; *CBW III* 389

126. Living Stones of God's Temple

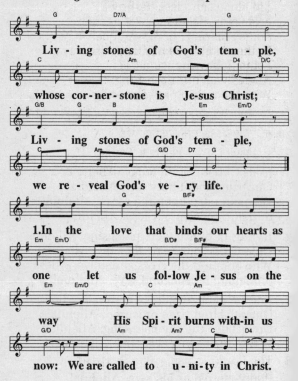

Liv - ing stones of God's tem - ple,
whose cor - ner - stone is Je - sus Christ;
Liv - ing stones of God's tem - ple,
we re - veal God's ve - ry life.

1. In the love that binds our hearts as
one let us fol - low Je - sus on the
way His Spi - rit burns with-in us
now: We are called to u - ni - ty in Christ.

2. In the faith in which we are re-born
   Let us follow Jesus on the way.
   The Spirit's breath within us blows:
   We proclaim God's word of life to all.

3. In the joy that gives our lives new hope
   Let us follow Jesus on the way,
   The cross, our sign of victory,
   As we bear his light to all the world.

4. In the yearning of our heartfelt pray'r
   Let us follow Jesus on the way,
   Made one with those who are oppressed
   We become their cry for God's own justice.

5. In the welcome offered to new life,
   Let us follow Jesus on the way;
   Sustained by living bread and cup,
   We announce the wonders of God's reign.

Text: © 1993 Madeleine Dubé; tr. © 1994 Bernadette Gasslein
Source: "Viens bâtir en Église," *Mission d'amour,*
   Éd. du Cénacle
Music: © 1993 Madeleine Dubé

127. Be Joyful, Mary, Heav'nly Queen

1. Be joyful, May, heav'nly queen,
   Gaude Maria:
   Your Son who died was living seen,
   Alleluia! Laetare, O Maria.

2. The Son you bore by heaven's grace,
   Gaude Maria:
   Did all our guilt and sin efface,
   Alleluia! Laetare, O Maria.

3. The Lord has risen from the dead,
   Gaude Maria:
   He rose with might as he had said,
   Alleluia! Laetare, O Maria.

4. O pray to God, O virgin fair,
   Gaude Maria:
   That he our souls to heaven bear,
   Alleluia! Laetare, O Maria.

Text: Anon., 17th century
Tune: REGINA CAELI, 8.8. with refrains
Music: CBW II 497; CBW III 460

128. He Stands at Our Door

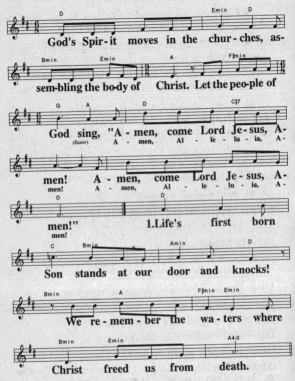

God's Spir-it moves in the chur-ches, as-

sem-bling the bo-dy of Christ. Let the peo-ple of

God sing, "A - men, come Lord Je - sus, A-
(Easter) A - men, Al - le - lu - ia, A-

men! A - men, come Lord Je - sus, A-
men! A - men, Al - le - lu - ia, A-

men!" 1.Life's first born
men!

Son stands at our door and knocks!

We re-mem-ber the wa-ters where

Christ freed us from death.

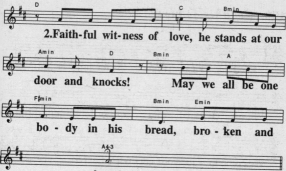

2. Faith-ful wit-ness of love, he stands at our door and knocks! May we all be one bo - dy in his bread, bro - ken and shared.

3. He has conquer'd all death:
   He stands at our door and knocks!
   May your word be a beacon
   To lead us through death to new life.

4. He has conquer'd all sin:
   He stands at our door and knocks!
   All creation births new life,
   Your reign breaking into our world.

5. The Lord of all life
   Stands at our door and knocks!
   The whole universe calls us
   To sing to the glory of God.

Text: M. Scouarnec; tr. and adapt. © 1992 Bernadette Gasslein
Source: "Aux Églises du monde," *Messe de l'apocalypse*, Ed. SM
Music: J. Akepsimas

129. Feed Us, O Lord

Feed us, O Lord, that we no long-er hun-ger.

Fill us, O Lord, that we no long-er thirst.

We come to you, your peo-ple's hearts are o-pen

Trust-ing, car-ing, lov-ing hearts,

Feed us, Lamb of God. 1. Jes-us, the Lord, left

this to his dis-ci-ples:

"Take, eat and drink, they're in my mem-o-ry."

2. Hear then our prayers,
   like those lost in the desert.
   Send manna down,
   so we, too, know your love.

3. Give us that bread,
   so we no longer hunger.
   Food for our lives,
   no more than this we need.

4. And, as we leave,
   the Christ abides within us.
   We share that Lord,
   that Love with all we meet.

Text and Music: © 1992 William J. Turner and the Archdiocese of Edmonton. Full accompaniment available from Rev. W. J. Turner, 627 Oxford Street East, London, ON N5Y 3J2

130. Your Very Life

Life- giv-ing bread, blessed and shared,
life - sav - ing cup poured out for all,
feast of the earth, feast of heav'n:
we be- come your ve - ry life.

1. Jesus, bread of all our hungers; Je - sus,
2. Jesus, bread of all our longings; Je - sus,

bread of all our hopes, bro - ken and blessed for
bread of all our needs, bread of your life so

all to share. Jesus, wine of all our thirsts;
free - ly giv'n. Jesus, wine of all our sor-rows,

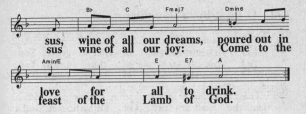

sus,   wine of all   our dreams, poured out in
sus   wine of all   our joy: Come to the

love   for   all   to   drink.
feast   of the   Lamb of   God.

© 1993 Michel Guimont

131. The Word of God for All the Earth

1. The Word of God for all the earth,
   the very Speech of God expressed,
   the Virgin mothered for our sake
   that all by love might be possessed.

2. The Spirit's overshadowing
   enfolded her in godly might
   to love and bear the Christ of God
   Emmanuel, the Light from light.

3. Let fiery spirits chant in praise
   of his unbounded graciousness:
   the Richest came in poverty
   to heal our barren woundedness.

4. O Jesus, Virgin-born, we sing
   on Mary's bright festivity,
   in joyful hope of that great Day
   when last you come to set us free.

Text: Verbum salutis omnium; tr. © *Dominican Friars of To-ronto.* Used by permission.
Tune: MELCOMBE, L.M.
Music: *CBW II* 68; *CBW III* 369

132. O First-Born Daughter

1. O firstborn daughter of God's grace, You
2. O true dis - ci - ple of the Lord, You
3. O wo - man, bear - er of our God, Now

lead the vast ar - ray Of all who sing God's
call us to de - clare The deep com - pas - sion
mid - wife at the birth Of God's own just - ice,

ho - ly name Through time to end - less
of your Son, God's peace be - yond com -
God's great day: The hope of all the

Refrain

day. Might - y God! a - cross the
pare.
earth.

spans of time Your mer - cy still we sing; With

Ma - ry we re - call your deeds and

joy - filled praise now bring.

Text: © 1993 Bernadette Gasslein
Tune: FOREST GREEN (Traditional English) or KINGSFOLD
Music: *CBW II* 730 (KINGSFOLD only); *CBW III* 502, 425

698

133. Amazing Grace

1. Amazing grace! how sweet the sound
   That saved a wretch like me!
   I once was lost, but now am found,
   Was blind, but now I see.

2. 'Twas grace that taught my heart to fear,
   And grace my fears relieved;
   How precious did that grace appear
   The hour I first believed!

3. The Lord has promised good to me,
   His word my hope secures;
   He will my shield and portion be
   As long as life endures.

4. Through many dangers, toils and snares,
   I have already come;
   'Tis grace has brought me safe thus far,
   And grace will lead me home.

5. When we've been there ten thousand years,
   Bright shining as the sun,
   We've no less days to sing God's praise
   Than when we'd first begun.

Text: John Newton, 1725-1807
Tune: NEW BRITAIN
Music: *CBW II* 673; *CBW III* 480

134. Joyful, Joyful We Adore Thee

1. Joyful, joyful we adore thee,
   God of glory, Lord of love;
   Hearts unfold like flowers before thee,
   Opening to the sun above.
   Melt the clouds of sin and sadness,
   Drive the dark of doubt away,
   Giver of immortal gladness,
   Fill us with the light of day.

2. All Thy works with joy surround thee,
   Earth and heaven reflect thy rays,
   Stars and angels sing around thee,
   Centre of unbroken praise,
   Field and forest, vale and mountain,
   Flowery meadow, flashing sea,
   Chanting bird and flowing fountain,
   Call us to rejoice in thee.

3. Thou art giving and forgiving,
   Ever blessing, ever blest,
   Wellspring of the joy of living,
   Ocean depth of happy rest!
   Ever singing, march we onward,
   Victors in the midst of strife,
   Joyful music leads us sunward,
   In the triumph song of life.

Text: Henry van Dyke (1852-1933), alt.
Tune: HYMN TO JOY, 87.87.D.
Music: *CBW II* 625; *CBW III* 406

135. Love Divine, All Loves Excelling

1. Love divine, all loves excelling,
   Joy of heaven, to earth come down.
   Fix in us thy humble dwelling,
   All thy faithful mercies crown.
   Jesus, thou art all compassion,
   Pure, unbounded love thou art;
   Visit us with thy salvation,
   Enter every trembling heart.

2. Come, Almighty to deliver,
   Let us all thy grace receive;
   Suddenly return, and never
   Nevermore thy temples leave.
   Thee we would be always blessing,
   Serve thee as thy hosts above,
   Pray, and praise thee, without ceasing,
   Glory in thy perfect love.

3. Finish then thy new creation,
   Pure and spotless let us be;
   Let us see thy great salvation,
   Perfectly restored in thee;
   Changed from glory into glory,
   Till in heaven we take our place,
   Till we cast our crowns before thee,
   Lost in wonder, love and praise.

Text: Charles Wesley, 1707-88
Tune: HYFRYDOL, 87.87.D.
Music: *CBW II* 536; *CBW III* 426

136. O Holy Spirit, Lord of Grace

1. O Holy Spirit, Lord of grace,
    Eternal fount of love,
    Inflame, we pray, our inmost hearts
    With fire from heaven above.

2. As thou in bond of love dost join
    The Father and the Son,
    So fill us all with mutual love,
    And knit our hearts in one.

3. All glory to the Father be,
    All glory to the Son,
    All glory, Spirit blest, to thee,
    While endless ages run.

Text: Chas. Coffin, 1679-1749; tr., alt. John Chandler, 1808-76
Tune: ST. ANNE, C.M.
Music: *CBW II* 640; *CBW III* 420

137. O God of Love, O King of Peace

1. O God of love, O King of peace,
    Make wars throughout the world to cease;
    Our violent ways help us contain;
    Give peace, O God, give peace again!

2. Whom shall we trust but you, O Lord?
    Where rest but on your faithful word?
    None ever called on you in vain;
    Give peace, O God, give peace again!

3. Where saints and angels dwell above,
    All hearts are joined in holy love;
    O bind us in that heav'nly chain;
    Give peace, O God, give peace again!

Text: Sir Henry Williams Baker, 1821-77, alt.
Tune: ROCKINGHAM
Music: *CBW II* 489; *CBW III* 382

138. Holy Spirit, Truth Divine

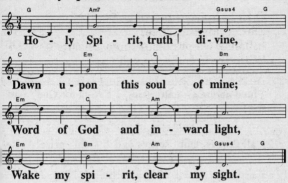

Ho - ly Spi - rit, truth di - vine,
Dawn u - pon this soul of mine;
Word of God and in - ward light,
Wake my spi - rit, clear my sight.

2. Holy Spirit, love divine,
   Glow within this heart of mine;
   Kindle ev'ry high desire,
   And my soul with joy inspire.

3. Holy Spirit, peace divine,
   Calm this troubled heart of mine;
   May I ever strongly live
   In the grace which Thou dost give.

Text: © S. Longfellow and A. Dickinson
Music: © 1986 Arthur Dickinson

139. Great Artist of the Universe

Great ar-tist of the u-ni-verse, Of land and sea and skies, Cre-a-tor God of all that is, Our source and fi-nal prize! Re-ceive our hymns of grateful praise, Re-ceive our joy-ful song. O may we bless you all our days, Give thanks our whole life long! long!

2. O gracious giver of all good,
   Of warmth and food and light,
   O everflowing stream of love,
   Our longing hearts' delight.
   Receive our psalms and joyful praise,
   The worship of our song.
   O may we bless you all our days,
   Give thanks our whole life long.

3. Consoling presence in our pain
   And shelt'ring dusk of night,
   Transforming radiance of the dawn,
   Our hope and future bright!
   Receive our psalms and hymns of praise,
   Rejoicing in our song.
   O may we bless you all our days,
   Give thanks our whole life long.

Text: Dolores Dufner, OSB
Tune: Terri Nehl, OSB;
© 1987 Sisters of St. Benedict, St. Joseph, MN 56374

140. God, Who Gives to Life Its Goodness

1. God, who gives to life its goodness,
   God, Creator of all joy,
   God who gives to all their freedom,
   God who blesses tool and toy:
   Teach us now to laugh and praise you,
   Deep within your praises sing,
   Till the whole creation dances
   God's love filling everything.

2. God, who fills the earth with beauty,
   God, who binds each friend to friend,
   God who names us co-creators,
   God who wills that chaos end:
   Grant us now creative spirits,
   Minds responsive to your mind,
   Hearts and wills your rule extending,
   All our acts by love refined.

Text: © Walter Henry Farquharson, b. 1936. Used by
permission.
Tune: ABBOT'S LEIGH
Music: CBW II 643, 536; CBW III 560, 691

141. L'Arche Hymn

1. Your name, Jesus Christ,
       let us sing on our journey,
   Proclaiming to all far and wide
       the good news of new birth.
   You alone are our life,
       and our peace and our love.
   Your name, Jesus Christ,
       we will sing on our journey.

2. Your name, Jesus Christ,
       let us praise on our journey.
   O Lord, let our voice echo yours
       and the joy of your heart.
   May the earth join our song!
       May the heavens resound!
   Your name, Jesus Christ,
       we will praise on our journey!

3. Your name, Jesus Christ,
       is the strength of our journey.
   You walk by our side as a shield
       in the darkness of night,
   Till the dawn of your day
       when the people you save
   Will sing your return
       as the end of our journey.

Text: Les Petites Soeurs de Jésus; tr. 1982 Norbert Brockman
    SM. Revised 1994 Bernadette Gasslein
Music: *CBW II* 554

142. Praise, My Soul, the King of Heaven

1. Praise, my soul, the King of heaven;
   To his feet thy tribute bring.
   Ransomed, healed, restored, forgiven,
   Who like me his praise should sing?
   Praise him! Praise him! Praise him! Praise him!
   Praise the everlasting King!

2. Praise him for his grace and favour
   To our people in distress;
   Praise him still the same for ever,
   Slow to chide, and swift to bless.
   Praise him! Praise him! Praise him! Praise him!
   Glorious in his faithfulness.

3. Lovingly he tends and spares us;
   Well our feeble frame he knows;
   In his hands he gently bears us,
   Rescues us from all our foes.
   Praise him! Praise him! Praise him! Praise him!
   Widely as his mercy flows.

4. Angels, help us to adore him;
   Ye behold him face to face;
   Sun and moon bow down before him;
   Dwellers all in time and space.
   Praise him! Praise him! Praise him! Praise him!
   Praise with us the God of grace!

Text: Henry Francis Lyte, 1793-1847, alt.
Tune: LAUDA ANIMA, 87.87.87.
Music: *CBW II* 650; *CBW III* 565

143. Forward in the Spirit

1. For - ward in the Spi - rit
with the life we share,
Nour - ished by God's pres - ence,
strength - ened by God's care.
Part - ners on our jour - ney
in the Word we meet.
Christ, our close com - pan - ion,
we, the wine, the wheat. ward.

2. Forward in the Spirit: now for many years,
   We have sought God's wisdom,
   we have known our fears.
   Walking with each other on a path that's sure,
   God will gently lead us, love forever endure.

3. We, a chosen people in our chosen land,
   Called to share the vision,
   honour your command.
   God of many nations, showing us the way,
   Teach us care and faithfulness,
   guide us ev'ry day.

4. Without hesitation, say to one and all,
   "Come and join our journey,
   answering the call."
   Challenge of our lifetime, following the Lord.
   Forward in the Spirit, that is our reward.

144. O Praise Ye the Lord

1. O praise ye the Lord!
   Praise him in the height;
   Rejoice in his word,
   Ye angels of light;
   Ye heavens adore him
   By whom ye were made,
   And worship before him,
   In brightness arrayed.

2. O praise ye the Lord!
   Praise him upon earth,
   In tuneful accord,
   All ye of new birth;
   Praise him who has brought you
   His grace from above,
   Praise him who has taught you
   To sing of his love.

3. O praise ye the Lord!
   All things that give sound;
   Each jubilant chord,
   Re-echo around;
   Loud organs, his glory
   Forth tell in deep tone,
   And sweet harp, the story
   Of what he has done.

4. O praise ye the Lord!
   Thanksgiving and song
   To him be outpoured
   All ages along:
   For love in creation,
   For heaven restored,
   For grace of salvation,
   O praise ye the Lord!

Text: Henry Williams Baker, 1821-77, alt.
Tune: HANOVER, 55.55.65.65.
Music: *CBW II* 649; *CBW III* 551

711

145. Alleluia! Sing to Jesus

1. Alleluia! Sing to Jesus!
   His the sceptre, his the throne;
   Alleluia! his the triumph,
   His the victory alone;
   Hark! the songs of peaceful Sion
   Thunder light a mighty flood;
   Jesus, out of ev'ry nation
   Has redeemed us by his blood.

2. Alleluia! not as orphans!
   Are we left in sorrow now;
   Alleluia! he is near us,
   Faith believes nor questions how:
   Though the cloud from sight received him,
   When the forty days were o'er
   Shall our hearts forget his promise,
   "I am with you evermore"?

3. Alleluia! Bread of heaven,
   Here on earth our food and stay!
   Alleluia! here the sinful
   Turn to you from day to day:
   Intercessor, friend of sinners,
   Earth's Redeemer, plead for us
   Where the voices of the blessed
   Join the chant victorious.

4. Alleluia! King eternal,
   You are Lord of lords alone.
   Alleluia! born of Mary,
   Earth your footstool, heav'n your throne:
   You within the veil have entered,
   Robed in flesh, our great high priest;
   You on earth both priest and victim
   In the eucharistic feast.

Text: William Chatterton Dix, 1837-98, alt.
Tune: HYFRYDOL, 87.87.D.
Music: *CBW II* 536; *CBW III* 426, 626

146. Sing of Christ, Proclaim His Glory

1. Sing of Christ, proclaim his glory,
   Sing the resurrection song!
   Death and sorrow, earth's dark story,
   To the former days belong.
   All around the clouds are breaking.
   Soon the storms of time shall cease;
   In God's likeness, people waking,
   Know the everlasting peace.

2. O what glory, far exceeding
   All that eye has yet perceived!
   Holiest hearts for ages pleading,
   Never that full joy conceived.
   God has promised, Christ prepares it,
   There on high our welcome waits;
   Ev'ry humble spirit shares it,
   Christ has passed th'eternal gates.

3. Life eternal! heav'n rejoices;
   Jesus lives who once was dead;
   Join with all the heav'nly voices;
   Child of God, life up your head!
   Patriarchs from distant ages,
   Saints all longing for their heav'n;
   Prophets, psalmists, seers and sages,
   All await the glory giv'n.

4. Life eternal! O what wonders
   Crowd on faith, what joy unknown,
   When amid earth's closing thunders,
   Saints shall stand before the throne!
   O to enter that bright portal,
   See that glowing firmament,
   Know, with you, O God immortal,
   Jesus Christ whom you have sent!

Text: 1 Corinthians 15:20; William Josiah Irons, 1812-83
Tune: HYMN TO JOY
Music: *CBW II* 625; *CBW III* 406, 510

147. Christ Is Made the Sure Foundation

1. Christ is made the sure foundation,
   Christ the head and cornerstone;
   Chosen of the Lord, and precious,
   Binding all the Church in one,
   Holy Sion's help for ever,
   And her confidence alone.

2. To this temple where we call you
   Come, Almighty Lord, today;
   Come with all your loving kindness,
   Hear your people as they pray,
   And your fullest benediction
   Give to us, O Lord, this day.

3. Grant, we pray, to all your servants
   What they ask of you to gain,
   What they gain of you for ever
   With the blessed to retain,
   And hereafter in your glory
   Evermore with you to reign.

4. Praise and honour to the Father,
   Praise and honour to the Son,
   Praise and honour to the Spirit,
   Ever Three and ever One,
   One in might and one in glory,
   While unending ages run.

Text: ca. 6th century, tr. John Mason Neale, 1818-66
Tune: REGENT SQUARE or WESTMINSTER ABBEY, 87.87.87.
Music: *CBW II* 528; *CBW III* 456, 430, 503

Music Index

SEASONAL PSALMS

HYMNS

Advent

Some advent hymns are equally useful
for the closing weeks of the liturgical year

Suitable for Baptism of the Lord and
feasts of John the Baptist

Christmas Day

Christmas Season

Christmas Day to Baptism of the Lord, inclusive

Communion Procession

GENERAL